# THE CHILD AND THE EUROPEAN CONVENTION ON HUMAN RIGHTS

**Programme on International Rights of the Child**
*Series Editor: Geraldine Van Bueren*

# The Child and the European Convention on Human Rights

DR. URSULA KILKELLY
*Lecturer in Law*
*University of Wales, Swansea*

**Ashgate**

**DARTMOUTH**

Aldershot • Brookfield USA • Singapore • Sydney

Published by
Dartmouth Publishing Company Limited
Ashgate Publishing Ltd
Gower House
Croft Road
Aldershot
Hants GU11 3HR
England

Ashgate Publishing Company
Old Post Road
Brookfield
Vermont 05036
USA

Ashgate website: http://www.ashgate.com

**British Library Cataloguing in Publication Data**
Kilkelly, Ursula
 The child and the European Convention on Human Rights
 (Programme on international rights of the child)
 1. European Convention on Human Rights 2. Children's rights -
 Europe 3. Children - Legal status, laws, etc.
 I. Title
 341.4'81'083'094

**Library of Congress Cataloging-in-Publication Data**
Kilkelly, Ursula.
 The child and the European convention on human rights / Ursula
 Kilkelly.
  p. cm.
 Includes bibliographical references and index.
 ISBN 1-84014-704-0 (hbk.)
 1. Children--Legal status, laws, etc.--Europe. 2. Children
 (International law) 3. Convention for the Protection of Human
 Rights and Fundamental Freedoms (1950) I. Title.
 KJC1018.K55 1999
 341.4'81'083--dc21                                99-44891
                                                        CIP


ISBN 1 84014 704 0

Printed and bound in Great Britain by MPG Books Ltd, Bodmin, Cornwall

# Contents

# Preface

The idea for this book arose principally from my modest fascination with the European Convention on Human Rights. In light of the Convention's unprecedented success in the enforcement of human rights in international law, I was interested in researching some particular area of its case law in context. In deciding that the particular focus of my research would be children, I was influenced by the almost universal ratification of the UN Convention on the Rights of the Child and the fact that the state reports of many European countries, including Ireland and the United Kingdom, were due to be considered imminently by the Committee on the Rights of the Child. This gave me the opportunity to study an alternative system of rights protection, in the form of the reporting mechanism administered by the UN Committee, as well as to establish a benchmark of rights and standards, according to which the case law of the Commission and Court of Human Rights on children could be roughly measured. It was, and is still my firm view that one of the most important ways to maximise the potential of the European Convention to protect children is to combine the widely accepted, detailed standards on children's rights set out in the UN Convention with the highly successful and influential European system of individual petition. This approach is particularly significant in States which have ratified the European Convention, but not the UN Convention, such as the United Kingdom, insofar as the former but not the latter, is binding on UK domestic courts and lawmakers.

The overriding aim of this book is to provide a comprehensive and detailed analysis of the case law of the European Commission and Court of Human Rights concerning children. It considers over 750 reported and unreported decisions of the Strasbourg institutions, including decisions on admissibility and merits from the Commission and judgments from the Court, dating from the institutions' establishment over forty years ago. As such, this book provides a wealth of sources on children's rights and other related issues, and it will act as a particularly valuable reference book for legal practitioners seeking to argue Convention points in domestic courts, as well as Government agents and officials working in all areas of their obligations under the Convention. However, the book is written as an academic text and as such it aims to make a valuable contribution to the study of both the Convention and children's rights by undergraduate and postgraduate students and researchers with an interest in human rights law.

The Court of Human Rights has developed several interpretive approaches and principles, which have furthered the Convention's potential to protect children. These are discussed, together with an introduction to the Convention, in Chapter 1. Chapter 2 provides an introduction to the application of the Convention to children by setting out how the case law defines the child and examining issues related to the child's status with particular reference to discrimination. Chapters 3 to 8 look in detail at specific aspects of the substantive rights of the child. Chapter 3 looks at the protection which the Convention offers children in conflict with the law, assesses the relevance to children of the Convention's liberty and fair trial provisions and examines efforts to adapt them so as to provide children with effective protection in systems of juvenile justice and detention. The rights of both children and their parents with regard to education are considered in Chapter 4 and the considerable potential of the Convention's education provision is examined in the context of children with special needs. Chapter 5 discusses the elements of a child's identity and in particular, presents an analysis of the case law on the child's right to information about his/her origins as well as the child's right to a name and nationality. The new area of participation rights is considered in Chapter 6, which examines to what extent the provisions relating to the civil and political rights of expression and participation apply to children. Chapter 7 examines the subject of the child's right to health care, together with the right of the child to have his/her life protected. The substantial case law of the Commission and Court on the child's right to physical integrity is considered in Chapter 8. The issues of physical and corporal punishment, together with the responsibility of the state to protect the child from various forms of abuse and neglect are also discussed. The following five chapters deal with the child and the family, a detailed introduction to which is provided in Chapter 9. Chapter 10 discusses the area of immigration law under the Convention, predominantly but not exclusively in the family context, and it also considers the potential of the Convention to protect the rights of immigrant and refugee children. Chapters 11, 12 and 13 deal with the case law on all aspects of family life, considering issues relating to the child and the family in relation to custody and contact, alternative care and adoption respectively. There is some overlap between chapters and sections although this is avoided where possible. In some areas, however, the discussion of a case from a different perspective is deemed appropriate, although repetition is kept to a minimum. In contrast to other texts on the Convention, the discussion is thematic, rather than led by the individual provisions of the Convention. The repetition of Convention provisions which this necessitated was unavoidable.

Recent years have seen a period of great change in systems for the protection of human rights at both domestic and European level. The incorporation of the Convention into the domestic law of the United Kingdom, by means of the Human Rights Act 1998, leaves the Republic of Ireland in isolation as the only Convention State yet to afford it binding status in domestic law. As a consequence, both the Convention and the enormous wealth of case law created by the Commission and Court of Human Rights occupy an unrivaled position in the domestic legal systems of Europe, and its status and influence are unprecedented at regional level as well as world-wide. 1998 saw fundamental change at European level too where the two tier system of the Commission and Court was replaced with a new, permanent Court of Human Rights in order to streamline its system of individual petition under Protocol 11. There are now forty States party to the European Convention and forty judges, one from each Convention State, sit on the Court. At the dawn of the 21st century, the Convention is finally European in the broadest sense, as it reflects the diverse religious, cultural, political, social and legal traditions of the European continent. It is hoped that its potential to protect the rights of children in Europe in this context is maximised.

Dr Ursula Kilkelly
University of Wales, Swansea
May 1999


ps In September 1999, I took up a position as a College Lecturer at the Department of Law, University College Cork, Ireland.

# Acknowledgements

This work originated as a doctoral thesis awarded from Queen's University Belfast in 1998 and it would not have come to fruition without the financial and academic support of the School of Law and the Centre for International and Comparative Human Rights Law at Queen's.

I have been fortunate enough to work with the European Commission of Human Rights in Strasbourg and I would like to acknowledge all those who made my work in the Commission possible, beneficial and enjoyable, but to Anna Austin and Karen Reid, two of the Secretariat's excellent lawyers, I owe a special debt of gratitude. As scholars of the Convention will know, the days before the website were dark indeed, although my incessant requests for information were always efficiently dealt with by the staff of the Human Rights Information Centre. I would also like to thank Montserrat Enrich Mas and Maud Buquicchio de Boer for providing me with access to much needed and hard sought after case law. I wish to show special appreciation to Jane Liddy, former Irish member of the European Commission of Human Rights, for her guidance, support and inspiration.

The writing of this book would not have been possible without the support of the Department of Law at the University of Wales (Swansea). I would particularly like to thank Professor Jenny Levin for her advice and editorial skills, and I am grateful also to my friend Ruth Costigan for her academic and personal support, which was much appreciated.

My research assistant Andrew Scott of the School of Law, University of Wales (Cardiff) spent many long and doubtless exciting hours tracking down illusive references and he was absolutely indispensable. Many thanks also to all at Dartmouth, especially Pauline Beavers, and to Professor Geraldine Van Bueren, the Series Editor.

Friends and family in Ireland and Wales have listened tirelessly to my plans for this project and inquired continuously as to its progress. I am hugely grateful for their vital moral and loving support.

Many sacrifices have been made by me and on my behalf to secure the completion of this book, but none like that made generously by my husband Cathal. His support and patience throughout have been immeasurable.

# Note on the Citation of Strasbourg Cases

## Court Reports

Judgments of the European Court of Human Rights reported before 1996 can be found in the Series A reports. Thereafter, they are reported in the Reports of Judgments and Decisions series. Many of the Court's judgments are also published in Sweet & Maxwell's unofficial European Human Rights Reports (EHRR) series. The EHRR citation is included where possible for ease of reference. Judgments are thus cited as follows:

Eur Court HR *Marckx v Belgium*, judgment of 13 June 1979, Series A no 31, 2 EHRR 330

Eur Court HR *Hussain v UK*, judgment of 21 Feb 1996, Reports 1996-I, no 4, p 252, 22 EHRR 1

## Commission Decisions and Reports

Decisions of the (now defunct) Commission of Human Rights were published in two stages, admissibility and merits. Not all admissibility decisions are reported, but those that are can be found in the Collection of Decisions series (CD), published up to 1974, or the Decisions and Reports (DR) series, from 1975 onwards. The Yearbook of the Convention also contains select admissibility decisions. Commission reports of the merits or detailing a friendly settlement were published in the DR series, or where they proceed to the Court, as an annex to the judgment. Unreported decisions can be obtained from the Human Rights Information Centre in Strasbourg, or from the website (www.dhcour.coe.fr/hudoc). The EHRR series has also published Commission decisions and reports, and this reference is provided where available. Commission cases are cited as follows:

No 8416/78 *Paton v UK*, Dec 13.5.80, DR 19, p 244, 3 EHRR 408

No 9471/81 *Warwick v UK*, Comm Rep, 18.7.86, DR 60, p 5.

# Series Preface

The concept of international children's rights has come of age, and the Programme on International Rights of the Child Series is the first series of volumes dedicated to exploring specific aspects of international children's rights. The series comprises both sole authored and edited volumes, and single disciplinary and multi-disciplinary monographs, all considering issues which are at the rapidly expanding boundaries of international children's rights.

Geraldine Van Beuren
Series Editor
Programme on International Rights of the Child
Queen Mary and Westfield College
University of London

# 1      The Application of the European Convention to Children

## Background to the European Convention

When the Council of Europe was formed in the aftermath of the Second
World War one its principal aims was to foster respect for human rights,
democracy and the rule of law among the nations of Europe. This was to
be achieved, *inter alia*, through the establishment of a collective guarantee
of human rights, which would bind all States that ratified it. More
importantly, a Commission and Court of Human Rights would be set up to
supervise state adherence to its standards. With the horrors of the war
fresh in their memories and the will to prevent their recurrence strong, the
drafting parties lost little time in drawing up the first European human
rights treaty[1] and on 4 November 1950 the Convention for the Protection of
Human Rights and Fundamental Freedoms was opened for signature.[2] The
Convention (known as the European Convention on Human Rights, or the
ECHR) came into force in 1958 when the requisite eight States had
accepted the compulsory jurisdiction of its main supervisory body, the
European Court of Human Rights. The first case was heard by the
Commission and then the Court almost straightaway and the right of an
individual to take a complaint against the State under the Convention was
thereby clarified and firmly established.[3] The right of individual petition
distinguishes the European Convention from other human rights treaties,
and this feature has allowed the Commission and Court of Human Rights
to establish the Convention's enviable reputation as a successful

---

[1]  See further Robertson & Merrills (1993) *Human Rights in Europe: A Study of
the European Convention on Human Rights,* 3rd ed, Manchester: MUP, pp 5-14
and Robertson (1951) 'The ECHR: Recent Developments', *British Yearbook of
International Law,* **28**, pp 359-365.

[2]  It was signed on behalf of the Governments of Belgium, Denmark, France, the
German Federal Republic, Iceland, Ireland, Italy, Luxembourg, the Netherlands,
Norway, Saar, Turkey and the United Kingdom. On 28 November 1950, it was
signed on behalf of Greece and Sweden.

[3]  Eur Court HR *Lawless v Ireland,* judgments of 14 Nov 1960, 7 Apr 1961 and 1
July 1961, Series A nos 1-3, 1 EHRR 1, 3 & 15.

mechanism for the protection and enforcement of human rights.   The Commission of Human Rights has heard tens of thousands of complaints, and in the last forty years its status has grown from a body, which filtered complaints for the Court, to a respected, judicial, human rights institution in its own right.  The Court has handed down over one thousand judgments under the Convention in that time and its contribution to international human rights law, as well as to the jurisprudence of many of its States Parties, is unrivalled.  The Convention has been either supplemented or amended by Protocol on eleven occasions.  Protocols One, Four, Six and Seven have added new rights and the remaining Protocols have made procedural amendments of varying significance.   Protocol Nine in particular extended to the individual the right to have a case referred from the Commission to the Court.  Moreover, Protocol Eleven, which came into force in November 1998, effected much needed reform of the Convention's complaint mechanism which, with the steady increase in complaints, had been operating under unsustainable pressure.  In particular, cases were taking over five years to reach the Court and with the number of cases likely to continue to grow, the system was in danger of grinding to a halt. As a result, it was resolved to streamline the process and to this end, the existing institutions were abolished and replaced with a single Court of Human Rights, which now sits in Strasbourg on a permanent basis.  One of the reasons for the increase in the case load of the Commission and Court was the expansion of the number of Parties to the Convention itself.  The last ten years has seen membership grow to forty states, including many of the relatively new democracies of Eastern Europe and the Balkans, meaning that the Convention and the reach of its guarantees are both European in the widest sense.[4]

## The European Convention and Children

The focus in the European Convention is on rights of a civil and political nature and its provisions reflect the concerns of the Governments in post war Europe.   For example, Article 3 prohibits torture, inhuman and

---

[4]   In addition to the original signatories, the following States are now parties to the Convention: Albania, Andorra, Austria, Bulgaria, Croatia, Cyprus, Czech Republic, Estonia, Finland, Former Yugoslavian Republic of Macedonia, Hungary, Iceland, Latvia, Liechtenstein, Lithuania, Malta, Moldova, Norway, Poland, Portugal, Romania, San Marino, Slovakia, Slovenia, Spain, Switzerland, Ukraine.

degrading treatment or punishment; Article 8 protects family life from arbitrary and unlawful state interference and Article 9 guarantees thought, conscience and religion.   Despite being inspired by the Universal Declaration of Human Rights, the European Convention does not reiterate its standards of social and economic rights.   Thus, the Convention does not recognise the right to social security, the right to an adequate standard of living, or cultural rights of any kind.   Specific reference to the important needs of childhood is absent too.   Nor does the Convention acknowledge that the family is the natural and fundamental unit of society.   Indeed, in contrast to the earlier Declaration on which it was based, the Convention lacks even the most basis recognition of the rights of the child.   Yet, despite these shortcomings, it does make provision for the protection of children in certain, specific areas.   Article 5 permits the detention of a minor for the purpose of educational supervision or for bringing him before the competent legal authority, thereby providing for the rehabilitation of minors in conflict with the law and their protection from harm.   Article 6, which recognises the right to a fair trial, provides that the press and public may be excluded from all or part of the trial where the interests of juveniles require.   This offers States the potential to restrict the right to a public trial where children are involved, in order to protect them from adverse publicity and protect their privacy during such proceedings.   Article 2 of the First Protocol to the Convention guarantees the right to education, and recognises the right of parents to ensure that the education and teaching of their children is in conformity with their own religious and philosophical convictions.   This latter concept affirms the dominance of the parental role in the rearing and education of children.   This is reflected too in Article 5 of the Seventh Protocol, which guarantees parental equality, during marriage and in the event of its dissolution, and also recognises the State's right to take measures considered necessary in the interests of the child. This provision has generated little case law, however, and it is Article 8, which guarantees the right to respect for family life, which has been most frequently invoked in children's cases.

In light of the fact that it makes few *express* references to the rights of the child, the equal entitlement of children to enjoy Convention rights needs to be highlighted, and its potential maximised.   It is significant therefore that Article 1 obliges States to secure Convention rights and freedoms to *everyone* within their jurisdiction.   This principle of equal entitlement to Convention rights is reinforced by Article 14, which prohibits discrimination in the enjoyment of Convention rights detailed below.   In theory, then, Convention rights are guaranteed to all, and there is little to prevent their application to children. In practice, the Commission and Court of Human Rights have refrained from placing express or general limits on the application of the Convention in children's cases. Moreover, they have adopted several dynamic interpretive principles, which have positive implications for the protection which the Convention offers children. These are outlined below, alone with some of the institutions' other more general approaches, which are central to the way in which children's cases are decided.


**Non-Discrimination**

The Convention's non-discrimination principle takes on added significance in seeking to maximise the general application of Convention provisions to children. Although not an equality provision, Article 14 prohibits discrimination in the enjoyment of Convention rights, and it may be relied upon by children and young persons, who can make out a claim. However, the protection, which Article 14 offers children, is limited by the fact that it is not a free standing provision. It can be invoked only in conjunction with one of the Convention's substantive provisions, and its scope to protect children's rights is restricted therefore by the Convention's considerable textual limits. Moreover, the effect of Article 14 is not such that all discriminatory treatment will be contrary to the Convention as such an approach would be unworkable. Instead, the Court has established that a difference in treatment which is capable of objective and reasonable justification will not fall foul of Article 14.[5] Despite the practical nature of this approach, it is clear that it may nonetheless be used to justify the unequal treatment of children under the Convention. In particular, where there are reasonable and objective grounds for treating children differently, either from adults or from each other, then the alleged discriminatory treatment will not contravene Article 14.[6]

Despite these limitations, the grounds on which discriminatory is forbidden under Article 14 are comprehensive. The text of the provision requires that Convention rights be secured without discrimination on any grounds, and the following are provided as examples only: sex, race, colour, language, religion, political or other opinion, national or social origin, association with a national minority, property, birth or other status.

---

[5]    See for example, Eur Court HR *Belgian Linguistic Case*, judgment of 23 July 1968, Series A no 6, 1 EHRR 252.

[6]    See further Chapter 2.

The reference to 'other status' indicates the open-ended nature of this list and the broad scope of the prohibition suggests that there is great potential for interpreting Article 14 in an expansive manner. In relation to children, it is important that the criterion of age has been found to fall within the scope of 'other status'.[7] Although the institutions have avoided giving express recognition to other grounds, including sexuality[8] and disability,[9] the fact that they have considered discriminatory treatment on such grounds indicates their tacit approval of such an interpretation.

The Court has developed its case law on Article 14 in a positive manner,[10] and the implications of this for the application of the Convention to children are illustrated briefly here. Firstly, the Court has found that the provision applies not only to those elements of a right which a State is obliged to guarantee, but also to the elements which it chooses to guarantee. For example, in the *Belgian Linguistics Case*, it found that although there was no obligation on the State to provide a particular system of education, where a State chooses to do so, it may not restrict access to it in a discriminatory manner.[11] The potential of this approach is clear and it may be useful, *inter alia*, in seeking to ensure equal access to education by children with physical disabilities for example.[12] Secondly, the scope of the substantive provision being invoked with Article 14 may influence the latter provision's scope of protection. Thus, if there is a positive obligation implicit in the substantive provision, then this may translate as an obligation to promote equality, rather than to protect against discrimination when the two provisions are read together.[13] Moreover, there is scope for argument as to whether a claim actually falls within the ambit of the main provision being invoked with Article 14. For instance (and this illustrates the former point too) Article 8 does not include an obligation to pay parental leave allowance. Nevertheless, it is sufficient for the purposes of Article 14 that the measure falls within the scope of respect for family life.

---

[7]  No *7215/75 v UK*, Comm Rep, 12.10.78, DR 19, p 66, 3 EHRR 63.

[8]  No 25186/94 *Sutherland v UK*, Comm Rep, 1.7.97, 24 EHRR CD 22, § 51. See further Chapter 2, pp 25-26.

[9]  No 29046/95 *McIntyre v UK*, Dec 21.10.98, unreported. See p 69 below.

[10]  See Harris, O'Boyle & Warbrick (1995), *Law of the European Convention on Human Rights*, London: Butterworths, pp 462-488 and Van Dijk & Van Hoof (1998), *Theory and Practice of the European Convention on Human Rights*, 3rd ed, The Hague: Kluwer, pp 710-730.

[11]  *Belgian Linguistics Case* judgment, *op cit*.

[12]  See further Chapter 4, pp 68-69. See also Chapter 10, pp 236-237.

[13]  Harris, O'Boyle & Warbrick, *op cit*, p 463.

In this way, a failure to award parental leave allowance to both parents will raise an issue under Article 14, taken together with Article 8.[14]  This illustrates the further point that despite its complementary nature, a violation of Article 14 may occur even if an infringement of a substantive provision is neither proven, nor even alleged.[15]  As a result, a measure, such as a denial to pay parental leave allowance to fathers will infringe Article 14, even though it may be compatible with Article 8, unless it can be reasonably and objectively justified.  In this way, Article 14 adds a further, important stage to the test of whether a Convention provision has been violated, and in the light of the extensive grounds on which discrimination is prohibited, it expands the protection which the Convention offers children generally.

## Principles of Interpretation

### *The Margin of Appreciation[16]*

The doctrine of the margin of appreciation is frequently decisive of the scope of protection which the Convention offers, particularly in children's cases.  The need to develop such a principle was first explained by the Court in the *Handyside* case in 1976.  Here, the Court said that due to their 'direct and continuous contact with the vital forces of their countries', domestic authorities are, in principle, in a better position than the international judge to give an opinion on whether a measure is necessary in

---

[14]  Eur Court HR *Petrovic v Austria*, judgment of 27 March 1998, Reports 1998-II, no 67.  See further Chapter 9, pp 210-212.

[15]  To reach the opposite conclusion would, the Commission said, deprive Article 14 of any practical value as the sole effect of the discrimination would be to aggravate the violation of another provision of the Convention. See *Belgian Linguistics Case*, Comm Rep, 24.6.65, Series B no 3, pp 305-306.

[16]  See further O'Donnell (1982), 'The Margin of Appreciation Doctrine: Standards in the Jurisprudence of the European Court', *Human Rights Quarterly*, **4**, pp 474-496; Macdonald, 'The Margin of Appreciation' in Macdonald et al (eds) (1993), *The European System for the Protection of Human Rights*. Deventer: Kluwer, pp 83-124, and  Lavender (1997) 'The Problem of the Margin of Appreciation' *European Human Rights Law Review* **4** pp 380-390. See further Chapter 9, pp 204-206.

a democratic society and proportionate with the legitimate aim sought to be achieved.[17] Arising from that fact,

> the State is allowed a certain measure of discretion, subject to European supervision, when it takes legislative, administrative or judicial action in the area of a Convention right.[18]

In the light of this definition, the doctrine appears to be directly relevant to those Convention provisions which permit limitations on rights that are necessary in a democratic society and proportionate to the pursuit of a legitimate aim. The margin of appreciation is thus widely associated with the rights contained in Articles 8 to 11, which guarantee, *inter alia*, the right to respect for family life; freedom of thought, conscience and religion; freedom of expression, and freedom of association respectively. However, there is also considerable evidence to support the view that the doctrine's application is actually wider in reach. Matscher, a former judge on the Court, describes it as an obligation to 'respect, within certain bounds, the cultural and ideological variety, and also the legal variety, which are characteristic of Europe'.[19] This reflects another dimension to the principle, which means that the scope of discretion enjoyed by Convention States will vary according to the circumstances of the case and the issue being considered. In this regard, one of the facts to be taken into account in determining its scope is whether there exists common ground between the laws of the Convention States.[20] Where common practice is apparent, then the margin of appreciation will be narrow and deviation from it will be difficult to justify. On the other hand, where a common approach is not widespread, then the discretion which the Court offers States will be generous.

While the margin of appreciation is a dominant theme throughout Convention case law, the broad degree of discretion which States enjoy with regard to respect for family life has a significant impact on the way in which children's cases are decided. This is largely due to the considerable judicial restraint exercised by the Court in considering whether domestic

---

[17] Eur Court HR *Handyside v UK*, judgment of 24 July 1976, Series A no 24,    1 EHRR 737, § 48-49.

[18] Harris, O'Boyle & Warbrick, *op cit*, p 12.

[19] See Matscher, 'Methods of Interpretation of the Convention' in Macdonald et al, *op cit*, pp 63-81, p 75.

[20] See for example Eur Court HR *Rasmussen v Denmark*, judgment of 28 Nov 1984, Series A no 87, 7 EHRR 371, § 40.

decisions on family law matters are compatible with Article 8. In particular, the Court has shown great reluctance to interfere with domestic decisions in matters such as the award of custody following divorce, or particularly the decision to place children with alternative carers. Although it purports to review whether such decisions are based on relevant and sufficient reasons, its examination of whether this was actually the case amounts to no more than a superficial examination of whether the decision was free from arbitrariness. Moreover, the Commission and Court have not always agreed on the scope of discretion which States enjoy in such matters,[21] although it is clear that the Court's more restrained approach has the effect of reducing the protection which the Convention offers children.[22] At the same time, the employment of the doctrine in such cases is not without justification given the Court's acceptance that due to the complex and sensitive nature of family law matters, it is necessary that the authorities closest to the situation and with direct contact with the parties enjoy a degree of latitude as to the decision made. It is important too that the relevant decision is taken at the most appropriate level and by the most appropriate authority, always subject to European review. Moreover, the doctrine is firmly grounded in Convention jurisprudence and it is, when appropriately applied, a necessary feature of a regional system of human rights protection. In particular, it plays an important role in the interpretation of the Convention and maintaining the credibility of its enforcement mechanism, and this is particularly important in the light of the scope of provisions such as Article 8.

Although the doctrine is a European construct, it is also relevant to the application of the Convention at domestic level, albeit in a different form. In any event, the use of the doctrine by both European and domestic courts should be closely monitored so that its improper application, perhaps as a convenient let-out clause in relation to potentially controversial decisions, or those which appear to impinge greatly on state sovereignty in a sensitive area, does not go unchallenged.

---

[21] Compare approaches in Eur Court HR *Olsson v Sweden*, judgment of 24 March 1988, Series A no 130, 11 EHRR 259 and *Olsson v Sweden,* Comm Rep, 2.12.86, 11 EHRR 301. See further Chapter 12.

[22] See further Chapters 9, 11, 12 and 13.

*Proportionality*

The principle of proportionality is an increasingly important theme in Convention case law. The Court has frequently reminded that:

> inherent in the whole of the Convention is a search for a fair balance between the demands of the general interest of the community and the requirements of the protection of the individual's fundamental rights.[23]

The principle of proportionality is one way in which this balance is achieved and its use throughout the Court's application of the Convention is now widespread. Nevertheless, it applies squarely to provisions of the Convention, which expressly permit restrictions on rights and freedoms and thus necessitate the achievement of a balance between competing interests. Article 8, for example, permits an interference with the right to respect for family life as long as it is proportionate to the aim which the measure creating the interference seeks to achieve.[24] Thus where a child is removed from his/her family, the Court will use the proportionality principle to consider whether an appropriate balance has been achieved between the interference with family life which it causes and the interests and rights of the child, which it serves to protect. However, the proportionality principle applies in other areas too, such as Article 14 where there must be an appropriate balance reached between the difference in treatment suffered and the aim which it pursues.[25] It is also employed to determine whether restrictions implicit in Convention rights are compatible with the Convention. For example, it is used when considering whether a restriction on the right of access to a court under Article 6 is justified by reference to the general interest which it serves.[26]

Overall, the principle of proportionality recognises that human rights are not absolute and that the exercise of an individual's rights must always be checked by the broader public interest. In the same way, the rights of children are not superior to the rights of parents or others in society, although the recognition in international law that children's interests should

---

[23] Eur Court HR *Soering v UK*, judgment of 7 July 1989, Series A no 161, 11 EHRR 439.
[24] See further Chapter 9, pp 199-206.
[25] See Chapter 2 for example.
[26] Eur Court HR *Osman v UK*, judgment of 28 Oct 1998, Reports 1998-VIII, no 95. See further Chapter 7, pp 143-145.

be *a*, if not *the*, paramount consideration in decisions affecting them highlights the difficulty in applying the Convention in children's cases.[27]

## Implicit Procedural Safeguards

While the margin of appreciation, discussed above, limits implicitly the protection which the Convention offers, the Court's emphasis on procedural aspects of Convention rights has arguably extended its scope and it is of great practical significance in a growing number of areas. It was first formulated in relation to Article 8, where the Court found respect for family life to include the right of parents to be involved in a decision-making process to a degree sufficient to provide them with adequate protection of their interests.[28] The Court has since expanded on the constituent elements of this principle and procedural protection is now an implicit part of respect for family life generally.

Notwithstanding that Article 6 contains important procedural rights, the development of procedural protection as an implicit part of certain substantive provisions permits the development of safeguards which are specific to the rights guaranteed and go beyond the scope of the fair trial provision. This is exemplified by the Court's development of the principle under Article 8, which applies to administrative as well as judicial decisions, and where the rights of parents to be consulted and informed about the decision making process concerning their children may be decisive as to whether their family life has been respected. It is also apparent from other areas, such as the right to life under Article 2, where considerable rights of procedural protection have been established.[29]

The following chapters highlight the scope for reading procedural guarantees into Convention provisions. This is particularly apparent in those areas where certain procedural rights are guaranteed expressly to children, as in Articles 5 and 6 in relation to areas of juvenile justice and detention.[30] Moreover, in the light of the procedural element implicit in Article 8, it is likely that the Court will find consultation with children to be essential for the effective protection of their rights too.[31]

---

[27] This dilemma is particularly evident in immigration case law. See further Chapter 10.

[28] Eur Court HR *W v UK*, judgment of 8 July 1987, Series A no 121, 10 EHRR 29. See further Chapter 9, pp 206-207 and Chapter 12, pp 284-289.

[29] See further Chapter 7, pp 141-146.

[30] See generally Chapter 3.

[31] See further Chapter 6, pp 117-120.

*Effective Protection*

In the light of its textual constraints, it crucial that the protection which the Convention offers children is maximised. At an early stage in Strasbourg jurisprudence, the Court established that the Convention was meant to protect rights which were practical and effective, and not those which were illusory and theoretical.[32] This interpretive approach has been further developed through the Court's case law and its effect has been to enhance considerably the scope of its various provisions. The basis for this approach is Article 1 of the Convention, which guarantees Convention rights to everyone, which is used as a platform from which the effective protection of Convention rights can be developed. The Court has consistently found that this provision imposes a positive obligation on States to ensure the equal application of the Convention to all those within its jurisdiction. For example, where a breach of a Convention right is attributable to a private, rather than a public individual, responsibility may nonetheless lie with the State for the violation as a consequence of its failure to provide adequate legal protection from the breach.[33] While responsibility for the actions of private individuals cannot be directly imposed on the State, nevertheless, the State must provide adequate legal protection from any treatment which falls foul of the Convention's standards. This is illustrated effectively by *A v UK*, in which a boy complained that he had suffered inhuman and degrading treatment at the hands of his father, for which the State was liable.[34] While the State was not directly responsible for the boy's ill-treatment, the obligation under Article 1 meant that it was responsible for failing to provide him with effective legal protection against any abuse contrary to Article 3.

This approach has subsequently been used to extend the scope of numerous other Convention provisions, and its effect is to find a requirement of legal protection to be implicit in substantive Convention provisions. Its potential to influence in a positive and dynamic manner the way in the Convention is applied to children is clear from the case law.[35]

---

[32] Eur Court HR *Airey v Ireland*, judgment of 9 Oct 1979, Series A no 32, 2 EHRR 305.

[33] For example, Eur Court HR *Costello-Roberts v UK*, judgment of 25 March 1993, Series A No 247, 19 EHRR 112.

[34] Eur Court HR *A v UK*, judgment of 23 Sept 1998, Reports 1998-VI no 90. See generally Chapter 8.

[35] See generally Chapters 7 and 8.

The approach is particularly important, however, where specific reference to the child's need for protection is lacking. This is illustrated by the cases of *T* and *V* against the UK in 1998 where the question arose as to whether two 11 year old boys had received a fair trial under the Convention, given that they were tried in an adult court.[36] Having regard to their young age and the application of the full rigours of the adult, public trial, the Commission concluded that the boys had been deprived of the opportunity to participate effectively in the determination of the criminal charges against them. As a result, they were denied a crucial ingredient of the concept of fair trial, in violation of Article 6.

## *Positive Obligations*

Also derived from Article 1 and inherently linked to the principle of effective protection is the principle of positive obligations.[37] It is derived from the recognition that the guarantee to secure Convention rights may entail obligations of a negative or a positive nature. While negative obligations are straightforward insofar as they require a State to refrain from taking action which interferes with a Convention right, the obligation to secure Convention rights may, in certain circumstances, require affirmative action. This principle was first applied by the Court in a children's case, where it established that there may be positive obligations inherent in an effective respect for family life. The Court concluded in the *Marckx* case that the State had failed to take appropriate action in fulfilment of its positive obligation under Article 8. In particular, by failing to recognise a child born outside marriage as a member of the mother's family the State, in breach of Article 8, had prevented the applicants from leading a normal family life.[38]

Some Convention provisions contain express positive obligations, such as Article 2, which says that everyone's right to life shall be protected by law. Obligations of a positive nature may be read into other provisions, although Article 8, whose reference to 'the right to respect', clearly facilitates such an interpretation.[39] For example, in relation to the

---

[36] See both No 24724/94  *T v UK* and No 24888/94  *V v UK*, Comm Reps, 4.12.98, unreported. See further Chapter 3, pp 58-60.

[37] See Harris, O'Boyle & Warbrick, *op cit,* pp 19-22.

[38] Eur Court HR *Marckx v Belgium*, judgment of 31 June 1979, Series A no 31, § 41, 2 EHRR 330.

[39] See also Connelly (1986), 'Problems of Interpretation of Article 8 of the ECHR', *International and Comparative Law Quarterly*, **35**, pp 567-593.

compulsory taking of children into public care, the Court has held that respect for family life includes a right for the parent to have measures taken with a view to his or her being reunited with the child and an obligation for the national authorities to take such action.[40]   However, the scope of the positive obligation inherent in a particular provision is not always clear and furthermore, it is for the Court to decide whether one exists at all.   In this regard, there is a thin line between finding that a certain measure constitutes a failure to respect, or an interference with family life.   Indeed the Commission and Court frequently take different approaches in this regard, although the consequences are rarely significant.[41]   This makes the application of the principle difficult to forecast although the factors taken into account in reaching the conclusion are the same in any event.[42]

*Evolutive Interpretation*

The Court has established that the Convention is to be interpreted as a living instrument and this has allowed it to maintain its relevance to social and legal standards.   This interpretive approach holds great promise for the application of the Convention to cases concerning children.   The Court firmly established this dynamic approach in the *Tyrer* case, which concerned whether the judicial punishment of a juvenile offender was compatible with the Convention.   In concluding that it was not, the Court noted that it could be influenced by the developments and commonly accepted standards in the policies and laws of the Member States of the Council of Europe.[43]

Insofar as interpreting the Convention in a fluid manner allows its standards to adapt and develop, this approach has obvious potential to enhance the protection which the Convention offers children, notwithstanding that their rights are given little express recognition among its provisions.   Further illustration of the importance of the approach is clear from the *Marckx* case.   While it was permissible when the

---

[40]   Eur Court HR *Eriksson v Sweden*, judgment of 22 June 1989, Series A no 156, 12 EHRR 183, § 71.
[41]   For example, see Eur Court HR *Keegan v Ireland*, judgment of 26 May 1994 Series A no 290, 18 EHRR 342, and No 16969/90 *Keegan v Ireland*, Comm Rep, 17.2.93, Series A no 290, p 26.   See further Chapter 9.
[42]   See further Harris, O'Boyle & Warbrick, *op cit*, pp 320-324.
[43]   Eur Court HR *Tyrer v UK*, judgment of 25 April 1978, Series A no 26, 2 EHRR 1, § 31.   See also Harris, O'Boyle & Warbrick, *op cit*, pp 9- 10.

Convention was drafted to treat children differently according to their parents' marital status, the need to reflect legal and social trends among Convention States required that the Court review this position in 1979.[44]

The potential of this approach is limited only by the constraints of the Convention itself. While provisions which are precisely worded will be more difficult to interpret in a dynamic fashion, those articles which are drafted in looser terms arguably lend themselves more naturally to such an interpretation.[45] The right to respect for private and family life under Article 8 illustrates this point effectively insofar as its lack of precision has permitted the continuous development and expansion of its scope to take account of legal, social and other change. For children, this provision appears incapable of exhaustive definition, and the obligations implicit in respect for private and family life continue to be developed through the Court's application of this approach. For example, a dynamic approach to the provision may require the recognition of the right of the child to information regarding his/her origins or birth parents as this right becomes more widely accepted in domestic and international legal systems. In addition, as national authorities increasingly offer the unmarried father the opportunity to enjoy legal equality with the mother vis-à-vis their children, this approach may emerge more decisively in the case law of the Court.[46] In the same way that the best interests approach has become the norm in cases of child care and the family, the fact that domestic legal systems continue to make increasing provision for the right of the child to be consulted will also have to be recognised by the Convention authorities.

*Reference to other International Instruments*

The requirement that the Convention must develop so as to maintain relevance to current legal and social conditions recognises that as a system of human rights protection it cannot operate in isolation from surrounding legal and social influences. Indeed, the Court has always drawn on factors outside of the Convention in applying its standards, and this is evident from its approach to the margin of appreciation where States will enjoy less discretion where their approach is out of line with commonly accepted modes in the Council of Europe and beyond. Among the sources of expertise upon which the Court frequently draws are the various legal

---

[44] *Marckx* judgment, *op cit*, § 41.

[45] Eur Court HR *Johnston v Ireland*, judgment of 18 Dec 1986, Series A no 112, 9 EHRR 203, § 57.

[46] See Chapter 11, especially pp 246-249.

instruments and treaties which make up both regional and international human rights law. For example, in the *Marckx* case the Court referred to the Council of Europe's Convention on the Legal Status of Children born outside Wedlock 1975 as evidence of an increasing acceptance of equal treatment for children regardless of their parents' marital status.[47] While the institutions have also referred to other regional and international treaties,[48] there is little doubt that  increasing reference to the almost universally ratified UN Convention on the Rights of the Child is a particularly important development in relation to the application of the European Convention to children.[49] Both the Commission and the Court have referred to provisions of the UN Convention in children's cases[50] and the Commission has gone further in attaching weight to the observations of the Convention's treaty body, the UN Committee on the Rights of the Child, where particularly relevant.[51]  In the absence of child-specific standards from the European Convention, the Convention on the Rights of the Child provides a clear and comprehensive code of children's rights. Given its almost universal acceptance, it is open to the Court to seek guidance from its principles and provisions where gaps in the Convention's text are identified. It is argued that the use of the Convention as persuasive authority in order to interpret Convention provisions in children's cases in

---

[47] ETS No 85. See *Marckx* judgment, *op cit*. For criticism of the Court's approach see Davidson, 'The European Convention on Human Rights and the 'Illegitimate' Child', in Freestone (ed) (1990), *Children and the Law: Essays in Honour of Professor HK Bevan,* Hull: Hull University Press, pp 75-106, at pp 95-96.

[48] In No *7626/76 X v UK*, Dec 11.7.77, DR 11, p 160 and Eur Court HR *Inze v Austria*, judgment of 28 October 1987, Series A no 126, 10 EHRR 394, § 32, the Commission and Court referred expressly to provisions of the European Convention on Adoption, ETS No 58. In Nos *5095/71, 5920/72 & 5926/72 Kjeldsen, Busk Madsen & Pedersen v Denmark*, Comm Rep, 21.3.75, Series A no 23, § 153, the Commission referred to the UNESCO Convention against Discrimination, 1960, UNTS vol 429, p 93, and also the Declaration on the Rights of the Child, 1959.

[49] UN Doc A/44/25.

[50] See *Costello-Roberts* judgment, *op cit*, § 36 referring to Article 16 and *Keegan* judgment, *op cit*, § 50, referring to Article 7.

[51] No 25599/94 *A v UK*, Comm Rep, 18.9.97, Reports 1998-VI no 90. See also No 24724/94 *T* Comm Rep, *op cit*, and No 24888/94 *V* Comm Rep, *op cit*.

the absence of other guidance is entirely acceptable, as long as the result is compatible with the object and purpose of the Convention itself.[52]

## The Teleological Approach

Pursuant to international law,[53] the European Convention on Human Rights must be interpreted in good faith in accordance with the ordinary meaning of the text and in the light of its object and purpose. This teleological approach ensures that the Convention is interpreted in a way, which aims to secure its purpose, i.e. the protection of human rights and freedoms and the maintenance and promotion of ideals, values and the rule of law in a democratic society.[54] In children's cases, this method of interpretation has proven significant in many areas, including education,[55] deprivation of liberty[56] and the right to adequate protection of physical integrity.[57] Moreover, reliance by the Court on the Convention's object and purpose requires that, in principle, permissible exceptions to the rights protected by the Convention be restrictively interpreted.[58] This is notable given that several provisions place express limits on the exercise of Convention rights, such as respect for family life, freedom of expression and freedom of religion.[59] It is also significant that that the exceptions to the right to liberty and to a public hearing in Articles 5 and 6 respectively apply only to children.

---

[52] The interpretation of the Convention should not be so dynamic as to lead to the creation of new rights, which would cause States to question the legitimacy of the Convention system. See Pellonpää, 'Economic, Social and Cultural Rights' in Macdonald et al, *op cit*, pp 855-874, at p 867.

[53] See Article 3 of the Vienna Convention on the Law of Treaties 1969, UNTS, vol, p 331.

[54] See further Harris, O'Boyle & Warbrick, *op cit*, pp 6-7 and Matscher, *op cit*, pp 68-70.

[55] Eur Court HR *Campbell & Cosans v UK*, judgment of 25 Feb 1982, Series A no 48, 4 EHRR 293. See further Chapter 4, pp 76-77.

[56] Eur Court HR *Bouamar v Belgium*, judgment of 29 Feb 1987, Series A no 129, 11 EHRR 1. See further Chapter 3, pp 42-44.

[57] Eur Court HR *X & Y v the Netherlands*, judgment of 26 March 1985, Series A no 91, 8 EHRR 235. See further Chapter 8, pp 174-175.

[58] See Matscher, *op cit*, pp 66-67.

[59] See generally Chapter 6 and Chapter 9.

**Prospects**

It is clear that, despite the apparent textual limits of the Convention for protecting the rights of the child, a number of factors have combined to show encouraging signs of its potential. The interpretive principles and general approaches of the Commission and Court, highlighted above, play an important role in this regard, and they identify clear ways in which the Convention's application to children can be taken forward. Thus, despite the limitations of the text, the Strasbourg institutions have already begun to apply the Convention in a positive way so as to extend its protection explicitly to children. Adopting a dynamic approach to interpretation and scope, placing emphasis critically on effective protection of Convention rights and the obligation, whether positive or negative, required to guarantee them, as well as relying on other established international standards in the absence of Convention guidance, can all play a significant role in ensuring that this potential is maximised.

# 2    Definition and Status of the Child

## Introduction

While the UN Convention on the Rights of the Child provides some guidance as to who is a child under international law,[1] the European Convention does not address specifically the age at which a person may enjoy its rights. Moreover, the line between ability and entitlement is blurred in children's rights, given that the age at which a child is *entitled* to enjoy Convention rights may be different from the age at which s/he is capable of *enjoying* them.[2] Notwithstanding that parents may be able to exercise some children's rights on their behalf, the issue is complicated further by the fact that the term *children* includes both the very young and those nearing adulthood, ignoring that not all such persons have the capacity to enjoy Convention rights, and that the ability to exercise those rights is acquired progressively. In the light of these conceptual difficulties, therefore, it is not surprising that neither the Commission nor the Court have attempted or found it necessary to identify a point in time after which children can be said to enjoy Convention rights. In the same way, they have failed to show support for the view that a minimum age limit should apply to the application of the Convention to children. The result is that there is neither an express nor an implicit limit on the application of Convention rights to children. This is reinforced by Article 1, which guarantees these rights to everyone and Article 14, which prohibits discrimination in the enjoyment of Convention rights on many grounds, including age.[3] Instead, the Strasbourg bodies decide each case on its merits, and conveniently leave the problematic issue of whether a child has the capacity to exercise Convention rights to the circumstances of each case.

---

[1]    UN Doc A/44/25. For background on the position in international law see Van Bueren (1995a), *The International Law on the Rights of the Child*, Dordrecht: Martinus Nijhoff, pp 33-38.

[2]    There is a wealth of academic writing on this and other related theory. See for example Freeman & Veerman (eds) (1992), *The Ideologies of Children's Rights*, Dordrecht: Martinus Nijhoff and Alston, Parker & Seymour (eds) (1992), *Children, Rights and the Law*, Clarendon: Oxford University Press.

[3]    See further Chapter 1, pp 4-6.

## The Definition of the Child

*When does Childhood begin? The Convention and the Unborn Child*

Although the question of whether children enjoy Convention rights has not been determined decisively by the Commission or the Court, the issue of when they apply to children has been addressed indirectly in the context of abortion and the right to life of the unborn child.  Article 2 of the Convention guarantees that everyone's right to life shall be protected by law, but, while the provision elaborates on other situations in which this right can be restricted, it is silent on whether the protection offered or the restrictions permitted extend to the child before birth.[4]  It is thus unclear whether abortion is compatible with Article 2 or conversely, whether its unavailability constitutes an unjustifiable interference with private life under Article 8 § 2.  The Commission's approach to this issue has been hesitant and the principal question, whether the right to life is enjoyed by the unborn child, is still largely unresolved.  However, it has reflected on the need to respect the divergence in laws and opinion regarding the availability of abortion in Convention States and, as long as the compatibility with the Convention is reviewed in each case, then a departure from its minimum standards will not be permitted.[5]

The case of *Brüggemann & Scheuten* raised the substantive issue for the first time in 1977, when two women complained that the absence of legal abortion violated their right to respect for private life under Article 8.[6] Rejecting their complaint, the Commission noted the wide range of medical, ethical and religious opinion on the subject of abortion among Convention States and consequently found that the lack of availability of abortion could not be found to violate the Convention, in the absence of

---

[4]  This is not surprising given that even the Convention on the Rights of the Child is ambiguous on this point.  On the issues which arose during drafting see Leblanc (1995), *The Convention on the Rights of the Child: United Nations Law Making on Human Rights*, Lincoln: University of Nebraska Press, p 66-73.  See also the declarations to the Convention entered by the UK and France in UN Doc CRC/C/11/Add.1, p 112 and UN Doc CRC/C/3/Add.15, p 11 respectively.

[5]  See Hogan, 'The Right to Life and the Abortion  Question under the European Convention on Human Rights', in Heffernan (ed) (1994), *Human Rights: A European Perspective*, Dublin: Round Hall Press, pp 104-116.

[6]  No 6959/75 *Brüggemann & Scheuten v Germany*, Comm Rep, 12.7.77, DR 10, p 100, 3 EHRR 244.

proof highlighting States' intentions to the contrary. As a result, therefore, it did not have to resolve

> whether the unborn child was to be considered as 'life' in the sense of Article 2... or whether it could be regarded as an entity which under Article 8 § 2 could justify interference for the protection of others. [7]

*Brüggemann* thus left open whether the unborn child is covered by Article 2 and in 1980, the Commission was faced with a fresh challenge which presented the argument from a different angle. The *Paton* case concerned whether laws permitting abortion violated the unborn child's right to life under Article 2.[8] In addressing the issue, the Commission examined the ordinary meaning of 'everyone' in the context of Article 2, as well as in the Convention as a whole. With regard to the latter, it noted that

> [i]n nearly all these instances the use of the word is such that it can apply only postnatally. None indicates clearly that it has any possible prenatal application although such application in a rare case ... cannot be entirely excluded.[9]

The same conclusion was reached with regard to the limitations on the right to life in Article 2, and here the Commission found that both the general usage of the term 'everyone', and the context in which it is employed in that provision, support the view that it does not include the unborn. The Commission then considered whether the term 'life' under the first sentence of Article 2 is to be interpreted as covering only the life of persons already born or also the unborn life of the foetus. On this, and in response to the specific claim that the right to life of the unborn was absolute, it drew the following conclusion. The 'life' of the foetus, it said, was intimately connected with, and cannot be regarded in isolation from, the life of the pregnant woman. If Article 2 were found to cover the foetus and, in the absence of any express limitation, its protection under this provision were seen as absolute, an abortion would have to be considered as prohibited even where the continuance of the pregnancy would involve a serious risk to the life of the pregnant woman. This would mean that the 'unborn life' of the foetus would be regarded as being of a higher value than the life of the pregnant woman. The 'right to life' of a person already born

---

[7]    *Ibid*, § 60.
[8]    No 8416/78 *Paton v UK*, Dec 13.5.80, DR 19, p 244, 3 EHRR 408.
[9]    *Ibid*.

would thus be considered as subject, not only to the express limitations in Article 2, but also to a further, implied limitation. On balance, it found that such an interpretation would be 'contrary to the object and purpose of the Convention', particularly given that, when the Convention was signed in 1950, all but one of the Convention States permitted abortion where necessary to protect the life of the mother. Moreover, since that time, national law on abortion has shown a tendency towards further liberalisation.

The Commission's view on whether the right to life of the unborn child was absolute is clear from *Paton*. What is still outstanding, however, is whether Article 2 can be said to provide *any* protection for the life of the foetus. Moreover, in the event that the protection of Article 2 is to be enjoyed by the unborn child, it is uncertain in what circumstances this will arise and whether, when it does, there will be implicit limitations on that protection. It may be relevant here that in the *Paton* case, the Commission referred to the equivalent provision in the American Convention on Human Rights, 1969. Article 4 of the American Convention expressly extends protection of the right to life to the unborn and this appears to highlight the absence of express protection in the European Convention. It also suggests that such protection is not implicit, although no formal conclusion has been drawn in this respect. In any event, the 'considerable divergence of views' among Convention States as to whether or not the Convention protects unborn life means that States must enjoy a level of discretion in this area, although the exact degree of discretion enjoyed is itself unclear.[10]

## When does Childhood End? Ages of Majority

Due to the fact that the Convention grants so few specific rights to children, there has been little need to define the point at which these rights no longer apply. As a result, neither the Commission nor the Court have considered the issue of when childhood ends in this context. The two specific references to minors in the Convention are made in Articles 5 and 6 respectively. Article 5 permits the detention of a minor for the purpose of educational supervision, or to bring him before the competent legal authority. Article 6 provides that the press or public may be excluded from

---

[10] For a criticism of the Commission's position see Peukert, 'Human Rights in International Law and the Protection of Unborn Beings' in Matscher & Petzold (eds) (1988), *Protecting Human Rights: The European Dimension, Studies in Honour of Gerard J Wiarda*, Koln: Heymanns, pp 511-519, at pp 515-518.

all or part of a trial where the interests of juveniles require. The fact that these two provisions use different terms in reference to children is curious, particularly given the fact that the liberty and fair trial provisions are considered to be inextricably linked. However, the importance of this distinction should not be exaggerated as the definition of these terms is, in any event, a matter for domestic law. Similar to other international instruments,[11] therefore, once a child falls within the definition of a minor or juvenile for the purposes of the relevant domestic law, then this will not be an issue when the matter is reviewed by the European Court, unless, of course, the age limit is arbitrarily or illegally applied. The application of the above provisions will thus be determined by the domestic situation, and once a minor is considered such under that system this is unlikely to be challenged in Strasbourg.

The use of minimum ages for the determination of a point in a child's life when particular activities become lawful (or unlawful where the age of criminal responsibility is concerned) reflects the child's lack of capacity, as well as the need to protect the child from exploitation and harmful influences.[12] Indeed, Convention case law recognises the fundamental principle that law should protect children's welfare and afford them the protection necessitated by their vulnerability and lack of maturity.[13] The setting of ages of majority and consent does not take into account the intellectual skills or abilities to carry out particular acts of any individual child. Moreover, legal rules which require persons to have reached a particular age before permitting them to consent to marriage and sexual relations, consume alcohol or vote, among other things, is both arbitrary and widely accepted.[14] Under the European Convention, this is reflected, *inter alia*, in Article 12, which provides that men and women 'of marriageable age' have the right to marry and found a family according to the relevant domestic law. The imposition on men and women of different age requirements for this purpose would arguably raise an issue of discrimination under Article 14, where this is not based on objective and

---

[11] Article 1 of the UN Convention on the Rights of the Child defines childhood as everyone under the age of 18 unless, under the law applicable to the child, majority is attained earlier, *op cit.*

[12] See Van Bueren (1995a), *The International Law on the Rights of the Child*, Dordrecht: Martinus Nijhoff, pp 36-39.

[13] No 24724/94 *T v UK*, Comm Rep, 4.12.98, unreported, § 91.

[14] *Ibid.* See Council of Europe Doc CDPS III.8 Obs (96) 1 *Ages at which children are legally entitled to carry out a series of acts in Council of Europe member countries.*

age requirements for this purpose would arguably raise an issue of discrimination under Article 14, where this is not based on objective and reasonable reasons.[15] Moreover, if the domestic law of a particular Convention State is out of step with the others, the wide margin of appreciation, which the State normally enjoys in setting minimum ages, is likely to be narrowed significantly in considering its compatibility with the Convention. This is illustrated by the comments of the Commission in a case, which challenged the fixing at 10 of the age of criminal responsibility. In considering this age to be 'relatively low' but not incompatible with the Convention, the Commission had regard to the lack of a commonly accepted minimum age for the imposition of criminal responsibility, and the fact that international law provides no specific guidance as to the age at which responsibility should be fixed.[16]

*Ages of Consent to Sexual Conduct*

In light of the fact that it is an important function of the law to protect children from harm, it is justifiable to impose ages of consent in the area of sexuality notwithstanding the interference with a person's private life which it causes.[17] Thus, it is clearly established that the prohibition of homosexual relations between an adult and a minor may serve to protect the minor's rights, with particular reference to his autonomy in sexual activities[18], in addition to the protection of general moral standards.[19] Moreover, according to the Commission, the criminal law should be used to protect from harm those individuals who are vulnerable because of their age and where there is an element of force or abuse of authority involved in

---

[15] See the concerns of the Committee on the Rights of the Child in this area. UN Doc CRC/C/38, § 275-299.

[16] No 24724/94 *T* Comm Rep, *op cit*, § 82-84. See further Chapter 3.

[17] See No *5935/72 X v Germany*, Dec 30.10.75, 19 Yearbook (1976), p 276. See also Eur Court HR *Dudgeon v UK*, judgment of 22 Oct 1981, Series A no 45, 4 EHRR 149, § 52.

[18] See for example No 5935/72 *X v Germany*, *ibid.*

[19] The Commission has accepted that prosecuting *some* homosexual conduct is aimed at both of these objectives. No 7525/75 *Dudgeon v UK*, Comm Rep, 13.3.80, Series B no 40. The criminalisation of homosexual conduct *per se* is not justifiable however. See *Dudgeon* judgment *op cit*, Eur Court HR *Norris v Ireland*, judgment of 26 Oct 1988, Series A no 142, 13 EHRR 186 and Eur Court HR *Modinos v Cyprus*, judgment of 22 April 1993, Series A no 259, 16 EHRR 485.

the adult-minor homosexual relationship.[20]    However, neither the Commission nor the Court has yet decided up to what age the protection of minors from homosexual relations is necessary, beyond finding that the fixing of such an age is a matter for the national authorities.[21]    Moreover, the age above which homosexual relationships are no longer subject to criminal law may be fixed within a reasonable margin and may vary according to the attitudes of society.[22]    The evolutive nature of the Convention's standards, which allows it to keep pace with social and legal trends throughout Europe, means that the setting of those ages will be subject to constant review at European level.    The effect of this is illustrated clearly by the case law in this area.

In 1975, the Commission found the age limit of 21 relatively high, although not beyond this reasonable margin.[23]    In 1978, it found that legislation which criminalised homosexual behaviour involving young men between the ages of 18 and 21 interfered with the right to respect for private life.[24]    However, it went on to find that the interference was justified given the risk that young men in this age bracket could be subjected to substantial social pressures, which could be harmful to their psychological development. In doing so, the Commission rejected that the fact that the age limit in most European countries was 18 meant that a higher age limit in the UK was incompatible with the Convention.    In particular, it noted that the age limit in each particular country must be established on its own merits.

In 1992, an Austrian law prohibiting men over 19 from engaging in homosexual acts with those under 18 years was found to be compatible with Article 8.    In particular, the Commission noted that the age of consent challenged was in fact lower than that in previous cases, from which the present case could not be distinguished.[25]    In 1995, a fresh challenge to the age of homosexual consent of 21 in the UK was averted when legislation

---

[20]    Criminal prosecution of the applicant did not violate Article 8 in No *7215/75 X v UK*, Comm Rep, 12.10.78, DR 19 p 66, 3 EHRR 63 where the victim had been forced to take part in homosexual acts with the adult applicant, or in No *22646/93 HF v Austria*, Dec 26.6.95, unreported, where the victim was the 15 year old employee of  the applicant, who was forced to have homosexual relations with him.

[21]    *Dudgeon* judgment, *op cit,* § 62.

[22]    No *5935/72 X v Germany, op cit.*

[23]    *Ibid.*

[24]    No *7215/75 v UK*, Comm Report, *op cit.*

[25]    No 17279/90 *AZ v Austria*, Dec 13.5.92, unreported.

was adopted reducing the age to 18 years and the case was settled as a result.[26]

It was not until 1997 that the fixing at 18 of the minimum age for lawful homosexual activities was challenged successfully before the Commission. In the *Sutherland* case, the applicant claimed that the fixing of this age of consent at 18, in contrast to the minimum age for lawful heterosexual conduct which is set at 16, amounted to discrimination with regard to his right to respect for his private life reading Article 8 with Article 14.[27] The Commission's principal focus here was whether there was a reasonable relationship of proportionality between the discriminatory treatment and the need to protect the rights of others. Its assessment took into account the State's margin of appreciation, which is narrow in such cases because the interference impinges on a most intimate aspect of affected individuals' private lives. However, in light of major changes in professional opinion in relation to the need to protect young male homosexuals and the desirability of introducing an equal age of consent, the Commission considered it necessary to review its case law in this area. In particular, it noted the increased support among professional bodies for an equal age of consent, as well as the fact that this equality of treatment is now recognised by the great majority of Convention States. The UK Government had advanced two arguments in favour of maintaining the existing inequality as regards the age of consent for homosexual and heterosexual conduct. Its first argument related to the need to protect vulnerable young men who do not have a settled sexual orientation from activities, which will result in considerable social isolation which they may regret with maturity. However, the Commission failed to find that this view was supported by evidence. The Government's second argument was that notwithstanding the European trend, British society was entitled to indicate its disapproval of homosexual conduct and its preference that children follow a heterosexual way of life. Again, however, the Commission could not accept that a society's entitlement to indicate disapproval of homosexual conduct could ever constitute an objective or reasonable justification for

---

[26] No *22382/93 Wilde, Greenhalgh & Parry v UK*, Dec 19.1.95, DR 80A, p 132, 19 EHRR CD 86. See s 145 Criminal Justice and Public Order Act 1994. In particular, all of the applicants had already reached 18 years.

[27] No *25186/94 Sutherland v UK*, Comm Rep, 1.7.97, 24 EHRR CD 22. The complaint of discrimination had been made in previous cases, but the Court and Commission had refused to consider it because of perceived overlap with the substantive issue. See for example, *Dudgeon* judgment, *op cit.*

inequality of treatment under the criminal law. Thus, despite the fact that these arguments emerged from a parliamentary debate of the matter,[28] the Commission failed to find that they offered a reasonable and objective justification for maintaining a higher minimum age of consent for male homosexual, than to heterosexual acts. In conclusion, this amounted to discrimination in violation of Article 8, together with Article 14.

In relation to discrimination on the grounds of sex, it is argued that the practice of setting different ages of consent for male homosexuals and lesbians under 18 years is also unlawful.[29]    The case law of the Commission has been negative on this point and based predominantly on the notion that gay men, as distinct from lesbians, often constitute a 'distinct socio-cultural group with a clear tendency to proselytise adolescents'.[30] In particular, it has taken the view that lesbians do not give rise to comparable social problems and for this reason, they are not analogous with male homosexuals for the purposes of Article 14.[31] However, in light of the Commission's decision to review its case law in the *Sutherland* case, it is certainly possible that a future challenge to this inequality of treatment would succeed. In particular, although it was not raised as part of the principal complaint, the Commission expressly referred to the potentially discriminatory difference in the age of consent for male homosexual conduct compared with lesbian relations in that case. Moreover, it refused to classify the complaint regarding the difference in the age of consent for heterosexual and homosexual conduct as a difference in treatment on the grounds of sexuality, preferring to leave open whether its basis was sexuality or gender. This serves to answer the question as to whether discrimination on the ground of sex with regard to ages of consent for homosexual and heterosexual conduct is consistent with the Convention.    In any event, legislation drafted subsequent to the Commission's opinion in the *Sutherland* case fixes the age of consent at 16, regardless of gender or sexual orientation.[32] This has the effect of making the argument academic, in the UK at least.

---

[28]    See HC Debates, 21 Feb 1994, Col 95-97.

[29]    Van Bueren, *op cit*, p 40.

[30]    No 5935/72 X v Germany, *op cit*. See Harris, O'Boyle & Warbrick (1995), *Law of the European Convention on Human Rights*, London: Butterworths, p 479 and Fawcett (1987), *The Application of the European Convention on Human Rights*, 2nd ed, Oxford: Clarendon Press, pp 302-304.

[31]    No *10389/83 Johnson v UK*, Dec 17.7.86, DR 47, p 72. See Harris, O'Boyle & Warbrick, *op cit*, p 479.

[32]    See the Sexual Offences Amendment Bill, 1998.

**The Status of the Child**

Various aspects of the status of the child have already been considered above, and it is apparent that in the context of non-discrimination under the Convention, children are subjected to different treatment to protect them from harm, rather than to deny them the effective enjoyment of Convention rights. Admittedly, the argument in favour of a measure which serves to protect the needs and rights of the child is strong. In this regard, it is notable that the Commission and Court have been considerably tolerant of laws and practices which treat children differently from adults, and both institutions have found such measures to be justified where the aim is to protect children from harm or negative influence.[33] In recognition of the possibility that certain measures, which fail to distinguish between the needs of children and adults, in doing so fail to protect children's interests, the Commission and Court have found such measures to be justified under Article 14 too.

The treatment of the child born outside marriage has been one of the most prevailing forms of discrimination and the inferior position of such children has had the traditional aim of depriving them of their rights. The response of the Commission and Court of Human Rights to this wholly unjustifiable discriminatory treatment has been both decisive and positive. The Strasbourg institutions have consistently found that treating children differently on the ground of their parents' marital status constitutes both a lack of respect for family life under Article 8, as well as discrimination, taking this provision, together with Article 14.[34]

In the *Marckx* case, an unmarried mother argued successfully before the Commission and the Court that the fact that she was required to take steps to have her biological tie with her daughter recognised in law constituted a lack of respect for their family life under Article 8 of the Convention.[35] In the Court's defining judgment in this case, it first established the general

---

[33] See No 11077/84 *Nelson v UK*, Dec 13.10.86, DR 49, p 170 and Eur Court HR *Bouamar v Belgium*, judgment of 29 Feb 1988, Series A no 129, 11 EHRR 1, § 67, in Chapter 3, pp 48 and 55.

[34] For a comparison of ECHR case law with US Constitutional law see Meeusen (1995), Judicial Disapproval of Discrimination Against Illegitimate Children: A Comparative Study of Developments in Europe and the United States, *American Journal of Comparative Law*, **43**, pp 119-145.

[35] No 6833/74 *Marckx v Belgium*, Comm Rep, 10.12.77, Series B no 29 and Eur Court HR *Marckx v Belgium*, judgment of 13 June 1979, Series A no 31, 2 EHRR 330.

principle that the right to respect for family life under Article 8 applies to 'legitimate' as well as 'illegitimate' families.[36]    With regard to what constitutes 'respect' for such a relationship, the Court held that family life implies the existence in law of safeguards which render possible from the moment of birth the child's integration into the family. It also found that this was something which was guaranteed to children, regardless of their parents' marital status. Although these principles were clearly important and set out in general terms, the Court applied them to the specific context of the relationship between an unmarried mother and her child. The narrow context notwithstanding, *Marckx* is authority for the principle that domestic law relating to family ties must enable all concerned to lead a normal family life. Moreover, on the facts of the case, the Court considered that where a regime does not automatically recognise the relationship between an unmarried mother and her child at birth and forces her to recognise her child by declaration with negative consequences, the normal development of family life is impeded.[37]    Given that automatic recognition of the tie between the parties did not occur at birth and the procedure, according to which the unmarried mother was required formally to recognise her child, was both complicated and time-consuming, these factors combined to violate the right to respect for family life of both mother and child.[38]

The clear presence of discrimination in this case - a married mother was not required to recognise her child in this way - was so fundamental as to necessitate the examination of a separate complaint under Article 14. Importantly, although they acknowledged the legitimate desire to encourage the traditional family, neither the Commission nor the Court accepted that this aim could be pursued in a manner which prejudiced the family not based on marriage.[39]    In particular, the argument that the tranquility of marital families might be disturbed by placing a child born

---

[36] *Marckx* judgment, *ibid*, § 31. In reaching this conclusion, it referred to Article 1, which guarantees Convention rights to 'everyone' as well as to Article 14. See further Chapter 1.

[37] *Marckx* judgment, *ibid*, § 36.

[38] *Ibid*. The Commission found that the very principle of requiring recognition constituted a disregard for the family life of the child born outside marriage. No 6833/74 *Marckx* Comm Rep, *op cit*, § 75.

[39] *Marckx* judgment, *ibid*, § 40. The Commission, similarly, rejected the argument that the need to treat the non-marital family less favourably with regard to matters of descent and relationship was among the principles generally accepted in democratic societies. See Comm Rep, *ibid*, § 93.

outside marriage on the same footing as a child born inside marriage was not a justification for the inferior treatment suffered by the former. Moreover, while discrimination between children on the grounds of their parents' marital status may have been permissible when the Convention was first drafted, subsequent recognition of the maxim *mater semper certa est* among the majority of Convention States rendered the difference in treatment discriminatory by present day standards. These were reflected, *inter alia*, in the Convention on the Status of Children Born Out of Wedlock adopted by the Council of Europe in 1975.[40] As a result both institutions found that the discrimination against the unmarried mother violated Article 14 together with Article 8.

Although *Marckx* was a landmark decision, its context was narrow insofar as it concerned predominantly the treatment of unmarried mothers and their children.[41] In 1986, however, the Court examined the complaint of a couple, who were prevented from marrying due to the lack of divorce in Ireland at the time, and their daughter born outside marriage.[42] The applicants in the *Johnston* case argued that the inferior position which they occupied under Irish law, in particular their inability to have their relationship recognised by law without the tie of marriage, amounted to a failure to respect their family life under Article 8. The Court noted that, under Irish law, the position of a child born outside marriage differed considerably from that of a child born inside marriage, and moreover, there were no means available to eliminate those differences.[43] It concluded, therefore, that there was an absence in Irish law of an appropriate legal regime reflecting her normal family ties and this amounted to a failure to respect the child's family life under Article 8.[44] In particular, the Court evinced that:

---

[40] ETS No 85. *Marckx* judgment, *ibid*, § 41-43. See also Chapter 1, pp 14-15.

[41] Legal reform in Belgium following the *Marckx* case allowed settlements to be reached in two similar cases. See No *10961/84 Le Mot & Others v Belgium*, Dec 13.5.86, DR 47, p 204 (settlement in Dec 8.10.87, DR 53, p 38) and No *11418/85 Jolie & Lebrun v Belgium*, Dec 14.5.86, DR 47, p 243 (settlement in Dec 8.10.87, DR 53, p 65).

[42] Eur Court HR *Johnston v Ireland*, judgment of 18 Dec 1986, Series A no 112, 9 EHRR 203.

[43] *Ibid*, § 74-75.

[44] The Commission reached the same conclusion. No 9597/82 *Johnston v Ireland*, Comm Rep, 5.3.85, 8 EHRR 214.

the normal development of natural family ties between the three applicants required the third applicant to be placed legally and socially in a position akin to that of a legitimate child.[45]

Importantly, therefore, the inferior treatment endured by the child in this case violated, not only her rights under Article 8, but those of her parents because of the close nature of the relationship between them.[46]  Unlike its consideration of similar facts in the *Marckx* case, the Court did not consider it necessary to examine the complaint under Article 14, although the presence of a clear element of discrimination in this case arguably demanded such a ruling.[47]

One year after *Johnston* and several after *Marckx*, the compatibility with the Convention of an Austrian law which gave inferior inheritance rights to a child born outside marriage was challenged before the Court.[48] The applicant in *Inze* had been born to unmarried parents and he complained that the law which gave preference to a son born inside marriage, over the son born outside marriage amounted to discrimination under the Convention.  In particular, while the former was principal heir and was as such entitled to take over his mother's farm, the latter was entitled only to unfavourable monetary compensation and this, he complained, violated Article 1 of the First Protocol, which guarantees the right to peaceful enjoyment of possessions, read together with Article 14. Agreeing with the applicant, the Commission noted that the case disclosed

a classic case of discrimination, namely legislation to the disadvantage of a minority based on a criterion - birth - which in itself has no intrinsic link with the matter to be decided.[49]

---

[45] *Johnston* judgment, *op cit*, § 72.

[46] *Ibid.* It is interesting in this regard that the claim of the child's parents that their situation breached their rights under Article 8 failed in this case.  See also Van Bueren (1996), 'Protecting Children's Rights in Europe - A Test Case Strategy', *European Human Rights Law Review*, 1, pp 171-180, at pp 171-172, who notes that the Court relied on consensus in finding a violation of the child's right but appeared to ignore similar consensus with regard to her parents' complaint.

[47] Judge De Meyer, in his separate opinion, believed that a violation of Article 14 should have been found for the sake of completeness.

[48] Eur Court HR *Inze v Austria*, judgment of 28 Oct 1987, Series A no 126, 10 EHRR 394.

[49] No 8695/79 *Inze v Austria*, Comm Rep, 4.3.86, 8 EHRR 498, § 55.  It found a breach of Article 1, Protocol No 1 together with Article 14 by 6 votes to 4.  In his dissenting opinion, Mr Schermers argued that in deciding which son was to

The Court agreed and went on to find that very weighty reasons would have to be advanced before a difference in treatment in this area could be compatible with the Convention.[50] This was partly due to the emerging consensus in relation to equality between children born inside and outside marriage, which the Court measured by reference to the ratification by nine Convention States of the European Convention on the Legal Status of Children born out of Wedlock, 1975.[51] Having considered the aims pursued by the Austrian legislature, including the need to prevent the division of hereditary farms on intestacy and recognition of the convictions of the rural population, the Court decided that they could not justify the treatment, which was found to violate Article 14, together with Article 1 of the First Protocol.[52] It is difficult to conceive any other outcome in a case which, in the words of the Commission, illustrated 'a classic case of discrimination'.

Through its judgments in the cases of *Marckx, Johnston* and *Inze* the Court has consolidated its position on the treatment of children born outside marriage. Its clear and decisive principles have undoubtedly contributed to the eradication of the status of 'illegitimacy' in Europe. The Convention has thus enjoyed significant success in the promotion of the equal treatment of all children in this context, and it has enhanced the legal status of such children both domestically and on a European and international level. It is significant also that the individual claims of the

---

get the farm, there will always be discrimination because only one son can obtain it. Sir Basil Hall made a similar point saying that rules of succession will always entail differentiation on the ground of birth and sex, where the older is preferred to the younger, the male to the female. These rules, he said, could be justified and the fact that a rule disadvantages a person does not mean it amounts to discrimination.

[50] *Inze* judgment, *op cit,* § 41.

[51] *Op cit.* The Court's reliance on this Convention has been criticised. See further Chapter 1, p 15, n 47.

[52] *Inze* judgment, *op cit,* § 43-45. Although the Court rejected the applicability of Article 1 of Protocol No 1 in the *Marckx* case, the provision was found applicable in Inze because it involved an actual, rather than a potential right to inherit. Austria's failure to implement promptly the findings of the Court in *Inze* led to a further application being declared admissible by the Commission. The case was settled when the Austrian Act on the Reform of the Law of Succession of 1989 entered into force. No *15154/89 Baumgartner v Austria*, Comm Rep, 16.2.93, DR 74, p 40.

children in the *Marckx* and *Johnston* cases were subjected to independent scrutiny by the Strasbourg institutions, and in *Johnston*, it was the claim of the child which succeeded where that of her parents failed.

## Future Challenges

Many of the concerns about the discriminatory treatment of children arise in the chapters which follow in the context of the substantive issues, to which they relate. However, certain aspects of the way in which the child is defined under the Convention are worth highlighting here. In particular, the Court has yet to confirm the Commission's opinion in the *Sutherland* case and so the compatibility with the Convention of applying different ages of consent for sexual activity depending on factors of gender and sexual orientation has yet to be decisively determined. A similar issue may arise in relation to applying different age limits for marriage on the grounds of gender.

Although the status of 'illegitimacy' has been all but eliminated in the legal systems of Europe, there are many residual issues which have yet to be eradicated.[53] Many of these require a delicate balance between recognising the rights of children born outside marriage, and protecting their best interests, and the latter factor is the key to unlocking the truly equal treatment of children in the context of the family. In particular, the Court's judgment in the *Inze* case, that any discrimination against children on the grounds of their parents' marital status must be supported by weighty considerations, should be applied throughout its case law to ensure that no difference in treatment, which cannot be shown to operate in the child's best interests, is permitted under the Convention.

---

[53] See, for example, Chapter 5, pp 95-101 and Chapter 9, pp 189-191.

# 3    Juvenile Justice and Detention

## Introduction

Among the Convention's most important provisions are Article 5, which protects the right to liberty, and Article 6, which guarantees the right to a fair trial.[1] The Court has consistently stressed the fundamental nature of these rights in a democratic society and through its case law it has developed a number of principles which are relevant to everyone, regardless of age. Notwithstanding that both provisions are detailed, comprehensive and clearly cover minors, neither recognises expressly that children may require protection beyond that enjoyed by adults.[2] This point was not completely ignored by the drafters of the Convention, however, and it is evident from the reference in Article 5 to the detention of a minor for the purpose of educational supervision and in Article 6 to the exclusion of the public from trial proceedings where the interests of juveniles require. In any event, while it is undisputed that children are entitled to the protection of these provisions, the absence of child specific standards in relation to liberty and fair trial matters may hinder their application to children somewhat. It is important, therefore, that the Court adopt a dynamic approach to the Convention's interpretation. Indeed, in some areas it has already begun to do so by placing emphasis on the need for effective protection of rights to liberty and fair trial and, where necessary, seeking guidance from other international standards, notably the UN Convention on the Rights of the Child.

---

[1]  See generally Harris, O'Boyle & Warbrick (1995), *Law of the European Convention on Human Rights*, London: Butterworths, 97-273 and Van Dijk & Van Hoof (1998), *Theory and Practice of the European Convention on Human Rights*, 3rd ed, The Hague: Kluwer, pp 343-479.

[2]  In contrast, see Article 10 § 2(b) of the International Covenant on Civil and Political Rights, 1966, UNTS vol 999, p 171, which provides that accused juvenile persons shall be separated from adults and brought as speedily as possible for adjudication. Article 14 § 4 of the Covenant provides that in the case of juvenile persons, the procedure shall be such as will take account of their age and the desirability of promoting their rehabilitation. See also Articles 37 and 40 UN Convention on the Rights of the Child, UN Doc A/44/25.

**The Scope of Article 5**

Article 5 guarantees the right to liberty, providing that no one shall be deprived of his liberty save in the circumstances set out in Article 5 § 1. The circumstances in which detention is specifically envisaged include, in brief, following conviction by a court (5 § 1 (a)); in order to bring a suspect before a legal authority (5 § 1 (c)); for the purpose of providing a minor with educational supervision (5 § 1 (d)); on the grounds of psychiatric illness (5 § 1 (e)) and with a view to deportation (5 § 1 (f)).[3] This list is exhaustive and the deprivation of liberty will only be compatible with the Convention therefore, where it falls within the scope of one of the sub-paragraphs in Article 5 § 1 and is otherwise lawful insofar as it pursues one or more of the aims set out in that provision. Moreover, according to the Court, the fundamental importance of the right to liberty requires that the express exceptions in Article 5 § 1 (a) to (f) must be narrowly interpreted.[4]

*Exercise of Parental Responsibility*

Notwithstanding these clear principles, the question arose in the *Nielsen* case as to whether the detention of a minor resulting from the exercise of parental responsibility fell within the scope of Article 5.[5] The applicant in this case was a 12 year old boy, who was at the centre of a custody dispute between his unmarried parents. His mother, who enjoyed sole parental responsibility, admitted him to the child psychiatric ward of a state hospital where he stayed for nearly six months in order to receive 'environmental therapy' for his 'neurosis'. His challenge to this detention under Article 5 failed as a slim majority of the Court found the provision to be inapplicable for two reasons. Firstly, and most importantly, the Court found that rather than being sanctioned by the Chief Physician of the hospital concerned, which would clearly have attracted state responsibility, the boy's placement was authorised by his mother, for whose actions the State was not liable. In particular, the detention was seen as a proper exercise of her parental rights, which, the Court said, constituted a fundamental element of family life, recognised under Article 8 of the Convention.[6] Indeed, the Court went

---

[3]   See the text of Article 5 § 1 for the full list of exceptions.

[4]   This is illustrated by the Court's approach in Eur Court HR *Bouamar v Belgium*, judgment of 29 Feb 1988, Series A no 129, 11 EHRR 1. See further below.

[5]   Eur Court HR *Nielsen v Denmark*, judgment of 28 November 1988, Series A no 144, 11 EHRR 175.

[6]   *Ibid,* § 61.

so far as to express the view that it *must* be possible for a child like the applicant to be admitted to hospital at the request of the holder of parental rights. The fact that the twelve year old disagreed with his mother was not important because the Court considered that he was still of an age at which it would be normal for such decisions to be made by a parent, even against his wishes. The Court's second basis for finding Article 5 to be inapplicable related to the nature of the detention. In this respect, the Court considered that restrictions on the boy's freedom of movement and his contacts with the outside world were 'not much different from those which might be imposed on a child in an ordinary hospital'.[7] It is clear therefore that where the detention of a child is ordered by a parent, and its nature does not constitute a deprivation of liberty, then it will assume a private character and fall outside the scope of Article 5. This is the case notwithstanding that there is no express exception to the right to liberty to that effect under the Convention.

The opinion of the Commission in *Nielsen* differed from that of the Court in almost every respect, although it was the conclusion drawn by a majority of eleven to one on the applicability of Article that proved decisive. In particular, the Commission was of the view that as the Chief Physician had taken the ultimate decision with regard to the boy's admission and the conditions in which he was kept, state responsibility was engaged.[8] The Commission also disagreed with the Court about the nature of the detention however. In this regard, it found it decisive that it concerned the

> detention in a psychiatric ward of a 12 year-old boy who was not mentally ill and that ... when he disappeared from the hospital, [the applicant] was found and brought back to the hospital by the police.[9]

It concluded, therefore, that the boy's hospitalisation constituted detention within the meaning of Article 5 and that he deserved the protection of that provision as a result.

The Commission's opinion as to the importance to be attached to parental consent to the detention also differed from that of the Court. In particular, it considered that parental consent could not be decisive as to

---

[7]   *Ibid*, § 70.
[8]   No *10924/84 Nielsen v Denmark*, Comm Rep, 12.3.87, Series A no 144, p 136, 9 EHRR 90, § 104-105.
[9]   *Ibid*, § 111.

whether the boy's detention fell within the scope of Article 5. While it acknowledged the right of parents to take decisions in matters which concern their children, it could not go so far as to find that they enjoyed an unrestricted power of decision over their children.[10] This approach was reflected in the dissenting opinion of the French Judge Pettiti, who noted that in a field as sensitive as psychiatric committal, unremitting vigilance was required to avoid abuse of both legal systems and hospital structures.[11] Due to their vulnerability, persons subject to committal decisions must be entitled to the protection of the law, and this point, the judge said, was even more important in the case of a minor who was already the victim of parental conflict.

The progressive nature of the Commission's opinion in *Nielsen* is apparent from the importance which it attached to the evolving capacity of the child. In particular, the expressed wish of the 12 year old applicant was a determining factor as to whether his placement in a psychiatric ward fell within the scope of parental rights. Notwithstanding that the boy's strong opposition to his placement was made perfectly clear from his various attempts to leave the hospital, the Commission did not see his case as exceptional, and it stressed the principle of attributing greater weight to the opinion of the child as s/he grows older and matures. In this regard, it recognised that, somewhere between very young (at which stage a child's opinion could hardly be decisive) and 17 years (where a placement against a child's own wishes could not be considered voluntary) the minor has a right to have his opinion considered in such matters.[12] On these grounds, and given that Jon Nielsen was 'a normally developed 12 year old child who was capable of understanding his situation and expressing his opinion clearly', his mother's consent could not legitimate his otherwise unlawful detention.[13]

Insofar as the judgment of the Court creates a further exception to the right to liberty where a child is detained with parental consent, *Nielsen* creates a clear disparity in the way in which Article 5 applies to children, as opposed to adults. In addition to being inconsistent with existing case law, which stresses the fundamental nature of the right to liberty and the need to interpret any exceptions narrowly, *Nielsen* also appears to be out of

---

[10] *Ibid*, § 117-118. See generally the issues raised in Chapter 6.

[11] *Nielsen* judgment, *op cit*.

[12] *Ibid*, § 125-126.

[13] *Ibid*, § 128. The Commission found no evidence that the applicant suffered from a mental illness which could characterise him as being of unsound mind for the purposes of Article 5 § 1(e). *Ibid*, § 133.

line with the standards in the UN Convention on the Rights of the Child, which came into force less than two years after the judgment.[14]   The anomaly which the judgment creates is complicated further by the Court's failure to clarify which issue, that of state responsibility or the nature of the boy's detention, was decisive in excluding the application of Article 5, or whether in fact the effect was cumulative. The seven judges who shared the minority view concluded that the nature of the detention, including the fact that the applicant, who was not mentally ill, had been placed in a psychiatric ward, was decisive in relation to whether the deprivation of liberty fell within the scope of Article 5.   Had the majority of the Court shared this view, would the same outcome have been reached overall? Admittedly, consideration of the nature of such detention has its difficulties, not least given that different factors necessarily apply when subjecting children, rather than adults, to essential medical treatment. However, it is arguably of greatest concern that parental consent to detention, in the face of complete opposition by a child, can cancel out the protection which Article 5 offers.   What this point fails to acknowledge is that the child's best interests may not always be a parent's primary concern, particularly where conflict exists between parents.   It is exacerbated further by its inconsistency with the Court's own standard that, where adults are concerned, voluntary detention cannot deprive the person concerned from the protection of Article 5.[15]

While the Commission's opinion in the *Nielsen* case is preferable to the extent that it is more in line with existing standards on children's rights, the Court's judgment is not devoid of merit.   Notwithstanding that it failed to consider that the child concerned had rights, respect for which was inconsistent with his detention against his will, the Court warned that parental responsibility was not unlimited and reminded the State that it should provide children with protection from potential abuse of parental authority.   Similarly, while it failed to find that the nature of the boy's placement had the characteristics of a deprivation of liberty, it nonetheless questioned the length of the detention, which at five and a half months, was clearly excessive, given that he was not mentally ill.

Harris et al argue that Article 5 may involve a positive obligation to control 'private detention'.[16]   Where children are concerned, this would

---

[14]   *Op cit.*
[15]   Eur Court HR   *De Wilde, Ooms & Versyp v Belgium*, judgment of 18 June 1971, Series A no 12, 1 EHRR 438.
[16]   Harris, O'Boyle & Warbrick, *op cit*, p 102.

require the State to protect a child from parental detention that went beyond the bounds of the right to respect for family life in Article 8. Although this is one way of balancing the rights of children and parents in this sensitive area, it appears to dilute the right of the child to liberty. In particular, it permits parents to place their children in detention as long as it can be justified as in their best interests, but without any test as to its legality or arbitrariness. This control is necessary given the risk that in the event of the abuse of parental authority and/or where a minor of sufficient age and maturity disagrees with the decision, there may be no-one to defend his/her rights in this regard.[17]    Moreover, in the light of the importance of the right to liberty in a democratic society, a right which is enjoyed by children and adults alike, a more preferable approach might be to consider the child's detention in the context of Article 5, rather than Article 8. This would permit questions as to whether particular treatment constitutes a deprivation of liberty, or whether it is arbitrary within the meaning of Article 5, to be determined according to the same strict rules which apply in adult cases. While measures of detention, such as normal hospitalisation and school detention, may not normally constitute a deprivation of liberty under Article 5,[18] the best interests principle reflected in Article 8 of the Convention, could be used to justify this position, while taking account of the child's views in relation to the conditions in which s/he is held. In any event, it is important in principle that the child's rights should be exercisable regardless of parental consent and conceptually, the issue should be framed in terms of the minor's control over his or her liberty, rather than parental or police control over it.[19]    This would also allow the application of Article 5 to the deprivation of liberty which occurs in welfare-oriented systems of juvenile justice or indeed in care, which the barrier of parental consent might otherwise preclude from challenge.[20]

---

[17]    Where the deprivation of liberty falls outside the scope of Article 5, there is no right under Article 5 § 4 to a review of its lawfulness. See below and Trechsel (1980), 'The Right to Liberty and Security of the Person - Article 5 of the European Convention on Human Rights in Strasbourg Case Law', *Human Rights Law Journal*, **1**, pp 88-135, p 121.

[18]    See Williams (1994), 'School Detention or False Imprisonment', *Childright*, **109**, p 15-16.

[19]    See further Murdoch (1993), 'Safeguarding the Liberty of the Person : Recent Strasbourg Jurisprudence', *International and Comparative Law Quarterly*, **42**, pp 494-522, at p 499.

[20]    No *21687/93 BH v Norway*, Dec 12.10.94, unreported. See also No *14013/88 Family T v Austria*, Dec 14.12.89, DR 64, p 176.

## Deprivation of Liberty

*Questioning of Child Suspects*

It is permissible under Article 5 § 1 (c) of the Convention to arrest or detain a person in order to bring them before the competent legal authority on suspicion of having committed an offence. Although this provision contains no express reference to minors, there does not appear to be any reason why it should not also apply to their detention in such circumstances. The fact that minors are not criminally responsible before a certain age does not preclude their interrogation where they are suspected of involvement in activities which would be punishable if they were criminally responsible.[21] This is justifiable with regard to the proper administration of justice and the protection of the rights of others.

The compatibility with Article 5 of questioning a child suspect at a police station was examined by the Commission in the *Sargin* case in 1981.[22] The ten year old girl at the centre of this case was taken by the police from her school to the station for questioning because her teacher suspected her involvement in school thefts. During her two hour stay at the police station, she was questioned for one hour, otherwise kept in an unlocked cell and released without charge after a police search had failed to locate any of the stolen property at her home. She complained that her treatment constituted a deprivation of liberty under Article 5 § 1 and § 3, which requires that an arrested person be brought promptly before a judge. Although the applicability of Article 5 was not influenced by the short duration of the girl's detention, the Commission concluded that while the girl had been questioned at the police station, she had been neither arrested nor detained. What was decisive in this regard was the intention of the police, who wished merely to obtain information from her regarding the school thefts and not to deprive her of her liberty within the meaning of Article 5. With respect, although this test may be consistent with the Court's case law on the issue,[23] it fails to take the special considerations of the case, particularly the suspect's young age, into account. Even though a

---

[21] No *8819/79 Sargin v Germany*, Dec 19.3.81, DR 24, p 158, 4 EHRR 276.

[22] *Ibid.*

[23] See Eur Court HR *Brogan v UK*, judgment of 29 Nov 1988, Series A no 145, 11 EHRR 117 and Eur Court HR *Murray v UK*, judgment of 28 Oct 1994, Series A no 300, 19 EHRR 193. Importantly, however, the applicants in these cases were arrested prior to questioning.

test based on the intention of the police may be justifiable where an adult is concerned, the vulnerability of a child in such circumstances must require a more subjective test to be adopted.    In this regard, however, the Commission described the girl's failure to comprehend the police action merely as 'regrettable', and appeared to ignore the significance of the failure of the police to inform her parents of her situation.  Nor, it appears, was she offered the assistance of a lawyer or other representative during her questioning.  It is arguable that where a police officer indicates by words or conduct that a suspect is not free to leave the station then there is an arrest for the purposes of Article 5.[24]  However, while in the absence of such instruction an adult may take the initiative to leave, it is unlikely that a ten year old child would act in a similar manner.  In *Sargin's* case, for example, it is unclear whether she was requested to go to the police station and consented to do so, or whether she believed she had an obligation to go.

While the decision is clearly out of line with current international standards on the way in which child suspects should be treated, nevertheless, the Commission recognised that the interrogation of children should be carried out in a manner respecting their age and susceptibility.  It also noted, importantly, that the suspect in *Sargin* did not allege that there were any irregularities in the way she was treated by the police and that she did not appear to have suffered as a result of the experience.

Article 5 § 2 requires that everyone arrested shall be informed promptly, in a language which he understands, of the reasons for the arrest and any charge against him.  This requires that the arrested person be told the essential legal and factual grounds for his arrest in 'simple, non-technical language that he can understand', so as to enable a challenge to its lawfulness to be made if appropriate.[25]  Moreover, where a person with a mental disorder cannot understand the information given to him, it must be given to a lawyer or other person authorised to act on their behalf.[26]  It is clear therefore that in order for children to enjoy effective protection of this right, its application must take their special needs and status into account.[27]  In order to be effective, the application of Article 5 § 2 to child suspects should require either that the police use language which children and

---

[24]  Harris, O'Boyle & Warbrick, *op cit,* p 100.

[25]  Eur Court HR *Fox,Campbell & Hartley v UK*, judgment of 30 Aug 1990, Series A no 182, 13 EHRR 157, § 40.

[26]  Harris, O'Boyle & Warbrick, *op cit,* p 130.

[27]  No 21528/93 *Bohuslav & Lausman v Austria*, Dec 12.10.94, unreported, where the applicants failed to exhaust domestic remedies.

young people can understand, or that an appropriate adult, who understands the situation, be present to explain the charge to the child. Such an approach would be consistent both with the overriding aim of Article 5 to prohibit arbitrary and unlawful detention, and with other relevant standards in international law.[28]

## Detention on Remand

Article 5 § 3 guarantees to those detained on reasonable suspicion of having committed an offence under Article 5 § 1 (c) the right to a trial within a reasonable time or release pending trial. The Court examined the application of this provision to minors in *Assenov v Bulgaria* in 1998 where it highlighted the specific needs of the minor in such circumstances.[29] Bulgarian national law expressly provides that minors should be detained on remand only in exceptional circumstances and as a result, the Court concluded that 'it was more than usually important that the authorities displayed special diligence in ensuring that the applicant was brought to trial within a reasonable time'.[30] On the facts, it had taken two years for the remanded applicant's case to come to trial. Given that that virtually no action was taken by the prosecuting authorities during one of those years, the Court concluded that the minor concerned had been denied a trial within a reasonable time in violation of Article 5 § 3. Notwithstanding that it was derived from the situation at domestic law, it is significant that the Court has acknowledged expressly that there is a greater burden on the domestic authorities to act diligently in bringing the accused to trial where a minor is concerned. In particular, it represents an advancement in the application of Article 5 to minors deprived of their liberty and signals an interpretation of the provision, which takes their age and vulnerability into account.[31]

---

[28] Article 37 (c) UN Convention on the Rights of the Child requires that every child deprived of liberty shall be treated in a manner which takes into account the needs of persons of his/her age, *op cit*.

[29] Eur Court HR *Assenov v Bulgaria*, judgment of 28 Oct 1998, Reports 1998, VIII, no 96.

[30] *Ibid*, § 157.

[31] See Article 37 (c) UN Convention on the Rights of the Child, *op cit*.

## Detention for the Purpose of Educational Supervision

Article 5 § 1(d) makes two express exceptions to the right to liberty, the first of which permits a minor's detention for the purpose of educational supervision. This sub-paragraph of the right to liberty is one of the few child-specific provisions in the Convention, and it reflects the important need to divert juvenile offenders or suspects from the criminal process. Notwithstanding that it provides for the minor's detention rather than his/her liberty, the provision has been interpreted in a dynamic manner by the Court, which has found that, in certain circumstances, it may place a strict positive obligation on States to put in place appropriate facilities. which ensure the education and reformation of juveniles in conflict with the law.

*Bouamar v Belgium* concerned the placement of a 16 year old boy on remand on nine successive occasions, totalling 119 days within the period of one year.[32] The placements had been made by a juvenile court pursuant to legislation which promoted the diversion of young offenders from the criminal process. The relevant provision of that law permitted the detention of a juvenile in a remand prison for up to 15 days, when it was 'materially impossible' to place him in a reformatory immediately.[33] The Court made a number of initial points before going on to consider whether the boy's detention was compatible with Article 5 § 1 (d). In particular, it established that the provision does not preclude the use of an interim measure as a preliminary to an educational placement. Nor does it require that this placement be immediate. However, in order to be consistent with Article 5, any interim measure of imprisonment must be speedily followed by actual application of an educational regime. The 'material impossibility' in this case was that Belgium did not have an appropriate institution in which to place the juvenile. As a result, it fell to the Court to examine whether the detention on remand fulfilled the requirements of Article 5 § 1(d) as regards its purpose of educational supervision. In short, the Court held that it did not, and found on the facts that:

---

[32]  Eur Court HR *Bouamar v Belgium*, judgment of 29 Feb 1988, Series A No 129, 11 EHRR 1.

[33]  Here, the material impossibility had arisen because there were no closed reformatories with educational facilities in his region and his difficult behaviour meant that available open reformatories were unwilling to accept him.

the detention of a young man in a remand prison in conditions of virtual isolation and without the assistance of staff with educational training cannot be regarded as furthering the educational aim.[34]

Moreover, the Court went on to find that taken together, the nine placement orders were incompatible with Article 5 § 1(d) as their 'fruitless repetition had the effect of making them less and less 'lawful' especially as proceedings were never instituted against the boy'.[35]

In finding a violation of Article 5, the Court limited itself to considering that the placements were incompatible with the Convention. Although it reached the same final conclusion, the Commission found that they were also inconsistent with domestic law.[36] In particular, it found it apparent from the decisions complained of that the juvenile courts had made the applicant's behaviour the basis for their repeated adoption of the remand measures, thus suggesting that the factor of punishment played an important role in the decision-making process. This contributed to its conclusion that the restriction permitted under Article 5 was used for a purpose other than that recognised, and its finding that it was unlawful under Article 18,[37] as well as unjustified under Article 5 § 1(d).[38]

*Bouamar* clearly establishes that Article 5 § 1(d) is to be interpreted narrowly to mean that where a State has chosen a system of educational supervision as its policy on juvenile delinquency, it is obliged to put in place appropriate institutional facilities which meet the demands of security and the educational objectives of the domestic law. Moreover, if the fulfilment of this obligation should necessitate the building or provision of appropriate reformatories then this action should be undertaken by the State, regardless of the cost. It is unfortunate that the Court failed to offer more specific guidance in relation to how the educational objective so clearly reflected in Article 5 § 1(d) should be achieved. However, it did advise that the placement must occur in a setting designed and with sufficient resources for the purpose. Nevertheless, *Bouamar* stops short of

---

[34] *Bouamar* judgment, *op cit*, § 52.

[35] *Ibid*, § 53.

[36] No 9106/80 *Bouamar v Belgium*, Comm Rep, 9.5.85, DR 42, p 28, 11 EHRR 24.

[37] Article 18 provides that the restrictions permitted to the Convention's rights and freedoms shall not be applied for any purpose other than those for which they have been prescribed.

[38] *Bouamar* Comm Rep, *op cit*, § 73-76.

placing a positive obligation on States to implement a system which favours the education of children in conflict with the law over their punishment. However, as long as there is a regime in place, the objective of which is the educational supervision of juvenile delinquents or offenders, then Article 5 § 1 (d) requires that it be used effectively for that purpose.

## Bringing a Minor before a Competent Legal Authority

The second specific exception to the minor's right to liberty in Article 5 § 1(d) provides for lawful detention for the purpose of bringing the minor before the competent legal authority. At first glance, there appears to be little to distinguish this provision from the preceding sub-paragraph, Article 5 § 1 (c), which permits detention for

> the purpose of bringing [a person] before the competent legal authority on reasonable suspicion of having committed an offence, or when it is reasonably considered necessary to prevent his committing an offence or fleeing having done so.

Presuming that the above exception also applies to minors, there is apparent duplication with regard to the detention sanctioned by Article 5 § 1 (d). However, the absence from Article 5 § 1 (d) of the words 'on reasonable suspicion of having committed an offence' is the obvious distinguishing feature. This appears to highlight the different objective pursued by Article 5 § 1 (d), although it is still unclear *when* a youth should be brought before a legal authority if not 'on reasonable suspicion of having committed an offence'. The *travaux préparatoires* suggest that one of the purposes of Article 5 § 1(d) was to recognise that minors in conflict with the law need to be treated differently from adults, by virtue of their vulnerability. Offering an explanation for the distinction in the terminology of the two provisions, the papers suggest that the detention of minors under Article 5 § 1 (d) is not concerned with the determination of a criminal charge, but with the removal of certain children from what are considered to be harmful surroundings.[39] In this situation, the children brought before the court under Article 5 § 1 (d) have committed no offence and their detention rightly falls outside the scope of Article 5 § 1(c). The

---

[39] Travaux Preparatoires iii 724, quoted in Fawcett (1987), *The Application of the European Convention on Human Rights*, 2nd ed, Oxford: Clarendon Press, p 90.

purpose of the former provision is non-punitive therefore, and its aim is to protect young people from harm and prevent them from sliding into criminality. The absence of 'arrest' from Article 5 § 1(d) supports this further.

In its limited case law on this aspect of the provision, the Commission has recognised that the minor's position in law is fundamentally different from an adult's, both before an offence has been proven and afterwards. In addition, it has noted the choice of measures available with respect to juveniles in conflict with the law in Member States of the Council of Europe, where emphasis is placed on the need to understand the minor's personality and to provide him/her with education and training. Indeed, Article 5 § 1(d) reflects this.[40]

The only clear situation to which Article 5 § 1(d) has been found applicable is the detention of a young delinquent in order to study his behaviour.[41] In this case, the Commission had to consider whether the detention of a 15 year old boy who was held for eight months 'under observation', which was ordered by the judge investigating him for a variety of offences, was unlawful under Article 5. Given that the applicant was a minor for the purpose of the provision and agreeing that he was deprived of his liberty being detained and forbidden to leave, the Commission had little difficulty finding Article 5 to be applicable. It went on to find that the detention fell within the meaning of Article 5 § 1 (d) because its purpose was to bring the minor before the competent legal authority. It failed to find, however, that the detention of the boy in these circumstances violated the provision. Even though the Commission expressed concern about the duration of the detention, this fact alone did not cast doubt either on the purpose of the detention or its conformity with Article 5. In reaching this conclusion, the Commission was undoubtedly guided by the fact that the decision to detain the youth had been taken by a juvenile court (a competent legal authority) and had been prompted by the ineffectiveness of earlier measures and the need to gain a better understanding of the boy's personality. These elements are important insofar as they confirm the lawfulness of the detention within the domestic system, as well as its purpose under Article 5 § 1 (d).

The practice of detaining a minor in order to supervise or assess his behaviour will be consistent with Article 5 § 1(d) therefore as long as it is carried out by lawful order and is considered to be proportionate in the

---

[40] No 8500/79 *X v Switzerland*, Dec 14.12.79, DR 18, p 238.
[41] *Ibid.*

circumstances.  However, the Commission's concern about the length of the detention flags this as a potential problem.  Although it is not a decisive factor in its compatibility with Article 5, the application of the provision requires that the minor enjoy the right under Article 5 § 4 to have the lawfulness of the detention reviewed at regular intervals.

## The Right to Challenge the Lawfulness of Detention

Article 5 § 4 provides that

> Everyone who is deprived of his liberty by arrest or detention shall be entitled to take proceedings by which the lawfulness of his detention shall be decided speedily by a court and his release ordered if the detention is not lawful.

The provision thus contains an important procedural safeguard, which requires that the person detained must be able to challenge the legality of his/her detention, both under domestic law and under the Convention.[42]  In relation to the former, the detention must comply both substantively and procedurally with domestic law.  To be compatible with the Convention, the imprisonment must fall within one of the specified exceptions to the right to liberty, and it must also be consistent with the purpose of Article 5, namely to protect individuals from arbitrariness.  In order to satisfy Article 5 § 4, it must be possible to challenge each element of the lawfulness of the detention and so a violation may occur either where the detained person does not have access to a body competent to conduct such a review or alternatively, where no such procedure is available in the circumstances. In relation to the former scenario, Article 5 § 4 must involve access to a 'court', although this does not necessarily have to be a court of law of the classic kind.  The body must have a judicial character, which requires it to be independent of the executive, and it must contain 'guarantees of judicial procedure appropriate to the kind of deprivation of liberty in question'.[43] Importantly, it is not sufficient that the body have advisory functions, as is clear from the text of Article 5 § 4, it must have the competence to decide the lawfulness of the detention and to order release if the detention is unlawful.  This is illustrated by the *Weeks* case in which the Court concluded that the Parole Board lacked the necessary powers for the

---

[42] Eur Court HR *Weeks v UK*, judgment of 2 March 1987, Series A No 114, 10 EHRR 293.
[43] *Ibid*, § 61.

purposes of Article 5 § 4. Notwithstanding that it had the requisite judicial character and was both independent and impartial, the functions of the Board were purely advisory, both in law and in substance. In particular, its recommendation on the release of a prisoner, whose detention it had the power to review, were not binding on the Home Secretary and it was therefore found to lack the power of decision required by Article 5 § 4. Although the respondent government implemented the *Weeks* judgment in 1991 by extending authority to the Parole Board to direct the Home Secretary to make a release, this amendment did not include the review of sentences of detention during Her Majesty's pleasure.[44] Not surprisingly, therefore, the Court found this situation to result in a violation of Article 5 § 4 in 1996.[45]

The second element of the remedy under Article 5 § 4 is that the detained person must have access to a procedure which complies with the provision. For example, in *Weeks* the Court found that the remedy provided by judicial review under the law of England and Wales was insufficient for the purposes of that provision. Weeks was sentenced to a discretionary life sentence and when, following his release he had his licence revoked, he claimed that judicial review was an inadequate means of challenging the lawfulness of his re-detention. The Court agreed, finding that the grounds on which judicial review lies, namely illegality, irrationality and procedural impropriety meant that the scope of its control was not wide enough to bear on the conditions essential for the lawfulness of the applicant's detention under Article 5 § 4. Thus, while it was a useful supplement to the procedure afforded by the Parole Board, it could not remedy the inadequacies of that procedure with regard to a person serving a discretionary life sentence.[46] The inadequacy of judicial review for the purposes of Article 5 § 4 was confirmed subsequently.[47] This notwithstanding, there is no guarantee to a right to judicial control of such scope as to empower a domestic court to substitute its own opinion for that of the decision-making authority.[48] However, it should be wide enough to determine the lawfulness of the detention both in relation to domestic law,

---

[44] See s 37 Criminal Justice Act 1991.
[45] Eur Court HR *Singh v UK,* judgment of 21 Feb 1996, Reports 1996-I, no 4, p 280, § 66.
[46] *Weeks* judgment, *op cit.* See Harris, O'Boyle & Warbrick, *op cit,* pp 154-155.
[47] *Singh* judgment, *op cit,* § 69.
[48] *Weeks* judgment, *op cit,* § 59.

as well as the conditions relevant to the aim of the restriction of liberty imposed under Article 5 § 1.[49]

*Right to a Speedy Review*

What amounts to a speedy determination of the lawfulness of detention, as required by Article 5 § 4, depends on the circumstances of each case and the importance of the right to liberty.[50]   Where the detention is short, however, it is important that the review procedure, including both the hearing and the handing down of the court's decision, is completed before the period of detention ends, so as to ensure that it has practical effect.[51]   It is arguable also that the application of the provision in children's cases will require particular expediency on behalf of the authorities.   This can be deduced from the Court's recognition that special diligence must be displayed in ensuring that a minor is brought to trial within a reasonable time under Article 5 § 3.[52]   It is also apparent from the specific application of this right to children in the UN Convention on the Rights of the Child.[53]

A regime which entitles adults to a review of the legality of detention, but which does not apply to children, does not appear to constitute discrimination under the Convention.   This arose in the *Bouamar* case where the applicant complained that, as a minor, he could not benefit from the right which adults enjoyed to have their detention reviewed within five days of their arrest. However, the Commission and the Court both agreed that because it stemmed from the protective, rather than the punitive nature of the procedure available to juveniles, the different way in which the criminal justice regime applied to them was objective and reasonable.[54]   It was thus compatible with Article 14.

---

[49]   *Ibid.* Judicial review has been found to be inadequate for this latter purpose. See *Weeks* judgment, *op cit*, § 57 and *Singh* judgment, *op cit*, § 69.

[50]   See for example, Eur Court HR *Sanchez-Reisse v Switzerland*, judgment of 21 Oct 1986, Series A No 107, 9 EHRR 71, § 55.   See generally, Harris, O'Boyle & Warbrick, *op cit*, pp 155-158 and Van Dijk & Van Hoof, *op cit*, pp 381-389.

[51]   *Bouamar* judgment, *op cit*, § 63.

[52]   *Assenov* judgment, *op cit*. See further above, p 41.

[53]   See Article 37 (d), *op cit*.

[54]   *Bouamar* judgment, *op cit*, § 67. See also Chapter 1, pp 4-6.

*Continuing Review at Reasonable Intervals*

Although Article 5 § 4 provides for the right to have the lawfulness of detention reviewed by a court, it has been found to have specific implications for those upon whom indeterminate sentences of detention have been imposed. Notwithstanding that such sentences generally include a punitive element, known as the tariff, the Court has established that the imposition of such an indeterminate sentence on a young person can only be justified by reasons based on the offender's perceived dangerousness to society.[55] In the light of the fact that this must involve taking into account any developments in the young offender as s/he grows older, and characteristics, which are susceptible to change with the passage of time, it is clear that new issues of lawfulness may arise in the course of such detention. As a result, the Court has recognised that, in accordance with Article 5 § 4, a young person must be entitled to take proceedings to have these issues decided by a court at reasonable intervals. Moreover, failure to have regard to the changes which inevitably occur as a young person matures would mean, according to the Court, that they 'would be treated as having forfeited their liberty for the rest of their lives', a situation which might raise an issue under Article 3.[56]

By contrast, where a mandatory life sentence is imposed, then the absence of discretionary factors means that Article 5 § 4 does not require a continuing remedy.[57] The same principle would appear to apply while the tariff of a discretionary sentence is still in force, meaning that there is no right to have the lawfulness of the detention reviewed during this period.[58] The Court has only considered the situation of a prisoner, whose tariff has expired, and it is unclear, therefore, whether the right to a continuing review applies to this situation, or to where the tariff has been quashed, but not replaced. The Commission examined this latter issue in 1998 where it found that, regardless of the status of the tariff, the inability of a young person, imprisoned at age eleven, to have his detention reviewed during the first five years of his sentence violated Article 5 § 4. Notwithstanding that

---

[55] Eur Court HR *Hussain v UK*, judgment of 21 Feb 1996, Reports 1996-I, no 4, p 252, 22 EHRR 1, § 52-54. In relation to the compatibility of sentencing with the Convention, see below, pp 52-55.

[56] *Singh* judgment, *op cit*, § 62.

[57] Eur Court HR *Wynne v UK*, judgment of 18 July 1994, series A no 294-A, 19 EHRR 333.

[58] Harris, O'Boyle & Warbrick, *op cit*, p 153.

the applicant's tariff had been quashed and not yet replaced, it was incompatible with the requirements of Article 5 § 4 as it applies to offenders sentenced at a very young age that 'a long period of time' had elapsed without the opportunity for a review of his detention.[59]    In particular, it could not be excluded that, after several years and following progress in maturation, a young offender could claim that new issues had arisen affecting the lawfulness of his continued detention. According to the Commission, the failure to provide him with the opportunity to make such a challenge breached the Convention.

It is uncertain whether the Court will choose to follow the Commission's opinion, which held the support of all but one of its members. The basis of the Government's argument was that the applicant's complaint was premature insofar as the tariff element of his sentence had been quashed through successful judicial review proceedings in the domestic courts, and had not yet been replaced. This may indeed find support among the Court. However, the view of the Commission is arguably correct because, regardless of whether or not a tariff was in force, it was the fact that a long period of time had passed without the possibility of having the legality of the detention reviewed, which gave rise to the violation.

*Procedural Guarantees under Article 5 § 4*

It was established in *Weeks* that a review body, which does not allow proper participation of the individual adversely affected by the contested decision, cannot be regarded as judicial in character as required by Article 5 § 4.[60] Moreover, it has subsequently become clear that certain guarantees of judicial procedure have been found to be implicit in the right to a review under Article 5 § 4, although the circumstances in which the proceedings take place must be taken into account in determining what safeguards must be provided. In this regard, particular guarantees have been found to apply to cases concerning juveniles, as well as those sentenced at a young age to an indeterminate life sentence.

In the *Bouamar* case, the Court found that the treatment of the minor, who appeared in person before the court reviewing the lawfulness of his

---

[59]    No 24724/94 *T v UK*, Comm Rep, 4.12.98, unreported, at § 135-136. See also No 24888/94 *V v UK*, Comm Rep, 4.12.98, unreported.

[60]    *Weeks* judgment, *op cit*, § 62-68. Subsequent amendments were made to the procedure entitling those before the Parole Board to have access to relevant documents. *Hussain* judgment, *op cit*.

detention was inadequate for the purposes of Article 5 § 4, in light of his young age at the time.[61]　In such a situation, the Court explained, it is essential that the minor should have the effective assistance of a lawyer, in addition to having the opportunity to be heard in person.[62] Notwithstanding that flexible and informal proceedings before a juvenile judge may be entirely consistent with the Convention, compatibility with Article 5 § 4 makes it essential that minors seeking to have the lawfulness of their detention reviewed must be present at the proceedings and must also enjoy the effective assistance of a lawyer.[63]

In the cases of *Hussain* and *Singh*, the Court considered whether the remedies available to the applicants, who were serving indeterminate life sentences imposed on them as minors, satisfied the procedural requirements of Article 5 § 4.[64]　Hussain's complaint was that at no time in the proceedings before the Parole Board did he have an opportunity to appear in person, and only at the fourth review was he finally shown the reports on him.　Similarly, Mr Singh complained that when the Parole Board considered his case, he was not entitled to attend, he had no opportunity to present oral evidence, nor was he entitled to question witnesses.　The Court criticised that neither applicant was present nor offered an oral hearing, factors which are essential to the fairness of such proceedings.[65]　This was particularly significant in light of the fact that the proceedings involved an assessment of the prisoner's character and mental state.　In view of the substantial term of imprisonment which may be at stake and the consideration of the prisoner's character and maturity, it concluded that Article 5 § 4 requires an oral hearing in the context of an adversarial procedure involving legal representation and the possibility of calling and questioning witnesses.　The circumstances in each case led to a violation of Article 5 § 4.

Strasbourg jurisprudence has been highly influential in the development of both the substantive and the procedural aspects of the right of those serving indeterminate sentences to have the lawfulness of detention

---

[61]　*Bouamar* judgment, *op cit*. See above pp 42-44.

[62]　No *15006/89 Abbott v UK*, Dec 10.12.90, unreported. The settlement reached in this case involved making legal representation available to minors who as wards of court were neither party to, nor represented in, the proceedings concerning their detention.

[63]　See the general discussion in Chapter 6.

[64]　*Singh* judgment, *op cit* and *Hussain* judgment, *op cit*.

[65]　*Singh* judgment, *ibid* and *Hussain* judgment, *ibid*, § 67-68.

reviewed. Importantly, the Court has recognised clearly the need to exercise vigilance in keeping the reasons for detaining young people for indeterminate periods of time under continuing review. The case law also acknowledges that special considerations must apply to juveniles in the criminal justice system, and in this regard, it is entirely consistent with the principle in the UN Convention on the Rights of the Child, that children should be detained only for the shortest appropriate period of time.[66]

## Sentencing

Article 5 § 1 (a) permits the lawful detention of a person following their conviction by a competent court. Although the Convention institutions may be required to examine the lawful nature of that detention, they are not permitted to review the appropriateness of a sentence of imprisonment.[67] Nevertheless, the Court has questioned the compatibility with the Convention of imposing a life sentence on a person under 18 years, whose offence does not appear to be serious, in circumstances other than where the aim of the sentencing judge is to grant the offender early release.[68] It has also been established that the sentencing of a young person to an indeterminate term of detention, which may be as long as that person's life, can only be justified by considerations based on a need to protect the public.[69] Any failure to keep the sentence under review in the light of inevitable developments in the young person's personality and maturity would mean that they would be treated as having forfeited their liberty for the rest of their lives. This might constitute inhuman and degrading treatment under Article 3.

In this regard, it is arguable that a sentence of detention during her Majesty's pleasure, which is imposed irrespective of the youth of the offender and any mitigating circumstances, amounts to arbitrary detention under Article 5, as well as inhuman punishment under Article 3. In the

---

[66] Article 37 (b), *op cit*. See also Palmer (1996), 'What has happened to Children's Rights in the Criminal Justice System?', *Cambridge Law Journal*, **55**(3), pp 406-409.

[67] *Weeks* judgment *op cit*, § 50. However, see the compatibility of judicial corporal punishment with the Convention in Chapter 8.

[68] *Ibid*, § 47. The Court and Commission indirectly questioned the need for such a severe sentence to be handed down in this case. See 9787/82 *Weeks v UK*, Comm Rep, 7.12.84, Series B no 97.

[69] *Singh* judgment, *op cit*, § 61.

cases of *T* and *V* against the UK the applicants, having received such a sentence, complained that this amounted to a violation of Article 3 because it is not terminable at any stage, any release is conditional, and it is linked to the perceived requirement of retribution rather than the well-being of the child.[70] However, the Commission rejected the complaint in light of the fact that a sentence of detention is primarily preventive in nature, and thus attracts the guarantees of Article 5 § 4 in respect of the right to have its lawfulness reviewed. It thus cannot be said that the young person has forfeited his liberty for life. Moreover, the fact that release is subject to potential recall does not disclose any element of inhuman or degrading treatment, not least because such re-detention would be subject to similar procedural guarantees.[71] Nor did it find the sentence to be arbitrary within the meaning of Article 5, notwithstanding its non-discretionary nature and the fact it was imposed mandatorily in respect of the offence of murder. Here it found that the sentence was clearly compatible with domestic law, both procedurally and substantively, and it went on to say that it was also consistent with the Convention, insofar as it fell within the scope of Article 5 § 1(a). With regard to the claim of arbitrariness, the Commission found that fixed term sentences could not be considered to be incompatible with Article 5, being such a common feature in many of the legal systems in Europe. Moreover, it noted the requirement that there must be some relationship between the ground of permitted deprivation of liberty relied on and the place and conditions of detention but, even assuming that Article 5 § 1(a) requires that sentences of detention for convicted children are geared exclusively to the individual considerations of rehabilitation and prevention, this was not at issue in these cases. In particular, it recalled that detention during Her Majesty's pleasure is an indeterminate sentence, according to which the decisive ground for continuing detention once the tariff has expired is the offender's dangerousness to society. The child's continuing detention therefore requires consideration of the individual circumstances of the particular child offender, albeit in this context and it is therefore compatible with Article 5.[72]

As long as the young offender upon whom an indeterminate period of detention is imposed enjoys the procedural guarantee of a right to have its

---

[70] No 24724/94 *T* Comm Rep, *op cit* and No 24888/94 *V* Comm Rep, *op cit*. The reports in these two cases are almost identical and only *T* is referred to hereafter.

[71] No 24724/94 *T* Comm Rep, *ibid*, § 107-112.

[72] *Ibid*, § 114-120.

legal basis reviewed, then the sentence will not in itself be incompatible with the Convention. Questions may arise however in relation to the application of a tariff in children's cases insofar as it is a period of detention fixed with reference to the perceived need for retribution and punishment, and not tailored to the individual child's need for rehabilitation. Although the Commission has accepted that in most cases the sentencing of children to detention will involve this punitive element, it has found that only a short tariff can be compatible with the Convention. This is based on the fact that young children can be expected to develop and mature in the years following their conviction and sentencing, and thus any sentence of detention to which they are subjected should be kept under continual assessment. [73]    In light of the fact that the right to take proceedings to have the lawfulness of detention reviewed is only to be enjoyed in respect of discretionary periods of detention,[74] the necessary review of the deprivation of a child's liberty will only be possible where the tariff is relatively short. While the case law provides no guidance as to what amounts to a short period in this regard, the Commission found the five year period to be too long when imposed on an eleven year old boy.

An additional procedural safety net is provided by Article 6 of the Convention in relation to the manner in which the tariff is fixed in cases of detention during Her Majesty's pleasure.[75] Importantly, Article 6 is applicable to the procedure, deemed to be judicial in nature, insofar as it constitutes the fixing of the punitive element of an otherwise indeterminate sentence. As a result, the Commission has established that where the tariff is set by the Secretary of State, the fact that he is a member of the executive will raise serious concerns about his/her independence and impartiality, in violation of Article 6.[76]

---

[73] *Ibid*, § 135-136.

[74] No 18757/91 *N v UK*, Dec 14.10.92, 15 EHRR CD 47 reiterating the view of the Court in *Weeks* judgment, *op cit*, and Eur Court HR *Thynne, Wilson & Gunnell v UK*, judgment of 25 Oct 1990, Series A no 90, 13 EHRR 666. This is evident in any event from the distinction between mandatory and discretionary life sentences.

[75] No 24724/94 *T* Comm Rep, *op cit*, § 122-129.

[76] The House of Lords found this practice to be unlawful too and had quashed the tariff set by the Secretary of State in these cases. See [1997] WLR 23. cf No 32003/96 *Bromfield v UK*, Dec 1.7.98, 26 EHRR CD 138 concerning the setting of the tariff for a sentence of custody for life.

*Discrimination in Sentencing Matters*

Although it is acknowledged that the criminal law cannot be expected to treat child and adult offenders in the same way, the Commission and Court have had difficulty clarifying exactly what difference in treatment is permissible. In *Nelson v UK* the applicant, who had been convicted in Scotland of attempted murder at the age of fifteen, complained that in contrast to his adult counterparts in Scotland and minors convicted of similar offences in England and Wales, he was not entitled to remission.[77] However, the Commission found that both differences in treatment were compatible with the Convention on the basis that they were objectively and reasonably justified. In particular, the Commission noted the importance of flexibility as an important prerequisite in the rules governing the detention of child offenders given that the personalities of persons sentenced at such an early age may change greatly in the course of their detention. The fact that the applicant in this case did not benefit from earlier release on licence, in contrast to other persons similarly placed, did not detract from the distinctive nature of this regime of detention which, the Commission found, was geared to deal more flexibly with child offenders. With regard to the complaint that minors in different regions of the UK were treated differently, this did not give rise to discrimination within the meaning of Article 14 because it was not related in any way to the personal status of the applicant. Although this approach allowed the Commission to sidestep the difficult issue of whether treating children differently according to the jurisdiction in which they were sentenced is compatible with the Convention, it is notable that the Committee on the Rights of the Child found this precise issue to be inconsistent with the principle of non-discrimination under the UN Convention on the Rights of the Child when it examined the UK report in 1995.[78]

## The Right to a Fair Trial

Convention case law frequently acknowledges the importance of the role which the right to a fair trial plays in a democratic society. Article 1 guarantees that the rights pertaining to a fair trial are to be enjoyed by everyone, including children, although it is arguable that systems of justice,

---

[77] No 11077/84 *Nelson v UK*, Dec 13.10.86, DR 49, p 170.
[78] UN Doc CRC/C/SR.205, § 8-11, 29.

which advocate dealing in a more flexible manner with children, highlight their increasing significance for minors. The guarantees of a fair trial, in particular the right to an independent and impartial hearing, assume great importance for juvenile offenders who may frequently be dealt with in informal proceedings.

Article 6 does not recognise specifically the importance of protecting the rights of children during criminal proceedings or any alternative procedure.[79]    Nevertheless, the Commission has highlighted the fundamental nature of the guarantee of impartiality in Article 6 § 1. In particular, it has questioned on a general level whether a system of juvenile justice, according to which the juvenile judge both investigates and determines the charge against the minor, is consistent with Article 6 and if so, what special considerations with respect to the trials of juveniles might serve as justification in this regard.[80]

In *Nortier v the Netherlands* the question of impartiality in such a system became the subject of the Commission and Court's scrutiny.[81]    The applicant, who was fifteen at the relevant time, complained under Article 6 that throughout the proceedings, i.e. during the pre-trial phrase as well as at the trial, his case had been dealt with by the same judge, who had taken all the relevant decisions. The personal impartiality of the judge was not doubted. However, the applicant argued that due to his involvement in the proceedings at the investigative stage, there was evidence to suggest that by the time the trial stage was reached, the judge had formed a concrete opinion as to his guilt and the likely sentence to be imposed. In other words, the cumulation of the judge's functions in his case resulted in his objectivity being compromised when he considered the penal charge against him.

Notwithstanding its misgivings, the Commission found the individual claim of bias to be unsubstantiated on the facts.[82]    It was not relevant whether the Dutch system as a whole conformed with Article 6, rather the

---

[79]    For discussion of the internationally recognised standards on juvenile justice see Van Bueren (1995a), *The International Law on the Rights of the Child*, Dordrecht: Martinus Nijhoff pp 169-205 and (1992b), 'Child Orientated Justice - An International Challenge for Europe', *International Journal of Law and the Family*, **6**, pp 381-399.

[80]    No *13924/88 Nortier v the Netherlands*, Comm Rep, 9.7.92, Series A no 267, § 60.

[81]    *Ibid* and Eur Court HR *Nortier v the Netherlands*, judgment of 24 Aug 1993, Series A no 267, 17 EHRR 273.

[82]    *Nortier* Comm rep, *ibid*, § 62-64.

issue was whether the way in which it was applied with regard to the minor in question gave rise to legitimate doubts as to the impartiality of the juvenile judge. In finding that it did not, particular weight was attached to the following circumstances. Firstly, a second judge heard witnesses at the request of the applicant's lawyer. Secondly and notably, there was no 'three way consultation' between the judge, the Public Prosecutor and the Child Welfare Council, as is normal practice in juvenile cases in the Netherlands. Thirdly, consistent with the case-law of the Court, the fact that the juvenile judge ordered the applicant's detention on remand was insufficient to raise doubts about his impartiality.[83] As the minor had confessed, no extensive judicial investigation was required in order to establish the facts and these factors combined to satisfy the Commission that the criminal charge against the juvenile had been determined in a manner consistent with Article 6.[84]

Dissenting members of the Commission expressed strong concern about the inconsistency with Article 6 of the Dutch juvenile justice system, and relied on the fact that minors were entitled to benefit from all the guarantees of Article 6 to find that the failure to offer such guarantees in this case breached that provision.[85] The difficult balance to be achieved between ensuring that the right to an impartial trial is guaranteed to juveniles and treating them in a sensitive and appropriate way throughout the criminal process is illustrated by the contrasting opinions of Mr Geus, who dissented, and Mr Trechsel, who concurred with the majority.[86] Mr Geus believed that Article 6 had been violated due to the failure to offer the applicant the guarantees of Article 6. Mr Trechsel, on the other hand, stressed the importance of building the confidence of a minor before the courts by having the same judge make the final determination on his/her case, as has been with the case from the outset. It is evident from the

---

[83] See Eur Court HR *Hauschildt v Denmark*, judgment of 24 May 1989, Series A no 154, where the Court found that, the fact that a trial judge has made decisions on the detention on remand of the accused at the pre-trial stage will only justify fears as to his impartiality in exceptional cases.

[84] *Nortier* Comm Rep, *op cit*, § 66-68.

[85] See the dissenting opinion of Mr Geus, joined by Mr Weitzel and Mr Marxer, *ibid.*

[86] Mr Trechsel was joined by Messrs Frowein and Schermers and Sir Basil Hall, *ibid.*

*Nortier* case that efforts to achieve this balance are on-going at domestic, as well as at regional or international level.[87]

The Court made much lighter work of the application in confining itself to the facts of the case.[88] It concluded, simply, that the allegations relating to bias on the part of the juvenile judge were unsubstantiated and it chose not to consider the broader picture of the importance of fair trial guarantees in juvenile justice cases. Nor did it consider whether it was consistent with the Convention to separate juveniles from the adult criminal process where to do so compromised their rights under Article 6. However, in his concurring judgment, Justice Morenilla referred expressly to the UN Convention on the Rights of the Child and attached considerable importance to the need to afford juvenile offenders special protection identified in the preamble and Article 40.[89] His judgment also attempts to place the complaint in the context of the need to set up

> juvenile courts under specific procedural rules to apply penal or protective measures aiming at the correction or re-education of the minor rather than the punishment of criminal acts for which he is not fully responsible.[90]

In addition, he finds commendable the attempts to develop a relationship of trust between the juvenile judge on the one hand and the minor and his parents or guardian on the other, although it is not clear how this relationship of trust is to be built up when the accused feels he is not receiving an impartial hearing.

The separate and dissenting opinions of various members of the Commission and Court in *Nortier* reflect the concern that the special considerations applicable to young persons should not be allowed to dilute the fundamental guarantees of Article 6. More recently, the Commission expressed the view that where a child is faced with a criminal charge and the domestic system requires a fact-finding procedure with a view to establishing guilt, it is essential that 'his age, level of maturity and intellectual and emotional capacities be taken into account in the procedures followed'.[91] The case in question concerned the circumstances

---

[87] See the UN Convention on the Rights of the Child, *op cit*, and Van Bueren, (1995a), *op cit*.

[88] *Nortier* judgment, *op cit*, § 31-37.

[89] *Ibid.* See also the opinion of Mr Justice Walsh.

[90] *Ibid.*

[91] No 24724/94 *T* Comm Rep, *op cit*, § 95 and No 24888/94 *V* Comm Rep, *op cit*.

of the Bulger murder trial in England in which two eleven year old boys were tried in an adult, criminal court for the murder of a two year old boy.[92] The question of whether the proceedings were compatible with Article 6 turned on the extent to which they had been modified so as to ensure that the right of the children to a fair trial was safeguarded. Even though the children were provided with defence counsel, the assistance of a social worker in court, and shortened court sittings to accommodate their limited concentration span, the public and formal nature of the proceedings was problematic. In particular, the children had been placed in a raised dock, and their trial had taken place in an adult court with intense public attention over a period of three weeks. These factors, the Commission concluded, must be regarded as a severely intimidating procedure for eleven year old children and must, in addition, have seriously impinged on their ability to participate in the proceedings in any meaningful manner. Most significantly, however, the boys had not given evidence during the trial and the Commission was satisfied that their psychological state was such that they could not realistically have been expected to do so. In these circumstances, it found that the primary purposes of the proceedings, the establishment of the facts of the case and the allocation of responsibility, were impaired. This was evidenced further by the fact that the trial judge, at the conclusion of the trial, was unable to determine the relative culpability of the two defendants. While it recognised that it can never be required that an accused give evidence, the Commission went on to find that:

> where the alleged offender is a child, the procedures adopted must be conducive to an active participation as opposed to passive presence. Otherwise the trial risks presenting the appearance of an exercise in the vindication of public outrage.[93]

In this regard, the Commission noted the distinction between public clamour and public interest and recognised that a closed trial would have given unsatisfactory assurances to the public. However, a modified procedure could provide, in a variety of ways, for selected attendance rights and appropriate reporting. As a result,

---

[92] *Ibid.*

[93] No 24724/94 *T* Comm Rep, *ibid*, § 97.

having regard to the age of the [two boys], the application of the full rigours of an adult, public trial, deprived [them] of the opportunity to participate effectively in the determination of the criminal charges against [them].

This situation led to a violation of Article 6.

In contrast, however, the Commission did not find that the proceedings had also amounted to inhuman or degrading treatment within the meaning of Article 3.[94] In response to the claim that the circumstances of the trial had been humiliating, the Commission noted that the eleven year old boys had been required to sit in a raised dock, separated from their parents with the formal panoply of the adult criminal trial, involving judge and counsel in wigs and gowns. In addition, the public nature of the trial meant that the location of the proceedings were known and open to the public and the press, which reported on them in detail, and which resulted in the atmosphere in the court room being highly charged. Moreover, at the end of the proceedings, the names of the boys were made public, with all the stigma which that entailed for them and their families. There was evidence that the proceedings had had a significant psychological effect on one of the boys, evidenced by his symptoms of post-traumatic stress disorder. Nor could it be ruled out that the process of the trial had had a detrimental effect on the other boy too, albeit to a lesser extent. In any event, the Commission noted that a significant part of the distress suffered by the two boys was attributable, simply, to the fact that they had committed a horrific crime and were being brought to face the consequences. It thus could not be concluded that the trial process had caused any particular psychological condition. Nor could the exact extent to which it augmented the already existing distress be determined, and consequently, the trial procedures did not inflict treatment of such a severity so as to breach Article 3.

**Future Challenges**

The unanimity of Commission members about their conclusions in the *T* and *V* cases suggests that the Court may indeed reach the same conclusion, with regard to the fair trial issue at least. Nevertheless, the significance of these cases lies beyond their individual circumstances. They present a challenge to the application of the Convention to children's cases. This and future challenges in this area are likely to provide a clear indication of the protection which the Convention offers to children in conflict with the law

---

[94] *Ibid*, § 73-89.

and current indications are that this may be extensive, particularly under Article 6, in light of the institutions' increasing reference to existing child-specific human rights standards.

Challenges to the detention of minors under Article 5 will undoubtedly expand its scope of protection, particularly given the acceptance of the principle in the UN Convention on the Rights of the Child that detention should be a measure of last resort and for the shortest appropriate period of time. Individual aspects of the detention of children may also be the subject of future challenge, either domestically or at European level, under Articles 5 and 3. Of particular relevance in this context may be the issue of appropriate detention for minors, especially their detention in conditions which are not conducive to rehabilitation or learning. The Convention position on the treatment of child suspects is also likely to come under fresh challenge, with regard both to their questioning by the police, as well as their detention on remand. In this context, as in others, the Court is likely to continue to draw on the more specialised children's rights standards set out in the UN Convention and, as long as it continues to do so in its interpretation of the rights of liberty and fair trial, then the outlook for their application to children can be considered to be very positive indeed.

# 4    Education

## Introduction

Article 2 of the First Protocol to the European Convention provides for the right to education and is thus the only provision that relates directly and specifically to children.  Notwithstanding that the right to education belongs to the child, Article 2 of the First Protocol also acknowledges the role of parents in the education of their children.  In particular, it obliges States to respect the religious and philosophical convictions of parents in the education and teaching of their children.  Although the right of the child to education is the dominant part of the provision, the emphasis on parental rights in education is reflected in the case law of the Commission and the Court.

## The Scope of Article 2 of the First Protocol

Article 2 of the First Protocol provides that

> [n]o person shall be denied the right to education.  In the exercise of any functions which it assumes in relation to education and to teaching, the State shall respect the right of parents to ensure such education and teaching in conformity with their own religious and philosophical convictions.

In contrast to the education provisions in other treaties,[1] Article 2 of the First Protocol is drafted in broad, non-descriptive terms.  The scope of the right is still largely undefined, however, although the provision has been subjected to broad interpretation in many areas, ensuring its relevance to the broader issues of education.

---

[1]  See Article 13 International Covenant on Economic, Social and Cultural Rights, UNTS vol 993, p 3, but especially Articles 28 and 29 UN Convention on the Rights of the Child, UN Doc A/44/25. On the latter see further Van Bueren (1995a), *The International Law on the Rights of the Child*, Dordrecht: Martinus Nijhoff, pp 232-261.

*First Sentence: The Right to Education*

In contrast to most other Convention provisions which begin: 'everyone has the right to...', Article 2 of the First Protocol is negatively formulated. While the consequences of this were uncertain at first, the Court has established that despite its negative formulation, Article 2 does contain a right to education which must be secured to all children.[2] The significance of the negative wording relates to the *scope* of the right which States must protect and in this regard, it has been suggested that it is a right to *freedom* of education which is involved here.[3] The Court has established that the provision permits States to recognise a right to education which stops short of requiring them to establish at their own expense education of any particular type or level, or even to subsidise such education.[4] The provision is thus limited to providing a right to avail of the 'means of instruction existing at a given time' and this interpretation suggests that the right to education enjoyed by the child may vary from one state to another. Importantly however, where developments in the education system of a particular State lead to the establishment of a new type of education, Article 2 of the First Protocol requires that access to it must be extended to all eligible persons. The provision's primary objective is therefore to guarantee a right of equal access to existing educational facilities.[5]

Article 2 does not specify the level or type of education to which every child is guaranteed, although it has been submitted that it includes entry to nursery, primary, secondary and higher education.[6] Although the Commission has suggested that the Convention is 'primarily concerned with elementary education',[7] this interpretation is neither consistent with

---

[2] Eur Court HR *Costello-Roberts v UK*, judgment of 25 March 1993, Series A No 247-C, 19 EHRR 112, § 27.

[3] Van Dijk & Van Hoof (1998), *Theory and Practice of the European Convention on Human Rights*, 3rd ed, The Hague: Kluwer, p 644.

[4] Eur Court HR *The Belgian Linguistics Case*, judgment of 23 July 1968, Series A no 6, 1 EHRR 252, § 3.

[5] See Van Dijk & Van Hoof, *op cit*, p 644.

[6] See Wildhaber, 'Right to Education and Parental Rights' Matscher & Petzold (eds) (1988), *Protecting Human Rights: The European Dimension, Studies in Honour of Gerard J Wiarda*, Koln: Heymanns, pp 531-551, at p 531.

[7] See No *5962/72 X v UK*, Dec 13.3.75, DR 2, p 50, and No *7671/76 15 Foreign Students v UK*, Dec 19.5.77, DR 9, p 185. See also Harris, O'Boyle & Warbrick (1995), *Law of the European Convention on Human Rights*, London: Butterworths, p 541.

case law, nor the broad wording and purpose of the provision.[8] Moreover, the Court has made no attempt to restrict the right to education in this way, although it has found that while States are not required to provide a certain level of education, they are obliged to make available access to existing education.

The relationship between the first and second sentences of the provision is clearly established. Importantly, the right to education set out in the first sentence belongs to the child and it is the dominant part of Article 2.[9] The second sentence must be read together with the first, and it is on to the right to education that respect for parents' religious and philosophical convictions must be grafted.[10] The significance of this approach is that parental convictions must never be respected in a manner which injures the right to education itself.

*Second Sentence:  Respect for Parental Convictions*

The second sentence of Article 2 of the First Protocol refers to respect for parental convictions in the education and teaching of their children and this also has implications for the scope of the provision as a whole. The Court has adopted a broad approach to the interpretation of 'education' and 'teaching'.[11]   Teaching or instruction has been found to refer to the transmission of knowledge and to intellectual development. Education on the other hand, includes 'the whole process whereby, in any society, adults endeavour to transmit their beliefs, culture and other values to the young'.[12] The meaning of education thus extends beyond theoretical instruction in the classroom to include the development and moulding of a child's character, which may take place in other situations, including in society generally.[13]   The fact that these terms are not interchangeable is apparent

---

[8]   See for example No 8844/80 *X v UK*, DR 23, p 228 and No *6094/73 Association X v Sweden*, Dec 6.7.77, DR 9, p 5.

[9]   See Eur Court HR *Campbell & Cosans v UK*, judgment of 25 Feb 1982, Series A no 48, 4 EHRR 293, § 40.

[10] Eur Court HR *Kjeldsen, Busk Madsen & Pedersen v Denmark*, judgment of 7 Dec 1976, Series A no 23, 1 EHRR 711, § 50.

[11] See Robertson (1951), 'The ECHR: Recent Developments', *British Yearbook of International Law*, **28**, pp 359-365, at p 363, for the differences in the French text (*éducation* and *enseignement*).

[12] *Campbell & Cosans* judgment *op cit*, § 33.

[13] See Nos 7511/76 & 7743/76 *Campbell & Cosans v UK*, Comm Rep, May 1980, Series A no 48, 3 EHRR 531.

from the reference to education *and* teaching and the obligation to respect parental convictions therefore has a potentially wide application. In particular, it is relevant not only to teaching in schools, but to all of the functions assumed by the State in the formal educational system. The Court's broad interpretation of the concepts of education and teaching also means that the parental right to have their views respected in their children's education is relevant beyond the school system, in the broader context of the way children are reared. For example, in certain circumstances, it may place an obligation on the domestic authorities to take the philosophical and religious convictions of parents into account in the exercise of their rights under a care order, in particular when placing a child with alternative carers.[14]

## State Discretion in Education

The vague wording of Article 2 of the First Protocol means that specific aspects of the right to education, such as at what age school attendance should begin, how long it should continue, what purposes the curriculum should serve and whether it should be free, are unclear.[15] These matters fall largely within the competence of the domestic authorities, although the Court reserves the right to review their compatibility with the Convention. The scope of the State's discretion in education is not clear-cut although a wide degree of discretion is enjoyed in relation to how the provision of education is organised. In particular, the regulation of education 'may vary in time and place according to the needs and resources of the community and of individuals'.[16] While it appears that the State may restrict entry to third or higher level education by establishing minimum standards of admission and imposing other conditions,[17] it is to be presumed that access to primary education under the Convention must be made open to all, regardless of merit.[18] Any attempt to restrict access to primary education would arguably injure the substance of the right guaranteed by Article 2 of

---

[14] Eur Court HR *Olsson v Sweden*, judgment of 24 March 1988, Series A no 130, 11 EHRR 259. See further Chapter 12, pp 273-276.

[15] cf Articles 28 and 29 of the Convention on the Rights of the Child, *op cit*.

[16] *Belgian Linguistics Case* judgment, *op cit*, § 5.

[17] No *5492/72 X v Austria*, Dec 16.7.73, Collection 44, p 63, No *8844/80 X v UK*, *op cit*, and also No *11655/85 Glazewska v Sweden*, Dec 10.10.85, DR 45, p 300.

[18] Harris, O'Boyle & Warbrick, *op cit*, p 541. See also the discussion on access to education by children with disabilities below.

the First Protocol and, as well as being inconsistent with that provision, would probably also contradict the spirit of the Convention as a whole, given the far-reaching consequences which it would have.[19] It is unclear whether restricted access to education at secondary level would also violate the Convention, although the fact that schooling at this level is compulsory in many Convention States supports a positive conclusion in this respect.[20]

Admittedly some financial outlay is necessary to guarantee the right to education, but the State is free to choose the means by which it complies with the Convention. As a result, the allocation of resources will not be the only means by which an effective right to education can be guaranteed, and the State may choose to organise its educational system in a way which complies with Article 2 of the First Protocol in order to achieve this aim. However, the negative formulation of the right to education would appear to preclude a challenge based on inadequate resources or the manner in which education is organised, as these are matters which fall within state discretion.[21] Moreover, where a child is denied education of a particular type, which is the parent's preference, then the limited scope of the right to education, together with the State's discretion in this area, will prevent a successful claim under Article 2 of the First Protocol. So, for example, parents who wish to have their disabled child educated in a main stream school, but are denied this opportunity because state policy is to provide only segregated schooling for such children, cannot invoke Article 2 of the First Protocol.[22] The manner in which the right to education is guaranteed

---

[19] See Van Dijk & Van Hoof, *op cit*, p 647.

[20] See individual state reports to the UN Committee on the Rights of the Child and Council of Europe Document CDPS III.8 Obs (1996) 1 '*Ages at which children are legally entitled to carry out a series of acts in Council of Europe Member countries*'.

[21] See No *14668/89 Simpson v UK*, Dec 4.12.89, DR 64, p 188 and No *14135/88 PD & LD v UK*, Dec 2.10.89, DR 62, p 292. See also Harris, O'Boyle & Warbrick, *op cit*, p 543. A reservation entered by the UK accepts the principle in the second sentence of Article 2 of the First Protocol only so far as it is compatible with the provision of efficient instruction and training, and the avoidance of unreasonable public expenditure. The validity and applicability of this reservation have yet to be determined. See No *28915/95 Pile v UK*, Dec 24.1.97, unreported. See also Cumper (1989), 'Muslim's Knocking at the Class Room Door', *New Law Journal*, **140**, pp 1067-1071.

[22] No 14135/88 *PD & LD v UK*, *op cit*. cf No 14668/89 *Simpson v Sweden, op cit*, where the parents of a dyslexic child disagreed with the local education authority's assessment of his needs which recommended placement in an integrated setting.

falls within the discretion of the State therefore and as long as the substance of the right is not infringed, the fact that the type of education received does not coincide with their parent's wishes will not itself violate the Convention.

Compulsory schooling, either in State schools or by means of private tuition, would appear to be compatible with Article 2 of the First Protocol, as long as it offers scope for the respect of parental convictions.[23] Moreover, the verification and enforcement of educational standards is an integral part of the right of the State to establish compulsory schooling. Consequently, where parents are given the freedom to educate their children at home, it is consistent with the Convention for the State to require them to cooperate in the assessment of their children's educational standards. The aim of this requirement is to ensure that a certain standard of literacy and numeracy is being achieved,[24] and thus it is the quality of the education, rather than its form which is important.[25]

## The Right to an Effective Education

Although the negative formulation of Article 2 of the First Protocol appears to mean that it stops short of obliging States to guarantee the right to education in a proactive manner, the Court has not ruled out that the right to education may place a positive obligation on the State.[26] It has held that the provision obliges States to ensure to children their right to education,[27] but it is still unclear what positive steps, if any, the domestic authorities are required to take to enable children to enjoy their right to education. However, it is important in this respect that Article 1 provides that Convention rights are to be secured to everyone. In addition, the Court has established that the Convention guarantees rights of a practical and effective nature.[28] In light of the fact that the right to education is clearly

---

[23] No *10233/83 Family H v UK*, Dec 6.3.84, DR 37, p 105.

[24] *Ibid.* See the declaration made by Ireland on ratification of the First Protocol, *op cit*, p 41. See also Fawcett (1987), *The Application of the European Convention on Human Rights*, 2nd ed, Oxford: Clarendon Press, pp 412-413.

[25] Van Dijk & Van Hoof, *op cit*, p 646.

[26] *Belgian Linguistics Case* judgment, *op cit*, § 3.

[27] *Costello-Roberts* judgment, *op cit*, § 27.

[28] Eur Court HR *Airey v Ireland*, judgment of 9 Oct 1979, Series A no 32, 2 EHRR 305, § 24; Eur Court HR *Marckx v Belgium*, judgment of 13 June 1979, Series A no 31, 2 EHRR 330, § 31. See further Chapter 1, pp 10-12.

of little use to a child who cannot benefit from it, these principles provide some basis for arguing that simply refraining from taking measures which infringe the right to education will be insufficient to guarantee that right under the Convention. Due to the wide discretion which States enjoy in securing the right to education, it is unlikely that a claim invoking the right to an effective education would entitle individual children to complain that particular teachers were failing in their job as educators. However, it is conceivable that the provision could be interpreted to place an obligation on Convention States to remove the obstacles in the way of children gaining access, or enjoying their right to education. For example, Article 2 of the First Protocol may require that the State facilitate access to education by a child with physical disabilities.[29] It is similarly possible to contend that the education received by a refugee child will be ineffective for the purposes of Article 2 of the First Protocol unless the child also receives necessary language tuition.[30] It is certainly arguable that, without affirmative action by the State, children in these and other situations will not be able either to enjoy the right to education or to take benefit from the education they receive. The argument that an effective right to education involves the taking of positive measures is strengthened further by reference to the principle of non-discrimination in Article 14. Under the Convention, States may thus be compelled to make adequate provision to ensure that all children enjoy equal access to the available educational facilities, and in this way, take benefit from an effective right to education.[31] The exact scope of such an obligation and how it is to be fulfilled would arguably be a matter of state discretion.

*Children with Disabilities*

The State enjoys considerable discretion with regard to how children with disabilities are educated and it is not the task of the Convention authorities to assess the standard of the special facilities which the State provides in the implementation of the right to education.[32] As long as the child's needs have been assessed by a competent authority therefore, the Court is unlikely to impose a contrary view unless it is established that the education received is clearly ineffective or discriminatory. The manner in

---

[29] See below.

[30] See further below and Chapter 10, pp 236-237.

[31] See further *Belgian Linguistics Case*, judgment, *op cit*, § 4.

[32] No 18511/91 *Dahlberg v Sweden*, Dec 2.3.94, unreported. No 14668/89 *Simpson v UK, op cit.*

which the domestic authority's decision is implemented may thus raise an issue under the Convention where the consequence is that the child in question does not enjoy the right to education on a par with his/her able bodied peers. This arose in *McIntyre v UK* in 1998 where a child with a physical disability relied on Article 2 of the First Protocol with Article 14 of the Convention to complain that she did not enjoy equal access to the educational facilities enjoyed by her classmates.[33] The applicant attended a mainstream school, but due to her increasing lack of mobility found that she was unable to gain access to the upper floors of the school building, to the science laboratory and other classrooms where her classmates took instruction. She argued that the local authority's failure to install a lift prevented her from enjoying her right to education, and amounted to discrimination on the grounds of her disability. Rejecting her complaint, the Commission noted that the applicant had been provided with a number of additional resources to accommodate her disability, including arranging that any disruption to her education be minimal and, in the light of her increased difficulty in climbing the stairs, leading to her fixed classroom being moved to the ground floor. Given that these and other alternative arrangements facilitated her receipt of an adequate education, the Commission found that the failure to install a lift in the school had not denied her the right to education. Moreover, the cost of installing a lift in a small, primary school was found to be high when balanced with the other demands of the area's schools and the girl's particular needs. As a result, the refusal to install a lift at the school was considered to be proportionate to the local authority's aim to provide educational facilities in a manner consistent with a practical and efficient use of resources.

While the Commission avoided deciding whether the words 'or other status' in Article 14 include physical disability as a status, its consideration of the *McIntyre* application on that basis arguably confirms that this is the case.[34] The Commission reiterated that the right to education is not absolute, but also stressed the need to balance the need and right of an individual child to have access to a full national curriculum with the resources available for education generally. The principle of proportionality is the key, therefore, to determining whether the measures adopted in any particular case will be compatible with the Convention as a whole.

---

[33] No 29046/95 *McIntyre v UK*, Dec 21.10.98, unreported.
[34] See also Chapter 1, pp 4-6.

## The Right to Provide Education

The right to education does not require States to establish new private schools; nor does it involve a duty to finance or subsidise private schools.[35] An interpretation which prohibits the establishment of private schools is unlikely, however,[36] and Article 2 may thus be said to comprise the right to provide, as well as the right to receive, education.[37] The extent to which this right depends on respect for parents' convictions under the second sentence of Article 2 is unclear.[38] It has been argued that a state monopoly of public schools may be consistent with Article 2 of Protocol No 1 as long as parents' philosophical and religious convictions are respected, although this approach may be too rigid to reflect the pluralism in education at which Article 2 was aimed.[39] In any event, the right to establish and run a private school, or to teach children at home, is not absolute,[40] and it may be subject to state regulation in order to ensure a proper educational system as a whole, with particular regard to quality of teaching.[41]

## Respect for Parental Convictions

Although it reflects the view that in the education and upbringing of their children, parents are superior in authority to the State,[42] the requirement that parents' convictions be respected in their children's education has its

---

[35]  No 10476/83 *X v Sweden*, Dec 10.85, 9 EHRR 247; No 7782/77 *X v UK*, Dec 2.5.78, DR 14, p 179 and *No 6853/74 40 Mothers v Sweden*, Dec 9.3.77, DR 9, p 27.

[36]  Nos *5095/71, 5920/72 & 5926/72 Kjeldsen, Busk Madsen & Pedersen v Denmark,* Comm Rep, 21.3.75, Series A no 23, § 153.

[37]  See Van Dijk & Van Hoof, *op cit*, pp 470-471.

[38]  See the argument in Opsahl, 'The Convention and the Right to Respect for Family Life' in Robertson (ed) (1973), *Privacy and Human Rights*, Manchester: MUP, pp 182-254.

[39]  Wildhaber, *op cit*, p 534 and *Kjeldsen, Busk Madsen & Pedersen* judgment, *op cit*, § 50.

[40]  This right belongs to the parents and not the school. No *11535/86 Jordebo Foundation of Christian Schools & Jordebo v Sweden*, Dec 6.3.87, DR 51, p 125.

[41]  *Ibid*. See also No *10233/83 Family H v UK*, *op cit*.

[42]  Duncan, 'The Child, the Parent and the State: The Balance of Power' in Duncan (1987), *Law and Social Policy: Some Current Problems*, Dublin: DULJ, pp 19-37, at p 19.

background in the desire to prevent the recurrence of the indoctrination of children by the State experienced during World War II. The provision aims to achieve pluralism in education also and it is this background which guided the Court's initial interpretation of Article 2 of the First Protocol from the parent's perspective. In particular, the Court has established that respect for parental convictions does not prevent the State from imparting, 'through teaching or education, knowledge of a directly or indirectly religious or philosophical kind'.[43] It merely requires that information be conveyed in an objective and pluralistic manner throughout the educational system.

The obligation to respect parents' religious and philosophical convictions, set out in the second sentence of Article 2, First Protocol, must be read together with the substantive right to education in the first sentence.[44] The duty to respect these convictions applies throughout the entire state education programme, and parental convictions must thus be observed in all the functions assumed by the State in the area of education. It is applicable, therefore, to matters of academic interest, all aspects of school administration, the supervision of the educational system and discipline issues.[45]

In an effort to identify the kind of convictions, which attract the protection of Article 2, First Protocol, the Court has distinguished between views and opinions, which fall within the scope of Article 10 of the Convention, and convictions, which must be respected under Article 2 of the First Protocol. However, it has limited the potential of parental influence in education by finding that the convictions to be taken into consideration are to be interpreted narrowly to include only those views, which attain a certain level of cogency, seriousness, cohesion and importance.[46] In determining whether these criteria have been satisfied in a particular case, the burden is placed on the parent to establish that their belief is part of a serious and cohesive thought process.[47] Moreover, the parent must prove that this thought process is the basis for the objection being made,[48] and that it was brought to the attention of the authorities.[49]

---

[43] *Kjeldsen, Busk Madsen & Pedersen* judgment, *op cit*, § 53.

[44] *Ibid*, § 50.

[45] *Campbell & Cosans* judgment, *op cit*, § 33-35.

[46] *Ibid*, § 36.

[47] *Campbell & Cosans* Comm Rep, *op cit*, § 93.

[48] No *9471/81 Warwick v UK*, Comm Rep, 18.7.86, DR 60, p 5.

[49] No *9303/81 B & D v UK*, Dec, 10.86, 9 EHRR 538.

*Religious Convictions*

The second sentence of Article 2 of the First Protocol recognises the importance of the parental role in the education and guidance of the child in religious matters and it is to be read in the context of the Convention as a whole, but in particular with Articles 8, 9 and 10.[50] The requirement to respect a parent's religious convictions in education thus reflects the right to respect for family life, the right to religious freedom as well as the right to freedom of expression respectively, and the emphasis is placed firmly on the religious freedom and expression of parents, rather than their children.[51]

While parents' religious convictions may be relatively easy to identify, what is problematic in the context of Article 2 of the First Protocol is the scope of the State's obligation to respect those convictions in education. Clearly, the State must respect religious beliefs in all aspects of the functions which it undertakes in the sphere of education and this requires that information or knowledge with a religious connotation may not be transmitted to pupils except in an objective and pluralistic manner.[52] However, the case law illustrates how applying this principle in practice may be problematic.[53] For instance, it may be difficult to distinguish between teaching children about different religions on the one hand, and religious instruction in a particular religion involving an element of prayer, on the other. While the former may be consistent with Article 2 as long as the content and mode of conveying the information is both objective and leaves adequate room for parental guidance,[54] compulsory child attendance at the latter class would appear to violate Article 2. This is highlighted by *Karnell & Hardnt v Sweden* where parents complained that the compulsory nature of religious instruction in state schools prevented them from educating their children in accordance with their religious convictions.[55]

---

[50] *Kjeldsen, Busk Madsen & Pedersen* judgment, *op cit,* § 52.

[51] This is consistent with the standard set out in Article 14 of the Convention on the Rights of the Child, which recognises the child's right to religious freedom, but makes its exercise subject to the guidance of the child's parents. See further Van Bueren (1995a), *op cit,* pp 156-159.

[52] *Kjeldsen, Busk Madsen & Pedersen* judgment, *op cit,* § 53.

[53] The Commission has itself pointed to this difficulty. No *21787/93 Valsamis v Greece,* Comm Rep, 6.7.95, Reports-VI no 27, § 38.

[54] *Kjeldsen, Busk Madsen & Pedersen* judgment, *op cit,* § 54, *mutatis mutandis.*

[55] No *4733/71 Karnell & Hardnt v Sweden,* Dec 28.5.73, 14 Yearbook (1971) p 664. See Boucaud (1989), 'The Council of Europe and Child Welfare: The Need for a European Convention on Children's Rights', *Human Rights Files No 10,* Strasbourg: Council of Europe, p 17. See also No *10491/83 Angeleni v*

The case was settled, illustrating the strength of the applicants' case, following the issuing of an order providing that religion would be taught as a separate subject, from which the children were free to withdraw. While permitting parents to withdraw their children from religious instruction appears to be sufficient to fulfil the obligation to respect religious convictions under Article 2, the Court is unlikely to find that the State need do more, notwithstanding that the process of withdrawing a child from such instruction may mark the child out to be different, when pressure to conform is great.[56]

There are circumstances in which exemption from religious instruction will be insufficient to respect parental convictions under the Convention, for example where a religion represents a way of life. This dilemma is illustrated by two cases concerning the compulsory participation of Jehovah's Witness children in school processions which celebrated a national holiday commemorating the beginning of the Greece-Italian war.[57] The girls' parents had expressly requested their exemption from religious education and any manifestation contrary to their pacifist religious convictions, including specifically commemoration of the national holiday. Nevertheless, both children were penalised for failing to attend the school on the day in question and received a one day suspension as a result. However, both the Commission and the Court rejected the view that this situation was incompatible with the rights of the children, or their parents under Article 2 of the First Protocol. Fundamentally, they disagreed with the applicants about the military nature of the procession and the challenge to the children's pacifist beliefs which it posed. Moreover, they were persuaded by the fact that the procession was fully integrated in the traditional nature of Greek schooling and culture, no exceptions being permitted to children's obligatory participation. As a result, the

---

*Sweden*, Dec 12.86, DR 51, p 41, 10 EHRR 123, in which Sweden's reservation precluded the finding of a violation in this regard.

[56] Hamilton & Watt (1995), 'A Discriminating Education - Collective Worship in Schools', *Child and Family Law Quarterly*, 7(4), pp 28-42, at p 33-34. It is the opinion of the Committee on the Rights of the Child that a system of withdrawing the child from religious instruction which requires the child to expose the faith of the child concerned may violate the child's right to privacy. See UN Doc CRC/C/15/Add.23, § 9.

[57] See *Valsamis* Comm Rep, *op cit* and Eur Court *Valsamis v Greece*, judgment of 18 Dec 1996, Report 1996-VI, no 27, p 2313, 24 EHRR 294 and the identical case of *No 24095/94 Efstratiou v Greece*, Comm Rep, 6.7.95 and Eur Court HR, judgment of 18 Dec 1996, Reports 1996-VI no 27, p 2347 and p 2367.

Commission concluded that mandatory participation in the procession did not amount to indoctrination; nor did imposition of a penalty for non-attendance violate Article 2 of the First Protocol.[58] The Court reached the same conclusion, although it raised a judicial eyebrow in relation to the compulsory nature of the parade and the penalty imposed for non-attendance, given the possibility that it would have a psychological impact on the girl.[59]

A large group of eight members dissented from the Commission, objecting to the mandatory nature of participation in the procession.[60] In particular, they found that this factor interfered with the children's freedom of religion under Article 9 of the Convention, insofar as the right to manifest a religion also implies a right to abstain from demonstrations which are not compatible with one's religious convictions. As it could not have pursued any legitimate aim and it was otherwise incompatible with the spirit of tolerance and openness which must prevail in a democratic society, they considered that the sanction imposed breached Article 9 in relation to the children, and Article 2 of the First Protocol in relation to their parents.

In addition to the fact that the conclusion of the Commission and the Court appears to be inconsistent with the general objectives of pluralism and tolerance in a democratic society,[61] the reliance of the institutions on their own assessment of the nature of the procession is also questionable in the circumstances of the case. Even considering that not all religious beliefs are worthy of respect under Article 2 of the First Protocol, nonetheless it is arguable that the parents' views on pacifism were significantly serious and important to warrant such protection. In line with the onus on parents to bring their views to the attention of the relevant authorities, they had, in this case, specifically requested exemption from the parade in advance. These factors notwithstanding, however, both institutions considered the issue of whether the nature of the procession infringed their pacifist beliefs was something which they could and did objectively decide, with decisive consequences.

---

[58]    *Valsamis* Comm Rep, *ibid*, § 36-41.

[59]    *Valsamis* judgment, *op cit*, § 31-32.

[60]    See the partly dissenting view of Mrs Liddy and Messrs Gozubuyuk, Marxer, Nowicki, Conforti, Bratza, Mucha and Perenic in *Valsamis*, Comm Rep, *op cit*.

[61]    See also the Council of Europe Recommendation 1201 (1993) on religious tolerance in a democratic society, particularly recommendation 16 ii. See (1996) *The Rights of the Child: A European Perspective*, Strasbourg: Council of Europe, pp 374-376.

The possibility that failure to exempt the children from the procession would have a detrimental effect on them caused the Court some concern. Moreover, the necessity of imposing such a severe measure for non-attendance at a parade was also questioned in the light of the possibility that it may impact psychologically on the children. While neither the Commission nor the Court considered whether the sanction itself violated Article 2 of the First Protocol, both institutions applied their conclusions as to the failure to respect the parents' beliefs *mutatis mutandis* to the complaint under Article 9 concerning the children's complaints.[62] This failure to undertake a separate examination of the child's complaint is unfortunate in the light of the Court's apparent conclusion that the right to respect for convictions in education belongs not to children, but to their parents.[63] The approach illustrated by a substantial minority of the Commission, which emphasised the child's right to be free to manifest his/her religious beliefs, is clearly preferable here.

*Respect for Religious Convictions through Private Schools*

Respect for the religious convictions of parents under Article 2 means that States cannot prohibit members of religious minorities from establishing their own schools. Thus, the State must tolerate separate schools if they are necessary to respect parents' religious convictions. Article 14 prohibits discrimination in the enjoyment of Convention rights and although there is no independent obligation on the State to fund separate schools, it is arguable that this provision read with Article 2 of the First Protocol entitles such schools to the same support as state schools. The circumstances in which this might arise are unclear however, given that the State is under no obligation to provide any particular form of education.[64] However, two related issues deserve attention here. Firstly, it may be possible to challenge state support which enables one religious minority to establish and maintain their school, but not another, by invoking Article 14, together with Article 2 of the First Protocol. Whether this situation would amount to a breach of the relevant provisions would depend on whether there

---

[62] *Valsamis* Comm Rep, *op cit*, § 50 and judgment, *op cit*, § 37.

[63] See Wildhaber, *op cit*, p 546. See also Van Bueren (1995a), pp 240-245, who discusses the case law on Article 2 of Protocol No 1 in the context of a child's right. See further below, pp 84-86.

[64] See also Harris, O'Boyle & Warbrick, *op cit*, p 548.

existed an objective and reasonable justification for the distinction.[65]   A separate issue might arise where failure to provide state support for a religious minority school results in the denial of the child's right to education due to the fact that the parents' religious beliefs cannot be respected in any other way.[66]   This may cause difficulty where the system of state schools is expressly committed to religious education of one kind and where the establishment of secular schools, for those who wish to avoid the strong religious ethos, is not facilitated.[67]

*Philosophical Convictions*

While it is relatively easy to identify convictions of a religious nature, philosophical convictions are not so easily defined, and according to the Court, the term is incapable of exhaustive definition.[68]   The most straight-forward example of the views which deserve protection relate to physical punishment.[69]   In finding that such views constitute philosophical convictions within the meaning of the provision, the Court noted that it was free to give 'philosophical convictions' an autonomous, contemporaneous and effective interpretation in the absence of guidance from the *Travaux Préparatoires*.[70]   This approach has attracted criticism from those who do not agree that parental views on corporal punishment are serious enough to

---

[65]   See No *7782/77 X v UK*, Dec, 2.5.78, DR 14, p 179 where the Commission found that the different levels of funding available to state schools and 'maintained' schools was justified because the subsidy offered to maintained schools was large and the advantages were considerable.

[66]   *Ibid.* See Hamilton, 'The Right to a Religious Education' in Bainham, Pearl & Pickford (eds) (1995), *Frontiers of Family Law,* Chichester: Wiley, pp 228-242, at pp 231-236, for a discussion of the conflict which may arise between a child's right to an effective education and respect for parent's religious convictions.

[67]   See Clarke (1986), 'Freedom of Thought in Schools: A Comparative Study', *International and Comparative Law Quarterly*, **35**, pp 271-301, at p 297.   See also the concerns raised by the Children's Rights Alliance (Republic of Ireland) in its report to the UN Committee on the Rights of the Child in Kilkelly (1997), *Small Voices: Vital Rights, A Submission to the UN Committee on the Rights of the Child*, Dublin: The Children's Rights Alliance, § 115-116.

[68]   *Campbell & Cosans* judgment, *op cit*, § 36.

[69]   *Ibid*, and *Warwick* Comm Rep, *op cit*. Cf No *17187/90 Bernard & Ors v Luxembourg*, Dec 8.9.93, DR 75, p 57 concerning parents' objections to moral education.

[70]   *Campbell & Cosans* Comm Rep, *op cit*, § 85-94 and judgment, *op cit*, § 36.

attract the protection of the Convention.[71] However, if the obligation to respect parental views in the education of their children is to remain relevant and effective in a modern context, the Court must adopt a dynamic approach to determining which views are worthy of respect. By establishing a threshold whereby only those views which are serious, important and coherent will require respect under the provision, and imposing a significant burden of proof on the parent seeking to rely on Article 2 of the First Protocol, the Court has placed a limit on the protection which the provision offers. In particular, the Court's test distinguishes effectively between mere parental preference regarding the way children are educated, which will fall outside the scope of the Convention, and those deeply held views, which impact significantly on the way children are treated through the educational process. In this regard, for example, the Court has found that views on physical punishment are to be distinguished from those held on other methods of discipline or discipline in general, because they relate to a 'weighty and substantial aspect of human life', namely physical integrity, the propriety of the use of the punishment and the prevention of any harm which its use might involve.[72] It is not insignificant therefore, that the basis of the parents' convictions in these cases was treatment which in itself raised an arguable claim under Article 3 of the Convention.[73] In addition, in the case of *Campbell & Cosans*, the Court recognised that corporal punishment was an integral part of the process by which the school moulded and developed the character of its pupils, making its relationship with the substantive right to education apparent.[74] Respect for a parent's convictions must not harm the fundamental right to education set out in the first sentence of Article 2. Thus in *Campbell & Cosans,* although one of the boys had not been subjected to the punishment with which he was threatened, the fact that he was suspended from school until he was prepared to accept it amounted to a violation of his right to education.[75] These factors all clarify why views on corporal punishment are considered to be more than 'mere preferences'

---

[71] See the dissent of Sir Vincent Evans, *Campbell & Cosans* judgment, *op cit*. See also Wildhaber, *op cit*, p 536.

[72] *Ibid*, § 36.

[73] *Ibid,* and *Warwick* Comm Rep, *op cit*. See further Harris, O'Boyle & Warbrick, *op cit*, p 546.

[74] *Campbell & Cosans* judgment, *op cit*, § 33.

[75] *Campbell & Cosans* Comm Rep, *op cit*, § 41. See Pogany (1982), 'Education: The Rights of Children and Parents under the ECHR', *New Law Journal*, pp 344-346.

of parents with regard to their children's schooling and why they deserve the protection of Article 2, First Protocol.

The above criteria notwithstanding, however, it is difficult to envisage in what other aspects of schooling the State might be compelled to take parents' views into account, especially given that the fundamental issue of language has been excluded.[76] The setting and planning of the curriculum falls within the competence of the State in principle at least,[77] and this includes the allocation of places in secondary schools and the way in which such schools are run.[78] Nor can the incorporation into the school curriculum of teaching of a philosophical or religious kind form the basis of a claim under Article 2 of the First Protocol, as this would risk a situation where all institutionalised teaching would become impracticable.[79] All that is required is that such instruction is given in an objective, critical and pluralistic way, and this principle was first established in the *Danish Sex Education* case, in which the Court found that the integration of sex education into the school curriculum, from which children could not be excused, did not constitute a failure to respect parents' convictions on the matter.[80] The manner in which the instruction was provided was decisive in this respect and in particular, the instruction did not attempt to indoctrinate a particular moral attitude, but merely conveyed information. As a result, the Court held that integration of the subject into the school curriculum did not affect the parents' right to

> enlighten and advise their children, to exercise with regard to their children natural parental functions as educators or to guide their children on a path in line with their own religious and philosophical convictions.[81]

Parents who wished to dissociate their children from integrated sex education were entitled to have them sent to private schools, which were heavily subsidised and bound by less strict obligations, or to educate them

---

[76] See further below.

[77] *Kjeldsen, Busk Madsen & Pedersen* judgment, *op cit.*

[78] No *7527/76 X & Y v UK*, Dec 5.7.77, DR 11 p 147.

[79] *Valsamis* Comm Rep, *op cit,* § 38 and No *9411/81 Mr & Mrs X & their Son v Germany*, Dec 7.82, 5 EHRR 276 where the parents disagreed with the technologically oriented ideology of the school.

[80] *Kjeldsen, Busk Madsen & Pedersen* judgment, *op cit,* § 53. The Court did not clarify whether parents' views on sex education amounted to religious or philosophical convictions for the purposes of the provision, although it clearly accepted that matters of a moral nature were involved.

[81] *Ibid*, § 54.

at home. Taking the situation as a whole therefore, the integration of sex education into the school curriculum did not violate Article 2 of the First Protocol.[82]

The separate opinion of Judge Verdross in this case highlighted the distinction between teaching about the biological science of reproduction and passing on information regarding sexual practices. Although he agreed that the school programme did not amount to indoctrination, the judge nonetheless argued that parents *could* object to information about sexual practices being given to their children. While this point has clear merit, it ignores the important public interest aim pursued by the Danish Government in making sex education compulsory for nine to eleven year olds. The Court's reference to the material situation, including an increase in teenage pregnancies, to which the relevant legislation was a response, illustrates the strong role played by the principle of proportionality in determining what constitutes respect for parents' convictions. In this case, making sex education compulsory for certain children pursued an important aim and the measure was thus proportionate to the means employed to pursue it, especially given the alternative offered by subsidised private education, although this will not always be the case.

While it appears that views held by parents about the content of the school curriculum will fall outside the scope of Article 2 of the First Protocol, it is unclear whether parental convictions about the way in which their children are educated will require respect in the same way.[83] For example, the views held by the parents of children with physical or learning disabilities about their education could be said to be part of a serious and cohesive thought process, or to otherwise satisfy the criteria set out in the physical punishment cases. In such cases too, there is a link between the effectiveness of a child's education under the first sentence and respect under the second sentence for the strongly held views of parents regarding the kind of education which they deem appropriate and necessary for their children. However, the Commission has failed to establish whether the view of a parent in that situation amounts to a philosophical conviction, and if so, what the State is obliged to do to respect that belief under Article 2 of the First Protocol. It has found that the education and teaching of a child must only conform with the parents' convictions as far

---

[82] The Commission reached the same conclusion. See *Kjeldsen, Busk Madsen & Pedersen* Comm Rep, *op cit.*

[83] For example, see Nos *10228/82 &10229/82 v UK*, Dec 3.84, 7 EHRR 141, concerning the parent's preference for their children to attend single-sex grammar schools.

as possible.[84] It is clear therefore, that even if such beliefs were to fall within the meaning of philosophical convictions, the principle of proportionality requires merely that they be respected as far as possible, given the limits of available resources and the need to address the needs of the wider school population. It does not require, for example, that the State provide special facilities to accommodate particular convictions, although it may affect the use of existing facilities.[85] In this regard, however, the State enjoys a discretion in the formulation of policy and practice on the education of such children, such as placing emphasis on integrated or special schooling or a mixture of both, and these factors together explain why such complaints have enjoyed little success. The Commission has noted that it is in keeping with current educational trends to educate children with special educational needs in an integrated setting, where that is compatible with their special education needs, the provision of efficient education for other children at the school, and the efficient use of resources. This approach appears to be consistent with international standards especially, the UN Convention on the Rights of the Child, which recognises the needs of children with disabilities for special care, while emphasising the importance of social integration and personal development.[86] Nevertheless, decisions relating to how to make the best use possible of the resources available to them in the interests of such children generally fall within the State's discretion. As a result, the Commission has failed to find that Article 2 of Protocol No 1 requires placing children who are severely brain damaged,[87] severely retarded in development,[88] have hearing difficulties,[89] physical disabilities[90] or are dyslexic[91] in a general school either where additional teaching staff would be needed or where such placement would be to the detriment of other pupils, rather than placing them in school with specialist facilities.[92] The effect of this is that where the needs of children with disabilities have been

---

[84] No 14135/88 *PD & LD v UK, op cit.*
[85] *Ibid.* See the UK reservation referred to above, p 66.
[86] See Article 23, *op cit.*
[87] No *14135/88 PD & LD v UK, op cit.*
[88] No *13887/88 Graeme v UK*, Dec 5.2.90, DR 64, p 158.
[89] No *25212/94 Klerks v the Netherlands*, Dec 4.7.95, DR 82, p 129.
[90] No *18511/91 Dahlberg v Sweden, op cit.*
[91] No *14668/89 Simpson v UK, op cit.*
[92] *Ibid*, No *25212/94 Klerks v the Netherlands, op cit* and No *13887/88 Graeme v UK, op cit.*

properly assessed[93] and their placement is consistent both with that needs assessment and as far as possible with parents' views about the child's needs, then no violation of the second sentence of Article 2 of the First Protocol will occur.[94] Whether such a placement amounts to a breach of the first sentence of that provision, where for example it proves completely ineffective, or constitutes discrimination in the enjoyment of the right to education, would depend on the facts of the individual case.[95]

## The Rights of Linguistic Minorities

Despite express recognition in other international instruments,[96] the rights of linguistic minorities receive no special treatment in the European Convention.[97] Moreover, notwithstanding that pluralism in education for minorities requires that policies designed to assimilate minorities be prohibited,[98] the Court has shown a tolerance for assimilation policies which appears to be out of line with its insistence on pluralism in other matters.[99]

---

[93] The right to be granted an education appropriate to the child's needs and aptitudes is not a civil right for the purposes of Article 6, which thus does not apply to any challenge to the assessment of such a child's needs. No *18511/91 Dahlberg v Sweden, op cit.* Nor is it necessary to afford the procedural guarantees of that provision - fairness, independence, impartiality of tribunal, expediency - to situations in which the assessment of the child's needs may be challenged. See No *14668/89 Simpson v UK, op cit.*

[94] See the reservation of the UK referred to above, p 66.

[95] See above, pp 68-69.

[96] See Article 30 Convention on the Rights of the Child, *op cit* and Article 5 of the UNESCO Convention against Discrimination in Education, 1960. See also the Framework Convention for the Protection of National Minorities, 1995 (ETS No 157). See further Packer & Myntti (eds) (1993), *The Protection of Ethnic and Linguistic Minorities in Europe,* Abo: Institute for Human Rights, Abo Akademi University.

[97] See Connelly (1993), 'The European Convention on Human Rights and the Protection of Linguistic Minorities', *Irish Journal of European Law,* 2, pp 277-293, especially pp 286-287.

[98] Cullen (1993), 'Education Rights or Minority Rights', *International Journal of Law & the Family,* 7, pp 143-177, at pp 157-159. Article 5 of the Framework Convention calls on States to refrain from policies or practices of assimilation of national minorities.

[99] See Harris, O'Boyle & Warbrick, *op cit,* p 548.

The *Belgian Linguistics Case* confirmed that the right to education under Article 2 of the First Protocol contains no linguistic requirement *per se*.[100] In particular, the Court has found that parents' linguistic convictions constitute neither religious nor philosophical convictions within the ordinary meaning of the provision. There is thus no obligation to respect linguistic convictions in the education of children; nor does the provision contain a right to have established or subsidised schools in which education is provided in a given language.[101] Although Article 2 of the First Protocol does not specify that instruction must be conducted in a particular language so as to safeguard the right to education, the Court has found that it

> would be meaningless if it did not imply in favour of its beneficiaries, the right to be educated in the national language or in one of the national languages, as the case may be.[102]

Yet, this does not place an obligation on States to respect the rights of children of linguistic minorities to be educated in their own language. Similarly, although Article 10 guarantees freedom of expression, it does not include the right to express an opinion in a language of one's choice, as this would imply a right to be taught in a language of one's choice, which is not found in the Convention.[103] Nor is it possible to invoke Article 2 of the First Protocol with the principle of non-discrimination in Article 14 in order to claim a right to obtain instruction in a language of one's choice.[104] For this reason, the claim of French-speaking parents, that the Belgian linguistic arrangements and the educational system based thereon treated their children differently from Dutch speaking children without objective

---

[100] *Belgian Linguistics Case* judgment, *op cit*, § 6. The Court referred to the *Travaux Préparatoires* which showed the express rejection of a Danish proposal for protection of linguistic minorities during the drafting of the Convention.

[101] *Ibid*, § 7.

[102] *Ibid*, § 3.

[103] No *1474/62 23 Inhabitants of Alsemberg & Beersel v Belgium*, 6 Yearbook (1963), p 332 in Van Dijk & Van Hoof, *op cit*, p 408. The Court has failed to find that this right is implicit in Article 2 of Protocol No 1 which provides for the right to education. See also Verdoot, 'The Right to Use a Language of One's Own Choice' in (1996) *Proceedings of the 8th International Colloquy on the European Convention on Human Rights*, Strasbourg: Council of Europe, pp 57-64.

[104] *Belgian Linguistics Case* judgment, *op cit*, § 11. According to the Court, this would lead to 'absurd results'.

or reasonable justification, failed before the Court on several counts.[105] However, the Court did find one minor practice to be inconsistent with Article 14, namely that Dutch-speaking children in a particular area could attend Dutch language schools in a bilingual district outside the neighbourhood, whereas French-speaking children in an equivalent Flemish area could not attend French language schools in the same bilingual district and were obliged to attend a local Dutch language school instead.[106] Overall, however, it found that the system, which was based on the principle of territoriality, aimed legitimately to protect the linguistic homogeneity of the region and although it caused hardship, the measures in question did not amount to arbitrary treatment.[107]

While the State is not obliged to set up or finance private schools in order to respect the rights of a linguistic minority, it is nonetheless arguable that the absence of necessary language tuition, for example, in the case of immigrant or refugee children, may raise concern about the effective or meaningful nature of the right to education provided under Article 2 of the First Protocol, alone or together with Article 14.[108] In particular, the failure to provide essential language tuition has the potential to injure the substance of the right to education itself, given that understanding is so intimately connected with the transmission of information.[109] While securing the right to send children to a private school reconciles the rights of minorities with the objective of pluralism, this is only true insofar as such schools are affordable and accessible.[110] Moreover, given that linguistic minorities are excluded from the protection of the second sentence of Article 2, it is unlikely that the practice of offering varying levels of support to different linguistic minorities would violate Article 2 with Article 14.[111] In any event, only differential treatment which cannot

---

[105] *Ibid.*

[106] *Ibid*, § 32.

[107] *Ibid*, § 7. Cf *Belgian Linguistics Case*, Comm Rep, 24.6.65, Series B no 1, where the Commission found several of the impugned aspects of the education system to have the effect of causing French-speaking children in Dutch-speaking regions to abandon their language. The Commission has also found restrictions on the school which a Greek speaking child could attend were justified. No *4372/80 X v Belgium*, Dec 2.2.71, 14 Yearbook (1971) p 398. See also Cullen, *op cit*, p 158.

[108] See above, pp 67-68.

[109] See Wildhaber, *op cit*, p 541.

[110] Hamilton, in Bainham, Pearl & Pickford, *op cit*, p 233.

[111] This was the issue in No *23716/94 SM & GC v UK*, Dec 29.11.95, unreported, which was struck off. See also Nos *18357/91 D & AH v Greece*, Dec 23.10.95,

be justified on reasonable and objective grounds will fall foul of Article 14.[112]    Although the Convention may require that the State tolerates independent or private schools of this kind, it would appear that, for the moment at least, it does not necessarily have to support them.

## The Right to Education - Parent or Child Right?

The Court has clearly recognised that the right to education set out in the first sentence of Article 2 of Protocol No 1 belongs to the child and that the parents' right to respect for their convictions in the second sentence is subsidiary in nature. However, while the wishes of parents are an important factor, they are clearly not the sole consideration. This is reflected in the fact that the exercise of the parental right under Article 2 is not absolute and may not in any way injure the substance of the child's right to education. Thus, it is the child, which enjoys a right of access to existing educational institutions; the child, which has a right not to be discriminated against in this regard, and the child, which is to be protected against indoctrination, an aim which the parental right in Article 2 sets out to achieve. Children are also entitled to benefit from their education and as a result they enjoy the right to official recognition of studies which have been successfully completed.[113]

Notwithstanding the above assertions, the child is not considered to have sufficient capacity to exercise his/her right to education[114] and the question is frequently asked whether education is truly a child's right, or whether it is more accurately considered a duty of the State, a responsibility of a parent, or even a parent's exercise of a child's right.[115] It is undoubted that, until recently, children were to a large extent perceived

---

unreported, where the refusal of the Greek authorities to award a licence for the establishment of a foreign language school despite a Court decision ordering it to do so violated Article 6.

[112] See No *7782/77 X v UK*, Dec, 2.5.78, DR 14, p 179 where the Commission found that the different levels of funding available to state schools and 'maintained' schools was justified because the state subsidy offered to maintained schools was large and the advantages were considerable.

[113] *Belgian Linguistics Case* judgment, *op cit*.

[114] Harris, O'Boyle & Warbrick, *op cit*, p 541.

[115] See Cullen, *op cit*, p 162. See also Van Bueren, 'Education: Whose Right is it Anyway?' in Heffernan (ed) (1994), *Human Rights: A European Perspective*, Dublin: Round Hall Press, pp 339-350.

as 'silent receptacles of knowledge', while the parental right to have a child educated in accordance with their convictions achieved a balance between the duty of the State and the right of parents with regard to serving the best interests of the child in education.[116] However, recognition of the fact that children with sufficient age and maturity have a right to a say and to actively participate in their own education is slowly gaining recognition.[117] As a result, the relationship between the parent and the State now falls to be re-examined in order to determine the duty which the State owes to consider the child's views and convictions.[118]

This view has not yet been given express recognition in Convention case law where the Court has drawn a clear line between the right of the child (to education) and the parental right (to have their beliefs respected) under Article 2 of the First Protocol.[119] In this regard, it has expressly rejected the child's claim made under the second sentence of the education provision.[120] Moreover, the right to education is seen as an integral part of the exercise of parental authority and custody.[121] Thus a person who loses parental authority as a consequence of a custody or adoption order can no longer claim a violation of Article 2 of Protocol No 1,[122] although the fact that children are taken into care does not necessarily cause parents to lose all their rights under this provision.[123] The Court has rejected the contention that any aspect of Article 8 guarantees either a personal or a parental right to education, although it has not excluded the possibility that measures taken in the field of education may interfere with the right to respect for family life.[124]

As long as the child's right to education is recognised as paramount, it would appear that any conflict between children and parents under the

---

[116] Van Bueren (1995a), *op cit*, p 240.

[117] See generally Chapter 6.

[118] Van Bueren (1995a) *op cit*, p 242. Boucaud makes this point with regard to Article 10 of the European Convention, *op cit*, p 18.

[119] Cf the dissenting view of Mr Kellberg in *Kjeldsen, Busk Madsen & Pedersen* judgment, *op cit*, pp 41-43.

[120] Eur Court HR *Eriksson v Sweden*, judgment of 2 June 1989, Series A, no 156, 12 EHRR 183, § 93.

[121] See for example No *7911/77 X v Sweden*, Dec 12.12.77, DR 12, p 192. See also Wildhaber, *op cit*, p 548.

[122] See No *7626/76 X v UK*, Dec 11.7.77, DR 11, p 160 and No *10929/84 Nielsen v Denmark*, Comm Rep, 12.3.87, Series A no 144, § 115.

[123] See Eur Court HR *Olsson v Sweden*, judgment of 24 March 1988, Series A no 130, 11 EHRR 259 in Chapter 12, pp 266-268.

[124] *Belgian Linguistics Case* judgment, *op cit*, § 7.

Convention may be resolved in a manner which guarantees the child's right to education as absolute. This is a straight-forward process in certain cases. In the *Danish Sex Education Case*, for example, the competing interests of parents and children were easily reconciled in a manner which reflected the child's best interests.[125] However, that the balancing exercise is not always as clear-cut is evident from the Jehovah's Witness cases, in which an issue of respect for religious convictions resulted in the suspension of two children from school. While the rejection of the child's complaint under Article 9 suggests that consideration of the issue from the child's perspective will meet with little success, the preference shown by many members of the Commission for this approach may add weight to its use in future cases.[126] The reliance on international instruments, which contain more detailed child-specific standards, assist this process and the principles and provisions of the Convention on the Rights of the Child are particularly valuable in this respect.

**Future Challenges**

Although the right to education has already been the subject of considerable case law before the Commission and Court from the perspective of parent and child, a number of issues have yet to be determined in this area. In particular, the extent of the obligation on the State to guarantee the right of education to all children is outstanding. This has particular significance for children with physical and other disabilities who do not enjoy equal access to education with their peers, as well as refugee and other children whose language difficulties hinder their ability to benefit from education. Moreover, the compatibility of school exclusions and suspensions with the Convention has also yet to be determined and, despite the scope of state discretion in this area, it is important that their use is proportionate to their purpose. While the inability to challenge an exclusion does not raise an issue under Article 6, given that the right to education does not fall within the meaning of civil rights in that provision, there is scope for arguing that it is inconsistent with the right to education itself insofar as it relates to the procedural aspect of that right. The fact that Article 1 secures Convention rights to everyone is significant in this context and it may be similarly relevant in the application of the education provision to the detention of children in circumstances

---

[125] See above, pp 78-80.
[126] See above, pp 73-75.

where they are not receiving adequate instruction or schooling. The cases of children with special educational needs have been highlighted above.

Despite the clearly articulated obligation to respect parents' convictions, States nonetheless enjoy a wide margin of discretion in the organisation of their educational systems. The failure of the Court to take a dynamic approach to the application of the Convention to linguistic minorities and respect for religious beliefs in education means that the case law on these issues is out of line with other international standards in these areas, although it remains open to review. In contrast, the case law on parental views on discipline is evidence of a modern, dynamic interpretation of the second sentence of Article 2 of the First Protocol. However, the scope of the State's obligation to respect parental convictions is still unclear, particularly in relation to the proportion of the burden which parents may be expected to share in ensuring that their desires for their children's education are realised.

# 5    Identity

## Introduction

The child's right to identity was given express recognition among the so called new rights in the UN Convention on the Rights of the Child, 1989[1] and its specific components are set out in Articles 7 and 8.[2]    Article 7 recognises the right of the child to be registered after birth, the right to acquire a nationality and, as far as possible, the right to know and be cared for by his/her parents.    In addition, Article 8 guarantees the right of the child to preserve his/her identity, the components of which include nationality, name and family relations. These standards are absent from the European Convention, although the Commission and Court have been called upon to examine disputes, the resolution of which is central to the different elements of the child's right to identity, namely, family relations, nationality and name.

## The Origins of the Child

The absence from the European Convention of express provision for the right of the child to identity has had consequences for the manner in which the Commission and the Court have dealt with related issues.    Disputes over the recognition of a child's biological and legal ties, which are determinative of the child's right to know his/her origins, have been resolved without special regard for the rights of the child.    While the consideration of such matters within the framework of the right to respect

---

[1]    UN Doc A/44/25.  See Cerda (1990), 'The Draft Convention on the Rights of the Child: New Rights', *Human Rights Quarterly*, **12**, pp 115-119.  See also Article 24 International Covenant on Civil and Political Rights, 1966, UNTS vol 999, p 171.

[2]    See Stewart (1992), 'Interpreting the Child's Right to Identity in the UN Convention on the Rights of the Child', *Family Law Quarterly*, **26**(3), pp 221-233. For a general account of the child's right to identity under international law see Van Bueren (1995a), *The International Law on the Rights of the Child*, Dordrecht: Martinus Nijhoff, pp 117-130.

for family life under Article 8 offers clear scope for balancing the rights of parents with those of their children, the approach of the Commission and the Court has been more passive than active in this regard.

*Paternity*

The Convention approach to the issue of paternity reflects the prevalence of the social and biological, over the legal reality in the recognition of family ties. For example, in 1993, a mother's inability to rebut the presumption that her husband was the father of her child, despite the fact that he had disappeared years before the birth, was successfully challenged before the Commission.[3] The Commission accepted that the generally recognised presumption that a married man is the father of his wife's children was reasonable and that there were good reasons for not overturning it easily. However, it went on to note that

> there are cases where it is clear that the presumption does not correspond to the real situation and, at least in some situations, the right to respect for private and family life in Article 8 may require that the real paternity is also legally recognised.[4]

This was clearly one such case and, in concluding that Article 8 had been violated with respect to both parents and child, the Commission attached weight to certain material facts, including that the child was unaware of her legal father's existence, that her biological parents had enjoyed a stable relationship a long time before her birth, and that her biological father was prepared to take responsibility for her.

The Court also believed that the irrebutable presumption violated Article 8, although it went further in its analysis of the situation. It held that

> respect for family life requires that biological and social reality prevail over a legal presumption which, as in the present case, flies in the face of both established fact and the wishes of those concerned without actually benefiting anyone.[5]

---

[3] No *18535/91 K, Z & S v the Netherlands*, Comm Rep, 7.4.93, Series A no 297-C, p 66, 18 EHRR 214.

[4] *Ibid*, § 40.

[5] Eur Court HR *Kroon & Others v the Netherlands*, judgment of 27 Oct 1994, Series A no 297-C, 19 EHRR 263, § 40.

Clearly, it was not the presumption itself, which gave rise to a violation of Article 8 in this case, but its irrebuttable nature. Despite this, the Court gave no guidance as to whether a presumption somewhere inbetween rebuttable and irrebuttable would raise an issue under Article 8. For example, would a presumption which is extremely difficult, but not impossible, to rebut be compatible with respect for family life?[6] The Court's reasoning in this case suggests that factors material to the determination of such a situation would include whether the presumption is consistent with 'the wishes of those concerned', and whether it can be said to 'benefit anyone', particularly the child at the centre of the issue.

The relevance of these factors was apparent in a paternity dispute which came before the Commission in 1994.[7] The complaint was brought by a man who, following an affair with a married woman who had subsequently had a child, was unsuccessful in seeking to establish the paternity of the child before the domestic authorities. In particular, the national courts had refused to order a blood test, which would have enabled the child's paternity to be established. In reaching its decision, the domestic authorities had relied on the view that the child's welfare was bound up inextricably with the family unit within which she was being raised, and that the risk of disturbing the stability of that family by allowing a blood test would be to her detriment. In finding that this did not involve a breach of Article 8, the Commission noted the basis for the domestic courts' refusal to order a blood test, in particular the significance attached to the best interests of the child. Moreover, it was unable to find anything unreasonable or arbitrary in this assessment of the child's interests and found it justifiable for the national courts to give greater weight to the interests of the child and the family in which he lived, than to the interest of the applicant in obtaining verification or otherwise of a biological fact. Although this decision may be considered reasonable in the light of the margin of appreciation which the State enjoys in the area of private and family life, it is unclear whether the Commission would have reached the same conclusion had it found that family life, rather than private life, existed between the applicant and his child. The Commission had decided on the facts that neither potential nor actual family life existed between the applicant and his alleged daughter. In particular, it noted that he had never cohabited with the mother, their relationship lasted only six months, the

---

[6]  See Andrews & Sherlock (1995), 'Respect for Family Life and Presumptions Regarding Paternity of Children', *European Law Review*, **20**, pp 414-416, at p 416.

[7]  No *22920/93 MB v UK*, Dec 6.4.94, DR 77A, p 108.

child was not planned and he did not see the child or form any emotional bond with her.[8] As a result, the refusal to allow him to discover the truth about his relationship with the child raised an issue under private, and not family life. The emerging question is this: while the obligation to respect *private* life did not include the ordering of blood tests to determine the applicant's biological tie with the child in question, would such an obligation have been required in order to respect *family* life? Clearly if the answer is no, then the distinction between private and family life is an academic one for this purpose. This is unlikely.[9] On the other hand, had family life been found to exist, it would arguably have been a material consideration in the determination of the case, although that is not to say that its very existence would have precluded the same negative outcome.

The applicant in the case above requested the Commission to consider that the refusal to order blood tests to determine the child's paternity also violated his (alleged) daughter's right to respect for family life. While there is little doubt that such a complaint brought by the child herself would have enjoyed success, the applicant did not have the right to represent the child in domestic law and so the Commission limited its examination of the complaint as it related to the applicant.[10] However, the Strasbourg authorities were not precluded from reviewing whether the treatment of the issue by the national courts - namely the accurate determination of relations between the applicant and the child - was arbitrary insofar as it failed to consider the child's right and need to have her origins determined. Nevertheless, the preference shown for raising the child in a family based on marriage reflects the importance of maintaining the current stable situation enjoyed by mother and child. Provided there is no obstacle placed in the way of the child later seeking to clarify paternal relations, then there would appear to be no problem with the decision as it stands.

## Paternity Proceedings

Due to the fact that paternity proceedings are decisive for civil rights and obligations, Article 6, which guarantees a fair hearing before an independent and impartial tribunal, has been found to be applicable to such disputes. In particular, the fact that the establishment of paternity

---

[8]  Cf Eur Court HR *Keegan v Ireland*, judgment of 26 May 1994, Series A no 290, 18 EHRR 342. See further Chapter 9, pp 191-193.

[9]  See Chapter 9, p 195.

[10]  See further discussion in Chapter 6, pp 123-126 and Chapter 11, pp 239-241.

determines the obligation to pay maintenance, the child's rights of inheritance and the legal, private and family relations between a parent and a child, requires that fair trial guarantees are enjoyed by the participants in paternity proceedings.[11] These proceedings may also raise an issue under Article 8 as effective respect for private and family life obliges States to make available an 'effective and accessible remedy' by which the alleged father could have established whether he is the biological father of the child.[12] There would appear to be no reason why this principle would not apply equally to such claims, when made by children themselves.

The application of a time limit beyond which paternity proceedings cannot be instituted is, in principle, consistent with the Convention, in the interests of good administration of justice.[13] This would appear to be the case regardless of whether the alleged father is seeking to establish a paternal link or to challenge an existing declaration of paternity when it becomes apparent subsequently that he cannot, after all, be the child's father. The Convention authorities have not expressed their view as to the length of time up to which paternity should be capable of being subject to challenge. However, a time limit of three years from the child's birth has been held not to be unreasonable in this regard. Moreover, it is acceptable that this time limit should be final,[14] even when new facts arise (including sterility) after the time limit expires.[15] The Commission has not yet examined whether an inaccurate determination of paternity gives rise to a failure to respect private and family life under Article 8. This question remains unanswered following its dismissal of a claim that, due to the advances in genetic testing, a paternity test carried out nearly forty years ago could not be considered scientifically reliable.[16]

It is clearly established that certain factors, such as the desire for legal certainty in family relations, difficulty of proof and the protection of the security and interests of the child may justify imposing restrictions on the access to a court in paternity matters.[17] In the case highlighted above, the

---

[11] No *8777/79 Rasmussen v Denmark*, Comm Rep 5.7.83, Series A no 87, p 19, 6 EHRR 94, § 66.

[12] *Ibid*, § 62.

[13] No *9707/82 X v Sweden*, Dec 6.10.82, DR 31, p 233. See discussion below.

[14] See No *24659/94 Judmaier v Austria*, Dec 28.6.95, unreported.

[15] No *9707/82 X v Sweden, op cit.*

[16] See No *24124/94 AS v Turkey*, Dec 24.10.95, unreported, inadmissible for procedural reasons.

[17] Eur Court HR *Rasmussen v Denmark*, judgment of 28 Nov 1984, Series A no 87, 7 EHRR 372, § 41.

applicant complained that the refusal to order a blood test prevented him from obtaining a determination of his civil right to contact, in violation of Article 6.[18] The Commission disagreed however and held that evidential difficulties did not constitute a denial of effective access to court. In particular, it found it significant that two higher domestic courts had given reasoned judgments against ordering a blood test, and there was, as a result, no violation of the right to fair trial.

An applicant cannot request that a specific test be carried out in order to establish or disprove paternity. *Andersson v Sweden* concerned the fact that the applicant had been ordered to pay maintenance following a minor forensic, genetic examination which, although it established in all probability that he was the father, did not eliminate the possibility that he was not.[19] On appeal, the applicant's request that a full genetic test be carried out was refused as it could not be expected to give any other result than the initial one. In response to his complaint that this decision violated Article 6, the Commission stressed that matters relating to evidence fell within the competence of the domestic courts. As a result, and finding that the decision of the domestic courts did not appear otherwise to be arbitrary, the Commission dismissed his complaint. It appears therefore that the margin of appreciation extended to the domestic authorities, usually the judiciary, in such matters will preclude the finding of a violation of Article 6 with regard to paternity proceedings, unless there is evidence of arbitrariness in the resolution of the matter at domestic level. For example, where a domestic court chooses to deny access to a genetic test, which is considerably more reliable than the one used in the establishment of paternity, without giving adequate reasons, this may give rise to an arguable claim before the European Court. In all such matters however, the importance of striking a balance between the interests of the individual in having paternity clarified, and the general interest, in the form of good administration of justice and expenditure of public funds, will be paramount.

As noted above, there is consensus in Strasbourg that the application of a time limit to paternity proceedings does not in itself infringe the Convention. However, there is a difference between the Commission and the Court with regard to whether a time limit which restricts the alleged father, but not the mother, from instituting proceedings is compatible with the Convention. The Commission, which holds the preferable view, found

---

[18] No *22920/93 MB v UK, op cit.* See above.
[19] No *15087/89 Andersson v Sweden*, Dec 1.7.91, unreported.

in *Rasmussen v Denmark* that such a difference in treatment is contrary to Article 8, taken together with Article 14.[20] In particular, it considered that there are no objective and reasonable grounds to justify the difference in treatment between men and women. Although the welfare of the child was the only legitimate basis for the differential treatment, the facts showed that there was a lack of proportionality between the means employed and the aim sought to be realised, not least because the operation of the time limit had caused the applicant to suffer both legal disadvantages and moral wrong.[21] The Commission also found that the welfare of the child would otherwise be properly considered were the applicant entitled to introduce paternity proceedings.

By contrast, the Court found that the authorities were entitled to think that time limits for the institution of paternity proceedings were justified by the desire to ensure legal certainty and to protect the interests of the child.[22] In addition, it agreed with the respondent Government that the interests of the mother coincided with those of the child and concluded that, given the lack of common European ground as to the regulation of paternity proceedings, the differential treatment in question did not violate the Convention. Although reflecting the wide margin of appreciation which the States enjoy in the area of family life, the Court's narrow view fails to recognise that the child has an autonomous right to identity which, beyond the interests which s/he shares with the mother, also deserves respect. The judgment also ignores the fact that, far from coinciding with the interests of the child, the mother's motivation may be entirely selfish and serve only to hinder the child's relationship with his/her father. This is recognised by the Commission's opinion, which is, as a result, preferable to that of the Court, not least because it achieves a more even balance between the rights of the parents and the individual interests of the child. In addition, however, the fact that the inequality of treatment found by the Commission to violate the Convention was rectified in Danish law prior to the judgment of the Court is an interesting one. Although this did not influence the Court's judgment, it is nonetheless a significantly positive step which serves to strengthen the position of the Commission on this matter.

---

[20] *Rasmussen* Comm Rep, *op cit,* § 83-88.

[21] In particular, the wife agreed to renounce the right to maintenance in return for the applicant's agreement not to introduce paternity proceedings. She later reneged on this agreement and sought maintenance, but when the applicant sought to introduce paternity proceedings the time limit was applied against him.

[22] *Rasmussen* judgment, *op cit,* § 41.

## Recognition of Family Ties

Article 8 guarantees the right to respect for family life and permits state interference with it only where it is in accordance with law, in pursuit of a legitimate aim and necessary in a democratic society under paragraph 2. Measures which interfere with family life will only be consistent with the Convention, therefore, where there is proportionality between the interference and the legitimate aim which it pursues, and where the measure pursues a pressing social need. In this regard, Article 8 is said to impose a negative obligation on States to abstain from taking action which interferes with family life. However, in certain circumstances States may be under an obligation of a positive nature with regard to guaranteeing respect for family life, although the type of action necessary to fulfil the positive obligation will be determined in each individual case.[23] Where this is the case, it is the approach of the Court to determine what is necessary to meet the positive obligation before then going on to consider whether the State has taken adequate measures in this regard. Whether respect for family life imposes on the State positive as well as negative obligations in a particular case has consequences for the protection which Article 8 guarantees in relation to the recognition of family ties.

It is well established under Article 8 that family life between an unmarried mother and her child is created by the fact of birth and the biological bond which it creates.[24] It is also clear that automatic and immediate transformation of this biological bond into a legal tie is essential in order to guarantee respect for family life. The fact that facilities for recognition may vary across Convention States means that domestic authorities enjoy a margin of appreciation with regard to the practicalities of how recognition takes place. Importantly, however, the Court established in the *Marckx* case that 'respect for family life implies the existence in law of safeguards that render possible, from the moment of birth, the child's integration in the family'.[25] In addition, it also found that domestic laws relating to family ties must 'enable all concerned to lead a normal family life'.[26]

---

[23] See further Chapter 9, pp 198-199.

[24] Eur Court HR *Marckx v Belgium*, judgment of 13 June 1979, Series A, no 31, 2 EHRR 330.

[25] *Ibid*, § 31.

[26] *Ibid*.

These principles highlight the importance of the legal recognition of family ties in enabling the child to be integrated into the family.[27] However, notwithstanding that the Court has acknowledged the significance of recognising in law the *de facto* family ties between parents and children, these principles have been narrowly applied. In *Marckx*, the Court found them to be applicable to the unmarried mother and her child. This meant that a law which required the mother to undertake a voluntary act of recognition in order to establish a maternal affiliation impeded the normal development of family life and thus constituted a violation of Article 8.[28]  In addition, because family life was found to include ties between near relatives such as grandparents, the fact that this situation also resulted in the child remaining a stranger to her mother's family gave rise to a further violation.[29]  There is a similar obligation on the State to respect the family life enjoyed by unmarried, but cohabiting parents and their child.[30]  In *Johnston*, the Court found that the normal development of natural family ties between such parents and their child required the child to be placed, legally and socially in a position akin to that of a child whose parents were married.

However, positive obligations to 'enable all concerned to lead a normal family life' and to facilitate the child's integration into the family will not flow automatically from the fact that family life within the meaning of Article 8 has been found to exist. For example, even if the relationship between an unmarried father and his child falls within the scope of Article 8, the State will not necessarily have to recognise in law his biological tie with his child.   In this respect, it is apparent from the case law of the Commission and the Court that the right to respect for family life enjoyed by the unmarried father may entail only negative rather than positive obligations.[31]

---

[27]  See Stewart, *op cit*, at pp 226-229 on family identity under the UN Convention on the Rights of the Child.

[28]  *Marckx* judgment, *op cit*, § 36.

[29]  *Ibid*, § 44-47.

[30]  Eur Court HR *Johnston v Ireland*, judgment of 18 Dec 1986, Series A, No 112, 9 EHRR 203, § 74.

[31]  The overlap between the approach of negative and positive obligations makes it difficult to determine the extent to which this is the case however.  See for example *Keegan* judgment, *op cit* and Comm Rep, 17.2.93, Series A no 290, p 26 and the discussion in O'Donnell (1995), 'The Unmarried father and the Right to Family Life', *Maastricht Journal of European and Comparative Law*, **2**(1), pp 85-96. See also Chapter 9, pp 198-199.

The reluctance to apply these principles to all cases where family life has been found to exist is not confined to the situation of the unmarried father and is apparent also with regard to its treatment of less traditional family arrangements. Notwithstanding the increasing number of children with alternative family styles, the Strasbourg authorities have refrained from acknowledging the rights of these children to lead a 'normal family life' in relation to requiring the recognition of family ties under Article 8. According to the Commission, a stable relationship between two women did not amount to family life within the meaning of Article 8, notwithstanding that they lived together as a family and shared parental tasks over the child born to one of them by artificial insemination by donor (AID).[32] Their relationship was found to raise an issue of *private* life, however, although Article 8 did not require the legal recognition of the tie between the child and his mother's partner in these circumstances. Here, the strength of the practical family arrangements between the parties meant that the failure to do so (and to grant parental authority as a result) did not interfere with the private or family life of either party.

The flip side of this situation was also argued before the Commission without success where a man, whose sperm donation had provided a lesbian couple with a child, claimed that the failure to recognise his biological link with the child breached Article 8.[33] Recalling that family life implies close personal ties in addition to parenthood, the Commission found it decisive that firstly, the applicant agreed to be a sperm donor to enable the lesbian couple to have a child together and secondly, that all parties had agreed that the lesbian couple would raise and have custody of the child. Overall, the Commission found that a situation in which a person donates sperm only to enable a woman to become pregnant through artificial insemination does not of itself give the donor a right to respect for family life with the child.[34] The fact that he babysat the child on a weekly

---

[32] No *15666/89 Kerkhoven, Hinke & Hinke v the Netherlands*, Dec 19.5.92, unreported.

[33] No *16944/90 G v the Netherlands*, Dec 8.2.93, 16 EHRR CD 38.

[34] For a discussion of the issues surrounding medically assisted birth see Haimes (1988), 'Secrecy: What Can Artificial Reproduction Learn From Adoption?', *International Journal of Law and Family*, 2, pp 46-61; Jones (1988), 'Artificial Procreation, Societal Reconceptions: Legal Insight from France', *American Journal of Comparative Law*, 36, pp 525-545; Liu (1994), 'The Parentage of Children Born as a Result of Natural and Assisted Reproduction', *Hong Kong Law Journal*, 23(4), pp 356-371; Dickens, 'Reproductive Technology and the 'New' Family, in Sutherland & McCall Smith (eds) (1990), *Family Rights:*

basis in the course of seven months of the child's infancy did not change that fact.

The harshness of the Court's failure to apply the *Marckx* and *Johnston* principles relating to the importance of legal recognition equally is evident from *X, Y & Z v UK*.[35] The applicants in this case were a female-to-male transsexual, his female partner and their child born by AID. Notwithstanding that they enjoyed family life within the meaning of Article 8, the Court failed to find that there was a positive obligation on the State to recognise formally the male applicant as the child's father. The basis to its decision was the absence of common European standards with respect to granting parental rights to transsexuals and reflecting in law the relationship between a child conceived by AID and the person performing the social role of father.[36] This lack of consensus meant that the State enjoyed a wide margin of appreciation when balancing the rights of the individuals concerned with those of the community. The community or public interest was served by the maintenance of a coherent system of family law which prioritises the best interests of the child. With regard to the rights of the individuals, the Court concluded that the social and legal disadvantages experienced by the child and her social father were unlikely to cause undue hardship in the circumstances. Overall, the Court was unconvinced that the registration of the applicant as her father would benefit the child concerned or indeed children conceived by AID in general. In conclusion, therefore, it refused to find implicit in Article 8 an obligation to recognise as the father of a child a person who is not the biological father.[37]

The Commission's alternative approach yielded an altogether different conclusion in this case.[38] It acknowledged that the legal value given to family relations can affect the social validity and family members' own sense of worth and security and in the child's case, noted that this could

---

*Family Law and Medical Advances*, Edinburgh: Edinburgh University Press, pp 21-41; Morgan, 'Undoing what comes Naturally - Regulating Medically Assisted Families', in Bainham, Pearl & Pickford (eds) (1995), *Frontiers of Family Law,* Chichester: Wiley, pp 75-94.

[35] Eur Court HR *X, Y & Z v UK*, judgment of 22 April 1997, Reports 1997-II no 35, p 619, 24 EHRR 143.

[36] *Ibid*, § 44.

[37] *Ibid*, § 52.

[38] No 21830/93 *X, Y & Z v UK*, Comm Rep, 27.6.95, Reports 1997-II, no 35, p 647.

play a role in her personal development and sense of identity.[39] While the parties may not suffer any direct or visible disadvantage as a result of the failure to recognise the mother's partner role as father, the lack of legal recognition might, it said, constitute a serious disadvantage in itself. In direct contrast to the Court, the Commission noted the increasing trend in Convention States towards the recognition of gender re-assignment and concluded that, where a transsexual who has undergone irreversible gender surgery lives with a partner of his former sex and child in a family relationship, there must be a presumption in favour of legal recognition of that relationship, the denial of which requires specific justification.[40] Having particular regard to the welfare of the child and her security within the family unit, therefore, the Commission found that the absence of an appropriate legal regime reflecting their family ties disclosed a failure to respect their family life.[41]

While the differing decisions of the Commission and the Court reflect their respective views on the treatment of transsexuals generally,[42] it was the way in which the Court reached its decision, rather than the decision itself, which attracts criticism here. In particular, although the Court's conclusion has some positive implications for the child's right to identity, its reasoning, in particular its failure to deal logically with the many complex, legal and moral rights issues raised by the facts of this case, was

---

[39] *Ibid, § 66.*

[40] *Ibid,* § 67.

[41] *Ibid,* § 68-71, by 13 votes to 5. The strongest dissenting opinion was delivered by Mrs Liddy, joined by Mr Reffi, whose opinion was concerned more with the appropriateness of transsexuals as fathers, rather than the right of those involved to have their practical and social family ties recognised by law. See also the dissenting opinion of Mr Bratza who despite acknowledging that a failure to legally recognise the relationship between the child and her mother's partner, would involve a possible detrimental impact on the identity of the child, felt that reservations about the sensitive, controversial and changing nature of the law necessitated erring on the side of caution in this case.

[42] The Commission's consistent view that the failure to permit a transsexual to have his birth certificate amended violates his/her respect for private life stands in direct opposition to that of the Court. See their respective opinions in the following cases: Eur Court HR *Rees v UK*, judgment of 17 Oct 1986, Series A no 106, 9 EHRR 56; Eur Court HR *Cossey v UK*, judgment of 27 Sept 1990, Series A no 184, 13 EHRR 622 and, Eur Court HR *B v France*, judgment of 25 March 1992, Series A no 232-C, 16 EHRR 1.

poor.[43] Firstly, in the light of Convention case law which acknowledges the importance of recognising family ties, the Court does not clearly set out the reasons why an exception should be made in the case of children born to a couple, one of whom is a transsexual. This is particularly pertinent given the acceptance of the practice by which the social parents (and not the sperm or egg donors) of a child born by AID are registered as such on the child's birth certificate.[44] In this case, the male applicant was treated as the father for the purposes of the AID procedure and this apparent discrimination, between transsexuals and non-transsexuals, was not addressed by the Court. Although the Commission considered the issue under Article 8, the Court failed to consider whether the differential treatment of the male party to the AID procedure on the grounds that he was registered female at birth was justified.

Regardless of the fact that the Court left unresolved whether registering the applicant as the child's father would harm or benefit the child born by AID, it paid little express attention to the child, whose rights to respect for family life and identity were also at stake. Although the interests of children in general were considered as part of the public interest issue, the failure to have regard to the rights of the individual child is unfortunate, especially as the child was listed as an applicant in this case. Indeed, this fact was highlighted by Judge Pettiti, who, in his concurring opinion, suggested that, in future, the parties should be encouraged to instruct a lawyer specifically to represent the interests of the child alone.[45] In addition, although the parties clearly agreed on their desire to have their family position legally recognised (although admittedly the child was only 5 years old at the time), this issue is also ignored by the Court, whose argument worryingly juxtaposes the rights of the child against her social father. Thus, while the Commission's reasoning appears to acknowledge that the child's right to identity is inextricably bound up with the child's right to a family in such cases, the Court acknowledged neither right.

This criticism notwithstanding, the Court appears to have deliberately left open whether it is in the child's interests to have the name of a person on his/her birth certificate, who is not the biological father. The fact that this occurs frequently in the case of children born by AID, who are not transsexuals, and children who receive 'new' birth certificates following

---

[43] It appears to match the expectations of some, however. See Harris, O'Boyle & Warbrick, *op cit,* p 313.

[44] For arguments for and against anonymity of donors see Haimes (1991), 'Gamete Donation and Anonymity', *Bulletin of Medical Ethics,* **66**, pp 25-27.

[45] See further Chapter 6, pp 124-126.

their adoption highlights that this issue is not straight forward. In this regard, the fact that the Court has chosen to postpone serious consideration of these questions to allow for their more decisive determination when European standards display a greater degree of consistency is positive. A future review of the compatibility of such circumstances with the Convention should, as Judge Pettiti suggested in *X, Y & Z*, be supplemented by a

> legal, sociological and ethical examination of the whole problem and the diversity of the rights and values to be attributed to each of the persons who go to make up a family.[46]

And it should, in particular, seek guidance from the UN Convention on the Rights of the Child and its interpretation by the UN Committee in this respect.[47]

## Access to Birth Information

While the Court's requirements relating to the recognition of family ties go some way to ensuring that basic information relating to the child is recorded officially, there is little suggestion that the Convention contains a guarantee of the child's right of access to information about his/her origins. However, it is arguable that between the lines of the Court's judgment in *X, Y & Z* is implicit concern that naming the child's father on a birth certificate has consequences for the future exercise of the child's right to identity. The Court suggested here that the fact that a transsexual parent was not registered as the father on the child's birth certificate did not prevent him from acting as such by supporting her, by giving her his surname and describing himself to her and to others as her father. Clearly, this approach attaches significance to the social reality and ignores the importance of the legal situation,[48] notwithstanding the Commission's concern that it might constitute a serious disadvantage to the child.[49] While the approach of the Court does not expressly take into account the child's right to identity, it

---

[46] *X, Y, & Z* judgment, *op cit.*
[47] See in particular UN Doc CRC/C/15/Add.20, § 14.
[48] Cf *Marckx* judgment, *op cit.*
[49] See above.

nonetheless leaves open whether it favours the child's right of access to birth information. In particular, it concluded that

> [i]t is impossible to predict the extent to which the absence of a legal connection between X (the transsexual) and Z (the child) will affect the latter's development.[50]

This highlights the Court's clear preference for abstaining at this stage from determining the matter in a way which favours registering the first applicant as the child's father. This position is based on the absence of a shared approach among the Convention States with regard to 'the manner in which the social relationship between a child conceived by AID and the person who performs the role of rather should be reflected in law'.[51]

The Court has also observed the lack of consensus among European countries as to whether the interests of the child are served by preserving the anonymity of the donor in this process, or whether the child should have the right to know the donor's identity.[52]    Although the restraint exercised is arguably consistent with the margin of appreciation enjoyed by the State in the absence of common practice in these areas, it is important to recognise that the Court does not exist merely to reflect in its case law the shared approaches among Convention States. It must also set standards in relation to the enjoyment of rights which are consistent with the Convention's object and purpose and, within its own sphere of competence, it must interpret the Convention in the light of modern day conditions.[53] Clearly in contentious areas, such as the issues of secrecy in adoption and more recently in artificial reproduction[54] the resolution of disputes and interpretation of the Convention will not be an easy process. By offering states a wide margin of appreciation with regard to such sensitive and important matters the Court is, rightly or wrongly, postponing its deliberation of them until it has acquired greater competence to do so properly.

---

[50]  *X, Y & Z* judgment, *op cit*, § 51.

[51]  *Ibid*, § 44.

[52]  *Ibid*.

[53]  See *inter alia* its judgment in the Marckx case, *op cit*.

[54]  See Price, 'Conceiving Relations: Egg and Sperm Donation in Assisted Procreation', in Bainham, Pearl and Pickford, *op cit*, pp 176-186. Haimes (1988), *op cit* and Van Bueren (1995b), 'Children's Access to Adoption Records - State Discretion or an Enforceable International Right', *Modern Law Review*, **58**, pp 37-53.

As early as 1989, however, the Court felt competent to determine whether a policy of confidentiality in the maintenance of social services records was compatible with the Convention.[55] In the *Gaskin* case, the Court found that it was in principle, particularly given the contribution which confidentiality makes to the overall effectiveness of the child care system, which aims to protect the interests of children. However, whether denying access to such information is compatible with the private or family life of an individual who seeks it will depend on whether that decision can be challenged before an independent authority.[56] This reasoning would appear to apply also to the use of confidential record systems for the processes of adoption and medically assisted reproduction. If this is the case, then denying access to information held in such records will violate Article 8, unless an independent authority exists to determine the merits of granting access in a particular case. However, the scope of the obligation as it applies to the child's right to receive information regarding his/her biological parents in these circumstances is still unclear. The Commission has accepted that States may consider it in the general interest to maintain certain links between the child and its natural family after adoption, although it is far from requiring such contact be maintained in any circumstances.[57]

Access to a child's birth certificate and other information which determines accurately a child's parenthood is crucial to a child's identity. The Commission and Court have also considered the importance of other records which shed light on a child's background. Article 10 of the Convention guarantees the right to receive and impart information,[58] but it does not include a right to seek it. In particular, it does not entitle an individual to gain access to a register which contains personal information relating to him[59] and it is unlikely therefore that the inability to gain access to information contained in an adoption register could be found to raise an issue under this provision.[60] A claim invoking respect for private and family life under Article 8 may enjoy success however. This was the basis

---

[55] Eur Court HR *Gaskin v UK*, judgment of 7 July 1989, Series A no 160, 12 EHRR 36, § 43.

[56] See further below.

[57] No *21632/93 GR, ER & KR v Austria*, Dec 30.11.94, unreported.

[58] See further Chapter 6, pp 127-128.

[59] Eur Court HR *Leander v Austria*, judgment of 26 March 1987, Series A no 116, 9 EHRR 433. cf Article 17 of the UN Convention on the Rights of the Child, *op cit*.

[60] See also Van Bueren (1995b), *op cit*, p 47.

of the *Gaskin* case, where the applicant, who had spent the majority of his life in care, sought access to information which the local authority held about him, to which he was denied. It was the nature of the information held about the applicant, which proved decisive in this case. According to the Commission, respect for private life requires that everyone should be able to establish details of their identity as individual human beings and that, in principle, they should not be obstructed by the authorities from obtaining such very basic information without specific justification.[61] Reflecting a clear and progressive view of the concept of identity and its importance in the circumstances of the case, the Commission found that

> an individual's entitlement to such information relating to his or her basic identity and early life is not only of importance because of its formative implications for his or her personality. It is also, by virtue of the individual's age and condition at the relevant time, information which relates to a period when the individual was particularly vulnerable as a young child and in respect of which personal memories cannot provide a reliable or adequate source of information.[62]

Due to the fact that the applicant had had very little contact with his biological family, as well as poor continuity of alternative care throughout his life, the file held by social services provided the only coherent record of his early childhood and formative years. Consequently, the refusal to allow him access to this information constituted an interference with his private life which could not be justified by reference to the need for confidentiality in the care system.

The Court reached the same conclusion, although its approach was to consider the state action as a failure to fulfil the positive obligation inherent in respect for private life. It acknowledged the importance of receiving information 'necessary to know and understand ... childhood and early development' and it noted, moreover, that persons who, like the applicant, have spent the majority of their lives in care, have a vital interest, protected by the Convention, in receiving that information.[63] It recognised that keeping confidential records was important to ensure the receipt of objective and reliable information, and to protect the contributors and other parties. In this regard, it found that a confidential system was in principle

---

[61] No *10454/ 85 Gaskin v UK*, Comm Rep, 13.11.87, Series A no 160, 11 EHRR 402, § 89.

[62] *Ibid*, § 90.

[63] *Gaskin* judgment, *op cit*, § 49.

compatible with the Convention in light of the State's margin of appreciation. However, according to the Court, such a system would only be proportionate under Article 8 if an independent authority were to decide whether access be granted where a contributor fails to answer or withholds consent. As no such procedure was available in the present case, there had been a violation of Article 8.[64]

The narrow scope of the *Gaskin* judgment clarifies that there is no general right of access to information about family ties or background, regardless of whether it is sought by children placed for adoption, or by those who have grown up in state care. Nor is there a general right under the Convention to know who one's parents are,[65] although the freedom to receive information does prohibit Governments from restricting a person from receiving information that others wish or may be willing to impart.[66]

Importantly, it was not the confidential nature of the social services record system which was offensive in *Gaskin*, but the fact that, where the authors of such records refused to allow the information to be passed on to the applicant, there was no independent procedure by which his right of access could be determined. Despite the fact that the absence of an independent authority to examine such disputes clearly led to the violation of Article 8 in this case, the Court did not offer any additional guidance as to the type of mechanism that would be consistent with the Convention in this regard. Nor did it suggest what criteria might be applied legitimately in determining whether access to records should be permitted.[67] This absence of guidance from the Court means that the State's obligation with regard to the access to such information, is unclear. What is clear, however, is that where the individual is able to establish the importance of the information to him then respect for his private life may oblige the State to allow him to see it. The significance of the information will only be a factor to be taken into account and thus establishing this is a necessary, but not a sufficient condition of access.[68]

---

[64] Five dissenting judges held the view that there was no lack of proportionality. See the joint dissenting opinion of Judges Ryssdal, Cremona, Golchklu, Matscher and Evans, *ibid.*

[65] *Gaskin* is not authority for a child's right to know the identity of his/her father. Van Bueren (1995a), *op cit*, p 124.

[66] *Leander* judgment, *op cit.*

[67] Pickford (1992), 'The Gaskin Case and Confidential Personal Information: whose secret?', *Journal of Child Law*, p 33.

[68] Harris, O'Boyle & Warbrick, *op cit*, p 311.

The Commission's opinion in *Gaskin* appeared to distinguish the complaint of the applicant, who had reached majority, from that of a child.[69] In this regard, the applicant's maturity was a significant factor in its conclusion that the decision to keep the file relating to his early years and background confidential from him was disproportionate to the aim which the system of confidentiality sought to achieve. Although it is suggested that the Commission has thereby limited the exercise of the right to seek such information to those who have reached the age of majority,[70] there is no suggestion of this distinction in the Court's judgment. Moreover, in the light of the strong statements which the Court made in support of the child's vital right and need to have access to information relating to his background, it is at least arguable that a similar claim introduced by a person under the age of 18 years would enjoy success. However, one area which may prove contentious in the future and to which the age of the applicant may be relevant is the purpose for which the information is sought. The applicant in *Gaskin* sought access to his confidential file in order to sue the local authority in negligence. Although this was not considered relevant by the Court, one judge, in his dissent, believed this to be decisive and concluded therefore that his claim in relation to accessing the information did not raise an issue of respect for private and family life.[71]

**Nationality**

Although the European Convention makes no reference to the child's right to acquire a nationality or the right to have that nationality respected, that has not prevented the Strasbourg authorities from examining related issues. For instance, a measure, which prevents a child from acquiring the nationality of the country in which s/he was born, may constitute an interference with the right to respect for private life under Article 8. Similarly, where a child is denied the right to acquire the same nationality as his/her parents, this may violate the right to respect for family life under that provision.[72] However, case law suggests that as long as the difference in nationality enjoyed by family members is of a *de jure,* rather than a *de*

---

[69] *Gaskin* Comm Rep, *op cit*, § 100.
[70] See Van Bueren (1995a), *op cit*, pp 124-125.
[71] See the dissenting opinion of Judge Walsh, *Gaskin*, judgment, *op cit*.
[72] See further Chapter 10.

*facto* nature, then this will not infringe the Convention.[73]  Should *de facto* separation arise, resulting in the parties living apart as a result of parents and children enjoying different nationalities, a claim could be made out under Article 8, the margin of appreciation offered to States in this area notwithstanding.

It is unclear whether the Convention places any obligation on the State to respect a child's nationality or national identity.[74]  However, it is well established that, although the Convention does not include a right to reside in a Convention State of which one is not a national, immigration law must be implemented consistent with Convention obligations.[75]  The right to respect for family life under Article 8 is frequently invoked in this regard although, importantly, its application in such circumstances appears to involve the imposition of purely negative, rather than positive obligations. For example, the Court has found that Article 8 does not require Convention States to allow a non-national spouse to enter and reside in order to respect a married couple's choice of residence.[76]  Nor does it oblige States to respect a family's decision as to residence, where the children, but not the parents, enjoy nationality of the chosen country.[77]  Hence, where either or neither parent enjoys nationality of the Convention State, the fact that their children have acquired nationality by virtue of their birth there will not entitle the family to remain in itself. This is particularly so where factors, such as those relating to public order, weigh in favour of their return to the parents' country of origin.  Emphasis is placed on the practicalities, rather than the legalities in such cases and both the child's national identity and the right to respect for his nationality appear to be ignored.  In these circumstances, it is arguable that the decision to deport a non-national parent naturally requires the deportation of their children, regardless of whether they are nationals of a Convention State, in contravention of Article 3 of the Fourth Protocol, which prohibits the expulsion of nationals.  However, the Commission has so far rejected any such claims by pointing out that the children themselves are not the subject

---

[73] No *5302/71 X & Y v UK*, Dec 11.10.73, Collection 44, p 29.

[74] Stewart suggests a distinction between a right to national identity and a right to a nationality where the latter is state-sanctioned and the other refers to the child's genuine identity. Stewart, *op cit*, p 232.

[75] Eur Court HR *Abdulaziz, Cabales & Balkandali v UK*, judgment of 28 May 1985, Series A, no 94, 7 EHRR 471, § 54-60.

[76] *Ibid*, § 68. Immigration rules of this kind must apply without discrimination.

[77] No *23938/94 Sorabjee v UK*, Dec 23.10.95, unreported.

of the deportation order, rather, that their departure to their country of origin is a consequence of their parents' deportation.[78]    Although this reasoning may be technically accurate, the Commission's approach amounts to judicial restraint designed to prevent the establishment of a precedent, which would have serious consequences for immigration law in Convention States.    However, it is regrettable that the Commission has failed to attach any real significance to the child's right to respect for his/her nationality in this respect, given its recognition in international law, if not in the Convention itself.[79]

Whether removal of a family member from a Convention State is compatible with Article 8 will depend on a number of factors, such as the extent to which family life is effectively ruptured, whether there are insurmountable obstacles in the way of the family living in the country of origin of one or more of them, and whether there are factors of immigration control or public order weighing in favour of exclusion.[80]    The Commission has adopted this approach when considering the situation where a parent is expelled with the choice of leaving behind the child which holds nationality of that State or having the child accompany him/her to their country of origin.[81]    In relation to the 'insurmountable obstacles in the way of the family living in the country of origin of one or more of them', the Commission views the nationality of the child as only one of a number of factors to be given consideration.[82]    This is the case whether the child was born in the Convention State, has another parent (a national) living there, and/or has lived and attended school there.    In fact, in the case of unlawful overstaying by a parent (where the birth of a child occurs during this overstaying thereby acquiring nationality) it does not appear to attach any significance to the factor of the child's nationality.[83]

---

[78]    *Ibid.*

[79]    See Article 7 § 1 UN Convention on the Rights of the Child, *op cit.*  Article 7 § 2 provides for the implementation of this right in accordance with national and international law and Article 8 provides for the right to have nationality, as part of a child's identity, preserved and re-established, where illegal deprivation has taken place.

[80]    See further Chapter 10, pp 219-229.

[81]    For example, see No *23938/94 Sorabjee v UK, op cit* and *No 24865/94 Jaramillo v UK*, Dec 23.10.95, unreported.

[82]    See further Storey (1990), 'The Right to Family Life and Immigration Case Law at Strasbourg', *International and Comparative Law Quarterly*, **39**, pp 328-344.

[83]    See No *11970/86 v UK*, Dec 7.87, 11 EHRR 48.

The means by which a child obtains nationality is also immaterial in determining whether his/her expulsion through the deportation of a parent violates his/her right to respect for family life. Thus, regardless of whether nationality is acquired by virtue of birth in a Convention State,[84] birth inside marriage to a legal resident of a Convention State,[85] or because a parent is a national of the Convention State and has passed on citizenship,[86] the legal nationality held by the child is not an important consideration. Indeed, the Commission has expressly stated that there is no material distinction between the different methods of acquiring nationality where the child is of an adaptable age and there are no effective obstacles to the child accompanying the parent being deported.[87] The practical approach adopted by the Commission in these cases sees the emphasis being placed, not on the legal nationality or identity of the child, but on the existence of effective obstacles to the child's accompaniment of the parent. Nor is the child's national identity taken into account when examining whether it is consistent with the Convention to require the child to accompany the parent.

The question of whether a child is at an adaptable age assumes importance in assessing whether obstacles exist to pursuing family life in the parent's country of origin. The Commission appears to attach considerable importance to whether the child is likely to adapt successfully to the new environment, although it has not found in any case that a child is unlikely to do so. Moreover, it has failed to establish even a benchmark age at which the child can be said to be 'adaptable' and has found children aged one[88] three,[89] four[90] and six[91] to be capable of adapting to a new environment. While there may be an objective basis for considering that children under the school-going-age are capable of adapting to new surroundings, the case law suggests the existence of a presumption in this regard, particularly in relation to some older children. For example, the Commission found in one case that there were no factors which would

---

[84] *Ibid* and No *8245/78 X v UK*, Dec 6.5.81, DR 24, p 98.

[85] See No *24865/94 Jaramillo v UK, op cit.*

[86] See No *22791/93 Maikoe & Baboelal v the Netherlands*, Dec 30.11.94, unreported.

[87] *Ibid.*

[88] See No *26985/95 Poku v UK*, Dec 5.5.96, 22 EHRR CD 94..

[89] See No *26609/95 Onyegbule v Austria*, Dec 16.10.95, unreported and No *23938/94 Sorabjee v UK, op cit.*

[90] See No *26985/95 Poku v UK, op cit.*

[91] See No *22791/93 Maikoe & Baboelal v the Netherlands, op cit.*

effectively prevent a ten year old boy who had been integrated into the school system in his country of birth from adapting to life with his family elsewhere.[92] The presumption of adaptability is also made with respect to the change in environment which occurs with deportation and the Commission appears to give inadequate consideration to the impact of such change even where it is likely to be dramatic. For instance, it has found that moving from the Netherlands to Surinam,[93] the UK to Kenya[94] and Columbia[95] and from Austria to Nigeria[96] would create little if any problem for children, regardless of age, and the sweeping generalisation that children can adapt, whatever the circumstances seems to dominate this case law. Although the Commission has taken subjective factors into account on occasion, it has never found them to be decisive. For example, in *Sorabjee*, the Commission decided that the deportation of a mother with sole custody of a child with British nationality was compatible with the Convention.[97] Two factors of importance in reaching this conclusion were firstly, that the child's British citizenship was 'not of particular importance' and secondly, that the child was deemed to be of an adaptable age. In relation to the former, it is arguable that to ignore the fact of nationality is to act contrary to customary international law, of which the right to reside in the country of one's own nationality is an essential part.[98] However, choosing to ignore the child's nationality may not be inconsistent with the Convention itself were the decision otherwise free from arbitrariness. Unfortunately, the Commission's consideration of the important factor of adaptability does not support this view. Thus, although it recognised the risk of the child experiencing problems when leaving her country of birth to face the hardship of living in a society where she may have difficulty integrating into the community, the Commission did not find this factor to be decisive. Overall, it emphasises the child's adaptable age, rather than his/her nationality, and its approach does not allow it to take into account additional subjective factors, such as the specific problems which the child will face following deportation. The fact that the Commission does not give adequate consideration to the issues suggests that such decisions are

---

[92]  No *26985/95 Poku v UK , op cit.*

[93]  No *22791/93 Maikoe & Baboela v the Netherlands, op cit.*

[94]  No *23938/94 Sorabjee v UK, op cit.*

[95]  No *24865/94 Jaramillo v UK, op cit.*

[96]  No *26609/95 Onyegbule v UK, op cit.*

[97]  No *23938/94 Sorabjee v UK, op cit.*

[98]  Mole (1995), 'Constructive Deportation and  the European Convention', *European Human Rights Law Review* **1**, pp 63-71, at p 64.

more political than legal in nature and highlights also a lack of proportionality in the way they are reached. The decision to ignore the child's nationality in such cases, particularly when the child has integrated into his/her country of birth, suggests that the child's state-sanctioned nationality reflects accurately the child's genuine identity. Moreover, it constitutes a failure to recognise the child's right to respect for his/her nationality in an area which is within the Convention's competence.

In light of the express recognition of the child's right to respect for his/her nationality in the UN Convention on the Rights of the Child,[99] it is submitted that greater importance should be attributed to this factor. This is particularly important where the child's nationality is not merely a legal status, but reflects the child's own identity following birth and integration into a Convention State.[100] Respect for the child's nationality in such circumstances would mean that a measure ordering the deportation of the child's parent would fall to be justified under Article 8 § 2 and, in particular, this factor would have to be taken into account when weighing up whether the interference is proportionate to the aim, which the deportation seeks to achieve.[101]

## The Right to a Name

Although the European Convention contains no explicit provisions on names,[102] the right to a name is protected under the right to respect for private and family life under Article 8 insofar as it corresponds to a person's right to identity.[103] The State has a legitimate role in regulating the use of names, which may be compatible with Article 8 where it aims to prevent arbitrariness, to maintain stability in the rules governing family names, and to preserve the unity of the family.[104] A refusal to permit a

---

[99] See above.

[100] Cf the Court's consideration of the integrated aliens cases in Chapter 10.

[101] See for example, No *22471/93 Singh v UK*, Dec 6.9.94, unreported.

[102] Cf Article 24 § 2 International Covenant on Civil and Political Rights, *op cit*, and Article 7 UN Convention on the Rights of the Child, *op cit*, which both provide that every child shall have a name.

[103] Eur Court HR *Burghartz v Switzerland*, judgment of 22 Feb 1994, Series A no 280, 18 EHRR 101, § 24.

[104] No *16123/90 Burghartz v Switzerland*, Comm Rep, 21.10.92, Series A no 280, p 36, § 62. See also No *18131/91 Stjerna v Finland*, Comm Rep 8.7.93, Series

change of surname will not necessarily constitute an interference under Article 8 § 1, but there may be a positive obligation on the State to respect private and family life in this way.[105] The absence of common ground between the domestic systems as to the conditions on which a change of name may be legally effected means that the State enjoys a wide margin of appreciation in this area.

While a decision permitting the change of a child's family name to that of her stepfather may be consistent with respect for her private and family life, it may nonetheless interfere with her birth father's rights under Article 8.[106] Where the best interests of the child outweigh those of her father, such as where the child has had little contact with him since birth, and has grown up and identified herself with the family newly created by her mother, then no interference will arise. On the other hand, a refusal to permit a child to change his/her surname to that of the mother's new family in similar circumstances would arguably be incompatible with the child's right to respect for family life. In such cases, respect for the child's family life would be likely to require the State to encourage the child's integration into the family newly created by the mother by permitting the change in surname.

The registration of the surname of children born outside marriage is a contentious issue and it is unclear whether the legitimate interest of the State extends to refusing to grant such a child the surname of one parent rather than another. The Court has not yet determined whether it is compatible with respect for family life to refuse to register children born outside marriage by their father's surname, rather than their mother's.[107] Such an approach would appear to be consistent with the Convention as long as it aims to maintain stability in the rules governing family names.[108] However, it may give rise to a violation of Article 14 where there is a difference in treatment between children on the grounds of their parents' marital status. For example, where children born inside marriage can be registered by the surname of either or both parents, but this is not a right enjoyed by children born outside marriage, then this would require

---

A no 299-B and No *18806/91 KAJMB v the Netherlands* Dec 1.9.93, unreported.

[105] No *26272/95 Sijka v Poland*, Dec 10.9.97, unreported.

[106] No *9290/81 X v the Netherlands*, Dec 5.83, 5 EHRR 581.

[107] No *24001/94 Gill & Malone v the Netherlands & UK*, Dec 11.4.96, unreported, was found inadmissible due to non-exhaustion of domestic remedies.

[108] No *18806/91 KAJMB v the Netherlands, op cit.*

justification under the Convention.[109] In this regard, subjecting children to different treatment on the grounds of the marital status of their parents must be supported by sufficiently weighty reasons and, notwithstanding the margin of appreciation, flexibility in this area should be encouraged.

Forenames, like family names, concern private and family life because they constitute a means of identification. Parental choice as to their child's first name is a 'personal, emotional matter' which falls within the private sphere.[110] Consequently, restricting the decision-making powers of parents in this regard may constitute a failure to respect their private and family life under Article 8, notwithstanding that state regulation aims to protect the interests of the child. According to the Commission, the interest of the State in such matters is legitimate because it serves to

> protect the child from any adverse consequences which may arise from the legal obligation to bear throughout their life a name which society as a whole may consider ridiculous, inappropriate or incomprehensible.[111]

The degree of inconvenience caused by domestic authorities, which refuse to register a particular name, is decisive in determining what is compatible with the Convention.[112] However, the wide margin of appreciation which States enjoy in this area and the legitimacy of state regulation of names means that it is difficult to make out a successful claim in this regard. This is illustrated by the *Guillot* case in 1996, where the French authorities refused to permit a child's parents to register their daughter as *Fleur de Marie*. Notwithstanding the upset experienced by the parents as a result, and the complications which resulted from the difference between the child's name in law and the name which she used on a day to day basis,

---

[109] No *20798/92 Maleveille v France*, Dec 26.10.95, unreported, concerned the fact that children born to unmarried parents were entitled to carry the name of both or either parent, whereas those born inside marriage could carry only the name of their father. This case was struck off. See also Van Nijnatien (1996), 'In the Name of the Third - Changing the Law on Naming Children in the Netherlands', *International Journal of Law, Policy and the Family*, **10**, pp 219-228.

[110] Eur Court HR *Guillot v France*, judgment of 24 Oct 1996, Reports 1996-V, no 19, p 1593, § 21-22.

[111] No *22500/93 Lassauzet & Guillot v France*, Comm Rep, 12.4.95, Reports 1996-V, no 19, p 1606, § 40.

[112] *Ibid*, § 23. See also Eur Court HR *Stjerna v Finland*, judgment of 25 Nov 1994, Series A no 280-B, 24 EHRR 195, § 42.

this decision did not breach their right to respect for family life.[113]    In reaching this conclusion, the Court attached considerable importance to the fact that the child was free to use the chosen name socially without hindrance, and it also took into account the subsequent agreement of the authorities to register the alternative name of *Fleur Marie*.

The Commission, in reaching the same conclusion, had been more strongly divided on the issue.[114]    Eleven dissenting members made the distinction between the choice of first name at birth and the ability of an adult to change his/her first name, and suggested that the former interfered with private and family life.    Mr Geus, with whom his colleagues agreed, found this situation to be disproportionate to the aim of protecting the child from suffering.[115]    The child's use of the name 'without hindrance', and the authorities' agreement to register the slight variation of the name both appear to support this conclusion.[116]

**Future Challenges**

Notwithstanding the absence of express standards relating to the various component elements of the child's right to identity, much of the Convention case law shows evidence of a relatively dynamic approach on the part of the Convention authorities.    The institutions have established a number of important principles, which form a solid platform for developing further the child's right to identity, in particular the child's right to know his/her origins, under the Convention.    The Court's decision to leave open whether the child's birth certificate should identify only the child's biological parents has merely postponed the consideration of this issue.    In this regard, future challenges to the policy of anonymity in both adoption and artificial reproduction practices may be made in the light of the child's own interests in finding out about his/her biological parents.    Increased awareness of the child's need and right to have access to essential birth information requires that the application of Article 8 to such complaints includes a consideration of the deeper moral, sociological and ethical rights issues involved.    Further test cases in the immigration area are also likely

---

[113] *Guillot* judgment, *op cit*, § 24-27.

[114] See *Lassauzet & Guillot* Comm Rep, *op cit*.

[115] See the dissenting view of Mr Geus, joined by Messrs Rosakis, Trechsel, Gozubuyuk, Weitzel, Martinez, Loucaides, Nowicki, Conforti, Bekes and Savby, *ibid.*

[116] See also No *27868/95 Salonen v Finland*, Dec 2.7.97, unreported.

to challenge the emphasis placed on the child's right to respect for his/her nationality in the light of concerns raised, although the absence of this right from the Convention means that the Commission's rigid position is likely to be adopted by the new permanent Court in this politically charged area.

# 6 Participation Rights

## Introduction

Although the rights to enjoy freedom of expression, association and religion are among the most established and widely recognised in international law,[1] their specific application to children has been slow.[2] The UN Convention on the Rights of the Child was the first international treaty to confirm the relevance of these so-called participation rights to children, and its provisions recognise the importance of consultation according to the principle of the child's evolving capacity.[3] This approach is epitomised by Article 12 which guarantees the child's right to express his/her views and have them given due weight in accordance with the child's age and maturity and also provides for the child's right to be heard, either directly or through a representative, in any judicial or administrative proceedings, which affect the child. Moreover, Articles 13, 14 and 15, which guarantee expressly to the child freedom of expression, freedom of religion and freedom of association respectively, establish the relevance of these provisions to children and the importance of child participation in a democratic, civil society.

The European Convention contains standard provisions on the freedoms of religion, expression and association,[4] but makes no special provision for children in these respects. The restrictions on the exercise of these limits and Article 1, which requires States to secure the enjoyment of Convention rights to everyone confirms their general application. However, the

---

[1] See the Universal Declaration of Human Rights adopted by GA Res 217A (III) of 10 December 1948, and the International Covenant on Civil and Political Rights, UNTS vol 999, p 171.

[2] These rights were not included in the early Declaration on the Rights of the Child in 1924 and 1959. Concern was also expressed about including them in the UN Convention on the Rights of the Child. See Detrick (ed) (1992), *The UN Convention on the Rights of the Child: A Guide to the Travaux Preparatoires*, Dordrecht: Martinus Nijhoff, p 231 and pp 250-251.

[3] UN Doc A/44/25.

[4] These rights are guaranteed by Articles 9, 10 and 11 respectively, and paragraph 2 of each provision sets out the circumstances in which limitations can justifiably be placed on the exercise of these rights.

Convention does not recognise that affirmative action may be necessary to enable children to enjoy these rights. Clearly, the effective enjoyment of these rights by young people who have yet to reach adulthood, but have acquired a certain capacity to enjoy them, may require the adoption of such measures. Neither the Commission nor the Court has had the opportunity to consider a positive obligation of this kind under the Convention. On the other hand, there has been no attempt to limit the child's enjoyment of these rights. Moreover, there is considerable potential for considering the right of the child to be consulted and especially the child's right to participate and enjoy legal representation in proceedings which concern him/her, under Articles 6 and 8 of the Convention.

## Consultation with the Child

Although the UN Convention on the Rights of the Child reflects the importance in international law of the child's right to be consulted,[5] this idea is not explicit in the text of the European Convention on Human Rights. Moreover, it has yet to be found to be implicit in the provisions which are relevant to the child, particularly Article 8 in relation to the family, and Article 2 of the First Protocol, with regard to education.[6] In its examination of family law proceedings, the role of the institutions has hitherto been passive, rather than dynamic. In particular, they have acknowledged and taken into account where consultation with children occurs at domestic level, but they have not yet constructed an obligation to do so.

The Commission and Court have made clear the importance of acting consistent with the child's wishes where possible.[7] Discussion of the substantive issue of the child's competence has been avoided however.[8] In particular, case law shows that a consistently wide margin of appreciation

---

[5] See Articles 5, 12, 14 and 18, *op cit*. For the Committee's interpretation of these provisions see UN Doc CRC/C/15/Add.34; UN Doc CRC/C/15/Add.20 and UN Doc CRC/C/15/Add.38.

[6] See Chapter 4, p 85.

[7] See Eur Court HR *Hokkanen v Finland*, judgment of 23 Sept 1994, Series A no 299-A, 19 EHRR 139, § 61.

[8] This is arguably the central issue in the debate. See Verhellen (1993), 'Children's Rights in Europe', *International Journal of Children's Rights*, 1, pp 357-376, at p 358.

is enjoyed by States with regard to the degree of consultation with children which occurs at domestic level and the weight attached to that opinion in reaching decisions on family matters. Thus, failure to consult the child or attach significant weight to his/her wishes has never been found to breach the Convention, although specific claims of this nature have yet to be brought by or on behalf of the children concerned. However, the Commission has found from an early stage that it is consistent with Article 8 of the Convention to refuse parental contact because this would involve acting contrary to the wishes of the children.[9] It has also noted that to award contact despite strong objections expressed by children as old as twelve and fourteen would result in serious mental conflict for them which would be detrimental to their normal development.[10] It is clear from Convention case law that the interests of the child are dominant in the assessment of whether the refusal to allow contact between parent and child in any circumstances is consistent with Article 8. In this way, the repeated refusal of a child to have contact with a parent will be taken into account in deciding the compatibility of denying such contact with Article 8.[11] The Court appears to have taken this a step further in the *Hokkanen* case.[12] Here, it found that the obligation under Article 8 to enforce an order for contact between a father and his daughter only violated that provision up to the point at which the child expressed the opinion that she no longer wanted to see him. From that point on, the domestic authorities could not have been expected to enforce the order for contact between them, and the violation of Article 8 ceased as a result. Thus, the establishment by the domestic courts that the child was against seeing her father was decisive with regard to the Court's determination of respect for the father's family life. According to the Commission, however, the fact that the child had expressed her wish not to see her father while in the company of her present carers, meant that little importance should be attached to it.[13] As a result, it found the failure to arrange contact violated Article 8, regardless.

---

[9]    No *514/59 X v Austria*, Dec 5.1.60, 3 Yearbook, p 198 and No *2707/66 Kurtz & Seltmann v Germany*, Dec 4.4.67, Collection 25, p 28. See the more recent case of No *24482/94 Bogdanski v Sweden*, Dec 29.11.95, unreported.

[10]   No *1329/62 X v Denmark*, Dec 7.5.62, Collection 9, p 28.

[11]   No *9018/80 X v the Netherlands*, Dec 4.7.83, Dr 33, p 9, 6 EHRR 133.

[12]   *Hokkanen* judgment, *op cit*.

[13]   No *19823/92 Hokkanen v Finland*, Comm Report, 22.10.93, Series A No 299, p 31, 19 EHRR 153. See more detailed discussion in Chapter 11, pp 257-258.

According to the Commission, it is important that the domestic authorities do not base a refusal of access solely on the negative attitude of a child, but refer also to the child's age and maturity in deciding what significance to attach to the child's opinion.[14] This reflects the principle of evolving capacity, which ensures that the significance attached to the child's opinion increases with the child's enhanced maturity and age.[15] However, it has avoided setting out guidelines as to the importance to be attached to these factors and the determination of capacity is a matter for the domestic authorities, which falls within the margin of appreciation.[16]

The Commission appears to recognise the right of the child with significant age and maturity to express an opinion regarding parental access and have that opinion given due weight.[17] However, it is unclear whether a refusal to take the view of a child into consideration, where the child has reached a suitable age and maturity, would violate the child's right to family life (or indeed the child's freedom of expression) or whether in such a case the infringement would arise more from the enforcement of access against the wishes of the child. In *Nielsen v Denmark*, the Commission found that the failure to consider the strongly expressed wishes of a mature 12 year old boy with regard to his placement in a psychiatric ward of a hospital contributed to the arbitrary nature of his detention, which was itself incompatible with the Convention.[18] The Court did not share this view however and found that the boy was still of an age at which it would be normal for such decisions to be made by a parent, even against his wishes.[19] While this judgment cannot be overlooked, it is

---

[14] *Ibid.*

[15] See Article 5 and Article 12 of the Convention on the Rights of the Child, *op cit*. This principle means that States do not have an unfettered discretion as to when to consider and when to ignore the child's views. See Van Bueren (1995a), *The International Law on the Rights of the Child*, Dordrecht: Martinus Nijhoff, pp 136-137.

[16] See No *24482/94 Bogdanski v Sweden, op cit* as well as No *21827/93 Eriksson & Alanko v Sweden*, Dec 30.11.94, unreported.

[17] It has not commented on who should determine the child's maturity and ability to understand.

[18] See No *10924/88 Nielsen v Denmark*, Comm Report, 12.3.87, Series A no 144, p 136, § 125-126.

[19] Eur Court HR *Nielsen v Denmark*, judgment of 28 November 1988, Series A no 144, 11 EHRR 175, § 61. It found that the detention fell within the scope of parental responsibility and outside the scope of Article 5. For further discussion of this case see Chapter 3.

relevant that is now over a decade old and in contrast to the almost unanimous opinion of the Commission in the same case, it conflicts clearly with the principles of the Convention on the Rights of the Child, whose standards now enjoy almost universal acceptance.

It is well established that there are procedural rights implicit in respect for family life under Article 8 of the Convention. This has been found to mean that parents must be involved in the decision-making process regarding their children's care to a sufficient degree to ensure the requisite protection of their interests.[20] This principle has not yet been extended to require the participation of children in family law proceedings. Resistance against imposing an obligation on States to consult with children may be derived from concern about pressurising children to express a view in circumstances which may cause distress, such as in custody disputes or where sexual abuse or neglect is alleged.[21] However, reliance on Article 12 of the UN Convention on the Rights of the Child here may resolve this dilemma by facilitating recognition of the right of children to express their views, rather than placing an obligation on them to do so. In particular, Article 12 does not oblige children to become delegated decision-makers. Instead, its aim is to make all decision making processes accessible to the child who wishes, and is able, to participate in them.[22] In the same way, it would clearly be consistent with the procedural rights implicit in Article 8 to require States to consider the child's opinion where it is expressed, rather than to require them to seek the view of the child in all cases.

### Representation and Participation in Civil Proceedings

The UN Convention on the Rights of the Child promotes the idea of providing the child with representation to facilitate expression of his/her views and this extends to legal and other relevant representation in judicial and administrative proceedings under Article 12 § 2.[23] In contrast, Article 6 of the European Convention entitles everyone to have effective access to a court to have their civil rights and obligations and any criminal charge

---

[20] Eur Court HR *W v UK*, judgment of 8 July 1987, Series A no 121, 10 EHRR 29, § 64. See further Chapters 9 and 12.

[21] See further Cantwell & Scott (1995), 'Children's Wishes, Children's Burdens', *Journal of Social Welfare and Family Law*, **17**(3), pp 337-354.

[22] Van Bueren (1995a), *op cit*, p 137.

[23] Article 12 § 1 and 2, *op cit*.

against them determined,[24] and this may require the State to appoint a legal advisor if the circumstances warrant it.[25] Thus, where a person is not in a position to represent himself or where the law makes representation compulsory, there is an obligation on the State to provide legal representation to those who cannot afford to pay for the services of a lawyer.[26] The relevance of this case law to the position of a minor is clear, although the status of a minor means that access to legal representation is even more fundamental to his/her enjoyment of the right of access to a court, than is normally the case. Convention case law offers no guidance as to the circumstances in which children should enjoy legal representation in civil cases under Article 6, although the issue here is not whether the child is entitled to representation, but rather, who should represent the child. Given that access to a lawyer is fundamental to the child's enjoyment of fair trial rights under Article 6, it is arguable that failure to make legal representation available to a child would infringe the substantive right protected by that provision. Moreover, it would also raise an important issue insofar as the lack of representation would have a detrimental impact on the child's effective participation in the proceedings which directly concern him/her and which is necessary to guarantee a fair trial. This argument is relevant to both private and public family law proceedings, and in this situation, a child of sufficient age and understanding who is unable to take part in such proceedings due to a lack of independent representation or other practical impediments could make an arguable claim under Article 6.[27] It is not clear whether the appointment to the child of an independent representative or a *Guardian ad Litem* in proceedings before the national authorities is necessary in order to secure the child's right to a fair trial under Article 6. However, respect for the child's rights under Article 8 supports the view that such independent

---

24 See generally Van Dijk & Van Hoof (1998), *Theory and Practice of the European Convention on Human Rights*,3rd ed, The Hague: Kluwer, pp 418-428 and Harris, O'Boyle & Warbrick (1995), *Law of the European Convention on Human Rights*, London: Butterworths, pp 196-202.

25 Eur Court HR *Golder v UK*, judgment of 21 Feb 1975, Series A no 18, 1 EHRR 524.

26 See Eur Court HR *Airey v Ireland*, judgment of 9 Oct 1979, Series A no 32, 2 EHRR 305.

27 See No *15006/89 Abbott v UK*, Dec 10.12.90, unreported, where the minor, who was a ward of court, made such a complaint in relation to criminal proceedings taken with a view to placing him in secure accommodation. The case was settled with an amendment to the law taking place.

representation is necessary, particularly where the child is vulnerable or of a young age. Were the Court to reach such a conclusion, it would leave issues relating to the quality of such representation and how it should be organised to the discretion of the State, as long as the substance of the right is not infringed.[28]

The right of access to a court is not absolute and its very nature calls for regulation by the State.[29] Restrictions on a minor's exercise of the right to a court will be consistent with Article 6 only where they pursue a legitimate aim to which they are shown to be proportionate.[30] Such limitations may be justified by the aim to protect the rights and interests of either individual children, or children generally. In addition, there may be reasons pursuant to the proper administration of justice which could also play an important role here. Time limits which restrict the right of access to a court may, for example, be consistent with Article 6 where there is proportionality between the effect of the time limit and the aim which it seeks to achieve.[31] Moreover, States enjoy discretion in laying down such limitations although they must not be such that the very essence of the right is impaired.[32]

## Representation and Participation in Criminal Proceedings

While Article 6 § 3 (c) guarantees the right to defence counsel in criminal proceedings, the right to choose a lawyer and have him/her appointed by the State is not absolute and is bound by the relevant provisions of domestic law.[33] It is important, however, that the right in Article 6 § 3 (c) relates to 'effective' legal assistance.[34] In children's cases, this would

---

[28]  *Ibid* and Roche (1995), 'Children's Rights: in the Name of the Child', *Journal of Social Welfare & Family Law*, **17**(3), pp 281-300, at p 285. Guggenheim (1994), 'The Right to be Represented but not Heard: Reflections on Legal Representation for Children' *New York University Law Review*, **59**, p 76.

[29]  *Golder* judgment, *op cit*, § 38.

[30]  No *12040/86 M v UK*, Dec 4.5.87, DR 52, p 269.

[31]  Eur Court HR *Stubbings v UK*, judgment of 22 Oct 1996, Reports 1996-IV, no 18, p 1487, 23 EHRR 213. See further Chapter 8, pp 180-182.

[32]  Eur Court HR *Osman v UK,* judgment of 28 Oct 1998, Reports 1998-VIII, no 95. See further Chapter 7, pp 143-145.

[33]  See further Van Dijk & Van Hoof, *op cit*, pp 471-473 and Harris, O'Boyle & Warbrick, *op cit*, pp 256-266.

[34]  Eur Court HR *Artico v Italy*, judgment of 13 May 1980, Series A no 37, 3 EHRR 1.

arguably require the lawyer to communicate with the child and his/her guardian throughout the proceedings and to explain developments to the child in a clear and precise manner so that s/he may be instructed.[35]  The Court has also established considerable procedural safeguards which apply to those seeking to challenge the lawfulness of detention under Article 5 § 4 either as a minor, or in relation to indeterminate sentences of detention imposed when a minor.  They include *inter alia* the right to be represented, as well as the opportunity to be heard in person at any proceedings.[36]

The Commission has found that where a child is faced with a criminal charge and a fact finding procedure is necessary to establish guilt, it is essential that his/her age, level of maturity and intellectual and emotional capacities be taken into account in the procedures followed.[37] According to the Commission, the establishment of juvenile courts is conducive to a fair trial under Article 6, although this does not mean that children may never be tried in an adult setting.  While Article 6 does not necessarily require that the accused understands the points of law raised or the evidential intricacies of the case, it is nonetheless implicit in the right to a fair trial that s/he is able to participate effectively in criminal proceedings.  Where the alleged offender is a child, therefore, the procedures adopted must be conducive to the child's active participation, although this can never require that the child be compelled to give evidence.  As a result of the fact that the child's ability to participate in a criminal trial may be significantly reduced by his/her age and immaturity, particularly where such proceedings are adult based and have not been adapted so as to guarantee the fairness of the child's trial in the circumstances, then this may, in certain circumstances, give rise to a violation of Article 6.[38]

## The Child's Right to Complain to the European Court

In terms of Strasbourg proceedings, the child's right to petition the Court is limited neither by the Convention nor by the Court's Rules of Procedure. Theoretically, therefore, children may lodge an application with the Court without the authority of their legal guardians or representatives, which is

---

[35] See further Chapter 3, pp 40-41.
[36] See further Chapter 3, pp 50-52.
[37] No 24724/94 *T v UK,*  Comm Rep, 4.12.98, unreported § 95-99.  See also No 24888/94 *V v UK*, Comm Rep, 4.12.98, unreported.
[38] See further Chapter 3, pp 58-60.

particularly important where a dispute between the child and his/her parents is at the centre of the application.[39] The Commission has rejected the proposition that a parent must represent the child before it[40] and has noted that the position of the child requires careful consideration and the avoidance of a restrictive or technical approach with regard to the right of individual petition.[41] Nevertheless, it has consistently held that the right to apply on the child's behalf is enjoyed only by a parent with parental responsibility, unless it can be shown that s/he is authorised to represent the child with respect to the application, or that the child expressed a wish in relation to that parent introducing a claim on his/her behalf.[42] Thus, the parent's right to make an application to the Commission on behalf of a child is related directly to the nature of the parent-child relationship in domestic law, and in practice, where a parent does not enjoy any parental responsibility, particularly custody, the Commission will not examine the complaint submitted on the child's behalf.[43] The Commission's basis for this approach is to prevent parents, who challenge the outcome of domestic proceedings in relation to matters like custody or contact before the Strasbourg institutions, from using the child as a pawn in the Strasbourg proceedings. Its aim therefore is to protect the child from exposure to parental conflict. Although this aim is laudable, it is uncertain whether the approach operates to protect the child's interests in all cases, in particular where the child is too young to express an opinion on the Strasbourg proceedings and there is no one else able or willing to bring a legitimate case on the child's behalf. In this regard, it is possible that the Commission's blanket refusal to examine complaints made on the child's

---

[39] See No *6753/74 X & Y v the Netherlands,* Dec 19.12.74, DR 2, p 118.

[40] In most cases children are represented by their parents before the Commission, although in some cases, the children enjoy their own legal representation. See for example *No 15416/89 D & E v the Netherlands*, Dec 1.93, 16 EHRR CD 34 and *Nielsen* judgment, *op cit*, where the applicant was granted legal aid under the Convention's legal aid scheme.

[41] No *23715/94 SD, DP & AT v UK*, Dec 20.5.96, unreported.

[42] See No *8045/77 X v Sweden*, Dec 4.5.79, DR 16, p 105; No *12246/86 Irlen v Germany*, Dec 13.7.87, DR 53, p 225 and No *22920/93 MB v UK*, Dec 6.4.94, DR 77, p 108. See further Chapter 11.

[43] See Buquicchio-De Boer, 'Children and the European Convention on Human Rights: A Survey of the Case-Law of the European Commission and Court of Human Rights' in Matscher & Petzold (eds) (1988), *Protecting Human Rights: The European Dimension, Studies in Honour of Gerard J Wiarda*, Koln: Heymanns, pp 73-89, at p 74.

behalf by a non-custodial parent may serve to preclude the consideration of important issues from the child's perspective. For example, in *Keegan,* an unmarried father complained on his child's behalf, as well as on his own, that his lack of involvement in her adoption proceedings meant that they went unchallenged thereby violating the right to respect for family life.[44] Had he not withdrawn this complaint, he would not have been entitled to pursue it before the Court given his lack of legal rights in relation to his child under Irish law.[45]   Yet, notwithstanding that the application concerned the father's rights in the adoption process, there was no one who would have brought a legitimate complaint on the child's behalf, as neither the adoptive parents nor the child's birth mother were likely to make that challenge.

The concern which prompted the Commission's approach, that the complaints made by parents on their child's behalf were not bona fide, but were made merely to bolster their own complaints, is a genuine one. At the same time, it is clearly preferable that children in such cases should be entitled to independent representation before the Court. It is submitted therefore that a measured response to both issues would be for the Court, or the parties, to arrange for the appointment of a Guardian *ad Litem* to children whose complaints require consideration and representation independent from their parents' or other co-applicants'.[46] Indeed, support for this view has already been expressed by some of the Court's judges.[47] Alternatively, in light of the fact that Article 36 of the Convention permits the Court to invite third party intervention in the interest of proper administration of justice, an independent third party could be invited to make submissions on behalf of the child in this context. A further option would be to create a post akin to the Advocate General in the European Court of Justice which would ensure that adequate consideration is given to the child's case where the facts of the case highlight a concern in that

---

[44] Eur Court HR *Keegan v Ireland,* judgment of 26 May 1994, Series A, no 290, 18 EHRR 342. See further Chapter 13, pp 310-311.

[45] He dropped this part of the complaint no longer believing it to be in her best interests given that by that time she had spent four years with her adoptive parents. *Ibid,* § 33-34.

[46] This could possibly be organised along the lines of the Court's limited legal aid facilities and it would require a change in the Rules of Procedure.

[47] See the comments of Judge Bonnici in Eur Court HR *Kroon & Others v the Netherlands,* judgment of 27 Oct 1994, Series A no 297-C, 19 EHRR 263 and Judge Pettiti in Eur Court HR *X, Y & Z v UK,* judgment of 22 April 1997, Reports 1997-II no 35, 24 EHRR 143.

regard. This would enable all children, and not only those whose interests are consistent with their custodial parents, to have their claims examined at Strasbourg level. It would also enhance the position of children in Strasbourg proceedings generally allowing the authorities to pay closer attention to the independent claims of the children involved.

### Freedom of Expression

Article 10 § 1 of the European Convention guarantees that everyone has the right to freedom of expression, but this right is not absolute and its exercise is subject to such formalities, conditions, restrictions or penalties as are prescribed by law and are necessary in a democratic society.[48] Unlike the equivalent provisions in the Convention on the Rights of the Child, Article 10 is clearly not specific to children and it appears to offer inadequate protection for children, who frequently need assistance or facilitation in order to exercise this right. In contrast, Article 13 of the Convention on the Rights of the Child provides for the *child's* right to freedom of expression, including the

> freedom to seek, receive and impart information and ideas of all kinds...orally, in writing or in print, in the form of art or through any other media of the child's choice.[49]

The contrast between Article 10 and Article 13 is stark. Although the European Convention provision also protects all kinds, forms and media of expression, it does not offer equal protection to each of these.[50] Nor does it impose a positive obligation on the State to provide the means and media to enable a child to exercise the freedom. Moreover, although it is theoretically possible to invoke Article 10 to argue that the child has the

---

[48] They must also pursue a legitimate aim such as respect for the rights and reputations of others, the protection of national security, public order or public health or morals. The right may also be restricted in order to prevent the disclosure of information received in confidence or for maintaining the authority and impartiality of the judiciary. See generally, Lester, 'Freedom of Expression' in Macdonald et al (eds) (1993), *The European System for the Protection of Human Rights*, Deventer: Kluwer, pp 465-491; Harris, O'Boyle & Warbrick, *op cit*, pp 372-416 and Van Dijk & Van Hoof, *op cit*, pp 557-585.

[49] See further Van Bueren (1995a) *op cit*, pp 131-150.

[50] See Harris, O'Boyle & Warbrick, *op cit*, p 379.

right to a say in decisions which affect him/her, case law does not support the application of the provision in this way.[51] Nevertheless, there are two important aspects to the freedom of expression and children, namely, the child's exercise of the right, and restrictions on its exercise by others in order to protect the rights of the child.

## *The Right to Information*

Although Article 10 protects the right to receive and impart information and ideas, it does not expressly recognise the right to seek information.[52] The recognition of the important function performed by the mass media[53] is reflected in the jurisprudence of the Court, however, in which great weight is attached to the role of press and television in ensuring effective enjoyment of the right to receive ideas and information on issues of general concern.[54] However, unlike the equivalent provision in the Convention on the Rights of the Child, Article 10 neither expressly nor implicitly encourages the freedom or exchange of information or ideas among children. Nor does it facilitate the child's freedom of expression through appropriate means.[55]

The absence from the provision of the right to seek information, together with the Court's finding that the right to access information is not implicitly protected by Article 10,[56] both have negative consequences for the usefulness of the provision for children. In particular, it appears to have little potential for children seeking to challenge access to state held records on matters of adoption, care and artificial reproduction.[57]

---

[51] *Ibid*, pp 372-416. See further Boucaud (1989),'The Council of Europe and Child Welfare: The Need for a European Convention on Children's Rights', *Human Rights Files No 10*, Strasbourg: Council of Europe and Buquicchio-De Boer, *op cit*, p 89.

[52] See further 'The Right to Information' in Loucaides (1995), *Essays on the Developing Law of Human Rights*, Dordrecht: Martinus Nijhoff, pp 3-31.

[53] See also Article 17 of the Convention on the Rights of the Child, *op cit*.

[54] See Harris, O'Boyle & Warbrick, *op cit*, p 406-407. See also various Council of Europe Resolutions in this area in (1996) *The Rights of the Child: A European Perspective*, Strasbourg: Council of Europe.

[55] On the importance of this in court proceedings see further Emery (1996), 'Representation for Children', *International Legal Practitioner*, **21**, pp 29-31.

[56] Eur Court HR *Leander v Sweden*, judgment of 26 March 1987, Series A no 116, 9 EHRR 433, § 74.

[57] See further Chapter 5.

Notwithstanding its failure to interpret Article 10 favourably in this area,[58] however, it is still open to the Court to find that there is a public right of access to official information about matters of legitimate public interest.[59] Moreover, it is significant that an issue may arise in the context of respect for private life under Article 8, where the information sought is necessary to facilitate knowledge and understanding of a person's childhood and early development.[60]   Yet, the Court has failed to express an opinion as to whether general rights of access to personal data and information may be derived by Article 8.[61]  Furthermore, the significance of the applicant's age (he had reached the age of majority) and the fact that it was the lack of a procedure by which access to the information was determined, rather than the confidential nature of the child care system itself which gave rise to the violation of Article 8, limits the application of the *Gaskin* judgment in cases where access is sought to information regarding their identity, in cases of adoption or artificial reproduction.[62]

## *Protection of the Child from Harmful and Exploitative Information*

It is well established that there are categories of information, access to which may be deemed to be contrary to the best interests of the child.[63] This idea of censorship is also reflected in Article 10 § 2 of the European Convention, which provides for restrictions on the exercise of the freedom of expression *inter alia* for the protection of health or morals or protection of the rights of others.[64]  It is indicative of the important position enjoyed

---

[58]  The Commission has found that the freedom to receive information guaranteed by Article 10 is primarily a freedom of access to 'general sources of information which may not be restricted by positive action of the authorities'.  See No *10392/83 Z v Austria*, Dec 13.4.88, DR 56, p 13.

[59]  Lester, *op cit*, p 482.

[60]  Eur Court HR  *Gaskin v UK*,  judgment of 7 July 1989,  Series A  no 160, 12 EHRR 36.  See further Chapter 5, pp 103-106.

[61]  *Ibid*, § 37.

[62]  See Van Bueren (1995a), *op cit*, pp 132-133 and see further Chapter 5.  See also Harris, O'Boyle & Warbrick, *op cit*, p 380.

[63]  Article 17(e) of the Convention on the Rights of the Child provides that States Parties shall encourage the development of appropriate guidelines for the protection of the child from information and material injurious to his or her well-being.  The exploitative use of children in pornographic materials is also prohibited under Article 34, *op cit*.

[64]  See also Van Bueren (1995a) *op cit*, pp 134-135.

by this freedom in a democratic society that any restrictions on its exercise are to be narrowly interpreted and must correspond to a pressing social need. Moreover, it is clear from Article 10 that there are duties and responsibilities implicit in the exercise of the freedom of expression, which may be taken into account when determining whether an interference with the freedom is proportionate to the legitimate aim pursued under Article 10 § 2.[65] All these factors are relevant to minors.

In a broad interpretation of the scope of Article 10, the Court has found that the freedom of expression applies to ideas and information which offend, shock or disturb the population as well as those which may be favourably received or regarded as inoffensive.[66] Nevertheless, the Strasbourg institutions have taken an active role in protecting young people from offensive material which, due to their impressionable age, may have a more detrimental effect on them than it would on adults. For example, although a magazine was not in itself 'manifestly liable to corrupt the young', the Commission found its censorship to be justified under Article 10 because its descriptions of film stars' lives as extravagant, loose and profligate presented a grave danger to adolescents who were much more prone than adults to seek models to imitate and emulate.[67]

This approach was confirmed in *Handyside* which concerned the seizure, forfeiture and destruction of an allegedly obscene publication, *The Little Red Schoolbook*, which was intended as a 'reference book' for children. The Commission found by a narrow margin that this measure was a justifiable interference with the freedom of expression under Article 10.[68] In particular, the Commission acknowledged the necessity of placing restrictions on obscene publications for the protection of morals, particularly those of young people and children and noted that all Convention States had legislated to restrict this freedom with regard to indecent, obscene or pornographic literature.[69] Although it admitted that there could be no uniform concept of morals applied equally throughout the

---

[65] See for example *Handyside v UK*, Judgment of 7 Dec 1976, Series A no 24 and Eur Court HR *Jersild v Denmark*, judgment of 23 Sept 1994, Series A no 298, 19 EHRR 1, which concerned the actions of a publisher and a television journalist respectively.

[66] *Handyside* judgment, *ibid*, § 49.

[67] No *1167/61 X & German Association of Z v Germany*, Dec 16.12.63, 6 Yearbook, p 204.

[68] No 5493/72 *Handyside v UK*, Comm Report, 30.9.75, unreported, § 139-155.

[69] *Ibid*, § 151. See also Boucaud, *op cit*, pp 34-36.

Council of Europe, it found that the opinion of the domestic court was decisive with regard to the tendency of the publication to deprave and corrupt the audience of young children at which it was aimed.[70] It went on to conclude by eight votes to five that the authorities had acted in good faith within the discretion afforded to them by taking measures necessary to protect morals.

The Court enjoyed greater consensus in finding that the restriction on the applicant publisher's freedom of expression was justified with regard to the need to protect the morals and rights of young people.[71] It also relied on the opinion of the English court that the book would have 'pernicious effects' on the morals of many of the children and adolescents who would read it.[72] In particular however, it was the intended readership of the Schoolbook that was significant, being aimed at 12 to 18 year olds, and the Court considered that it was easily within the comprehension of even the youngest of those readers. Attaching special significance to the capacity of the person to be protected thus appears to make the State's intervention easier to justify, particularly when its aim is to protect a specific category of the population, which is especially vulnerable.[73]

The approach of the Strasbourg authorities to this issue is unlikely to have changed much in the two decades since its consideration of *Handyside*, notwithstanding the increased awareness of the opposing right of the child to information enumerated in the Convention on the Rights of the Child. In *Handyside*, the Court failed to draw an analogy between the material disseminated and the distribution of general pornography because the latter was not aimed at children to the same extent.[74] Nor was the Court

---

[70] *Ibid*, § 155. The Commission cited the domestic court in relation to the book's 'attacks on traditional child/parent and child/teacher relationships' which 'undermine many of those influences which might otherwise provide restraint' and its failure to mention that smoking pot and sexual intercourse for girls under the age of 14 are illegal.

[71] The Court ruled by 13 votes to 1. *Handyside* judgment, *op cit*.

[72] *Ibid*, § 52.

[73] This factor was also dominant in Eur Court HR *Muller v Switzerland*, judgment of 24 May 1988, Series A no 133, 13 EHRR 212, § 36, where the Court, in finding reasonable the view of the domestic courts that paintings with their emphasis on sexuality in some of its crudest forms were liable grossly to offend the sense of sexual propriety of persons of ordinary sensitivity, noted that there was no age-limit imposed on those seeking admission to the art exhibition in question.

[74] *Handyside* judgment, *op cit*, § 56.

influenced by the fact that no prosecution had occurred in any of the other Convention States where the publication was also available.[75] Notwithstanding the contribution of children to the *Little Red Schoolbook*, the Court conceptualised the issue as one of child protection, rather than rights. As a result, it would probably reach the same conclusion today, although the need to find an appropriate balance between the protection of the child from harmful information and recognising the child's right of access to appropriate information may play a greater role in a contemporary examination of the question.

Although it has been submitted that the complaint of a minor regarding access to the *Little Red Schoolbook* may have met with greater success,[76] the Convention position is unclear in this regard. The Commission dismissed the complaints made by two minors (aged 13 and 17) and their mother, who claimed that the banning of the handbook violated their right to receive information under Article 10.[77] Their application failed on the grounds that the second edition of the book, which was not substantially different from the first, was freely available. Thus, it was found to be irrelevant in the *Handyside* case that the second edition of the Schoolbook had not been subjected to the same measure of censorship as the first, despite being similar to it, yet its availability precluded a finding of a violation of Article 10 when the situation was examined from the child's perspective.

The Strasbourg approach to the protection of children from the negative effects of commercial speech is similar to that outlined above, and in this area too, the issue of the target audience and the responsibility enjoyed by the broadcaster is central to the consideration of the case. Importantly, the Commission has recognised that within the context of restricting the freedom of commercial expression children have a 'right...to be protected against indirect advertisement in television programmes primarily aimed at a young audience'.[78] Hence, restrictions placed on the freedom of

---

[75] *Ibid.*,§ 54. Moreover, the Court found that the absence of prosecution against the revised edition suggested that the competent authorities wished to limit themselves to what was strictly necessary in accordance with Article 10, at § 55.

[76] Van Bueren (1995a), *op cit*, p 135.

[77] No *5528/72 X, Y & Z v UK*, Dec 4.3.76, DR 5, p 5.

[78] It was also considered to be aimed at the right of companies to be protected against unfair competition. *16844/90 Nederlandse Omroeprogramma Stichting (Netherlands Broadcasting Programme Foundation) v the Netherlands*, Dec 13.10.93, unreported. See Recommendation 952 (1982) on international means to protect freedom of expression by regulating commercial advertising and

expression, which aim to protect children in this way will probably be consistent with Article 10. For example, when the makers of a special feature programme aimed at the nine to twelve year age group, in which the name of a holiday resort and a soft drink were mentioned on two separate occasions, were found to have flouted Dutch media legislation, the Commission failed to find that this violated Article 10.[79] Even though it had not been the intention of the Broadcasting Foundation to promote one product over another, the Commission found that the interference with their rights was reasonable in the light of the (young) target audience of the programmes in question and their specific position in the Dutch broadcasting system. While this decision is welcome insofar as it applies Article 10 in a manner which protects children from commercial exploitation through television, its scope is unclear. For example, is it equally consistent with the Convention to ban advertising aimed directly at children, such as the advertising of toys, during the broadcasting of children's programmes? Clearly, any such interference would have to be proportionate to the aim to protect children from harm and this will, as always, depend on the circumstances of the case.

**Freedom of Religion**

According to Article 9 of the European Convention everyone has the right to freedom of thought, conscience and religion.[80] This right includes freedom to change religion as well as the right to manifest religion or belief through worship, teaching, practice and observance, although a limit may be placed on the freedom to manifest one's religious beliefs in certain circumstances.[81] Article 9 does not place any specific restriction on the

---

to protect freedom of expression by regulating commercial advertising and Recommendation (84) 3 on principles of television advertising in (1996), *The Rights of the Child: A European Perspective*, Strasbourg: Council of Europe.

[79] No *16844/90 Nederlandse Omroeprogramma Stichting v the Netherlands, ibid.*

[80] See further Harris, O'Boyle & Warbrick, *op cit*, pp 356-371; Van Dijk & Van Hoof, *op cit*, pp 541-557 and Fawcett (1987), *The Application of the European Convention on Human Rights*, 2nd ed, Oxford: Clarendon Press, pp 235-250.

[81] Limitations must be prescribed by law and be necessary in a democratic society in the interests of public safety, the protection of public order, health or morals or for the protection of the rights and freedoms of others.

right of children to enjoy such rights, however.[82] The Convention appears to envisage a parental role in the exercise by the child of his/her freedom of religion[83] and in particular, Article 2 of the First Protocol requires States to respect the religious convictions of parents in the education of their children. Although the stated aim of this provision is to protect the child from religious indoctrination by the State, rather than the protection of the religious integrity of individual pupils, it is also considered important that any instruction the child receives from the State leaves scope for parental guidance.[84] In addition, the obligation to respect the religious convictions of parents in the exercise of their children's education applies as part of the exercise of parental responsibility.[85] Thus, the right to determine a child's religious education is considered to be an inherent part of the right of custody, which may be relinquished along with other parental duties in certain circumstances.[86] Although exercise of the child's freedom of religion is not subject expressly to parental consent or guidance, it is implicit that in most circumstances parents are entitled to bring up children in their own religion.[87] However, the Convention authorities have yet to determine the weight to be attached to the child's rights where there is conflict between a parent and child with respect to the child's religion. Nevertheless, it is important that the limits set out in Article 9 § 2 apply to the manifestation of religious beliefs, and not to the freedom to choose religion itself.

---

[82] Cf Article 14 UN Convention on the Rights of the Child, *op cit*, which does not offer children the right to change religion. See Van Bueren, 'The Struggle for Empowerment: the emerging civil and political rights of children' Defence For Children International (1990), *Seminar on the Implementation of the Convention on the Rights of the Child,* Syracusa Italy, 24-28, September, 1990, pp 59-62.

[83] Article 14 § 2 UN Convention on the Rights of the Child, *op cit*, which says that States shall respect the rights and duties of parents to provide direction to the child in the exercise of his/her right in a manner consistent with the evolving capacities of the child.

[84] Eur Court HR *Kjeldsen, Busk Madsen & Pedersen v Denmark*, judgment of 7 December 1976, Series A, no 23, 1 EHRR 711, § 53. See further Chapter 4.

[85] See Eur Court HR *Olsson v Sweden*, judgment of 24 March 1988, Series A, no 130, § 95. See further Chapter 12.

[86] No *5608/72 X v UK*, Dec 14.12.72, Collection 44, p 66.

[87] See Eur Court HR *Hoffmann v Austria*, judgment of 23 June 1993, Series A, no 255-C, 17 EHRR 293. See Harris, O'Boyle & Warbrick, *op cit*, p 317.

There is little guidance available from the Court in relation to the exercise by a child of his/her religious freedom,[88] although existing case law suggests that it is difficult to make out a successful claim under this provision. In *Valsamis v Greece* the suspension from school of two children who refused to participate in a school procession commemorating the beginning of the Greece-Italian war, which they believed to be contrary to their religion, was found to be compatible with Article 9.[89] Decisively, neither the Commission nor the Court found the procession to be inconsistent with the girls' religious beliefs as Jehovah's Witnesses, disagreeing with them as to its military nature. However, it is arguable that, in the light of the importance of the freedom of religion in a democratic society, the applicants should have enjoyed the benefit of the doubt in this regard given the subjective nature of the question at issue, i.e. whether the parade in question had a military colour which was irreconcilable with their religious beliefs, and the absence of domestic authority on the matter.[90] Moreover, finding that their treatment interfered with their freedom of religion under Article 9 would have allowed the Court to consider whether this measure was proportionate to the aims of public order etc under Article 9 § 2. The necessity and importance of undertaking such a balancing exercise would take on added significance in light of the fact that the child's right to education, denied as a result of the penalty imposed, was at stake.[91]

Both the Commission and the Court found that as the obligation to take part in the school parade did not infringe her parents' religious convictions, it did not *mutatis mutandis* interfere with the pupil's freedom of religion under Article 9.[92] Moreover, the fact that she enjoyed exemption from religious instruction and Orthodox mass meant that a balance had been

---

[88]  This is consistent with the limited case law on Article 9 generally which, it is suggested, reflects the cautious approach of the institutions in this area. Harris, O'Boyle & Warbrick, *op cit*, p 356.

[89]  No *21787/93 Valsamis v Greece*, Comm Rep, 6.7.95, Reports 1996-VI, no 27 and Eur Court HR *Valsamis v Greece*, judgment of 18 Dec 1996, Reports 1996-VI, no 27, p 2313. See the identical case of Eur Court HR *Efstratiou v Greece*, judgment of 18 Dec 1996, Reports-VI, no 27, p 2347. See further Chapter 4, pp 72-75.

[90]  See also Harris, O'Boyle & Warbrick, *op cit*, p 358.

[91]  Indeed, one third of the Commission took this view and went on to find that the one day suspension imposed on the children was disproportionate to the aim of protecting public order under Article 9 § 2. *Valsamis*, Comm Rep, *op cit*.

[92]  *Valsamis* Comm Rep, *op cit* and judgment, *op cit*.

achieved between her freedom of religion and the demands of school discipline. Given that the scope of Article 9 is wider than that of Article 2 of the First Protocol, however, this provision should arguably have entitled the girl to greater protection under the Convention. Arrangements had been made for her to be excluded from religious instruction and other religious activities without disrupting order within the school. It is difficult to envisage, therefore, why refusing to exempt her from the parade, in relation to which she had made a prior request, which she similarly believed to be incompatible with her religion, could be considered to be consistent with that provision.

On a positive note, the Court raised a judicial eyebrow to the possibility of requiring pupils to parade outside the school on a national holiday on pain of suspension from school, even if only for a day.[93] It also questioned implicitly whether there might be more expedient educational methods, which would be better suited to the aim of perpetuating historical memory among the younger generation.[94] These remarks are important because they leave open the possibility that a future challenge to the consistency of such a measure with the child's right to education under the First Protocol or, more importantly, Article 9 would enjoy success.[95] In any event, the inability to have the child's disciplinary sanction subjected to legislative review constituted a denial of an effective domestic remedy in respect to the alleged violation of a Convention right, in breach of Article 13.[96]

Other case law also suggests that the approach of the Commission has been to promote pluralism, rather than to protect the religious freedom of a particular minority grouping in society. For instance, the Commission dismissed the claim made by a Muslim University student that the requirement to remove her head scarf for a photograph taken for identification purposes was incompatible with her religious beliefs.[97] In doing so, it noted that by choosing to pursue her higher education in a secular university the applicant had submitted to the rules restricting the

---

[93] *Valsamis* judgment, *ibid,* § 31.

[94] *Ibid,* § 32.

[95] It is noted that the Court sometimes resists applicants' attempts to raise under Article 9 issues which can be dealt with under other provisions such as Article 8 where the case concerns the custody of children. See Harris, O'Boyle & Warbrick, *op cit,* p 359.

[96] *Valsamis* judgment, *op cit,* § 43-49.

[97] See No *16278/90 Karaduman v Turkey,* Dec 3.5.93, DR 74, p 93 as well as No *18783/91 Bulut v Turkey,* Dec 3.5.91, unreported.

freedom of students to manifest their religion, which aimed to ensure harmonious co-existence between students of different beliefs. It stressed that, particularly in countries where the great majority of the population belong to one particular religion, manifestation of the observances of that religion, without restriction as to place and manner, may constitute pressure on those who do not practice it.[98] Thus, where secular universities have laid down dress regulations for students, they may ensure that certain fundamentalist religious movements do not disturb public order in higher education or impinge on the beliefs of others. Applying this rationale, the interference with the student's freedom of religion under Article 9 was justified on the grounds of public order.

The Commission has accepted that banning a particular religious practice under domestic law is a justifiable interference with religious freedom and thus Article 9 cannot be invoked in order to justify a practice which is contrary to national law. In particular, the Commission has found that marriage is not solely a manifestation of religious belief, but falls also to be considered under Article 12 which provides for legislation to govern the exercise of the right to marry.[99] Even though it may be consistent with Islamic law to marry a 12 year old girl, therefore, the fact that sexual intercourse with a girl under the age of 16 is unlawful under domestic law was decisive in the Commission's finding that the prosecution of the adult husband did not violate Article 9 or Article 12. Thus, although the practice of marrying very young reflected the manifestation of a particular religious belief, the fact that domestic legislation consistent with the Convention provided protection for the rights and health of young people in such circumstances meant that, indirectly, a limit was placed on the freedom of religion to this end.

**Freedom of Assembly**

While the inclusion of the right or freedom to assemble or associate with others in a public place among the provisions of the UN Convention on the Rights of the Child arguably confirms the relevance of this right to children, it is also possible that the provision was included for the sake of

---

[98] Cf the view in *Valsamis* Comm Rep, *op cit*, and judgment, *op cit*, that a member of a minority religion should take part in the procession with all the other students for the purposes of school discipline.

[99] No *11579/85 Khan v UK*, Dec 7.7.86, unreported.

completeness.[100] Nevertheless, the right, given its ordinary meaning, can be said to have every relevance to children, who during their teenage years, tend to gather in groups, regardless of whether they live in a rural or urban location. However, Convention case law on Article 11, which guarantees the right to freedom of peaceful assembly and to freedom of association emphasises that the provision aims to protect the right of individuals to 'come together for the expression and protection of their common interests'.[101] Article 11 is thus applicable to situations in which the right to demonstrate (and to be protected from counter-demonstrators) or to join a trade union are at issue, rather than any right to casually associate with whomever one wishes. The Commission confirmed the inapplicability of the provision to the latter situation in 1997, when it rejected the complaint that a ban on the entry and use of a shopping centre by a number of black youths violated Article 11.[102] The applicants' complaint failed on the ground that they had no history of using the shopping centre for any form of organised assembly or association and thus it did not raise any issue under Article 11, which contains, *inter alia*, a right for individuals to associate 'in order to attain various ends'. Thus, any restrictions placed on the activities of young people, either by the State or a private party, such as their parents, will be unlikely to raise an issue under this provision unless it is established that their gathering serves a particular purpose.

**Future Challenges**

While there have been few specific applications brought by children themselves challenging their civil rights, there is clearly considerable potential for invoking the European Convention in this area. The acceptance of the principles of child participation and consultation, dominant in international law is also increasing in the legal systems of Convention States, at least insofar as children enjoy greater access to independent legal representation in proceedings which concern them. This is also reflected in the Council of Europe's Convention on the Exercise of

---

[100] See Article 15, *op cit.*

[101] See Harris, O'Boyle & Warbrick, *op cit*, 417-434, at p 417 and Van Dijk & Van Hoof, *op cit*, pp 586-601.

[102] No 33689/96 *Anderson & Ors v UK*, Dec 27.10.97, 25 EHRR CD 172. The applicants claim under Article 14 was dismissed as their action under s 20 Race Relations Act 1976 was still pending before the domestic courts.

Children's Rights, which has yet to come into force.[103]    There is thus no shortage of relevant standards to which the Court can refer in considering a challenge to the failure to consult or involve the child in a decision making process which concerns him, particularly in the area of family law under Article 8, where a similar right has been guaranteed to parents. Similarly, the right of the child to participate in criminal proceedings is also in an early stage of development and it is clearly conceivable that this will emerge as an obligation on States to develop appropriate systems of juvenile justice to ensure that young people enjoy a fair trial.

While there are many aspects of Article 10 and the freedom of expression which have yet to be applied specifically to children, particularly in the contexts of having their views heard and gaining access to certain information, it is likely that laws placing strict limits on the availability of information perceived to be harmful, on the internet for example, may raise an issue under this provision. The search for an appropriate balance between the freedom of expression and the need to protect children will be revisited in an age of unprecedented data and information exchange.

Similarly, given the increasing diversity of European society and the extension of the Convention's scope into Central and Eastern Europe, issues relating to respect for religious freedom will continue to arise. According to the Court, democracy does not simply mean that the views of a majority must always prevail, but requires that a balance be achieved to ensure the fair and proper treatment of minorities, avoiding any abuse of a dominant position. In responding to these challenges, whether brought by children or their parents, greater adherence to this view will be decisive in ensuring the protection of religious freedom.

---

[103] DIR/JUR (95) 12 Rev, Council of Europe, Strasbourg, 8.9.95. See also Killerby (1995), 'The Draft European Convention on the Exercise of Children's Rights', *The International Journal of Children's Rights*, **3**, pp 127-133.

# 7      Life, Health and Health Care

## Introduction

Within the Council of Europe, issues relating to social and economic rights were originally seen as falling within the remit of the European Social Charter, the sister treaty to the European Convention, which came into force in 1965.[1] Nevertheless, it is a falsehood that social, economic and cultural rights fall outside the scope of protection of the European Convention. For example, the right to education, traditionally classified as a social right, is guaranteed by Article 2 of the First Protocol and Article 1 of the First Protocol contains the right to peaceful enjoyment of possessions, an economic right. Admittedly, the Convention does not share detailed provisions on the right to health care or an adequate standard of living with the Social Charter or the UN Convention on the Rights of the Child,[2] and its relevance to children may be said to be undermined as a result. However, as in other areas, a number of factors have helped to reduce the significance of its apparent inadequacy in this regard. For instance, the fact that the constituent elements of many Convention rights are not defined means that the Court enjoys discretion to interpret them in a manner which has consequences for the protection of social and economic rights.[3] Evidence of this is outlined below. Moreover, the Court has expressly stated that, as a matter of principle, the fact that an interpretation of the Convention may extend into the sphere of social and economic rights

---

[1]   ETS No 35 and revised by ETS No 163. See generally Drzewicki, Krause & Rosas (eds) (1994), *Social Rights as Human Rights: A European Challenge*, Abo: Institute for Human Rights, Abo Akademi University.

[2]   UN Doc A/44/25. See further Leary, 'The Social and Economic Rights of the Child' in Defence For Children International (1993), *Selected Essays on International Children's Rights*, Vol 1, Geneva: DCI, pp 15-43 and Van Bueren (1995a), *The International Law on the Rights of the Child*, Dordrecht: Martinus Nijhoff, pp 293-327.

[3]   Melchior, 'Rights not covered by the Convention' in Macdonald et al (eds) (1993), *The European System for the Protection of Human Rights*, Deventer: Kluwer, pp 593-601.

should not be a decisive factor against it.[4]  Through the adoption of a dynamic approach in many areas, the Commission and Court have enhanced considerably the protection which the Convention offers children in this area, especially in relation to aspects of the right to life, health and health care.[5]  Although a positive interpretive approach alone cannot compensate for the absence of substantive Convention provisions protecting these rights,[6] nonetheless, the case law suggests that the Convention's potential to protect children in this area has not yet been exhausted.

## The Right to Life

It has been described as curious that Article 2 of the Convention guarantees that 'everyone's right to life shall be protected by law', but, unlike other Convention provisions, it does not recognise the existence of the right to life itself.[7]  Insofar as it entails an obligation to protect everyone's right to life, Article 2 has the potential to be broadly interpreted.  It has been questioned, for example, whether a State would be in default for failing to take measures to reduce deaths on the roads.[8]  However, its meaning is clarified by Fawcett's explanation, that it is the *right* to life which must be protected by law, and not life itself.[9]  Article 2 does not guarantee protection against all threats to life, therefore, but safeguards against 'intentional deprivation and careless endangering of life'.[10]  The fact that the right to life must be protected by law explains why the procedural, rather than the substantive aspect of Article 2 dominates Strasbourg jurisprudence.

---

[4]   Eur Court HR *Airey v Ireland*, judgment of 9 October 1979, Series A no 32, 2 EHRR 305, § 26 concerning the interpretation of Article 6 to require civil legal aid in certain circumstances.

[5]   See Chapter 1, pp 6-16.

[6]   See Pellonpää, 'Economic, Social and Cultural Rights' in Macdonald et al (Eds), *op cit*, pp 855-874.

[7]   Van Dijk & Van Hoof (1998), *Theory and Practice of the European Convention on Human Rights*, 3rd ed, The Hague: Kluwer, p 297.

[8]   *Ibid.*

[9]   Fawcett (1987), *The Application of the European Convention on Human Rights*, 2nd ed, Oxford: Clarendon Press, p 37.

[10]   Van Dijk & Van Hoof, *op cit*.

In any event, it is unclear what consequences the wording of Article 2 has for the nature of the obligations which flow from the provision. The fact that the first sentence of Article 2 § 1 is followed by a prohibition of intentional deprivation of life[11] suggests that the provision stops short of imposing positive obligations on domestic authorities. It is inconceivable therefore that Article 2 could be found to require States to maintain an adequate health service, although the withdrawal of medical facilities in an individual case may raise an issue under this provision.[12]     However unlikely it is that the Court would find a positive obligation to flow from Article 2 in this respect, a dynamic development of this kind should not be ruled out given that such an interpretation would be consistent with the Convention's object and purpose.[13]

## Procedural Safeguards

In 1995 the Court confirmed that there is a procedural aspect implicit in the obligation to protect the right to life under Article 2,[14] something which had been developed by the Commission, *inter alia,* in a number of children's cases.   One such case concerned the fact that an unqualified nurse had been appointed to a position of some authority within the health service and was later found responsible for the deaths and serious injuries of children on her ward.[15]     Notwithstanding that the offender was subsequently prosecuted successfully and a public inquiry was held to establish the facts of the case, the parents of the children argued that this was inadequate for the purposes of Article 2.   They claimed that where

---

[11] Article 2 § 1 says that the deprivation of life shall not be regarded as inflicted in contravention of this article when it results from the use of force which is no more than absolutely necessary: a. in defence of any person from unlawful violence; b. in order to effect a lawful arrest or to prevent the escape of a person lawfully detained or c. in action lawfully taken for the purpose of quelling a riot or insurrection.

[12] Such a case would fall more naturally under Article 3 however. See for example Eur Court HR *D v UK*, judgment of 2 May 1997, Reports 1997-III, no 37, p 777, 24 EHRR 456.

[13] Harris, O'Boyle & Warbrick (1995), *Law of the European Convention on Human Rights*, London: Butterworths, pp 40-41.

[14] Eur Court HR *McCann, Farrell & Savage*, judgment of 27 Sept 1995, Series A No 324, 21 EHRR 97.

[15] No *23412/92 Taylor, Crampton, Gibson & King v UK*, Dec 30.8.94, 18 EHRR 215.

unlawful killing has been threatened or has occurred in an environment for which it is responsible, the State is required to seek out the perpetrator and bring him/her to justice, compensate the victims and establish a mechanism by which lessons could be learned and repetition of similar attacks prevented. This interpretation of the procedural requirement under Article 2 was rejected, in favour of a more minimalist one, however. In particular, the Commission noted that

> where a State or its agents potentially bear responsibility for loss of life the events in question should be subject to an effective investigation or scrutiny which enables the facts to become known to the public, and in particular to the relatives of any victims.[16]

Thus the fact that neither the criminal proceedings nor the inquiry addressed the wider issues relating to the organisation and funding of the health service, or the pressures which might have led to a ward being run subject to such shortcomings, did not mean that the procedural requirement in Article 2 was unfulfilled. To the contrary, the Commission found that the inquiry which took place satisfied the requirements of the provision insofar as it was independent of the parties, had full access to relevant documentation and witnesses and made its findings and recommendations public. In the absence of an inquiry, it is unclear whether the fact that the nurse in question had been prosecuted successfully would have been sufficient for the purposes of Article 2.[17] What is certain, however, is that an investigation into circumstances of death which is inadequate or too lengthy will raise an issue under Article 6 of the Convention, which places a reasonable time requirement on certain civil and criminal proceedings.[18]

The Commission's finding that Article 2 includes a right to an inquiry where 'the state or its agents potentially bear responsibility for loss of life' is highly significant insofar as it is a broad interpretation of the text of Article 2, which prohibits intentional killing. Consistent with this view, the Commission has recently found that Article 2 requires States to establish a judicial system whereby the cause of death, and possibly the responsibility

---

[16] *Ibid.*

[17] It is likely that the availability of a civil remedy alone would be insufficient to satisfy the requirements of Article 2 although this will depend on the facts of the case. See further below and the discussion of related issues in Chapter 8.

[18] No *21166/93 Family D v France*, Comm Rep, 17.5.95, unreported. On length of proceedings generally see Harris, O'Boyle & Warbrick, *op cit*, pp 222-230 and Van Dijk & Van Hoof, *op cit*, pp 446-450.

of doctors, may be established where, for example, the death of a child occurs during surgery.[19] The Strasbourg institutions reserve the right to review the compatibility of such a procedure with the Convention, although where the authorities do not appear to have assessed arbitrarily the evidence before them, and there is no evidence of negligence on the part of hospital staff, then it is unlikely that a violation of Article 2 will be found.[20]

Under Article 2, the right to life must be secured by the State putting in place effective criminal law provisions to deter the commission of violent offences, supported by law-enforcement machinery. Indeed, the Court took this interpretation one step further in the *Osman* case in 1998.[21] Ahmet Osman was a young boy when his school teacher developed an obsession with him, which led to a serious campaign of harassment, several attacks on his home and an eventual shooting incident where Ahmet was injured, and his father was killed. Both the education authorities and the police were involved from an early stage, but according to the facts established by the Commission, there were no factors which, judged reasonably, rendered it foreseeable with any degree or probability that the stalker would carry out an armed attack on the family. However, the applicants argued that the police had failed to take the necessary measures to safeguard life under Article 2. The Commission, having found that there was no violation of that provision,[22] referred the case to the Court and it fell to the Court, therefore, to determine whether the facts disclosed a failure by the authorities to protect the right to life of the boy and his father. Considering the obligation to protect life under Article 2, the Court first established that this may involve an obligation to take preventive operational measures to protect an individual whose life is at risk from the criminal acts of another. This is not an obligation which will apply in every case and, according to the Court, its application depends on matters such as resource restrictions, operational choices and public policy considerations. Consequently, whether the authorities have violated their positive obligation to protect life, in the context of the duty to prevent and suppress

---

[19] No *20948/92 Isiltan v Turkey*, Dec 2.5.95, unreported. The seizure of a child's body to enable such an investigation to take place does not violate the child's or the parent's rights. No *25274/94 Scharpf v Germany*, Dec 18.1995, unreported.

[20] No *27594/95 Santaniemi v Sweden*, Dec 10.9.97, unreported.

[21] Eur Court HR *Osman v UK*, judgment of 28 Oct 1998, Reports 1998-VIII, no 95, § 113-123.

[22] No *23452/94 Osman v UK*, Comm Rep, 1.7.97, Reports 1998-VIII, no 95.

offences against the person, will depend on the circumstances. In particular, it will only arise where it is established that the authorities

> knew or ought to have known at the time of the existence of a real and immediate risk to the life of an identified individual . . . from the criminal acts of a third party and that they failed to take measures within the scope of their powers . . . which might have been expected to avoid that risk.[23]

Having considered the facts of the case in detail, the Court concluded that this was not the case in *Osman*. In particular, it held that there was no decisive stage in the sequence of events leading up to the shooting where the police knew or ought to have known that the lives of the Osman family were at real and immediate risk. As a result, and having regard to the need for the police to discharge their duties in a manner which is compatible with the rights and freedoms of others, particularly the presumption of innocence, the Court concluded that there had been no violation of Article 2 in this case.[24]

However, the applicant also sought to challenge the police immunity rule, which prevented him from having his claim for negligence against the police authorities for failing to investigate and suppress the criminal acts of the stalker determined by the domestic courts. The Court considered this complaint in the context of a restriction on the right of access to a court under Article 6.[25] In brief, it found that the application of the police immunity rule, imposed by the domestic courts on public policy grounds, served to confer a blanket immunity on the police for their acts and omissions during the investigation and suppression of crime. The Court added that although there were legitimate public interest considerations for protecting the police from negligence actions, it must be open to a domestic court to have regard to the presence of other public interest considerations which pull in the opposite direction to the application of the rule. The failure to distinguish between degrees of negligence, or harm suffered meant that all applicants, no matter how deserving their claim, were prevented from having their claims examined on the merits. As a result,

---

[23] *Ibid*, § 116. The Court rejected the Government's submission that the failure to act must be tantamount to gross negligence, finding that standard too rigid and inconsistent with the obligation under the Convention to ensure practical and effective protection of its rights.

[24] Its conclusion was reached by 17 votes to 3. *Ibid*, § 169.

[25] *Ibid*, § 131-154.

the operation of the immunity rule constituted an unjustifiable restriction on the right of access to a court.

While this case has clear implications for the way in which the domestic courts in the UK consider such claims in negligence, on a wider scale, it marks further progress in the Court's procedural approach to the right to life. Most importantly, from the child's perspective, the judgment reflects a positive development in the application of Convention provisions to children. In particular, one of the factors to which the Court attached weight in reaching its conclusion under Article 6 was the fact that the case involved the alleged failure to protect the life of a child. Implicitly, then, the obligation which fell on the State under Article 2 was amplified by the fact that it was the life of a young child that was at risk.

Although Article 2 engages the responsibility of the State to take all measures to protect life, the State's responsibility does not appear to extend to cases where the error is made by a private doctor, detached from a public hospital.[26] This questionable decision of the Commission has not been confirmed by the Court, and it stands in direct contrast to case law which states clearly that the State cannot absolve itself of responsibility by delegating its obligations to private bodies of individuals.[27] In any event, it is argued that state liability must be incurred for any infringement of the right to life in an area of government responsibility, and this should not be influenced by the public or private status of the parties directly responsible. Any other perspective would appear to be unsustainable in the light of the fundamental nature of the right to life and the guarantee, under Article 1, that Convention rights are to be secured to everyone.[28]

Article 2 enjoins the State to take appropriate steps to safeguard the lives of those within its jurisdiction and it is this aspect of the right to life which has been the subject of recent judicial activity in Strasbourg. In *LCB v UK*, the applicant complained that the failure of the State to warn her father of the possible risk to her health which would be caused by his participation in the nuclear tests on Christmas Island in 1957 amounted to a breach of Article 2.[29] In the light of the fact that she had developed

---

[26] No *19158/91 Family de Gerando v France*, Dec 29.6.94, unreported. The Commission also referred to the fact that regardless, the procedural aspects of Article 2 were sufficient.

[27] Eur Court HR *Costello-Roberts v UK*, judgment of 25 March 1993, Series A no 247-C, 19 EHRR 112, § 27. See further Chapter 8, pp 167-168.

[28] See further Chapter 1, pp 12-13.

[29] Eur Court HR *LCB v UK*, judgment of 9 June 1998, Reports 1998-III, no 76.

leukaemia as a child, the Court had to consider whether, in the circumstances of the case, the State had done all that could have been required of it to prevent her life from being put avoidably at risk. In finding that it had, and consequently that there had been no violation of Article 2, the Court found it significant that there was a lack of certainty surrounding the causal link between exposure of a father to radiation and leukaemia in a child subsequently conceived. Nevertheless, it found that if, at the time, it was considered likely that her father's exposure to radiation might have engendered a real risk to her health, then the State would have been required to advise her parents to monitor her health. Thus this case observed a further clear development in the procedural element of the right to life under the Convention to the extent that where state action creates a real risk to health, then Article 2 imposes an obligation to inform the potential victim of that risk.[30]

*The Right to Life of the Unborn*

Although it refers to everyone's right to life, Article 2 does not expressly state to whom the right to life belongs, and leaves open whether it applies to the unborn child.[31] It is unclear therefore whether abortion is compatible with Article 2, or conversely, whether its unavailability constitutes an unjustifiable interference with private life under Article 8 § 2. The Court has so far avoided pronouncing definitively on whether the scope of Article 2 extends to life before birth[32] and the Commission has conveniently ignored opportunities to clarify the matter.

---

[30] Similar reasoning was used to interpret the positive obligation to respect family life in another recent case. Eur Court HR *Guerra v Italy*, judgment of 19 Feb 1998, Reports 1998-I, no 64, 26 EHRR 357.

[31] See Freeman (1984), 'The Unborn Child and the ECHR: To Whom Does Everyone's Right to Life Belong?', *Emory International Law Review*, 8(2), pp 615-665 and Hogan, 'The Right to Life and the Abortion Question under the European Convention on Human Rights', in Heffernan (Ed) (1994), *Human Rights: A European Perspective*, Dublin: Round Hall Press, pp 104-116. See also Chapter 2, pp 19-21.

[32] Eur Court HR *Open Door Counselling and Dublin Well Woman v Ireland*, judgment of 29 Oct 1992, Series A No 242, 15 EHRR 244, § 66 where a prohibition on the circulation of information on abortion services outside the State violated Article 10. See also Eur Court HR *Bowman v UK*, judgment of 19 Feb 1998, Reports 1998-I, no 63, 26 EHRR 1, where the Court found that the prosecution of the applicant for distributing details of the abortion views of

It is clear that Article 2 does not offer specific protection to the right to life of the unborn child.[33]    With regard to whether such protection is implicit in this provision, the Commission considered in the *Paton* case that Article 2 could conceivably be interpreted in one of three ways.[34]  The first possible interpretation is that Article 2 applies only after birth.  The second possibility is that the unborn child is entitled to enjoy the protection of Article 2 subject to limitations, and the third possible interpretation is that the provision recognises the right to life of the unborn child as absolute.  The Commission rejected this latter interpretation because of its implication that the right to life of the foetus would be regarded as being of a higher value than the life of the pregnant woman, whose right to life is also protected by Article 2.  It also found this interpretation to be contrary to the object and purpose of the Convention in light of the fact that, at the time of drafting, many Convention States allowed abortion where it was necessary to protect the life of the mother.  However, the Commission did not find it necessary to decide between the other two interpretations due to the nature of the case being examined and it is thus unresolved whether Article 2 protects the right to life of the unborn subject to limitations, or at all.[35]

The Commission has recognised the considerable divergence of views among Convention States as to whether the Convention protects unborn life and consequently it has concluded that they must enjoy a level of discretion in this area.[36]    This approach, which reflects perceived sensitivities in this controversial area, is evident throughout its case law.  For instance, the termination of a pregnancy in its tenth week in order to protect the physical or mental health of a pregnant woman has been found not to violate Article 2.[37]  Moreover, an abortion after fourteen weeks on the grounds that 'the pregnancy, birth or care for the child may place the mother in a difficult situation of life' has been found to be consistent with

---

election candidates prior to a general election violated her freedom of expression under Article 10.

[33]  No 8416/78 *Paton v UK*, Dec 13.5.80, 19 DR p 244, 3 EHRR 408.

[34]  *Ibid.*

[35]  *Ibid.*

[36]  See Peukert, 'Human Rights in International Law and the Protection of Unborn Beings' in Matscher & Petzold (eds) (1988), *Protecting Human Rights: The European Dimension, Studies in Honour of Gerard J Wiarda*,    Koln: Heymanns, 511-519,  at p 518.

[37]  No *8416/78 Paton v UK, op cit.*

the Convention.[38]    After fourteen weeks, however, it becomes unclear whether the termination of a pregnancy on these grounds is compatible with Article 2. Notwithstanding the uncertainty surrounding the level of protection which the Convention affords to the unborn child, therefore, it is arguable that where it constitutes a serious risk to her physical or emotional health, a mother enjoys an unlimited right to terminate her pregnancy within a specific period of time.[39]    The Commission has thus failed to clarify in what circumstances Article 2 may apply to the unborn child, although the application of the margin of appreciation supports the view that the grounds on which abortion is permissible under the Convention are broad.

In determining whether the unborn child enjoys the right to life, a question arises as to who is entitled to complain on the child's behalf. The obvious answer here is that a parent will be entitled to invoke Article 2 in this way, where an abortion has been performed without the consent of one of them.[40]    Where the abortion is performed without the mother's agreement, or where the issue is the broader one of sterilisation without consent, then this may be more appropriately dealt with under Article 3, which contains an absolute prohibition on treatment which is inhuman and degrading, or under Article 8, which protects the right to physical integrity as part of the right to respect for private life.[41]

Where abortion is unavailable to some-one who requests it and the parties concerned enjoy a family relationship, then it would seem more appropriate to invoke Article 8 and the right to respect for family life. In this regard, the question to be answered is whether the unavailability of abortion constitutes an interference with family life that can be justified with regard to the need to protect the rights of the unborn child. It is not yet established whether the unborn child is an entity within the meaning of

---

[38] No *17004/90 H v Norway*, Dec 19.5.92, DR 73, p 155.

[39] *Ibid.*

[40] In this regard, the Commission rejected the claim of a religious minister on the basis that he was not a victim under the Convention. No 11045/84 *Knudsen v Norway*, Dec 85, DR 42, p 247.

[41] An early case had suggested that sterilisation may involve a breach of the Convention. See No 1287/61, *X v Denmark*, unreported in Van Dijk & Van Hoof, *op cit*, at p 302, fn 43. However, the Commission recently dismissed as manifestly ill-founded the claim of a woman that she had been sterilised against her consent on the grounds that her ability to take both civil and criminal action in the domestic courts to challenge the surgeon's action sufficiently protected her right to respect for private life under Article 8. No 20393/92 *MD v Austria*, Dec 17.1.96, unreported.

'protection of the rights of others' under Article 8 § 2,[42] and thus the question of whether a mother could be forced to carry a child for a full term in order to protect the rights of the unborn child remains unanswered. However unlikely this prospect, it is by no means certain that the rights of the mother will always prevail where there is direct conflict between her rights and those of the foetus. Importantly, it has been recognised that pregnancy is not a uniquely private situation and consequently, there is no right of access to abortion under Article 8.[43] However, the rights of the mother have been found to be superior to those of the father in relation to the termination of pregnancy.[44] Although he may be so closely affected by the termination of the pregnancy that he can claim to be a victim under the Convention, the Commission has found that any interpretation of his right in connection with the mother's abortion must be preceded by consideration of the mother's rights, she being the person primarily concerned by the pregnancy's continuation or termination.

**The Right to Health Care**

There is clearly no right to an adequate standard of health or health care under the European Convention. Provision for medical care is implicit in certain provisions, however, especially Article 8, which protects *inter alia* the right to physical and psychological integrity as part of the right to respect for private life. In addition to refraining from interfering with this right, Article 8 may require the State to take positive measures to respect it. In particular, where the State has an obligation to provide medical care, an excessive delay of the public health service in providing a medical service to which the patient is entitled may raise an issue under the Convention. In order to rely on Article 8 in this way, the patient would have to establish that the delay has, or is likely to have, a serious impact on his/her health.[45] In addition, where the failure to provide medical services would result in a life-threatening situation, this might raise an issue under the right to life under Article 2,[46] or under Article 3, which prohibits inhuman and

---

[42] No *6959/75 Bruggemann & Scheuten v Germany*, Comm Rep 12.7.77, DR 10, p 100, 3 EHRR 244.

[43] *Ibid* and No *24844/94 Reeve v UK*, Dec 30.11.94, unreported.

[44] No *8416/78 Paton v UK, op cit.*

[45] No 32647/96 *Passannante v Italy*, Dec 1.7.98, 26 EHRR CD 153.

[46] No *6839/74 X v Ireland*, Dec 4.10.76, DR 7 p 78.

degrading treatment. For example, the Commission has found admissible a complaint regarding the failure of the authorities to observe, counsel or treat a suicidal prisoner.[47] Here, a mother alleges that the treatment of her son, in particular his segregation for 23 hours every day, amounted to inhuman and degrading treatment having regard to his medical condition, and she claims also that the prison authorities failed to take adequate and appropriate measures to secure effective protection of his life.

Compulsory medical treatment, however minor, may constitute an interference with the right to respect for private life. However, such treatment will not infringe the Convention as long as there is proportionality between the interference which it creates and the need to protect the public interest which it serves. This has been found to be particularly important where children are concerned, because they have limited possibilities to protect their own rights.[48] The same principle applies to dental treatment, where the Commission has found it significant that parents are free to choose the dentist to carry out the treatment required and may appeal any decision to carry out treatment.[49] These are clearly relevant factors to be taken into account in deciding whether compulsory medical treatment of children, which is against the wishes of their parents, will be consistent with respect for private and family life. In this regard, the Commission has found it compatible with Article 8 to take a child into care in order to carry out an operation, even where the child's parents preferred the non-surgical option.[50] The child's tragic death during surgery was found not to affect the fact that, at the time of the domestic decision, there were reasonable and sufficient reasons for taking the child into care. It is clear that the State enjoys a margin of appreciation in relation to respect for family life under Article 8 in such cases, as well as the manner in which it safeguards the child's right to health and life.

*Preventive Health Care*

Immunisation plays a significant role in preventive health care world-wide and its impact in the reduction of death and serious diseases among children is well documented.[51] In this context, the European Commission

---

[47] No 27229/95 *Keenan v UK*, Dec 22.5.98, 26 EHRR CD 64.

[48] No *22398/93 JR, GR, RR & YR v Switzerland*, Dec 5.4.95, DR 81, p 61.

[49] *Ibid.*

[50] No *16071/93 Wedberg and Hillblom v Sweden*, Dec 11.4.96, unreported.

[51] See Henderson 'Immunisation: Going the Extra Mile' in (1998) *The Progress of Nations*, New York, UNICEF.

has considered the compatibility of vaccination programmes with the Convention, and in doing so it has attempted to balance the right of the child (and children generally) to preventive health care with the right of parents to decide what is in their child's best interests. Notwithstanding that Article 2 obliges the State to take appropriate steps to safeguard life and to refrain from taking life intentionally, neither obligation is called into question by the implementation of an immunisation programme designed to protect the health of society. According to the Commission, this is despite the fact that a small number of fatalities occur as a result of the programme.[52] While proper liaison with parents, and informed health visitors are desirable, precautionary measures in the administration of a vaccine programme, the compatibility of a particular system of control and supervision with Article 2 will depend on the circumstances of the case.[53]

The failure to inform parents adequately of the risks involved in vaccinating their children arguably denies them the opportunity to make a decision with full knowledge of the facts and may give rise to a violation of Article 8 insofar as it interferes with choice making within the family. So far, however, the Commission has dismissed the complaints of parents, that the severe damage or death suffered as a result of vaccinations violated Article 8.[54] Although a decision to have a child vaccinated may not be based on a technical appreciation of the special risks involved, the Commission has accepted as common knowledge that immunisation schemes involve certain risks. As a result, it is legitimate for the State to leave checks for contra-indications to clinical judgement and, with regard to a voluntary scheme at least, respect for family life does not oblige the authorities to provide specific, detailed information to parents on either contra-indications, or the risks associated with particular vaccines.[55]

Compulsory screening may constitute an interference with family life however, particularly where non-compliance is a punishable offence.[56] Yet again, however, the interference is likely to be justifiable under Article 8 §

---

[52] No *7154/75 Association X v UK*, Dec 12.7.78, DR 14, p 31; No 26536/95 *Boffa et al v San Marino*, Dec 15.1.98, unreported, involving compulsory vaccination against Hepatitis B.

[53] No *7154/75 Association X v UK, op cit.*

[54] *Ibid.*

[55] See also No *8452/79 Godfrey v UK*, Dec 4.2.82, DR 27, p 94 and No *10787/84 Wain v UK*, Dec 12.85, 9 EHRR 122.

[56] No *10435/83 Acmanne & Ors v Belgium*, Dec 10.12.84, DR 40, p 251. In contrast, a voluntary vaccination programme does not interfere with family life. No *7154/75 Association X v UK, op cit.*

2 as necessary to protect public health.  Compulsory vaccination schemes will thus be compatible with the Convention insofar as they fall within the margin of appreciation enjoyed by the State in looking after the nation's health.[57]  It is uncertain whether respect for family life requires the State to provide specific and detailed information to parents on the risks associated with vaccines where the immunisation is compulsory.  However, it is unlikely that an inability to access relevant information with regard to compulsory vaccination will contradict either Article 10, which guarantees freedom of expression, or Article 9, which protects the freedom of thought, conscience or religion.[58]  This cannot be ruled out however.[59]

The lack of success enjoyed by those seeking to challenge compulsory vaccination programmes is not surprising given the role of the public health care system and the importance of the child's access to it.  Importantly in this area, the Commission has accepted that parents' wishes may not always coincide with their child's best interests and its recognition of the child's right to health, and the duty of the State to protect it, are positive developments in this context.  At the same time, there would appear to be little or no basis in the Convention for arguing for an individual right to be vaccinated in the event of an epidemic for example.  Any positive obligation to protect life or physical integrity under Articles 2 or 8 respectively would have to take into account the right of the State to take measures perceived to be in the interest of public health generally.

The Convention does not provide for a right to compensation where vaccination, either voluntary or compulsory, results in serious damage or death.[60]  Complaints relating to the inadequacy of compensation payments or even exclusion from a compensation scheme fall outside the scope of the Convention's substantive provisions therefore.  Article 13 may provide scope for a right to compensation, however, where the injury results from a violation of a Convention provision.  Thus, where the administration of a vaccine causes damage in violation of the right to respect for private and family life, the State may be required to provide an effective remedy for

---

[57] No 10545/83 *Acmanne & Ors v Belgium, ibid.*
[58] No 26536/95 *Boffa et al v San Marino, op cit.*
[59] See *Open Door  Counselling and Dublin Well Woman* judgment, *op cit*, which concerned the right of access to information on abortion services available outside the State.
[60] No *8542/79 Godfrey v UK, op cit* and No 10787/84 *Wain v UK, op cit.*

that violation in the form of a compensation payment in certain circumstances.[61]

*Standards of Treatment in Health Care*

Notwithstanding that the Convention does not set out specific conditions for the treatment of sick children,[62] the Commission has found it implicit in Article 2 that there is a positive obligation on the State to put in place regulations in hospitals, which are sufficient to ensure the protection of the life of the sick.[63] In theory, the standard of hospital care given to a particular patient could be challenged by invoking Article 3, given that complaints regarding the conditions of detention in a psychiatric institution have been considered under this provision.[64] However, the usefulness of Article 3 in this context is reduced by the fact that it only prohibits treatment, which deliberately causes severe mental or physical suffering.[65] Moreover, according to the Commission, the medical authorities have the power to decide on the therapeutic methods to be used to preserve the physical and mental health of patients for whom they are responsible.[66] The established rules of medicine applied in this situation are decisive in principle in this regard and, although patients are entitled to the protection of Article 3 as a general rule, a measure which is a therapeutic necessity cannot be regarded as inhuman or degrading. Nevertheless, before reaching a conclusion in such a case, the medical necessity for the treatment must be shown convincingly to exist.[67] In the absence of such evidence, it would be open to the Court to find a violation, although a margin of appreciation will inevitably apply.

---

[61] No *8452/79 Godfrey v UK, op cit*. On the effectiveness of remedies see Harris, O'Boyle & Warbrick, *op cit*, pp 616-617 and on Article 13, pp 443-461.

[62] On the standards in the UN Convention on the Rights of the Child, see Leary, *op cit*, pp 30-36.

[63] No *20948/92 Isiltan v Turkey, op cit*.

[64] Eur Court HR *Ashingdane v UK*, judgment of 28 May 1985, Series A no 93, 7 EHRR 528. However, the Strasbourg authorities have hesitated to find that conditions of detention in mental hospitals fall below the standard in Article 3. See Harris, O'Boyle & Warbrick, *op cit*, p 88.

[65] See further Chapter 8, pp 160-166.

[66] No *14551/88 Persson v Sweden*, Dec 3.5.93, unreported.

[67] *Ibid*. Here the Commission failed to find a violation of Article 3 where it was alleged that the medical care of a boy with physical and mental disabilities was inadequate and that his care had been assigned to inexperienced staff.

Article 8 is particularly relevant to the treatment, which a child enjoys while receiving hospital care. On the one hand, the right to respect for private life will require that the child is entitled to a degree of privacy although this will necessarily be balanced with considerations pertaining to the general interest under Article 8 § 2. For example, it is arguable that Article 8 entitles the child to enjoy any correspondence which s/he receives during a hospital stay without arbitrary interference by the hospital authorities.[68] Moreover, Article 8 requires that family life be respected while the child is in hospital and the inability of parents to enjoy private visits with their child may raise an issue under this provision. Any legal restriction placed on contact between a parent and child, beyond the normal limits on visiting hours, must satisfy the requirements of Article 8 by being in accordance with law.[69] Moreover, the conditions of the visits must be consistent with respect for their family life. Thus, a fair balance is to be struck between the interests of the parent being able to visit their child under acceptable conditions and the State's interest in ensuring adequate care of patients, considering also the interests of other visitors.[70] Relevant factors here will be whether the parent has a reasonable opportunity to visit the child in hospital without being unnecessarily disturbed, taking into account the physical surroundings (whether the child is in a ward with other children for example) and having regard to the character of the hospital as a public institution.

*Interfering with Family Life to Protect the Health and Life of the Child*

Although the child's right to health is not guaranteed under the Convention, Article 8 justifies the removal of the child from his/her family where it is necessary to protect the child's health or well-being.[71] Any measure of this kind must satisfy the requirements of Article 8 § 2, and the interference with family life which it creates must be balanced by relevant and sufficient reasons based on the need to protect the child. The margin of appreciation which the State enjoys in relation to the making of a care order in such circumstances means that the Strasbourg authorities are reluctant to interfere with a domestic decision of this kind.[72] As a result,

---

[68] See Eur Court HR *Golder v UK*, judgment of 1 June 1973, Series A no 18, 1 EHRR 524, relating to prisoner correspondence.

[69] No *14551/88 Persson v Sweden*, Comm Rep, 14.4.94, unreported, § 74 - 91.

[70] *Ibid*, § 66.

[71] See also above.

[72] See further Chapter 12, pp 263-271.

the Commission has frequently accepted that an interference with family life is justifiable under Article 8 § 2 where the physical or mental health of the child is at risk.[73] Moreover, where children are found to be living in deplorable conditions without light or heat, their removal into care has also been found to be compatible with the Convention.[74] The Commission has been seen to attach considerable weight to living standards in its consideration of whether a decision awarding custody to a parent is consistent with respect for family life of the other parent. For example, in one case it found that the economic and educational benefits which would accrue to children living in South Africa partly justified the interference with the father's family life which would result from their move there with their mother.[75] The advantage of better living conditions is unlikely to be anything other than a contributory factor in its assessment of such a case, however, and a care order based solely on this justification would arguably be inconsistent with respect for family life under Article 8. This is consistent with the Commission's more decisive view that only the most pressing grounds can justify removing a child from the family, even when material conditions are poor.[76]

## The Right to a Healthy Environment

One of the dynamic departures in Article 8 jurisprudence is marked by the *Lopez Ostra* case, in which the Court found the right to a healthy environment to be an implicit part of the right to respect for private life and home.[77] In this case, a mother of two children complained that the legal installation and operation, a few metres from her home, of a treatment plant which gave off pestilent smells, persistent noise and pollutant fumes made her living conditions unbearable and caused her and her children serious health problems. The Commission and Court agreed that serious pollution

---

[73] See No *4004/69 WX & HX v UK*, Dec 16.3.70, Collection 33, p 18; No *5132/72 X v Denmark*, Dec 12.8.71, Collection 43, p 57, and No *12651/87 Grufmann v Sweden*, Dec 9.5.89, DR 61, p 176.

[74] No *8059/77 X & Y v Germany*, Dec 3.10.78, DR 15, p 208.

[75] No *9867/82 X v UK*, Dec 10.82, 5 EHRR 489. No *2707/66 Kurtz & Seltmann v Germany*, Dec 4.4.67, Collection 25, p 28, which concerned whether a better standard or living existed in former West Germany, than in the former East.

[76] No *8059/77 X & Y v Germany, op cit*.

[77] Eur Court HR *Lopez Ostra v Spain*, judgment of 9 Dec 1994, Series A no 303.

can affect the physical well-being of a person thereby interfering with his private life or depriving him of enjoyment of the amenities of his home.[78] In considering the balance between the interests of the individual and the community as a whole, the cause and effect relationship between the applicant's daughter's health problems and the pollutant emissions from the plant was deemed to be established.[79]    Importantly, both institutions concluded that, although the authorities were not directly responsible, they had tolerated the plant by allowing it to be built on Government land and subsidising its construction.[80]    As a result, the respondent State was held liable for the breach of Article 8, in terms of the risks which the pollution caused to the child's health.    It is uncertain whether state responsibility would be incurred where the treatment plant is a purely private venture, although the necessity of planning permission would invoke some degree of state responsibility.    In any event, it is arguable that Article 8 places a positive obligation on the State to protect the well-being of everyone within its jurisdiction from the effects of serious environmental pollution, regardless of whether the perpetrator is a private or a public company.    This view is supported by the conclusion of the Court in the *Guerra* case in 1998, where it found that the authorities had failed to fulfil the obligation to respect private and family life in this respect.    In particular, they had failed to provide the applicants with information about the risks which they might face by continuing to live in a town particularly exposed to danger in the event of an accident at the factory in question.[81]

**Health Education**

The importance of accessing information necessary to safeguard the right to life and health and to protect children from risks of the abuse of such rights has been highlighted above under various Convention provisions. Notwithstanding that the provision of family planning education is an important aspect of the right to health care,[82] it has not yet been found to be

---

[78]    *Ibid*, and No *16798/90 Lopez Ostra v Spain*, Comm Rep, 8.8.92, Series A no 303, p 60.

[79]    *Lopez Ostra* judgment, *op cit*, § 51.

[80]    *Ibid*, § 58.

[81]    *Guerra* judgment, *op cit*, § 56-60.

[82]    See Article 24 § 2(f) of the Convention on the Rights of the Child, *op cit*, which the Committee has interpreted to mean that young people should be provided with sex education. UN Doc CRC/C/15/Add.34, § 14.

implicit in the right to respect for private and family life. The Commission has recognised that Article 12, which guarantees the right to marry and found a family, may call for sex education in certain Convention States.[83] In addition, instruction on sex and pregnancy, imparted in a biological or emotional context, amounts to education within the meaning of Article 2 of the First Protocol.[84] The negative formulation of the right to education would appear to preclude reliance on Article 2 of the First Protocol to require domestic authorities to provide sex education to children in schools.[85] However, a system which integrates the subject into the school curriculum on a compulsory basis must present the material in an objective and pluralistic manner so as to ensure that parents' convictions in the education of their children are respected.

In the *Danish Sex Education Case*, several parents complained that the integration of sex education into the school curriculum as a compulsory subject infringed their right under Article 2 of the First Protocol, to have their children educated in conformity with their religious and philosophical beliefs.[86] Their claims were rejected however and both the Commission and the Court made a number of important points in doing so.[87] Firstly, it was established that instruction on sex and pregnancy falls within the scope of Article 2 of the First Protocol, where the child's right to receive such education in the first sentence is dominant over respect for parental convictions in the second sentence.[88] The Convention thus requires domestic authorities to respect the beliefs of parents only insofar as they do not interfere with the child's right to education. Secondly, the second sentence of Article 2 does not entitle parents to object to the integrated teaching of certain information, but rather obliges States in the fulfilment

---

[83] Nos *5095/71, 5920/72 & 5926/72 Kjeldsen, Busk Madsen & Pedersen v Denmark*, Comm Rep, 21.3.75, unreported, § 162.

[84] *Ibid*, § 148.

[85] See further Furmiss & Blair (1997), 'Sex Wars: Conflict in and Reform of Sex Education in Maintained Secondary Schools', *Journal of Social Welfare and Family Law*, **19**(2), pp 189-202. See also Chapter 4, pp 78-79.

[86] See the concerns of the Committee on the Rights of the Child in relation to the parental right to withdraw children from sex education. UN Doc CRC/C/15/Add.34, § 14.

[87] Nos *5095/71, 5920/72 & 5926/72 Kjeldsen, Busk Madsen & Pedersen v Denmark*, Comm Rep, *op cit*, and Eur Court HR *Kjeldsen, Busk Madsen & Pedersen v Denmark*, judgment of 7 Dec 1976, Series A, no 23, 1 EHRR 711.

[88] *Kjeldsen, Busk Madsen & Pedersen* Comm Rep, *ibid*, § 149 and judgment, *ibid*, § 50.

of its functions in education to ensure that material in the school curriculum is conveyed in an objective and pluralistic manner.[89]  On the facts of the case, the purpose of sex education in Danish schools was found not to impose a particular morality (or lack of it) on children, but rather provided them with objective information on biological and other facts of human life.[90]  Thus, although it involved moral considerations, these were general in character and did not overstep the boundaries of what a democratic state may regard as in the public interest.   Thirdly, the introduction of sex education into schools on a compulsory basis served the public interest, especially given that the importance of imparting knowledge in sexual matters to children had become clear in the light of increased teenage pregnancies and sexually transmitted diseases in many countries.[91]  It also found it reasonable that schools should be chosen as the centres for such education.  In achieving a balance that was proportionate in the circumstances, it was noted that the relevant legislation did not affect the right of parents to advise their own children in line with their convictions and the Court attached significance to the fact that parents who wished to disassociate their children from integrated sex education could send their children to private schools which were highly subsidised and bound by more lenient obligations, or alternatively, they could educate them at home.[92]

Sex education thus clearly falls within the State's role as educator and in fulfilling this role, the authorities must take care that information is portrayed in an objective manner, whatever the context.  The State is required to regulate the distribution of suitable sex education material and to ensure that the border between sex education and pornography is not crossed. Educational materials distributed by private persons may also be regulated by the State in the light of the duties and responsibilities which pertain to the exercise of the freedom of expression under Article 10, and

---

[89]  *Kjeldsen, Busk Madsen & Pedersen* Comm Rep, *ibid,* § 153 and judgment, *ibid,* § 53.

[90]  *Kjeldsen, Busk Madsen & Pedersen* Comm Rep, *ibid,* § 164 and judgment, *ibid,* § 54.

[91]  *Kjeldsen, Busk Madsen & Pedersen* Comm Rep, *ibid,* § 163 and judgment, *ibid.*

[92]  *Kjeldsen, Busk Madsen & Pedersen* judgment, *ibid,* § 54.  Contrast the Court majority of six votes to one with the Commission's split decision, the vote of the President being cast against the finding of a violation.  The minority of the Court followed Judge Verdross' opinion that objective information on sexual activity given at too early an age could violate the religious convictions of parents under Article 2.

restrictions may legitimately be placed on this right where it is necessary to protect health or morals.[93] As a result, those distributing material aimed at promoting sex education for young people must pay particular attention to the quality of the publications which they circulate, taking care not to distribute information which may be considered pornographic.[94]

**Future Challenges**

The ruling in 1979 that the Convention could be interpreted in a way that extended its remit into social and economic rights has provided to be a sound basis for such development. The use of this and other dynamic interpretive approaches have meant that the absence from the Convention of express guarantees of social and economic rights has not been decisive for the protection which the Convention offers children in this area. Nor has the Convention's potential in this regard yet been reached.

The considerable development of the procedural guarantees under the Convention in this area suggests that the emphasis on remedies and procedures is likely to continue. It is extremely significant that the Convention has been found to impose an obligation on the police to take preventive protective measures in certain circumstances, as well to conduct criminal investigations with due care. These principles have particular merit with regard to the right to challenge the actions or omissions of the police with regard to their investigative duties.

Also significant has been the development of the right to information regarding the risks to health and life. Although the scope of this obligation is not yet clear, it may be possible to invoke it in challenging preventable environmental and industrial disasters, such as oil spills, leaks from nuclear or other power stations, and even the alleged danger posed by mobile phone masts. Other prospective challenges may arise in relation to the national health service, where inadequate medical treatment, or a delay in treatment, may raise an issue under Article 3 or Article 8, where it can be established that it has had a detrimental impact on the child health. The ability to challenge acts and omissions of this kind in the domestic courts will no doubt be decisive as to whether they will breach the Convention and further development of positive and procedural obligations under Articles 2, 3 and 8 is likely in this regard.

---

[93]  See further Chapter 6, pp 128-132.
[94]  Nos *6782, 6783, 6784/74 X, Y & Z v Belgium*, Dec 1.3.77, DR 9, p 14.

# 8    Abuse and Neglect

## Introduction

The absence of children's rights standards from the European Convention on Human Rights is probably most critical with regard to the need to protect the child from harm or physical ill-treatment. In contrast to the UN Convention on the Rights of the Child, which places a comprehensive obligation on States to protect children from all forms of violence, abuse and maltreatment,[1] the European Convention contains no such provision, specific to children or otherwise. Notwithstanding the absence of more specific standards, however, the Convention has been invoked with growing success in relation to the issues of corporal punishment, physical punishment within the family and the protection of the child from abuse and neglect generally. Both Article 8, which guarantees both the right to physical integrity as part of private life as well as the right to respect for family life, and Article 3, which contains an absolute prohibition on inhuman and degrading treatment have proven relevant in this context. Moreover, the application to these provisions of various dynamic interpretive approaches has led to considerable enhancement of the protection which the Convention affords children in this area.

## Protection under Article 3

### Physical Punishment

Article 3 of the Convention prohibits torture, inhuman and degrading treatment and punishment.[2] Due to the absolute nature of the prohibition, only ill-treatment which attains a minimum level of severity will fall within its scope and a breach of the provision is thus particularly difficult to

---

[1]    See Article 19, UN Doc A/44/25.

[2]    See generally Harris, O'Boyle & Warbrick (1995), *Law of the European Convention on Human Rights*, London: Butterworths, pp 55-89 and Van Dijk & Van Hoof (1998), *Theory and Practice of the European Convention on Human Rights*, 3rd ed, The Hague: Kluwer, pp 309-334.

establish. It is important to children, however, that the assessment of whether this level is reached is a relative one. In particular, the Court has held that it

> depends on all the circumstances of the case, such as the duration of the treatment, its physical or mental effects and, in some cases, the sex, age and state of health of the victim.[3]

This principle thus offers adequate scope for interpreting Article 3 in a way which offers protection to children from physical assault or abuse.

This was first illustrated in the *Tyrer* case,[4] which concerned a judicial sentence of three strokes of the birch imposed by an Isle of Man court on a 15 year old boy convicted of actual bodily harm.[5] Considering whether the treatment constituted degrading punishment contrary to Article 3, the Court noted that the humiliation involved must attain a particular level depending on all the circumstances of the case. Tyrer's sentence had been carried out in private by a police constable three weeks after it was passed, and he was not found to have suffered any physical or psychological effects. The fact that the punishment was administered by a stranger over the boy's bare posterior aggravated the degrading nature of the punishment, although it, alone, was not the determining factor. Nor was it decisive that the punishment took place in private, because while publicity may be relevant, the Court found that its absence will not necessarily prevent it from falling within the prohibited category because the victim may be humiliated in his/her own eyes. It was the cumulative effect of these factors, therefore, that persuaded the Court that the punishment was degrading. Nevertheless, the Court was clearly convinced more by the humiliating nature of the judicial punishment, than by the facts of the particular case in finding that the treatment violated Article 3.[6] This is epitomised by its statement that:

---

[3] Eur Court HR *Ireland v UK*, judgment of 18 Jan 1978, Series A no 25, 2 EHRR 25, § 162.

[4] Eur Court HR *Tyrer v UK*, judgment of 25 April 1978, Series A, no 26, 2 EHRR 1.

[5] On compatibility of sentencing with the Convention see Chapter 3, pp 52-55.

[6] See also Edge (1994), 'Dancing to the Beat of Europe', *New Law Journal*, **144**, p 770.

his punishment, whereby he was treated as an object in the power of the authorities, constituted an assault on precisely that which it is the main purpose of Article 3 to protect, i.e. dignity and physical integrity.[7]

Moreover, having established that the Convention should be interpreted in the light of present day conditions, the Court went on to apply this principle by finding that in considering the case, it could not but 'be influenced by the developments and commonly accepted standards in the penal policy of the Member States of the Council of Europe'.[8] Thus, the *Tyrer* judgment also confirmed the absolute nature of the prohibition of degrading treatment, as the Court rejected that public support for the use of the punishment in the Isle of Man was relevant to its compatibility with the Convention.[9] It thereby reinforced Article 3 as a non-derogable standard, which prohibits treatment for which there can be no justification, and in the application of which, no national adjustment may be made to take account of local sensitivities.

Given the weight attached by the Court to the official and institutional nature of the punishment in *Tyrer*, it is arguable that its severity was merely an aggravating factor. This emphasis on the institutional setting of the punishment made it difficult to determine what degree of severe or humiliating punishment a young person would have to experience outside the institutional setting before Article 3 could be invoked successfully.[10] Procedural obstacles and friendly settlements denied both the Commission and the Court an early opportunity to determine how the provision would apply to a less severe case of corporal punishment.[11] Complaints found

---

[7]    *Tyrer* judgment, *op cit*, § 33. See also No 5856/72 *Tyrer v UK*, Comm Rep, 14.12.76, Series B no 24, pp 22-30.

[8]    *Tyrer* judgment, *op cit*, § 31. The Isle of Man was the only territory in the Council of Europe still applying the punishment of birching to juveniles.

[9]    This support was noted by dissenting members of the Commission and the Court. Mr Mangan, dissenting from the Commission, found that 'the whipping ordered ...was no more physically severe than what many parents or teachers...consider themselves justified in administering to their offspring or pupils', *Tyrer* Comm Rep, *op cit*.

[10]    See Zellick (1978), 'Corporal Punishment in the Isle of Man', *International Comparative Law Quarterly*, **27**, pp 665-671 and Bonner (1979), 'The Beginning of the End for Corporal Punishment', *Modern Law Review*, **42**, pp 580-586.

[11]    It appears that the issue of physical punishment before the Strasbourg organs is an all British affair with the cost of defending about 30 cases before the

admissible by the Commission have included that of a 14 year old who was subject to three strokes of the cane which left her scarred for a couple of months,[12] and those of two sisters who received blows from a tawse across the hand and the buttocks respectively.[13] Notwithstanding that they were not considered on their merits by the Commission or the Court, the large sums paid to the applicants in settlement of these cases suggests that the punishment was severe enough to breach Article 3.[14] This view is supported further by *Warwick*, where the Commission found that one stroke of a cane given to a 16 year old girl constituted degrading punishment, in violation of Article 3.[15] Here, however, the Commission distinguished judicial corporal punishment from school corporal punishment, finding that the institutionalised character of the former was not evident as a matter of principle in cases of moderate school physical punishment.[16] This did not preclude such treatment from falling foul of Article 3, however, but merely served to recognise the different circumstances in which the punishment was administered. The element of humiliation was nonetheless important in *Warwick*, in which it was decisive that the punishment involved

> physical injury inflicted by a man, in the presence of another man, on a 16 year old girl who under domestic legislation is a woman of marriageable age.[17]

---

Commission in 1985 estimated at about £4 million. Khan, 'Corporal Punishment in Schools' 7(1) *Education and the Law* (1995) 1-11, at p 3.

[12]   No 7907/77 *Mrs X v UK*, Dec 2.7.78, DR 14, p 205. See further Khan (1995), 'Corporal Punishment in Schools', *Education and the Law*, 7, p 1-11, at p 3.

[13]   No 10592/83 *v UK*, Dec 1.86, 9 EHRR 277.

[14]   One applicant was awarded £1,200 compensation and the Government also undertook to inform the local educational authorities that corporal punishment may, in certain circumstances, amount to treatment contrary to Article 3. No 7907/77 *Mrs X v UK*, Comm Rep, 17.12.81, 24 *Yearbook* (1983), p 402. In the latter case, the children received £3,000 and £1,500 respectively. See No 10592/83 v UK, Comm Rep, 16.7.87, DR 52, p 150.

[15]   No 9471/81 *Warwick v UK*, Comm Rep, 18.7.86, DR 60, p 5, § 86-88.

[16]   *Ibid.* The local education authority had not drawn up any formal guidelines on the use of the punishment in schools, suggesting that the institutional character was lacking.

[17]   *Ibid*, § 87.

The injury was not trivial given that its effect lasted over one week and it could not be excluded that the punishment had an adverse psychological impact. As a result, it was the combined physical and emotional effects of the treatment which led to the conclusion that it was degrading within the meaning of Article 3.[18] The Commission used the same reasoning to find that a 15 year old boy, who had been caned four times through his trousers, had also been the victim of degrading treatment contrary to Article 3, noting that the punishment had caused him significant pain and humiliation.[19] In particular, the Commission found in *Y v UK* that the boy's treatment was both unacceptable and unjustifiable, regardless of who administered it and any pedagogical reasoning behind it.

On the same day as it decided the *Y* case, the Commission gave its opinion in the case of *Costello-Roberts*, also against the UK.[20] Costello-Roberts was a 7 year old boy who was given three 'whacks' on the bottom with a gym shoe by his headmaster and he complained that this treatment violated Article 3.[21] The Commission found that in all the circumstances the mild punishment at issue did not amount to degrading treatment within the meaning of that provision.[22] In its consideration of the case, the Court expressed reservations about the automatic nature of the punishment, which was imposed when the boy reached a certain number of demerit points for misbehaviour, as well as the three day wait.[23] Nevertheless, it went on to distinguish the present case from *Tyrer* on the grounds that both factors of severity and humiliation were of a lesser degree and concluded therefore that there was no violation of Article 3.[24] In particular, the Court

---

[18] *Ibid.* The Education (No 2) Act 1986 abolished corporal punishment in public schools.

[19] No 14229/88 *Y v UK*, Comm Rep, 8.10.91, Series A no 247, 17 EHRR 240, § 43-45. The case was settled with a payment of £9,000 being made to the applicant.

[20] No 13134/87 *Costello-Roberts v UK*, Comm Rep, 8.10.91, Series A no 247, p 66, 19 EHRR 119.

[21] He also complained under Article 8. See below, p 175.

[22] *Costello-Roberts* Comm Rep, op cit, § 39-42.

[23] Eur Court HR *Costello-Roberts v UK*, judgment of 25 March 1993, Series A no 247-C, 19 EHRR 112.

[24] Moreover, four dissenting judges expressed the view that the punishment was degrading because of its official and formalised nature, the fact that it had been meted out without the adequate consent of the mother, and because it had involved the headmaster whacking a lonely and insecure seven year old boy

noted that the boy in this case was much younger than *Tyrer*, he had suffered no severe effects from the punishment, which was administered over his trousers, after a much shorter delay and the official nature of the humiliation suffered by *Tyrer* was also absent here.

The Court's approach places emphasis clearly on the institutional or official setting of the punishment, rather than on its severe or degrading nature and its effect is thus to place a conceptual limit on the potential of Article 3 to protect children from certain types of physical punishment. For example, it poses particular difficulty for those seeking to invoke Article 3 in a case of physical punishment administered by a parent or child-minder, where the institutionalised setting is obviously absent. Moreover, the Court's approach in *Costello-Roberts* ignores that, in accordance with the *Tyrer* criteria, the notion of degrading punishment can be experienced as much during a severe beating, as during a slap or a severe telling off in front of peers or members of the public. A preferable approach to such cases would be to consider that all physical punishment is capable of infringing a child's dignity and physical integrity, which it is the purpose of Article 3 to protect.[25] The Court could then go on to consider whether on the facts of an individual case the minimum level of severity necessary to breach Article 3 has been attained. The application of the threshold will ensure that Article 3's important standard is not trivialised, but merely adapted to changing circumstances.

These conceptual difficulties will not pose a problem where the physical punishment is severe in itself. This was evident in a recent case against the UK in which punishment administered with a garden cane on a 9 year old boy on two or three occasions within the period of one week was found to be degrading within the meaning of Article 3. At least some of the strokes were inflicted directly onto the bare skin and they caused severe bruising which was visible several days later. Moreover, the injuries were considered to be sufficiently serious to merit the initiation of criminal proceedings against the boy's stepfather, and this was a relevant factor,

---

after a three-day gap. See the Dissenting Opinion of Judges Ryssdal, Vilhjalmsson, Matscher and Wildhaber, *ibid.*

[25] The Committee on the Rights of the Child disagrees with physical punishment *per se* due to the infringement which it involves on the child's dignity. See UN Doc CRC/C/15/Add.34. See Editorial (1993), 'Corporal Punishment and the Abuse of Children', *Practitioner's Child Law Bulletin*, 6, pp 26-27.

notwithstanding that he was acquitted in the domestic court.[26]    On consideration of these facts, and noting the similarity with the cases of *Warwick* and *Y v UK*, the Commission had little difficulty finding that the treatment suffered by the boy amounted to degrading punishment.[27]  The Court reached the same conclusion.[28]  Thus, the *A* case reinforces that only physical punishment which causes physical injury or humiliation of a particular severity will fall within the scope of Article 3.  There is as yet no evidence to suggest that punishment of a mild nature, such as slapping, will reach the level required to breach that provision.[29]

The threat of treatment contrary to Article 3 may raise an issue under that provision in certain circumstances, provided it is sufficiently real and immediate.[30]  In the context of physical punishment however, a breach of Article 3 will only be found where humiliation or debasement attaining a level of severity has actually been experienced.[31]  Thus, a risk or threat of such treatment will be insufficient to breach Article 3, although the Commission has refused to exclude that

> young and sensitive children may suffer adverse effects by the use of violence around them and by the very fact that they are themselves under the threat in principle of corporal punishment if they misbehave.[32]

According to the Court, pupils attending a school where corporal punishment is in use are not humiliated solely because they are at risk of being subjected to such treatment; nor are feelings of apprehension or disquiet sufficient to amount to a breach of Article 3 in this way.[33]

---

[26]  See further below pp 167-170.

[27]  No 25599/94 *A v UK*, Comm Rep, 18.9.97, Reports 1998-VI, no 90, § 39-41.

[28]  Eur Court HR *A v UK*, judgment of 23 Sept 1998, Reports 1998-VI no 90, § 21.

[29]  Smith (1999) 'To Smack or not to Smack?  A Review of A v UK in an International and European Context and its Potential Impact on Physical Parental Chastisement', *Web Journal of Current Legal Issues* 1.

[30]  See for example Eur Court HR *Soering v UK*, judgment of 7 July 1989, Series A no 161, 11 EHRR 439.  See Harris, O'Boyle & Warbrick, *op cit*, pp 74-80.

[31]  Eur Court HR *Campbell & Cosans v UK*, judgment of 25 Feb 1982, Series A no 48, 4 EHRR 293, § 28.

[32]  No *7511/76 & 7743/76 Campbell & Cosans v UK*, Comm Rep, 5.80, Series A no 48, 3 EHRR 531, § 122.

[33]  *Campbell & Cosans* judgment, *op cit*, § 26-31.  Cf the comments of the dissenting judges in *Costello-Roberts* judgment, *op cit*, that 'given that corporal punishment was being progressively outlawed elsewhere, it must have appeared

**State Responsibility for Breaches of Article 3**

While there has never been any doubt that Article 3 prohibits acts of torture, inhuman and degrading treatment or punishment carried out by an official or agent of the State, the question of whether the provision could be used to challenge the conduct of private individuals was left unanswered until very recently. It was first addressed in *Costello-Roberts,* where the applicant who had received corporal punishment from the headmaster of the private school which he attended, complained that his ill-treatment constituted a violation of Article 3, for which the State was responsible.[34] The Court established its dynamic approach to the issue of state responsibility in this case, and took Article 1, which guarantees that Convention rights are to be secured to everyone, as its starting point in this regard. It deduced from that provision that the responsibility of the State is engaged if a violation of one of the rights in the Convention results from non-observance of its obligations. Given the case's educational context, it found it relevant that a school's disciplinary regime falls within the scope of the right to education. As no distinction can be made in the way in which the right to education is guaranteed, the State will be responsible for any treatment of children which falls foul of Article 3, regardless of whether they attend state or independent schools.[35] In its consideration of the matter, the Commission had found that the State may also be liable to protect the right to respect for private life of pupils in private schools, to the extent that corporal punishment in such schools may involve an unjustified interference with a child's physical and emotional integrity under Article 8.[36] Hence, as long as a punishment entails adverse effects for a child's physical or moral integrity severe enough to violate either Convention provision, state responsibility will be incurred. Although the treatment in *Costello-Roberts* failed to attain the minimum level of severity required for this purpose, the judgment nonetheless means that the State cannot absolve itself from responsibility by delegating its obligations to private individuals or bodies.

---

all the more degrading to those remaining pupils in independent schools whose disciplinary regimes persisted in punishing people in this way'.

[34] *Costello-Roberts* judgment, *op cit.* See further above, pp 164-165.

[35] *Ibid*, § 27.

[36] *Costello-Roberts* Comm Rep, *op cit*, § *45-55.*

The Court extended the notion of state responsibility even further in 1998, in the case of *A v UK*.[37] The applicant, who was a nine year old boy, complained that the State's failure to protect him from the physical beatings of his stepfather amounted to a violation of Article 3. Having found that the punishment inflicted on him was degrading within the meaning of that provision,[38] the Court went on to examine the more difficult issue of whether the State could be held responsible for the punishment which was administered by a private person in the capacity of *loco parentis*. In this regard, the Court found that Article 1, read together with Article 3, required states to take measures designed to ensure that individuals within their jurisdictions are not subjected to inhuman or degrading treatment or punishment, even where it is administered by private individuals. Importantly, the Court noted that children must have state protection, in the form of effective deterrence, against serious breaches of personal integrity due to their vulnerability. In light of the fact that the boy's stepfather was acquitted by a domestic court of ill-treatment, which was severe enough to fall within the scope of Article 3, the Court concluded that the level of protection provided by the State was inadequate in this regard.[39]

The Commission's consideration of the matter was significantly more comprehensive and hence provides greater guidance as to the scope of the State's obligation to protect children from ill-treatment.[40] While it recognised that a State cannot guarantee through its legal system that inhuman and degrading treatment can never be inflicted by one individual on another, the Commission found that state responsibility will be incurred where it is shown that the domestic legal system, in particular the relevant criminal law, fails to provide practical and effective protection of the rights guaranteed by Article 3. In determining whether such protection was provided, the Commission attached importance to the international recognition of the need to protect children from all forms of ill-treatment and noted in particular Article 19 of the UN Convention on the Rights of the Child, which requires states to take all appropriate measures to 'protect the child from all forms of physical or mental violence, injury or abuse'.[41] In terms of the protection available to the applicant, the Commission noted

---

[37] *A* judgment, *op cit.*

[38] See further above, p 165-166.

[39] *A* judgment, *op cit*, § 22-24.

[40] *A* Comm Rep, *op cit*, § 42-55.

[41] *Ibid.*

that the relevant English law provides criminal sanctions against assault. However, it went on to find that

> the protection afforded in this area by the law to children within the home is significantly reduced by the defence open to parents...that the acts in question were lawful, as involving the reasonable and moderate physical punishment of the child. [42]

However, it was the operation of this defence which caused the Commission most concern. In particular, it noted that, in such cases, the burden lies on the prosecution to negative the defence, by satisfying a jury beyond reasonable doubt that the punishment was not in all the circumstances reasonable or moderate. The defendant is thus not required to substantiate the reasonable and moderate value of the punishment applied. The fundamental problem in this case, however, was that the jury, which was required to consider this defence, was provided with little guidance as to the meaning of reasonable and moderate chastisement. This is significant, not least because this imprecise expression had led the UN Committee on the Rights of the Child in 1995 to express its concern about the possibility of it being interpreted in an arbitrary and subjective manner.[43] The Commission added its own concern to the UN Committee's, noting that the jury did not receive direction on the relevance of such factors as the age or state of health of the applicant, the appropriateness of the instrument used in his chastisement, the suffering experienced or the relevance, if any, of the defence claim that the punishment was 'necessary' and 'justified'. As a result, and unconvinced by the Government's reliance on reported cases where convictions had been obtained in cases involving excessive physical punishment, the Commission concluded that domestic law had failed to provide the applicant with adequate and effective protection against corporal punishment which was, in the circumstances, degrading within the meaning of Article 3.

It is significant that the Commission has provided such detailed consideration of the factors relevant to this case. Similarly, the Commission's reference to the Convention on the Rights of the Child, as

---

[42]  *Ibid*, § 50.

[43]  UN Doc CRC/C/15/Add.34, § 16.  See further Kilkelly (1996), 'The UN Committee on the Rights of the Child - An Evaluation in the Light of Recent UK Experience', *Child and Family Law Quarterly*, **8**(2), pp 105-120, at pp 114-115.

well as the observations of the UN Committee following its consideration of the UK's implementation of the Convention, is illustrative of a dynamic approach. In particular, it is evidence of how reliance on the child-specific standards of the UN Convention in order to interpret the European Convention in children's cases can produce positive results. Moreover, in States which have incorporated the European Convention, but not the Convention on the Rights of the Child, this approach provides an opportunity to cite the latter Convention's higher, more detailed standards in domestic courts.

**Protection under Article 8**

Article 8 can be used to protect children from ill-treatment in two ways. The most direct form of protection is provided by the right to physical integrity, which must be respected as part of private life under Article 8. Secondly, it is clearly justifiable to remove a child from the family where it is necessary to protect the child's rights and best interests. In this regard, the child only enjoys the protection of Article 8 indirectly, as the focus is on balancing the interference with family life with the need to protect the child, and not on the latter in itself. Nevertheless, case law on Article 8 illustrates how the provision protects children through the rejection of parents' disproportionate and competing claims to family life.

*Interfering with Family Life to Protect the Child from Abuse*

While Article 8 permits the authorities to remove children from the family environment where it is necessary to protect them, its aim is to prevent the abuse of such powers by the State.[44] In this regard, only those measures which fulfil a pressing social need will be compatible with the Convention and hence, there must be proportionality between the interference with family life and the need to protect the child under Article 8 § 2. The special position of domestic authorities, which are close to the sensitive and complex factual issues to be determined in such cases, requires them to enjoy a degree of latitude with regard to the way in which Article 8 is respected. This margin of appreciation means, therefore, that the Strasbourg institutions exercise judicial restraint insofar as they rarely interfere with domestic decisions to remove children from the family where

---

[44]   See further the discussion in Chapter 12.

abuse or neglect is suspected or confirmed, as long as the reasons put forward in support of the care order are relevant and sufficient.

As early as 1960, the Commission found it compatible with the Convention that a father, who had assaulted his children, was denied contact with them, even when the children themselves complained that this breached their right to respect for family life.[45] Similarly, in 1963, the decision to award custody of a child to her mother, where her father had been convicted of indecently assaulting her, was found to be consistent with Article 8.[46] If the relevant parent has been convicted of abuse by the domestic courts, then the Strasbourg decision, that the removal of the children from his/her care is a justifiable interference with family life, will be relatively clear cut. However, if the issue of abuse or maltreatment has not been judicially determined, evidence of such ill-treatment may nonetheless constitute a relevant and sufficient reason for removing the child from a parent's care. For instance, where a child is brought to hospital with injuries consistent with maltreatment, in the absence of proof that they were inflicted by the parent, the injuries may in themselves cast doubt over the sufficiency of the parent's supervision in a manner which serves to justify the removal of the child into care.[47] In this way, the Commission may avoid considering whether the allegation of abuse was false and the care order unjustified, although a complaint found admissible in 1998 may require consideration of this substantive issue.[48] The case concerns the wrongful removal of the child from her family after employees of the local authority erroneously identified the mother's cohabitee as the child's abuser. This allegation is contested by the family, including the child herself, who argue therefore that her removal from the family was an unjustified interference with her family life, for which the State was responsible.[49] Although the outcome of this case may turn on the availability of means to challenge the local authority's actions, existing Commission case law is relevant to the substantive issue. In particular, it has found that the decision to place a child on the abuse register, without

---

[45] No *900/60 X & Y v Austria,* Dec 8.5.62, Collection 9, p 34.

[46] No *1449/62 X v the Netherlands,* Dec 16.1.63, 6 Yearbook (1965) p 262.

[47] No *12805/87 Nowack v Sweden,* Dec 13.3.89, DR 60, p 212 and see also No *16184/90 Lavender v UK,* Dec 7.5.90, unreported.

[48] No *28945/95 TP & KM v UK,* Dec 26.5.98, 26 EHRR CD 84.

[49] See the decision of the House of Lords in the case of *X (Minors) v Bedfordshire County Council & M (A Minor) v Newham Borough Council & Ors* [1995] 2 AC 633. See also the discussion of remedies below and Chapter 12, pp 292-293.

having the allegation of abuse judicially determined, was justified in order to protect the child's health and rights under Article 8.[50] In reaching this decision, the Commission found it significant that putting the children's names on the register did not constitute a finding of fact or of guilt, that the parent did not show that she had suffered any prejudice as a result and most importantly, that it did not adversely affect her custody or access to her children.[51]

*Positive Obligations to Prevent Abuse*

It is well established that in certain circumstances Article 8 may require the taking of positive measures to protect effective family life. The scope of this obligation varies from case to case and in determining whether it exists at all, the Court must have regard to the fair balance that has to be struck between the general interest of the community and the interests of the individual.[52] In striking this balance, the aims mentioned in the second paragraph of Article 8 may be of relevance and it is arguable therefore that a pro-active measure taken to protect a child from abuse would fulfil a legitimate aim under Article 8 § 2, which could not be counteracted by any stronger public interest. Although the Court has not yet had the opportunity to determine the scope of a positive obligation in this regard, the Commission has considered related issues. For example, where a divorced mother and her children complained that their harassment by their husband and father violated Article 8, the Commission found that in such circumstances

> the responsibility of the State is engaged and that it is under a positive obligation to secure the applicants' rights by providing adequate protection against this type of deliberate persecution.[53]

However, it is as yet unclear what kind of action is necessary to ensure 'adequate protection' of this kind.

---

[50] No *17071/90 VW v UK*, Dec 7.1.91, unreported.

[51] See No *16586/90 McCallister & Lorance v Netherlands*, Dec 1.12.93, unreported, which concerned the return of a child to her father in America despite her mother's allegation that he had sexually abused her causing them to flee to the Netherlands. The applicants had failed to exhaust domestic remedies.

[52] See further Chapter 9, pp 198-199.

[53] No *20357/92 Whiteside* v UK, Dec 7.3.94, DR 76, p 80.

The Court may have the opportunity to determine this matter in the context of Article 3 if a case found admissible by the Commission in 1998 proceeds before it.[54] The complaint here is brought by five siblings who submit that the gross neglect and maltreatment which they suffered at the hands of their parents over a five year period amounted to inhuman and degrading treatment. They further submit that the local authority was aware of their ill-treatment, but failed to take adequate preventive measures in response. It will fall to the Court to determine, therefore, whether the positive obligation to protect children from under Article 3 extends beyond imposing criminal sanctions for such ill-treatment, and requires intervention by the State in such circumstances in accordance with the fulfilment of statutory duty.[55]

*Neglect*

It is perhaps more difficult for the supervisory bodies to determine whether the reasons for removing children from the family home are relevant and sufficient where the issue is one of child neglect, rather than physical abuse. Nevertheless, the Commission has yet to find that the child's separation from a parent in these circumstances is inconsistent with Article 8. However, it has established that only the most pressing grounds can justify the disruption of existing family ties, even where the material conditions of a family are poor.[56] Severe conditions of neglect and an inability to meet a child's medical and welfare needs may thus justify the removal of children from parental care.[57] In certain circumstances, it will also be consistent with Article 8 to take children into care where they are living in unsanitary and impoverished conditions.[58] The role played by

---

[54] No *29392/95 KL & Others v UK*, Dec 28.5.98, 26 EHRR CD 113. See the House of Lords decision in this case in *X (Minors) v Bedfordshire County Council & M (A Minor) v Newham Borough Council & Ors, op cit.*

[55] On remedies for such abuse see below and see the relevant discussion on protection under Article 3 above. See further Wright (1998) 'Local Authorities, the Duty of Care and the European Convention on Human Rights', *Oxford Journal of Legal Studies* **18**, pp 1-28, especially pp 21-25.

[56] No *8059/77 X & Y v Germany*, Dec 3.10.78, DR 15, p 208 and No *11588/85 U & GF v Germany*, Dec 15.5.86, DR 47, p 259.

[57] *Ibid* and No *25291/94 Lajtner v Poland*, Dec 17.1.95, unreported.

[58] No *5132/71 X v Denmark*, Dec 12.7.71, Collection 43, p 57 and No *8059/77 X & Y v Germany, op cit.*

poverty undeniably complicates matters and raises the question of what the State is obliged to do to provide assistance in such cases. For example, where children are found to be suffering from neglect as a result of poverty or inadequate family support, can the permanent removal of the child from the family home be supported by relevant and sufficient reasons, where it is arguably the State which is at fault in failing to provide such assistance earlier? Notwithstanding the economic implications of such an approach, it is certainly arguable that respect for family life requires the provision of family assistance in order to prevent state intervention at a later stage to protect the health of the children. In particular, a positive obligation to respect family life under Article 8 could, in certain circumstances, require the adoption of appropriate measures in order to prevent the separation of family members. This approach might also assist in the promotion of good practice. Whereas the Commission and Court are free to encourage that pro-active measures be taken prior to the removal of a child from the family, according to the current approach, States are not compelled to give such advice their attention. The development of a positive obligation in this area, consistent with Article 8 jurisprudence in other areas of family life,[59] would require that support and assistance be provided to the family prior to the removal of the children on the grounds of neglect. This approach would help to give the Court some purpose in this area and would also make the Convention's protection of children and the family practical and effective.

*The Right to Physical Integrity*

It is well established that physical integrity is a component of respect for private life which deserves respect under Article 8. This principle was conceived in the case of *X and Y v the Netherlands* which concerned the impossibility of having criminal proceedings instituted against the perpetrator of a sexual assault of a 16 year old girl with mental disabilities.[60] The difficulty arose from a gap in Dutch criminal law which required a complaint to be made by the victim of an indecent assault before criminal proceedings could be instituted. Notwithstanding that she was unable, due to her disability, to make the complaint herself, the law did not permit anyone to make the complaint on her behalf. Deciding the case, the Court recalled that there is a positive obligation to respect private life, the

---

[59] See generally Chapters 11 and 12.

[60] Eur Court HR *X & Y v Netherlands*, judgment of 26 March 1985, Series A No 91, 8 EHRR 235.

nature of which will depend on the particular aspect of private life that is at issue. The Court went on to note that States enjoy a discretion as to the choice of means designed to secure compliance with Article 8. Although recourse to the criminal law is not necessarily the only answer, the protection of the civil law was found to be insufficient in the circumstances given the kind of wrongdoing inflicted on the young applicant and the fact that fundamental values and aspects of private life were at stake.[61]

The Court considered the issue of physical integrity again in *Costello-Roberts*, this time in the context of school physical punishment.[62] The seven year old applicant in this case received three 'whacks' of a gym shoe on the bottom as an automatic punishment for minor breaches of school rules. The treatment was not severe enough to breach Article 3,[63] but, according to the Court, this did not preclude it from raising an issue under Article 8, but it did provide a point of reference in this regard. Moreover, the Court did not exclude the possibility that there might be circumstances in which Article 8 could be regarded as affording protection, which goes beyond that given by Article 3 in relation to disciplinary measures. The fundamental difference between the two provisions is that unlike the latter provision, the right to respect for private life is not absolute. Furthermore, the Court has found that not every act or measure which may be said to affect adversely a person's physical integrity will give rise to an interference with that right. This is the case in the field of education for example, where sending a child to school necessarily involves a level of interference with the child's private life.[64] However, there is scope for discussion about the degree of interference that is permissible in this context. According to the Court, the treatment complained of did not entail adverse effects for his physical or moral integrity sufficient to bring it within the scope of the prohibition contained in Article 8 and there was thus no violation of that provision. The contrasting view of the Commission is outlined below.

Notwithstanding its conclusion that the scope of protection offered by Article 8 may be broader than that under Article 3, the Court has applied the test of severity to both provisions in a manner which makes it difficult to distinguish the protection of one provision from that of the other. In

---

[61] *Ibid*, § 27.

[62] *Costello-Roberts* judgment, *op cit*.

[63] See further above, pp 164-165.

[64] *Ibid*, § 36. The Court was here citing its judgment in Eur Court HR *Belgian Linguistics Case*, judgment of 23 July 1968, Series A no 6, 1 EHRR 252.

particular, by requiring that, similar to Article 3, only treatment which reaches a particular level of severity will raise an issue under Article 8, the Court has placed a limit on the potential of the latter provision in terms of protecting the child from physical punishment. In this regard, for example, it is difficult to envisage the Court finding a particular type of treatment to be compatible with Article 3, but in breach of Article 8 and its approach lacks clarity for this reason. This notwithstanding, it is positive that the Court did not wish to be seen to approve corporal punishment as part of a school disciplinary regime. Moreover, the Court's reference to the UN Convention on the Rights of the Child is also significant, although its reference to Article 16, the child's right to privacy, is a curious choice.

In contrast to the Court, the Commission found the boy's physical punishment violated Article 8 and its approach was also different from that of the Court.[65] The Commission took as its starting point the fact that corporal punishment constitutes an obvious interference with the physical integrity of the individual and a lack of respect for private life. It went on to note, however, that consent to such punishment may avoid an interference under Article 8 § 1, and considered, importantly, that in the case of children or young persons, consent may be given by parents on their behalf. The scope of parental rights in this respect cannot be unlimited and on the facts of the case, the mother's act of enroling the boy in the school could not be treated as a waiver of his right to physical integrity. In the absence of parental consent to the treatment, therefore, the corporal punishment constituted an interference with the boy's private life. As to whether this was justified under Article 8 § 2, the Commission noted that the government had failed to produce any social, educational, health or moral justification for the punishment. Nor had an explanation been offered to the boy's parents, other than the fact that he had accumulated the requisite number of demerit points which, according to the school's disciplinary practice, warranted physical chastisement. Accordingly, the Commission found no basis on which the interference could be justified and it reached the inevitable conclusion that the punishment violated Article 8.[66]

The Commission's opinion in *Costello-Roberts* is preferable to that of the Court not least because, having clarified that the protection offered by Article 8 may in certain circumstances be broader than that of Article 3, it carries this argument through to its natural conclusion. In particular, while

---

[65] *Costello-Roberts* Comm Rep, *op cit*, § 45-55.
[66] This conclusion was reached by nine votes to four.

the conclusion that the punishment administered was not severe enough to amount to degrading treatment under Article 3 was correct, the Commission justified going on to examine the complaint under Article 8, eventually finding a violation of that provision. Notwithstanding that the Commission's reasoning on the Article 8 issue was not adopted by the Court, it nevertheless remains a valuable interpretation of the provision and its potential in relation to cases of mild physical punishment is clear. It is also important that Article 8 so interpreted provides a context in which other disputes regarding physical ill-treatment, which might be considered justifiable, can be resolved. In particular, the Education Act 1997 of the UK provides staff with a right to restrain pupils by force 'reasonable in the circumstances' for the purpose of preventing a pupil from committing an offence, causing personal injury, or engaging in any behaviour prejudicial to the maintenance of good order and discipline at the school.[67] While such ill-treatment may not be severe enough to violate Article 3, it will fall squarely within the scope of Article 8 as an interference with the right to physical integrity. Whether this will be justifiable under this provision will depend on a number of factors, including whether the State has offered guidance as to what is reasonable in the circumstances.[68]

The Court's case law on the issue of state responsibility for ill-treatment committed in the private sphere arguably applies to Article 8 as it does to Article 3.[69] The fact that the punishment which infringes the child's right to physical integrity is administered by a parent or guardian will not preclude the Court's consideration of its compatibility with the Convention therefore. The wide scope of parental authority with regard to what is best for the child may prevent the Court from finding that treatment, which falls short of the standards required to breach Article 3, constitutes an interference with the child's private life. The Commission has acknowledged from an early stage that parental choices and rights in the upbringing and education of their children are paramount as against the State.[70] Parental rights are not absolute, however, and a ban on corporal punishment within the family will not interfere with family life, where it is unaccompanied by sanctions or other legal implications.[71] The

---

[67] S 4 Education Act 1997, adds a new s 550a to the Education Act 1996, under which corporal punishment was abolished.

[68] See the relevant discussion of *A* Comm Rep, *op cit*, above.

[69] See further above.

[70] No *8811/79 7 Individuals v Sweden*, Dec 13.5.82, DR 29, p 105.

[71] *Ibid.*

compatibility with Article 8 of criminalising the corporal punishment of children by their parents is uncertain, and would be likely to depend on the circumstances. In any event, it is arguable that the margin of appreciation which States enjoy under Article 8 has been reduced by the complete ban on physical punishment in schools,[72] the increasing number of Convention states in which physical punishment of children by those in loco parentis is now prohibited[73] and of course by the fact that all European Convention States have ratified the UN Convention on the Rights of the Child, under which an extensive range of ill-treatment and abuse is prohibited.[74]

**Remedies for Abuse**

Although Article 13 expressly requires that a remedy be made available at domestic level for a violation of a Convention right,[75] the right to legal protection from abuse and ill-treatment has been found to be implicit in Articles 3 and 8 also. This remedial protection has been further enhanced by the Court's interpretation of Article 6 in the context of the right of access to a court, meaning that the scope of the Convention for responding to the violation of its provisions has been broadened significantly. There is now considerable overlap in the protection provided by Articles 3, 8, 6 and 13 in this regard.

The obligation to provide access to an effective remedy under Article 13 arises where the applicant has an 'arguable' claim that he is a victim of a violation of the Convention. The link between the arguability of a claim in domestic proceedings and the ultimate success of an application at Convention level has proved contentious in physical punishment cases. In *Costello-Roberts*, the Court found it adequate for the purposes of Article 13 that the Convention argument would be substantively effective in a civil action in the domestic court.[76] Thus, Article 13 was not violated notwithstanding the likelihood that the civil action would be dismissed on the ground that the punishment constituted reasonable and moderate

---

[72]  S 548 Education Act 1996.

[73]  Smith, *op cit*.

[74]  See Article 19, *op cit*.

[75]  See generally Harris, O'Boyle & Warbrick, *op cit*, pp 443-461 and Van Dijk & Van Hoof, *op cit*, pp 696-710. See also Fawcett (1987), *The Application of the European Convention on Human Rights*, 2nd ed, Oxford: Clarendon Press, pp 289-291.

[76]  See *Costello-Roberts* judgment, *op cit*, § 40.

chastisement according to domestic law. According to the Court, therefore, the effectiveness of a remedy within the meaning of Article 13 does not depend on the certainty of a favourable outcome, and the Court will not speculate as to what decision the domestic courts would have reached.[77] What is decisive is that there exists a *possibility* of a civil action being remedially effective. In contrast, the Commission's opinion in *Costello-Roberts* was that because the applicant had no prospect of bringing a successful assault claim in the domestic courts, there was no effective remedy for the purpose of Article 13.[78] This is the case notwithstanding its own conclusion that the treatment complained of was not severe enough to breach Article 3.[79] While the Court's judgment takes precedence here, it is significant that in finding the domestic remedy to be inadequate for the purposes of Article 13 the Commission has tended to attach significance to the failure of the domestic courts to consider the criteria for a breach of Article 3.[80] Importantly, this reasoning re-emerged as part of the basis for the breach of the substantive right in Article 3 in *A v UK* in 1998.[81]

The Court's judgment in *Costello-Roberts* means that as long an aggrieved individual can raise the substance of a Convention complaint before the domestic authorities then there will be no violation of Article 13. More recently, the Court has noted that the scope of the obligation under that provision varies depending on the nature of the applicant's complaint under the Convention.[82] In particular, the nature of the right safeguarded under Article 3, in particular the fundamental importance of the prohibition on torture, inhuman and degrading treatment in that provision, has implications for Article 13. Thus in *Aydin v Turkey*, where the public prosecutor failed to conduct an effective and thorough investigation of the complaint of a 17 year old girl that she was raped and tortured by members of the Turkish security forces, she was found to have been denied an

---

[77] *Ibid*, § 41.

[78] *Costello-Roberts* Comm Rep, *op cit*, § 59.

[79] See above, pp 164-165.

[80] *Warwick* Comm Rep, *op cit*, and *Y* Comm Rep, *op cit*, § 56. Despite the merit of this approach, the Commission in *A v UK* followed the Court's approach. See above.

[81] *A* judgment, *op cit*. See above, pp 168-170.

[82] Eur Court HR *Aydin v Turkey*, judgment of 25 Sept 1997, Reports 1997-VI, no 50, 25 EHRR 251, § 103.

effective remedy for an alleged violation of her rights under Article 3.[83] This amounted to a violation of Article 3, not least because the failure to investigate her complaint in the criminal context deprived her of establishing the facts which would have also formed the basis of any civil proceedings, which she wished to institute.

The scope of Article 6 is broader than Article 13, in particular, because it embodies the right to a court, of which the right to institute proceedings in civil matters is a constituent part. While this right is not absolute, the Court has clearly established that any limits placed on it must be proportionate to the aim which they seek to achieve.[84] It is not yet clear whether the situation in which it is impossible to have a complaint against the social authorities considered on its merits in civil proceedings constitutes a restriction on the right of access to a court which is proportionate to the public interest aim which it attempts to serve. A complaint in this regard, made by a number of children who seek to challenge the State's failure to protect them from the abuse which they suffered at the hands of their parents has been found admissible by the Commission.[85] Their challenge in negligence was rejected by the domestic courts on grounds of public policy and, should the applicants successfully establish that the refusal of the domestic court to examine the merits of their case resulted from the automatic application of a rule granting immunity to the social authorities in such cases, rather than on the basis of their individual complaint, then their claim under Article 6 is likely to succeed.[86]

Given that redress for abuse experienced by children may not in reality be available to them until they reach adulthood, it is crucial that such victims should not be prevented from instituting civil proceedings by the application of a time limit or other practical impediments. For example, where the abuse was experienced by a child in the care of the State, it may

---

[83] The Court added that the requirement of a thorough and effective investigation into an allegation of rape in custody at the hands of a State official also implies that the victim be examined, with all appropriate sensitivity, by medical professionals with particular competence in this area and whose independence is not circumscribed by instructions given by the prosecuting authority as to the scope of the examination. *Ibid*, § 107.

[84] See Eur Court HR *Osman v UK*, judgment of 28 Oct 1998, Reports 1998-VIII, no 95. See further Chapter 6, pp 144-145.

[85] No *29392/95 KL & Others v UK, op cit* and No *28945/95 TP & KM v UK, op cit*.

[86] See *Osman* judgment, *op cit*. See also Wright (1998), *op cit*.

be possible to argue that access to the confidential files held by the social services is necessary to ensure effective access to a court under Article 6.[87] The compatibility with the Convention of imposing a time limit on the institution of such proceedings arose in the *Stubbings* case.[88] Here the Commission found that a strict time limit, which precluded victims of sexual abuse (as an intentional injury) from instituting civil proceedings after a certain period of time, violated Article 6 together with Article 14.[89] The Commission was not satisfied that it was either reasonable or proportionate to allow flexibility in the application of the time limits where a victim of unintentional injury lacks the knowledge required to bring an action, but to exclude it entirely where a victim of intentional injury lacks the requisite knowledge. Arguments as to legal certainty, prevention of stale claims and injustice to defendants apply to both categories of victim, and there were thus no apparent obstacles to allowing the courts to examine whether it was equitable to proceed in cases other than those of negligent injury.

In disagreeing with the Commission, the Court recognised that children are entitled to state protection from sexual abuse in the form of effective deterrence. [90] However, it attached greater weight to the purposes served by limitation periods in personal injury cases in reaching the opposite conclusion. While noting the lack of uniformity among Convention States regarding the length of civil limitation periods or the date from which they are reckoned, the Court also commented on the developing awareness in recent years on the 'range of problems caused by child abuse and its psychological effects on victims'.[91] Importantly, it highlighted the

---

[87] Although the applicant in *Gaskin* sought access to such information in order to pursue a claim in negligence, the purpose for which the information was sought was not considered by the Court which found the inability to challenge the denial of access to violate Article 8. See Eur Court HR *Gaskin v UK*, judgment of 7 July 1989, Series A no 160, 12 EHRR 36 and Chapter 5, pp 103-106.

[88] No 22083/93 *Stubbings v UK*, Comm Rep, 22.2.95, Reports 1996-VI, no 18, p 1515, 19 EHRR CD 32, and Eur Court HR *Stubbings v UK*, judgment of 22 Oct 1996, Reports 1996-IV, no 18 p 1487, 23 EHRR 244. See the background to the case in Palmer (1996), 'Limitation Periods in Cases of Sexual Abuse: A Response under the European Convention', *European Human Rights Law Review*, **2**, pp 111-119.

[89] *Stubbings* Comm Rep, *ibid*, § 49-68.

[90] *Stubbings* judgment, *op cit*, § 51.

[91] *Ibid*, § 54, 56.

possibility that, in the near future, rules on limitations of actions may have to be amended to make special provision for this group of claimants. These sound observations notwithstanding, however, the Court went on to find that, as long as the essence of the right was not impaired and the restrictions on the exercise of the right were proportionate to the legitimate aim pursued, the time limits were compatible with the Convention.[92] Reaching the same conclusion with regard to Article 6 together with Article 14, it adopted the reasoning that firstly, there was no difference in treatment between the victims of child sexual abuse and victims of other deliberate wrongdoing and secondly, that the victims of intentionally and negligently inflicted harm could not be said to be in analogous situations for the purposes of Article 14. In an extremely weak conclusion, the Court observed that any comparison which could be drawn between the categories of victim, and any difference in treatment which might be apparent, could be justified as reasonable and objective and within the State's margin of appreciation.[93]

In contrast to this very disappointing decision stand the two dissenting judgments, which place clear emphasis on the particular problems experienced by victims of child abuse in identifying, as adults, the causes of their psychological problems.[94] Both judges believed that the margin of appreciation afforded to the State had been too great and that the application of the strict time limit operated in a manner which infringed the rights of victims of child sexual abuse. These reasoned decisions are clearly preferable to the Court's judgment, although it is positive that the door to a future challenge to the application of a strict time limit appears to have been left open by the Court's comment that special protection for victims of child sexual abuse in this context may be warranted in the near future.

The right of access to a court does not grant the victim of a criminal offence the right to institute criminal proceedings.[95] As noted in *Stubbings* and elsewhere,

---

[92] *Ibid*, § 56-57.

[93] *Ibid*, § 73-74.

[94] Only one judge, Judge Macdonald, found a violation of Article 6 together with Article 14 and two, Judge Macdonald and Judge Foighel found a violation of Article 6 alone. *Ibid*.

[95] Eur Court HR *Helmers v Sweden*, judgment of 29 Oct 1991, Series A No 212-A, § 28.

children and other vulnerable individuals are entitled to State protection, in the form of effective deterrence from such grave types of interference from essential aspects of their private lives.[96]

While the criminal law may not always be necessary to provide this protection, effective deterrence is indispensable and criminal protection is essential where fundamental values and essential aspects of private life are at stake.[97]  In such circumstances, the failure to make criminal remedies available for such behaviour may raise an issue of compatibility with the Convention.

While Article 13 contains the right to an effective remedy, the Court has found standards of legal protection to be implicit in Articles 3 and 8 also.  In *X & Y v Netherlands* and *A v UK*, for example, the lack of adequate legal protection from an interference with physical integrity and degrading treatment respectively gave rise to violations of the relevant substantive Convention provisions.  According to the Commission,

[t]he essence of the applicant's complaints under Articles 3 and 8 of the Convention concerns the inadequacy of the domestic law to protect his substantive rights under these Articles.  As held by the Court [in Costello-Roberts] Article 13 does not go so far as to guarantee a remedy before a national authority in such circumstances.  It follows that there has been no violation of Article 13 in the present case.[98]

Article 13 thus offers greater protection than Articles 3 and 8.  This is welcome in light of the criticism leveled at the Court's approach to Article 13,[99] as well as its curious absence from the Human Rights Act 1998, which brings the Convention into the law of the UK.

## Treatment of Victims in Legal Proceedings

Where a victim of abuse chooses to participate in legal proceedings against the alleged perpetrator, the experience can be traumatic, particularly for

---

[96] *Stubbings* judgment, *op cit*, § 64. See also *X & Y* judgment, *op cit* and *A* judgment, *op cit.*

[97] *X & Y* judgment, *op cit*, § 27.

[98] *A* Comm Rep, *op cit*, § 66.

[99] See the criticisms of Harris, O'Boyle & Warbrick, *op cit*, p 443 and Van Dijk & Van Hoof, *op cit*, p 697.

victims of sexual abuse. As a result, certain techniques have been adopted to minimise the detrimental impact of the trial on the alleged victim, including the use in court of video evidence that is pre-recorded or statements previously made. While their aim of protecting the alleged victim is necessary and important these developments must not encroach upon the right of the accused to a fair trial, in particular the right under Article 6 § 3(d) to cross examine witnesses, insofar as they involve the use of evidence that is for the most part unchallengeable.[100]  Although all evidence must normally be produced in the presence of the accused at a public hearing with a view to adversarial argument, the use in evidence of other statements previously made is not in itself inconsistent with Article 6 provided that rules of the defence have been respected. The admissibility of evidence is primarily governed by domestic law and as a rule it is for the national courts to assess the evidence before them.[101]  It is unclear therefore, whether the admission of hearsay evidence in child sexual abuse proceedings is consistent with Article 6, although its general admissibility in continental jurisdictions suggests that it is, in principle.[102]

Reflecting the need to balance the rights of both the victim and alleged accused, Article 6 does not grant the latter an unlimited right to secure the appearance of witnesses in court and it is for domestic courts to decide whether it is necessary or advisable to hear a particular witness.[103] However, the rules of the defence require that the defendant be given an adequate and proper opportunity to challenge and question witnesses against them either when these statements are made, or at a later stage of proceedings.[104]  In this regard, if a particular witness was not heard by the trial courts, it may be sufficient for the purposes of a fair trial that she was examined by the investigating judge in the presence of the applicant's lawyer at an earlier stage in the proceedings. It may also be relevant that the defence had ample opportunity to put questions to her.[105] Although it is preferable to hear a witness in person, the Commission held in the *Finkensieper* case that a court's decision not to summon a particular witness is not necessarily arbitrary or unreasonable given the sensitive

---

[100] See No *25205/94 Kremers v the Netherlands*, Dec 19.10.95, unreported.

[101] See, for example, No *19525/92 Finkensieper v the Netherlands*, Comm Rep, 1.7.95, Reports 1996-II, no 5.

[102] See, for example, O'Doherty (1996), 'Recent Cases on Hearsay Evidence in Civil Child Sexual Abuse Proceedings', *Irish Law Times*, **14**(12), pp 284-287.

[103] No 25205/94 *Kremers v the Netherlands, op cit.*

[104] *Ibid.*

[105] *Ibid,* and *Finkensieper* Comm Rep, *op cit.*

nature of the case and the problems which a victim of sexual abuse may suffer giving evidence.[106] This would appear to be the case only as long as the statement of the relevant witness is not the only evidence on which the court bases its conviction.[107] It is unlikely therefore that the same would hold true if the alleged victim provided the only uncorroborated evidence of the abuse.[108]

It is also uncertain whether it is consistent with a fair trial to allow a witness to appear in court, but to permit him/her to refuse to answer emotionally burdensome questions, or be cross examined in the absence of the accused.[109] Here, a balance must be achieved between the position in which the defence is placed and the victim's right to respect for private life, which deserves special protection in proceedings for sexual abuse. In reaching this balance, it may be relevant for instance, that information in the case file is substantiated by other expert witnesses and that, although the accused may not be present, his lawyer is free to cross examine.[110] Nor has the Commission found that a refusal to grant a defendant a psychiatric assessment of a child victim in order to establish the child's credibility and trustworthiness violates the right to fair trial.[111] Here it agreed with the domestic court which had heard the child, that it was for the court to decide the question of credibility.

The right of the child to privacy in such proceedings is expressly recognised by Article 6 which provides that the public and media may be excluded from legal proceedings where it is in the interests of the child. However, it is not clear whether this extends to the public reporting of such cases and whether the reporting of proceedings concerning child sexual abuse in a manner which identifies the child victim may violate either Article 8 or Article 6. In particular, where the abuse occurs within the family, the publication of information relating to the alleged abuser may

---

[106] *Finkensieper* Comm Rep, *op cit*, § 67.

[107] *Ibid*, § 68.

[108] Dissenting members of the Commission expressed the view that because the information which the relevant witness could provide was of considerable importance in evaluating the charges against the applicant, and the fact that the reason which she refused to testify was not verified, the use of the statement together with the fact that no attempt was made to hear her before the court did not take sufficiently into account the rights of the defence. *Ibid*.

[109] No *25206/94 Hols v the Netherlands*, Dec 19.10.95, unreported.

[110] *Ibid*.

[111] No *20708/92 HS v Sweden*, Dec 11.1.94, unreported.

lead to the identification of the child victim. Concern may also be expressed about the child's right to privacy during and subsequent to legal proceedings and the compatibility of exposing the child's identity in such circumstances may raise an issue under the Convention. However, it is unclear how a balance is to be struck between the right of the press to provide information to the public under Article 10 and the child's right to privacy under Article 8 in this area, although the proportionality of any restriction would be decisive.

## Future Challenges

In many ways, the case of *A v UK* is a milestone in the use of the Convention to protect children from ill-treatment. While its most important feature was the successful use of Article 3 to protect children from physical abuse in the private sphere, the reference to the UN Convention on the Rights of the Child to fill the gaps in Convention jurisprudence is evidence of a positive and dynamic approach to the application of the Convention to children. The case also highlights the Convention's potential to protect children from physical abuse masquerading as parental discipline and this positive approach is likely to continue particularly given the growing intolerance of physical punishment among Convention States.

Dynamic interpretation of Article 3 and Article 8 means that the Convention's scope is increasingly broad and this has consequences for the protection of children from abuse and neglect. Possible areas for future development include the concept of a positive obligation to protect children from abuse and neglect, as well as the availability of legal protection and remedies where the authorities fail to remove a child from an abusive environment, or remove a child in error in this regard. Future challenges may also occur in relation to the right of the child and/or adult to enjoy effective access to court to seek remedies for abuses experienced in childhood and relating also to their participation in such proceedings. Issues surrounding the victim's participation in criminal proceedings including evidential matters, are also likely to be raised under Article 6, and the balance to be reached between the fair trial rights of the accused and the need to treat the victim of abuse with respect and dignity is a difficult one in this respect.

# 9  Definition and Treatment of the Family

## Introduction

The protection which the European Convention on Human Rights affords the family, both as a unit and in terms of its individual adult and child members, is unrivalled in international law. The source of much of this protection is Article 8 of the Convention, which guarantees the right to respect for private and family life and prohibits any state interference with that right which is not in accordance with law, in pursuit of a legitimate aim and necessary in a democratic society. The scope of Article 8 is very broad and it has been interpreted in a dynamic fashion by the Commission and Court of Human Rights. In addition, Article 12 guarantees the right to marry and found a family and the important role played by parents in the education of their children is recognised in the second sentence of the education provision in Article 2 of the First Protocol to the Convention. Further express protection is offered to the family by Article 5 of the Seventh Protocol which guarantees equality between spouses as regards their children both during marriage and in the event of its dissolution.

## Definition of the Family

Given the extensive protection which flows from Article 8[1] the definition of the family within the meaning of that provision is crucial because it circumscribes the provision's scope. Importantly, the concept of family life has evolved steadily in the lifetime of the Commission and the Court and indeed, one of the most positive features of their case law is the way in which family life has been interpreted so as to take account of social change.[2]

---

[1]  See generally Van Dijk & Van Hoof (1998), *Theory and Practice of the European Convention on Human Rights*, 3rd ed, The Hague: Kluwer, pp 504-522; Harris, O'Boyle & Warbrick (1995), *Law of the European Convention on Human Rights*, London: Butterworths, pp 302-355.

[2]  Harris, O'Boyle & Warbrick, *ibid*, p 312.

According to the wording of the provision, family life is located squarely within the private sphere, where it is entitled to function free from arbitrary state interference.[3] Notably, however, Article 8 protects family life, rather than the family itself,[4] and this means that the existence of family relationships is not always sufficient to attract the protection of Article 8. Although the Strasbourg institutions have developed certain useful criteria to determine the applicability of Article 8, as a matter of principle, they decide on the existence of family life on the facts of each case. Importantly, the Court and Commission have always maintained a flexible approach to the interpretation of family life, bearing in mind the diversity of modern family arrangements, the implications of divorce and medical advance. Notwithstanding that it is essential to adopt a dynamic approach to the family life concept if it is to remain relevant to today's legal and social conditions, the case by case approach means that it is not always possible to enumerate those relationships which constitute family life, and those which do not.[5]

Although as a rule, the existence of family life depends on whether there are close personal ties between the parties, an increasing number of family relationships enjoy the automatic protection of Article 8. One such situation is where marriage is involved and a child born to parents who are lawfully and genuinely married will be *ipso iure* part of that relationship from the moment and by the fact of the child's birth.[6] Once established, family life does not come to an end upon divorce,[7] or when the parties no longer live together.[8] Nor is it terminated by a decision to place a child in

---

[3]    O'Donnell (1995a), 'Protection of Family Life: Positive approaches and the ECHR', *Journal of Social Welfare and Family Law*, **17**(3), pp 261-280, at p 262.

[4]    There is some confusion over the use of the terms family life, respect for family life and the right to respect for family life. See Connelly (1986), 'Problems of Interpretation of Article 8 of the ECHR', *International and Comparative Law Quarterly*, **35**, pp 567-593 and also O'Donnell (1995b), 'The Unmarried father and the Right to Family Life', *Maastricht Journal of European and Comparative Law*, **2**(1), pp 85-96, at p 89.

[5]    Duffy (1982), 'The Protection of Privacy, Family Life and Other Rights under Article 8 of the European Convention on Human Rights', *Yearbook of European Law*, **2**, pp 191-238, at p 194.

[6]    Eur Court HR *Berrehab v the Netherlands*, judgment of 21 June 1988, Series A no 138, 11 EHRR 322, § 21.

[7]    No *8427/78 Hendriks v the Netherlands*, Comm Rep, 8.3.82, DR 29, p 5, 5 EHRR 223.

[8]    *Berrehab* judgment, *op cit*.

care.[9]  Although subsequent events, such as adoption[10] or expulsion[11] may break the tie of family life, the Court has established that this can only happen in exceptional circumstances.[12]

The Court established at an early stage that Article 8 applies automatically to the relationship between a mother and her child, regardless of her marital status.[13]  Although the *Marckx* case extended the application of Article 8 to the family outside marriage, however, unmarried parents and their children do not always benefit from a presumption of family life.  In the *Johnston* case, the Court found that the relationship between two adults, who lived together, but were unable to marry due to the lack of divorce under Irish law at the time, and their daughter deserved the protection of Article 8.  In reaching this conclusion, the Court was persuaded by the stable nature of their relationship and the fact that it was otherwise indistinguishable from the family based on marriage.[14]  Although this extension of Article 8 to include the family outside marriage does not apply to all non-marital relationships, parents who live together with their children as a family, are especially likely to enjoy the automatic protection of Article 8.

## *Unmarried Fathers and their Children*

Although family life will normally exist between unmarried parents and their children who live together, the Court has frequently held that cohabitation is not a *sine qua non* of family life, irrespective of the parents' marital status.[15]  Traditionally, however, where the father was neither married to, nor cohabiting with the mother and their child, he did not enjoy the protection of Article 8 unless he could prove that, in addition to the

---

[9]  Eur Court HR *Andersson v Sweden*, judgment of 25 Feb 1992, Series A, no 226, 14 EHRR 615, § 72.

[10]  No *7626/76 X v UK*, Dec 11.7.77, DR 11, p 160.

[11]  No *14830/89 Yousef v UK*, Comm Rep, 30.6.92, unreported, § 43.

[12]  Eur Court HR *Boughanemi v France*, judgment of 24 April 1996, Reports 1996-II no 8, p 593, 22 EHRR 228.  See further Chapter 10, p 216.

[13]  Eur Court HR *Marckx v Belgium*, judgment of 13 June 1979, Series A no 31, 2 EHRR 330, § 31. See further Chapter 2, pp 27-29.

[14]  Eur Court HR *Johnston v Ireland*, judgment of 18 Dec 1986, Series A no 112, 9 EHRR 203.

[15]  For example, see *Berrehab* judgment, *op cit* (divorced father) and Eur Court HR *Kroon & Ors*, judgment of 27 Oct 1994, Series A no 297-C, 19 EHRR 263 (unmarried).

blood link, he enjoyed close personal ties with his child by reference to emotional or financial commitment.[16] The effect of this approach was that the unmarried father occupied an unfavourable position in relation to his children, when compared with the married father, whose relationship with his children amounted to family life by the fact of birth inside marriage, regardless of his commitment to them.    This approach attracted much criticism,[17] but it was defended by the Commission with reference to the need to protect the child.    In particular, due to the varying level of commitment shown by unmarried fathers to their children, as well as the diversity of relations between them, the Commission found that the situation of a child born outside marriage required a distinct legislative framework, which took into account the difficulties involved.[18]    Thus, while the structures of marriage provide some protection for the child in the event of its dissolution, this protection is absent where the parents are not married.  Taking this into account, the Commission's approach was to consider that an unmarried father could only benefit from the protection of Article 8 where he had demonstrated a level of commitment to his child, either in terms of financial dependency and/or frequent and regular contact. It was a consequence of this approach that family life was treated as revolving around marriage to a large extent.[19]

There is evidence that this perspective is changing however. The *Boughanemi* case in 1996 involved an immigrant who argued that his expulsion from France would violate the right to family life, which he enjoyed, *inter alia*, with his son.[20] Here, the Court held that

> [t]he concept of family life on which Article 8 is based embraces, even when there is no cohabitation, the tie between a parent and his or her child, regardless

---

[16] See No *22920/93 MB v UK*, Dec 6.4.94, DR 77A, p 108; *No 14501/89 A & A v the Netherlands*, Dec 6.1.92, DR 72, p 118 (financial dependency and contact); *14247/88 C v UK*, Dec 3.7.92, DR 73, p 27 (contact); No *18280/91 MV v Malta*, Dec 9.4.92, unreported (lack of genuine interest).

[17] See O'Donnell (1995b), *op cit,* and  Bainham (1989), 'When is a Parent not a Parent? Reflections on the Unmarried Father and his Child in English Law', *International Journal of Law and the Family*, **3**, pp 208-239.

[18] No *9530/81 v Germany*, Dec 3.84, 7 EHRR 134; No *13557/88 N v Denmark, op cit.*

[19] O'Donnell (1995b), *op cit*, p 90.

[20] *Boughanemi* judgment, *op cit.*

of whether or not the latter is legitimate. Although that tie may be broken by subsequent events, this can only happen in exceptional circumstances.[21]

Applying this principle, the applicant's relationship with his son born outside marriage, and with whom he had had little contact, was found to amount to family life within the meaning of that provision.

This approach was followed by the Commission and the Court in subsequent immigration cases,[22] where neither a father's delay in recognising his child, his failure to support the child financially, nor his decision to leave the child in the care of relatives when emigrating to a Convention State constituted exceptional circumstances in this regard.[23] Moreover, the presumption that Article 8 automatically applies to the relationship between parent and child, regardless of its nature, has also been applied in the wholly domestic case of *Söderbäck*.[24] Here, an unmarried father and his daughter were found to enjoy family life despite the fact that they had never cohabited or enjoyed regular contact. The Court's approach in these two cases suggests therefore that the presumption in favour of family life has now been extended finally to unmarried fathers and their children.

*Potential Family Life*

Until recently however, only unmarried fathers who could provide evidence of their contact with and commitment to their children were entitled to the protection of Article 8. Difficulties arose therefore where the child's mother had prevented the development of a family life between the unmarried father and his child. In order to ensure that fathers in such circumstances were not unjustly deprived of the protection of Article 8, the Court established that potential family life may be sufficient to attract the protection of the provision, where actual family life did not yet exist. This arose in the *Keegan* case, where the applicant's daughter had been placed

---

[21] *Boughanemi* judgment, *ibid*, § 35.

[22] No 24889/94 *McCullough v UK*, Dec 12.9.97, 25 EHRR CD 34. See Liddy (1998), 'The Concept of Family Life Under the ECHR', *European Human Rights Law Review*, 1, pp 15-25, at p 18.

[23] See Eur Court HR *C v Belgium*, judgment of 7 Aug 1996, Reports 1996-III no 12, p 915 and Eur Court HR *Ahmut v the Netherlands*, judgment of 28 Nov 1996, Reports 1996-VI, no 24, p 2017, 24 EHRR 62.

[24] See Eur Court HR *Söderbäck* v Sweden, judgment of 28 Oct 1998, Reports 1998-VII, no 94. See further below and Chapter 13, pp 304-306.

for adoption by the child's mother without his consent or knowledge, thereby depriving him of the opportunity to establish close personal ties with her.[25] Due to the nature of the relationship between the child's parents - they cohabited, planned the pregnancy and intended to marry - the Court found that the potential family life between father and child meant that their relationship fell within the scope of Article 8, notwithstanding that they had met on only one occasion.

Despite the progressive nature of the Court's approach in *Keegan* and its objective that Article 8 should apply where any other decision is unjust, the effect of the judgment is that the applicability of Article 8 in such circumstances will depend entirely on the nature of the father's relationship with the mother. This is highlighted by a Commission case considered subsequently, where an unmarried father also sought to rely on potential family life with his daughter to invoke the protection of Article 8.[26] In this case, however, a number of factors mitigated against adopting the *Keegan* approach. In particular, the parents had neither lived together nor planned the child, the mother was married to some-one else who, she claimed, was the child's father. On the basis of these facts, the Commission rejected that the applicant's relationship with his daughter, who he had never seen, amounted to potential family life and Article 8 was found to be inapplicable.

According to this approach, the question as to whether the relationship between a father and his child falls within the scope of Article 8 is determined with reference to the parents' actions pre- and post-natally, as well as their marital status. This is clearly unsatisfactory insofar as it resembles the unjustifiable concept of 'illegitimacy', which permitted discrimination against children principally because of their parents' behaviour. Admittedly, the reasoning aims to distinguish between unmarried fathers who are committed to their children, but who do not enjoy a stable loving relationship with them for whatever reason, and fathers who appear to lack genuine commitment. Moreover, the fact that Article 8 protects the right to respect for family life, requiring genuine commitment in addition to the biological link between an unmarried father and his child, facilitates such an approach, and its overriding aim, according to the Commission, is to protect the interests of the child. The approach is effective insofar as it can be used to preclude a man from

---

[25] Eur Court HR *Keegan v Ireland*, judgment of 26 May 1994, Series A no 291-A, 18 EHRR 342, § 45. See further Chapter 13, p 311.

[26] No *22920/93 MB v UK*, *op cit*.

claiming the protection of Article 8 where his child is conceived as a result of an act of rape or incest, for example, although it may also be applied to divert the application of Article 8 in cases where the child is the unplanned result of a brief sexual encounter.[27]    The requirement of commitment is useful therefore insofar as it distinguishes between such relationships and those based on loving stable ties, thereby preventing the former from requiring the protection of Article 8.

The meritorious objectives of this approach notwithstanding, it fails to take into account that the determination of family life is merely the first step in the application of Article 8 and that the existence of family life does not of itself determine the scope of the obligations which flow from that provision.    For example, finding family life to exist between a rapist and the child born to his victim as a result does not necessarily entitle him to rights of contact or care of the child.    This point appears to have escaped the Commission, although a recognition of the various sensitivities at play in family law cases, whose basis may lie in conflict between the mother and the father, may have influenced its approach.

The traditional approach to the existence of family life outlined above is also flawed insofar as its consequence is to apply Article 8 to children's cases in a discriminatory manner.    For this reason at least, it is argued that the Court's approach in the *Boughanemi* and *Söderbäck* cases should be applied to all Article 8 case law.[28]    This would involve implicit acceptance of the fact that birth always creates family life between a child and both parents, whatever the nature of their relationship.    Fundamentally, it would permit the application of Article 8 in a way that ensures that all children enjoy the right to respect for family life, regardless of their parent's behaviour or status.    According to this approach, a presumption in favour of family between parent and child would exist allowing the Court to go on to consider, in greater detail perhaps, whether the interference with that relationship is justified under Article 8 § 2 with regard to the interests of the child.    It would apply, therefore, regardless of whether the interference comes in the form of a refusal to award parental responsibility, custody or contact, or the placement of the child for adoption.    Although factors such as the nature of the parents' relationship, and/or the nature of the father's relationship with his child may be factors relevant to weighing up the interests at stake, these factors would not be decisive for the outcome of the

---

[27]    No *24848/94 Bellis v Greece*, Dec 22.2.92, unreported.
[28]    See above, pp 190-191.

application as before.[29]   The Court is likely to confirm this approach to the interpretation of family life in future cases, and it will thereby reaffirm the flexibility of the family life concept in a way which secures its adaptability to a range of family structures in order to afford equal protection to all children in this respect.[30]

*Modern Family Structures*

The flexible approach to the existence of family life has enabled the Commission and Court to adapt the concept to the challenges brought by modern family arrangements.  This is highlighted particularly by a case in which the relationship between a female-to-male transsexual and his child born by artificial insemination by donor (AID) was found to constitute family life.[31]   In reaching this conclusion, the Court found it significant, firstly, that their relationship was otherwise indistinguishable from that enjoyed by the traditional family and secondly, that the transsexual participated in the AID process as the child's father.  The clear merit of this approach is that it places emphasis on the social, rather than the biological reality of the situation, and in this regard, the Court did not consider that the father's status as a transsexual or the child's conception by AID were relevant to its conclusion that family life existed between them.  Although the emphasis on the *de facto* ties of family life which the parties enjoyed in this case is also evident in other case law, *X, Y & Z* is the first case in which the concept of family life was extended formally to include parental relationships without a blood tie.  However, the Court concluded that respect for the relationship of family life between the transsexual father and the child born to his partner by AID did not require its formal legal recognition.  This illustrates that although the concept of family life applies to relationships of blood, marriage and adoption of a certain type, the measures required to respect these relationships may not always be the same.[32]

---

[29]   See *Söderbäck* judgment, *op cit,* and in Chapter 13, pp 304-306.

[30]   See also Van Bueren (1995a), *The International Law on the Rights of the Child*, Dordrecht: Martinus Nijhoff, p 67.

[31]   Eur Court HR *X, Y & Z v UK*, judgment of 22 April 1997, Reports 1997-II, no 35, p 619, 24 EHRR 143, § 37.  See also Chapter 5, pp 98-101.

[32]   In contrast, the Commission found by thirteen votes to five that respect for the applicants' family life did require its legal recognition. No 21830/93 *X, Y & Z v UK*, Comm Rep, 27.6.95, Reports 1997-II, no 35, p 647.

In the *Kerkhoven* case in 1992, the Commission failed to find that a stable relationship between two women and the child born to one of them by AID fell within the scope of family life.[33] Notwithstanding that they lived together as a family and shared parental tasks in relation to the child, the Commission preferred to deal with their claim for legal recognition in the context of private life, although it gave no clear reasons for its distinction. The Dutch member of the Commission, Mr Schermers, dissenting from the majority in *X, Y & Z* found that there was no distinction between the situation of the parties in that case and the *de facto* family ties enjoyed by parents of the same sex in *Kerkhoven*. In his view, there was no reason why all forms of durable relationships between parents and their children should not fall within the meaning of family life under Article 8. In particular, he said that the

> [p]rincipal elements of family life are mutual affection, which may exist between persons - irrespective of their sex - and between children of one or both of these persons, and the wish of such persons to found and/or maintain a 'family unit' by establishing a joint household, either through marriage or cohabitation.[34]

This reasoning, which is arguably consistent with the approach of the Court in *X, Y & Z*, includes same sex relationships in the concept of family life. It has not yet been accepted by the majority of the Commission and the Court has yet to consider this issue. However, if the concept of family life is to continue to reflect modern social and legal conditions, it arguably should be extended to include a stable same-sex union for the reasons outlined by Mr Schermers.

Further challenges to the concept of family life are likely to arise in the light of medical advance, in particular the increasing use of egg and sperm donation procedures. While it is significant that the absence of a biological link will not preclude a relationship from constituting family life, a mere blood or genetic link may be insufficient for this purpose. This is illustrated by the Commission's decision that the relationship between a sperm donor and the child born as a result does not necessarily amount to family life under Article 8.[35] Notwithstanding their blood tie, the fact that he had undertaken babysitting duties on a weekly basis provided

---

[33] No *15666/89 Kerkhoven, Hinke & Hinke v the Netherlands*, Dec 19.5.92, unreported.

[34] *X, Y & Z* Comm Rep, *op cit.*

[35] No *16944/90 G v Netherlands*, Dec 8.2.93, 16 EHRR 38.

insufficient evidence that they enjoyed the close personal ties necessary to attract the protection of Article 8.

Whether the presumption in favour of family life between parents and their children applies to children born into second relationships, inside marriage or not, or children born from an extra marital affair, has yet to be determined. In dealing with such claims to family life, the Commission has determined the application of Article 8 on a case by case basis, taking into account the *de facto* ties between the parties.[36]

## The Extended Family

From an early stage, the Court has recognised that the concept of family life may include extended members of the child's family. It was first established in the *Marckx* case that family life may exist between children and their grandparents since they play a 'significant part in family life'.[37] This approach is positive insofar as it recognises the importance and relevance of relationships between extended family members. This is confirmed further by the inclusion of the relationship between siblings, both as children[38] and as adults,[39] in the concept of family life. The Court has not yet determined whether the relationship between an uncle or aunt and his/her nephew or niece falls within the meaning of family life and the Commission's approach is to require particular evidence of close personal ties, in addition to their blood link before finding Article 8 to apply. This is also true in immigration cases, it seems, where the claim that family life existed between an uncle and his nephew, whom he had adopted and maintained despite the fact that his birth parents still lived in India, was rejected by the Commission.[40] The opposite conclusion was reached in another case which was settled before it reached the Court, where family life was found to exist between an uncle and his nephew, in the light of the fact that the boy stayed for weekends with his uncle, who was deemed by

---

[36] See No *11418/85 Jolie & Lebrun v Belgium*, Dec 14.5.86, DR 47, p 243. cf No *7289/75 & 7349/76 X & Y v Switzerland*, Dec 14.7.77, DR 9, p 57.

[37] *Marckx* judgment, *op cit*, § 45. See also No *12402/86 Price v UK*, Dec 9.3.88, DR 55, p 224 and No *12763/87 Lawlor v UK*, Dec 14.7.88, DR 57, p 216.

[38] Eur Court HR *Olsson v Sweden*, judgment of 24 March 1988, Series A no 130, 11 EHRR 259.

[39] *Boughanemi* judgment, *op cit*, and also Eur Court HR *El Boujaidi v France*, judgment of 26 Sept 1997, Reports 1997-VI, no 51, p 1980.

[40] No *7229/75 X & Y v UK*, Dec 15.77, DR 12, p 21.

the domestic authorities to be a 'good father figure' to him.[41]    It remains to be determined whether relations more typical of nephew/uncle relations would similarly attract the protection of Article 8.

## *Adoptive and Foster Parents*

Although the relationship between adoptive parents and children will, in principle, attract the protection of Article 8,[42] it is unclear whether ties between a child and his/her foster parents will amount to family life in the same way.  The Commission has found such a relationship to amount to private life only,[43] although the success of a future challenge will depend on the circumstances of the claim being made.  If there is no birth family making a similar claim of family life, and the child has been cared for by the foster family and developed strong ties with them, it is likely that their relationship will enjoy the protection of Article 8, the absence of formal legal ties notwithstanding.  Moreover, it is important that a child, who is otherwise deprived of a family environment, is entitled to have the personal ties which s/he develops with the foster family given legal recognition and protection under Article 8, particularly in the event of long-term fostering.

## **Compatibility with Article 8**

The existence of family life merely determines the applicability of Article 8.  From this point, the Court goes on to examine the substance of the applicant's complaint under Article 8 § 2.  While the more common approach is to determine whether the State's interference with family life is justified, the issue of whether there is a positive obligation to respect family life, which must be satisfied to comply with Article 8, may arise in certain circumstances.

---

[41] No *16580/90 Boyle v UK*, Comm Rep, 9.2.93, Series A no 282, p 26, 19 EHRR 181. See further Chapter 12.

[42] No *9993/82 X v France*, Dec 5.10.82, DR 31, p 241, 5 EHRR 302; *Söderbäck* judgment, *op cit*.

[43] No *8257/78 X v Switzerland*, Dec 10.7.78, DR 13, p 248.  However, see the comments of Mr Schermers dissenting in No *12366/86 Rieme v Sweden*, Comm Rep, 2.10.90, Series A no 226-B, 16 EHRR 169.

*Positive Obligations*

It is well established that respect for family life may in certain circumstances require affirmative action in order to secure the enjoyment of that right.[44]    However, the identification of circumstances in which compliance with Article 8 will require positive action is not without difficulty.[45]    In particular, the Court has acknowledged that the notion of respect is not clear-cut and, due to the varying conditions and circumstances in Convention States, what is required to ensure respect for family life will vary considerably from case to case.[46]    This diversity entitles States to a wide margin of appreciation in the manner in which they guarantee the right to respect for family life and determining the scope of any positive obligation to respect family life is thus a balancing exercise between the interests of the individual applicant and the general interest of society to which the legitimate aims listed in paragraph 2 of Article 8 are relevant.[47]

This means, for example, that even though the relationship between an unmarried mother and her child requires the adoption of measures designed to ensure the child's integration into his/her family from the moment of birth, the same is not true of every other family life relationship.  This was illustrated in the case of *X, Y & Z* where the Court found family life to exist between a child born by AID and her transsexual father, but it declined to require the State to respect their relationship by permitting him to register on her birth certificate as her father.[48]    Other family life relationships, such as that between the unmarried father and his child,[49] and that enjoyed between a child and his/her grandparents[50] also appear to require less 'respect' in the form of the adoption of affirmative measures.  There is no

---

[44]    *Marckx* judgment, *op cit*. See further Chapter 1, pp 12-13.

[45]    Harris, O'Boyle & Warbrick, *op cit*, p 321.

[46]    Indeed, the case law shows a diversity of opinion among the members of the Commission and Court as to which approach is appropriate in particular cases. For example, see No *10454/85 Gaskin v UK*, Comm Rep, 13.11.87, Series A no 160, p 27, 11 EHRR 402 and Eur Court HR *Gaskin v UK*, judgment of 7 July 1989, Series A no 160, 12 EHRR 36.

[47]    Eur Court HR *Hokkanen v Finland*, judgment of 23 Sept 1994, Series A no 299, 19 EHRR 139.  An earlier view was that the positive approach rendered paragraph 2 irrelevant. See Connelly, *op cit*, p 572.

[48]    *X, Y & Z judgment, op cit.*

[49]    See O'Donnell (1995a), *op cit.*

[50]    See No *12402/86 Price v UK*, *op cit*. See further Chapter 12, pp 280, 287- 288.

uniform approach in this regard, however, and the existence of positive obligations will depend on the facts of the individual case. In any event, this distinction in treatment is likely to become more apparent in the light of the Court's new found preference for the automatic application of Article 8 in such cases.[51]

## Negative Obligations

Article 8 § 2 requires States to refrain from taking action which interferes unjustifiably with family life and this principle of negative obligations is the dominant approach of the Strasbourg institutions in this area. Further to Article 8 § 1 which guarantees the right to respect for private and family life, home and correspondence, Article 8 § 2 provides that

> [t]here shall be no interference by a public authority with the exercise of this right except such as is in accordance with the law and is necessary in a democratic society in the interests of national security, public safety or the economic well-being of the country, for the prevention of disorder or crime, for the protection of health or morals or for the protection of the rights and freedoms of others.

In order to be consistent with Article 8, therefore, any interference with family life must fulfil all of the criteria listed in paragraph 2 of the provision. In particular, the interference must be in accordance with law, it must pursue one of the legitimate aims listed in the second paragraph and it must be necessary in a democratic society or proportionate to the pursuit of that aim. The Strasbourg authorities consistently accept that any measure which infringes upon family life constitutes an interference with it. For example, restricting contact between parent and child, refusing a parent entry to a country to join a spouse or child, or placing a child with foster or adoptive parents automatically interferes with family life and as a result, this limb of the test poses little difficulty. In contrast, whether the measure in question is in accordance with law, has a legitimate aim and is necessary in a democratic society is more difficult to determine. It is the question of the proportionality of the interference which is the most common stumbling block for applicants seeking the protection of Article 8.

---

[51] See above, pp 190-191.

*In accordance with Law:*  A measure which constitutes an interference with family life will only be compatible with Article 8 where it is in accordance with law.  According to the Court's well-established guidelines, the phrase 'in accordance with law' refers not only to domestic law, but also to the rule of law, meaning that the law which provides for the interference must contain a measure of protection against arbitrariness by public authorities.[52] While it is possible to complain that the measure creating the interference does not have a legislative basis,[53] it is also a source of common complaint that the law, which is in place, is too broad or vague.  It may be arguable, for example, that the scope of powers conferred on social workers to remove children from care or restrict contact with their parents is too broad.[54]  In the *Olsson* case for example, the parents made such a complaint about the law which authorised taking children into care.  Although the Court acknowledged that the Swedish law was written in general terms, it accepted that it satisfied the legal requirements of Article 8 § 2.  In doing so, the Court commented that absolute legislative precision is unattainable in the area of child care and acknowledged that the need to avoid excessive rigidity and keep pace with changing circumstances means that many laws are inevitably couched in vague terms.  Such laws do not necessarily violate Article 8, because it is impossible to formulate a law to cover every eventuality of taking a child into care.  Moreover, to confine the authorities to where harm has occurred may reduce the effectiveness of protection.

Nor is a law which confers a discretion in itself inconsistent with the requirement of foreseeability, as long as the scope of discretion and the manner of its exercise are indicated with sufficient clarity to give the individual adequate protection against arbitrary interference.[55]  For example, the Commission and the Court have agreed on this basis that legislation permitting children to be taken into care where their health or development are jeopardised, but without requiring proof of actual harm, satisfies the test of legality under Article 8.[56]  What is important here is that

---

[52]  *Olsson* judgment, *op cit*, § 61 and Eur Court HR *Johansen v Norway*, judgment of 7 Aug 1996-III, p 979, 23 EHRR 33, § 53-59.

[53]  See Eur Court HR *Olsson (No 2) v Sweden*, judgment of 27 Nov 1992, Series A no 250, 17 EHRR 134, § 67.

[54]  See further Harris, O'Boyle & Warbrick, *op cit*, pp 340-341.

[55]  *Olsson* judgment, *op cit*, § 62.

[56]  *Andersson* judgment, *op cit*, § 62 and No *10465/83 Olsson v Sweden*, Comm Rep, 17.4.91, Series A no 130, § 132-142. This criterion was introduced into the law of England and Wales in The Children Act 1989.

there exist safeguards against arbitrary interference in the form of subjecting the exercise of statutory powers to review by the administrative courts.

The requirement of legality also refers to the quality of the law in question, requiring that it be accessible to the persons concerned and formulated with sufficient precision to enable them, if need be with appropriate advice, to foresee, to a degree that is reasonable in the circumstances, the consequences which a given action may entail.[57]

*Legitimate Aim: The Best Interests of the Child:* It falls to the State under Article 8 § 2 to identify the aim which it pursued as a basis for the interference with family life under Article 8 § 1. Respondent States consistently submit either 'the protection of health or morals', or 'the protection of the rights and freedoms of others' as legitimate reasons for taking measures which interfere with family life and the Strasbourg institutions rarely refuse to accept their claims. Where the complaint relates to the separation of family members due to the enforcement of immigration laws, States frequently invoke the aims of protecting the economic well-being of the country and preventing disorder and crime.[58] In typical domestic family law cases, however, the aim most frequently cited is the need to protect health or morals, and this has been applied as an individual, rather than a social value.[59] More specifically, the aim of protecting the child's health (physical, psychological or emotional) has been accepted as a legitimate basis for interfering with a parent's right to respect for family life.[60] The same is also true with regard to the aim of protecting the rights and freedoms of others, although there is rarely any enumeration of what individual rights or freedoms are being protected in a given instance. In cases involving children, the best interests test is now the accepted principle by which the consistency with Article 8 § 2 of state interference with family life is determined.[61] However, the Strasbourg case

---

[57] *Andersson* judgment, *op cit*, § 75.

[58] See further Chapter 10, pp 219-221.

[59] See No *911/60 X v Sweden*, Dec 10.4.61, Collection 7, p 7 and also Opsahl, 'The Convention and the Right to Respect for Family Life' in Robertson (ed) (1973), *Privacy and Human Rights*, Manchester: MUP, pp 216-217.

[60] See *Hendriks* Comm Rep, *op cit.*

[61] The only reference to this principle in the Convention is in Article 5 of Protocol no 7 which provides that equality of rights and responsibilities between spouses and in relation to their children shall not prevent States from taking such measures as are necessary in the interests of the children.

law reflects more the traditional form of the best interests principle, which is associated with the concept of welfarism,[62] than the remoulded, dynamic principle contained in the UN Convention on the Rights of the Child, which takes into account the child's evolving capacity and right to be heard.[63] Moreover, the Convention authorities have failed to highlight the factors to be taken into account in applying the best interests principle, or what weight should be attached to each factor.[64] To the contrary, these matters are deemed to fall appropriately within the margin of appreciation which States enjoy in their application of the Article 8[65] and this discretion is in turn offered by the State to its agents - judges, social workers - who are charged with determining what is in the child's best interests.[66]

It is similarly unclear what level of importance should be attached to the child's best interests to ensure compatibility with Article 8. The principle of paramountcy enjoys occasional, but not consistent, support throughout the family life case law. Admittedly, an approach which treats the child's interests as the sole consideration in such cases would make it difficult to balance the rights of the child with the right to respect for family life of parents and/or other family members. Notwithstanding that an approach, according to which the child's interests are treated as paramount, is enjoying increasingly widespread acceptance,[67] the context of Article 8 which, like many ECHR provisions, requires the reconciliation of competing interests, demands that all relevant factors be given adequate consideration, without placing the interests of the children and the parents in an unnecessarily adversarial context.

---

[62] This is illustrated by the Commission's opinion in *Hendriks* Comm Rep, *op cit*, § 121. See further Chapter 12, pp 251-255.

[63] Article 3, 5 and 12, UN Doc A/44/25. See Van Bueren, *op cit*, pp 45-46.

[64] Nor does the Convention on the Rights of the Child. See Van Bueren (1995a), *op cit*, p 47-48. However, the welfare principle has itself been criticised for being indeterminate. See Dupaix (1987), 'Best Interests Revisited: in Search of Guidelines', *Utah Law Review*, **3**, pp 651-573 and Elster (1978), 'Salamonic Judgement: Against the Best Interests of the Child', *University of Chicago Law Review*, **54**, pp 1-45.

[65] Importantly, domestic law, which imposes the best interests standard, is likely to be accompanied by guidance such as the 'welfare checklist', to be used by courts and other domestic authorities. See Hoyal (1993), 'The Children Act 1989 and the European Convention', *Legal Action*, pp 22-23.

[66] See further below, pp 204-206.

[67] It is enshrined in English law in s 1 Children Act, 1989.

While the approach of the institutions to the best interests principle may be criticised for being minimalist, the compatibility with the Convention of a measure which interferes with family life in order to protect the child is nevertheless determined ultimately by the application of the proportionality principle in the latter stage of the Article 8 test.    Although specific examples of how this is applied in practice are provided in the individual contexts of custody and contact, alternative care and adoption in the chapters which follow, it is useful to highlight the general principles, which the Court has developed in its application of the test at this stage.

*Necessary in a Democratic Society:*  It is well established that the question of whether the State has struck an appropriate balance between the interference with family life and the aim of protecting the interests and rights of the child is answered by applying the principle of proportionality. According to the Court, this involves considering whether in the light of the case as a whole, the authorities had 'relevant and sufficient reasons' for taking the contentious measures.[68] Although the Court has required the existence of 'strong reasons' to justify an interference in some cases, this suggests not a different test, but one that varies with the facts of the case and the demands of proportionality.[69] The more far reaching and severe the interference with family life, therefore, the stronger the reasons required to ensure its consistency with Article 8.  This approach means, for example, that stronger reasons are needed to justify a prohibition on contact between a parent and child in care, than a restriction on such contact.[70]

In the light of the Court's move towards an approach, according to which family life between parents and their children is presumed to exist, it is likely that this stage of the Article 8 test will become more detailed and comprehensive.  Having found family life to exist between an unmarried father and his child in *Söderbäck* for example, the Court went on to weigh up factors previously considered relevant to whether family life existed, such as the nature of the father's relationship with his daughter, in determining whether the interference with that family life was justified.[71] While this approach is not likely to lead to greater success before the Court for such applicants, it is arguably a more fair and just way to apply Article

---

[68] *Olsson* judgment, *op cit*, § 87. See also *Hokkanen* judgment, *op cit*.
[69] For criticism see the dissenting opinion of Judge Lagregren in *Andersson* judgment, *op cit*. See also Harris, O'Boyle & Warbrick, *op cit*, p 350.
[70] See further Chapter 12, pp 276-280.
[71] See further Chapter 13, pp 298-300.

8, not least because it permits the merits of more cases to be examined under Article 8 § 2.

*The Margin of Appreciation:*[72] In following the above test, the Court has experienced difficulty in reviewing national policy on such issues, particularly in the absence of a common European understanding about child care and the legitimate nature of state interference. In this regard, it has recognised the diversity in approaches to child care and state intervention among the States of the Council of Europe, and it takes this into account when examining such cases under the Convention. It has particular regard to the fact that

> perceptions as to the appropriateness of intervention by public authorities in the care of children vary from one Contracting State to another, depending on such factors as traditions relating to the role of the family and to State intervention in family affairs and the availability of resources for public measures in this particular area.[73]

The Court has also recognised that due to their proximity to the sensitive and complex issues being determined at national level, the domestic authorities are better placed to make an assessment of the circumstances of each case and to determine the most appropriate course of action. In care cases, for example, the national authorities benefit from direct contact with the persons concerned, at the very stage when care measures are being envisaged or immediately after their implementation.[74]   As a result, the State enjoys a degree of discretion with regard to the manner in which family life is respected under Article 8 and this is reflected in the way in which the balance between the interference and its aim is assessed. However, the margin of discretion afforded to competent national authorities will vary in the light of the nature of the issues and the seriousness of the interests at stake.[75]  Although a wide margin is permitted in assessing the necessity of taking a child into care, stricter scrutiny is required with regard to further limitations, such as restrictions on parental contact, and of any legal safeguards designed to secure effective protection

---

[72] See also Chapter 1, pp 6-8.

[73] *Johansen* judgment, *op cit*, § 64.

[74] *Olsson (No 2)* judgment, *op cit*, § 90.

[75] See Eur Court HR *The Sunday Times v UK (no 1)*, judgment of 26 April 1979, Series A no 30, 2 EHRR 245, § 59.

of the right to respect for family life guaranteed to both parents and children.[76]

It is not the task of the Strasbourg institutions to take the place of the competent domestic authorities by undertaking a fresh examination of all the facts and evidence in a case. At the same time, the Court does not limit its review to ascertaining whether the State exercised its discretion in relation to respecting family life reasonably, carefully and in good faith.[77] What falls to the Court is to review, as a whole, the decisions taken by the domestic administrative and judicial authorities in the exercise of their power of appreciation.[78]    This degree of discretion is taken into consideration in every children's case in the light of the considerations outlined above. While it is inescapable that this discretion limits the scope of the Court's powers to examine domestic decisions, it has not prevented it from finding that the domestic authorities have gone beyond the discretion offered to them in acting inconsistently with Article 8.[79]  There has been much debate about the extent of the Court's power to review domestic decisions, including the suggestion that the Court should hear witnesses if it is to undertake a proper review of national decisions.[80]  On the other hand, there is also support for the Court to adopt a purely procedural approach to their review of issues of child-care, which would defer all determination of substantive issues to the domestic authorities.[81]  Such a

---

[76] This is due to the fact that such limitations entail the danger that the family relations between the parents and a young child will be effectively curtailed. *Johansen* judgment, *op cit*, § 64.

[77] *Ibid.*

[78] For example, see *Hokkanen* judgment, *op cit*.

[79] However, it is sometimes unclear whether the burden falls on the applicant to show the inadequacy of domestic action or on the State to show that its authorities have taken adequate steps in this regard.  See Harris, O'Boyle & Warbrick, *op cit*, p 350.

[80] See the dissenting opinion of Judge Lagergren in *Olsson (No 2)* judgment, *op cit*.  See also Harris, O'Boyle & Warbrick, *op cit*, p 350.  However, moves to hear witnesses in Strasbourg might give rise to speculation that the Court is seeking to act as a fourth instance.

[81] See the view of Mr Schermers in No 11373/85 *Eriksson* v Sweden, Comm Rep, 14.7.88, Series A no 156, and Harris, O'Boyle & Warbrick, *op cit*, p 351. Cf the dissenting opinion of Judges Pinheiro Farinha, Pettiti, Walsh, Russo and De Meyer in *Olsson* judgment, *op cit*. See also Cohen-Jonathan, 'Respect for Private and Family Life' in Macdonald et al (eds) (1993), *The European System for the Protection of Human Rights*, Deventer: Kluwer, 405-444, at p 440.

deliberate move to limit the Court's jurisdiction is unlikely however, not least because it would be inconsistent with the Convention's object and purpose to exempt state action in a particular area from the Court's scrutiny.

## Procedural Safeguards implicit in Family Life

Article 6 contains a procedural safeguard in the form of the right to have civil rights and obligations determined by a court. However, its procedural protection applies to family law proceedings only insofar as they involve determination of a civil right of contact, custody or guardianship.[82] It is important, therefore, that Article 8 provides further protection covering administrative and other proceedings, and decision-making processes at domestic level. In particular, the Court has found implicit in Article 8 a procedural safeguard which requires parental involvement in any decision-making process concerning their children to a degree sufficient to provide them with a requisite protection of their interests. This is particularly important given the circumstances and the serious nature of the decisions to be taken.[83] Notwithstanding its significance, the same principle has yet to be developed in relation to the involvement of children in such proceedings. Admittedly, it has yet to be argued before the Court that respect for family life requires that the views of the child be sought and given consideration, or that the child should be represented independently where decisions fundamental to their private and family life under Article 8 are being made. In the light of the fact that international law has given express recognition to the child's right to participate in this way, particularly under Article 12 of the Convention on the Rights of the Child, however, the Court is likely to need little encouragement to adopt such an interpretation either under Article 8, or Article 6.[84]

The Court has acknowledged that there is a difference in the protection afforded by Articles 6 and 8 in this context. Although Article 6 contains a procedural safeguard, it is to be distinguished from Article 8 by the nature

---

[82] See further Harris, O'Boyle & Warbrick, *op cit*, pp 174-196.

[83] Eur Court HR *W v UK* judgment of 8 July 1987, Series A, no 121, 10 EHRR 29, § 64. See also the separate judgments in *R, O* and *B v UK*, handed down on the same day.

[84] See further Chapter 6, pp 117-120.

of the procedural protection which the latter provision offers. According to the Court,

> not only does the procedural requirement implicit in Article 8 cover administrative procedures as well as judicial proceedings, but it is ancillary to the wide purpose of ensuring proper respect for family life.[85]

This may explain why the same facts may be examined appropriately under both provisions, where the situation complained of has repercussions for family life as well as the conduct of the judicial proceedings, this approach is considered appropriate.[86] In practice, however, this double examination is seldom undertaken and the issue is usually considered under one provision with the finding that no separate issue arises to warrant its further examination under the second.[87]

## *Family Law Proceedings and Article 6*

Given that family law proceedings have particular characteristics and the potential to change substantially family relations, a careful balance must be reached between the interests of the parties involved in such proceedings and the proper administration of justice. However, the fundamental right to a fair trial must never be infringed and in the *De Vries* case, for example, a domestic court's infringement of a whole series of rules, which resulted in an appeal against a decision to deprive a parent of guardianship being submitted out of time, was found to violate Article 6.[88] In particular, the decision to reject the father's appeal against a decision that had serious implications for his relations with his children could not be justified by any factor pertaining to the proper administration of justice.[89]

Article 6 is applicable to care proceedings as a whole and thus the Court has not found it necessary to consider whether particular children's hearings, such as those under Scots law, are consistent with the provision.

---

[85] Eur Court HR *McMichael v UK*, judgment of 24 Feb 1995, Series A no 308, 20 EHRR 205, § 91.

[86] *Ibid*, § 92.

[87] See No 173873/90 *Johansen v Norway*, Comm Rep, 17.1.95, Reports 1996-III, no 13, p 1015, § 106 and No *12574/86 Nyberg v Sweden*, Comm Rep, 31.8.90, Series A no 181, p 42, 14 EHRR 870, § 150-153.

[88] No *16690/90 De Vries v the Netherlands*, Comm Rep, 13.10.93, unreported, § 48.

[89] *Ibid*, § 49.

However, the Court has recognised that, notwithstanding their particularly sensitive and complex nature, the right to a fair trial is as important in family law proceedings as elsewhere. Regardless of how they accommodate the sensitive and complex matters before them, family proceedings must not jeopardise the rights of the parties involved under Article 6, or Article 8 for that matter. There may be good reasons in the domain of family law for opting for an adjudicatory body that does not have the composition of a court of law of the classic kind. However, as a matter of general principle, the right to a fair, adversarial trial means the opportunity to have knowledge of and comment on the observations filed or evidence adduced by the other party.[90] The exclusion of parents from family proceedings, which consequently denies them the opportunity to cross examine their children, will be consistent with Article 6 as long as it is necessary to exclude the influence of the interested parties and hear the children in their absence.[91] Where only one parent is excluded, in some cases this may raise an issue under Article 6 with regard to the principle of the equality of arms.

Confidential or *in camera* proceedings are likely to be consistent with Article 6 given the nature of the proceedings as a whole and particularly, the fact that they concern the welfare and future of a child.[92] In this regard, Article 6 expressly states that the press and public may be excluded from all or part of a trial in the interests of children, although this would appear to apply to the hearing, rather than the public pronouncement of the judgment. Failure to reveal the identity of prospective adopters in adoption proceedings is also consistent with the right to a fair trial given the nature of such proceedings.[93] In contrast, however, a legal situation which as a rule denies the unmarried father standing in adoption proceedings,[94] and an oral hearing within those proceedings, is incompatible with the right to a fair trial.[95]

---

[90] *McMichael* judgment, *op cit*, § 80. See also No *17771/91 R v Switzerland*, Comm Rep, 9.9.93, unreported, § 46-53.

[91] No *8893/80 X v Austria*, Dec 5.3.83, 31, p 66.

[92] See No *18280/90 MV v Malta, op cit*. See also (1996) *New Law Journal Digest*, p 1425.

[93] *Ibid.*

[94] *Keegan* judgment, *op cit*. See further Chapter 13, p 311.

[95] No *17771/91 R* Comm Rep, *op cit*, § 41-45 where the applicant's lack of oral hearing violated Article 6.

*Length of Family Proceedings*

The impact of the length of family law proceedings on their outcome has implications for Article 8 as well as Article 6. Effective respect for family life requires that future relations between parent and child be determined solely in the light of all relevant considerations and not by the mere effluxion of time.[96] Any procedural delay may thus lead to a *de facto* determination of the issue before the court and thus the relevant authorities are under a duty to exercise exceptional diligence where there is a danger that a procedural delay will have an irreversible effect on the parties' family life.[97] Although the unnecessary duration of proceedings may be a factor in considering whether the proceedings as a whole were consistent with Article 8, their length may also fall to be considered under Article 6, which provides for the right to a fair trial within a reasonable time. What is reasonable in this context depends on all the circumstances of the case and, there is no absolute time limit for different types of proceedings. Factors which are of decisive importance in determining the consistency of the length of particular proceedings with Article 6 are the complexity of the proceedings, the conduct of the applicant and the conduct of the relevant administrative and judicial authorities.[98] The Court will consider the cumulative effect of these elements and decide on the basis of the case as a whole whether the length was excessive. Where several levels of jurisdiction are involved,[99] or where the complexity of the proceedings is evident from the amount of evidence, preparation of expert reports and other in-depth investigations being conducted, it is unlikely that the length of proceedings will be found to be excessive.[100] In general, where procedural delays can be attributed to the conduct of the applicant then the State will not be held responsible for the delay. Similarly, where the domestic authorities can demonstrate their awareness that such proceedings

---

[96] *W* judgment, *op cit*, § 65.

[97] Eur Court HR *H v UK*, judgment of 8 July 1987, Series A, no 120, § 85.

[98] *Olsson (No 2)* judgment, *op cit*, § 99. In cases where the delay is unjustifiable, a settlement may be easily reached. See No *20609/92 Wills v UK*, Dec 17.5.94, unreported.

[99] *Olsson (No 2)* judgment, *op cit*, § 106; *Hokkanen* judgment, *op cit*, § 72 and Eur Court HR *Eriksson v Sweden*, judgment of 2 June 1989, Series A, no 156, 12 EHRR 183, § 74-75.

[100] No *19823/92 Hokkanen v Finland*, Comm Rep, 22.10.93, Series A no 299, 19 EHRR 153, § 136-146.

by their very nature require to be dealt with urgently, then no violation will occur.[101]

## Family Assistance

The Court's flexible approach to the interpretation of Article 8 means that the provision of family assistance falls within the scope of the right to respect for family life. However, the Commission has found that the Convention does not guarantee the right to state assistance for the family, either in the form of financial support or day care places for children.[102] Thus, a challenge to Swedish policy, which replaced financial support for children with day care places in order to achieve greater representation of women in the work-place, was unsuccessful. In particular, the Commission found that respect for family life cannot be interpreted so as to oblige States to provide financial assistance to enable a parent to take care of children in the home. Thus, where a parent chooses to stay at home, there is no positive obligation on the State to replace his/her lost income in order to respect family life under the Convention. However, it is unclear whether an obligation of either a positive or negative kind should be ruled out in all circumstances. It might arise, for example, where the parent's decision to stay at home was an enforced, rather than a voluntary one, such as where the parent had to provide care for a child with special needs. Even more uncertain, however, is whether the payment of family allowances to households with children, or a system of tax relief which favoured families with children would be compatible with the provision.[103]

It is arguable that providing financial assistance to one parent, but not the other, raises an issue of discrimination on the grounds of gender. However, the Commission and the Court have expressed conflicting views as to whether such differential treatment is consistent with Article 14, together with Article 8. In the *Petrovic* case, the applicant father complained about the refusal to grant him parental leave allowance as a full

---

[101] No 16817/90 *Paulsen-Medalen v Sweden*, Comm Rep, 4.9.96, unreported, § 51-58.

[102] No *11776/85 Andersson & Kullman v Sweden*, Dec 4.3.86, DR 46, p 251.

[103] See Melchior, 'Rights not covered by the Convention' in Macdonald et al (eds), *op cit*, p 601.

time carer, when it was awarded to mothers.[104]  Although Article 8 does not contain a right to parental leave, the complaint fell within the scope of that provision because the payment was designed to promote family life.  The Commission and Court disagreed, however, as to whether the differential treatment of mothers and fathers with regard to the payment of a parental leave allowance was justified.  The Commission, relying on the fact that the advancement of equality between the sexes was a major goal in the member states of the Council of Europe, failed to find that weighty reasons existed for the difference in treatment which it found to be exclusively based on the ground of sex.[105]  The lack of a common standard with regard to the payment of benefits reflected the substantial diversity of social-security systems across Europe, but could not absolve the State from granting those benefits without discrimination.  The Court, in contrast, focussed on the fact that at the material time, there was no common standard in the field as the majority of Convention States did not provide for parental leave allowances to be paid to fathers.  This absence of a common standard permitted the Court to grant to the Austrian authorities a wide margin of appreciation within which the difference in treatment complained of could be justified.

The Commission's decision in this case was a positive development, which reflected the move towards common parental responsibilities, evident at European and international level.  In direct contrast, the Court's judgment leaned heavily on the absence of common standards in the area to find that the State enjoyed a wide margin of appreciation in this area.  Curiously, the Court seemed keen to emphasise that its consideration of the situation related to the end of the 1980s, when the relevant Austrian legislation awarding parental leave allowance to mothers was first enacted.  In light of the fact that Austrian law extended this payment to both parents in 1990, the Court said it would be difficult to criticise the Austrian legislature (presumably by finding a violation of the Convention) for introducing legislation in a gradual manner, which was, all things considered, progressive in Europe.  More importantly, however, the Court distinguished between the denial of parental leave to fathers and the refusal to grant related benefits, suggesting arguably, that the latter would indeed violate the Convention.  These points notwithstanding, the Court found it

---

[104] No *20458/92 Petrovic v Austria*, Comm Rep, Dec 15.10.96, and Eur Court HR judgment of 27 March 1998, Reports 1998-II, no 67.

[105] In particular, the Commission found that there was no reason why a father who was willing to do so, could not personally take care of a newborn child, *ibid.*

surprisingly easy to justify discrimination which, according to two dissenting judges, perpetuated the traditional distribution of roles and could also have negative consequences for the mother.[106]

## Future Challenges

According to Judge Pettiti

> [t]he growing number of precarious and unstable family situations is creating new difficulties for children of first and second families, whether legitimate, natural, successive, or superimposed.[107]

Thus although the Commission and the Court have been responsible for a dynamic development of the family life concept, it is clear that the twentieth century will present new challenges, not least those highlighted above. The institutions have shown a willingness to adapt their approach to family life, evident in the extension of the concept to include a parent-child relationship without a blood or legal tie, which is necessary if the relevance of Article 8 to the modern family is to be ensured. However, 'thoughtful consideration of the identity of the family and the meaning of family life' will be necessary before the Court determines the applicability of Article 8 to modern family arrangements, including those to which Judge Pettiti refers. In addition, other permutations of family life, including the relationship between half-siblings, children and foster parents, and children of first and second relationships have yet to be examined, although it is positive in this respect that the Court appears to favour the presumption of family life in many cases where a blood or legal tie exists, leaving the substantive issues to be decided more appropriately under Article 8 § 2.

The other area likely to endure further expansion is in relation to the procedural protection of respect for family life under Article 8, as well as under Article 6. In particular, the need for independent representation for children in family proceedings will undoubtedly arise before the Court, both in terms of providing the child with an independent means to express his/her opinion and safeguarding the child's individual interests. The lines

---

[106] See the dissenting opinions of Mr Bernhardt and Mr Spielmann, *Petrovic* judgment, *ibid.*

[107] Concurring Opinion of Judge Pettiti in *X, Y & Z* judgment, *op cit.*

defining the scope of Article 8 have not yet been finally drawn and it is envisaged that future challenges will arise from its interpretation from the child's perspective. These are highlighted further in the Chapters which follow.

# 10    Immigrant and Refugee Children

**Introduction**

Notwithstanding that the European Convention does not guarantee specific rights to immigrants and refugees, there is now a considerable body of case law on the compatibility of immigration and asylum law measures with its provisions.[1] Moreover, while the Court has consistently recognised the rights of States to control their borders,[2] it has also stressed the requirement that immigration law and practice must be implemented consistent with all of the Convention's provisions. The application of the Convention to immigrants and refugees, regardless of nationality or status is assured therefore, although certain provisions have proven to be more useful than others in protecting the rights of such children.

Article 8, which guarantees the right to respect for private and family life, has been used frequently with varying degrees of success in the immigration context. In particular, it has been invoked where parents and/or their children are being deported from a Convention State, or where they are refused entry for the purposes of family reunification. Article 3, which prohibits torture and inhuman and degrading treatment, has also been invoked in these cases in relation to the treatment of children on entry and during deportation from a Convention State. In addition, the right to liberty under Article 5 is applicable to the detention of refugees prior to deportation from, or on their arrival into a Convention State. Despite the usefulness of these provisions, the absence of specific protection for the immigrant and refugee children means that positive approaches to the interpretation of relevant provisions must be adopted in order to secure protection of their rights. Thus, Article 1, which requires the State to

---

[1]    See Storey (1990), 'The Right to Family Life and Immigration Case Law at Strasbourg', *International and Comparative Law Quarterly*, **39**, p 328-344 and Villiger, 'Expulsion and the Right to Respect for Private and Family Life - An Introduction to the Commission's Case Law' in Matscher & Petzold (eds) (1988), *Protecting Human Rights: The European Dimension, Studies in Honour of Gerard J Wiarda*, Koln: Heymanns, pp 657-662.

[2]    Eur Court HR *Abdulaziz, Cabales and Balkandali v UK*, judgment of 28 May 1985, Series A No 94, 7 EHRR 471, § 67.

secure Convention rights to everyone, can be used to argue that the right to education, for example, is enjoyed by non-national children.[3] Similarly, Article 14, the non-discrimination provision, may be invoked by such children who do not enjoy their rights equally with other children in a Convention State.[4]

## Family Life in Immigration Cases

Article 8 is a valuable provision insofar as it provides a basis for challenging the separation of parents from their children as a result of a decision to deport or refuse entry to one or the other. Before Article 8 can be invoked, however, those seeking to rely on the provision must prove that the relevant relationship falls within the meaning of family life. While the general principles used to determine the existence of family life apply in the immigration context too - the trend is towards finding the relationship between parents and children will always constitute family life[5] - the Commission and Court have traditionally taken a strict approach to the application of Article 8 in such cases, in light, *inter alia*, of the State's right to control its borders.[6]

The Court established in the *Berrehab* case that cohabitation is not a *sine quo non* of family life and it went on to find that family life existed between a divorced man and his daughter, notwithstanding that they no longer lived together.[7] Despite this principle, the Commission *has* taken into account whether the parties live together in deciding whether family life exits in immigration cases.[8] It is also apparent from immigration cases that the extent to which the parties depend on each other financially or emotionally will be relevant to the existence of family life too.[9] In *Berrehab* for instance, the facts that the applicant was the child's co-

---

[3] See Chapter 1, pp 11-13 and Chapter 4, pp 67-68.

[4] See Chapter 1, pp 4-6.

[5] See Chapter 9, pp 187-197.

[6] See Sherlock (1998) 'Deportation of Aliens and Article 8 ECHR', *European Law Review*, **23**, pp 62-75, at p 68.

[7] Eur Court HR *Berrehab v the Netherlands*, judgment of 21 June 1988, Series A no 138, 11 EHRR 322, § 21.

[8] For example see Nos *7289/75 & 7349/76 X & Y v Switzerland*, Dec 14.7.77, DR 9 p 57.

[9] For example see No *7229/76 X & Y v UK*, Dec 15.12.77, DR 12, p 32.

guardian and that he contributed to her upkeep on a monthly basis helped to substantiate the claim that their relationship was one of family life.[10]

More recent deportation cases have highlighted the adoption by the Court of a more principled approach to the existence of family life. In particular, it appears to favour a presumption that family life exists between parent and child, which can only be ruptured in exceptional circumstances. In *Boughanemi v France,* for example, the applicant's relationship with his son born outside marriage amounted to family life notwithstanding that he enjoyed no parental rights in relation to his son, contributed nothing to his upkeep or education and failed to recognise him until ten months after he was born.[11] In addition to presuming that family life exists between parent and child, the exceptional circumstances in which the tie may be broken have not yet been found to exist.[12] Thus in *C v Belgium* the Court found that the applicant's imprisonment, his deportation and the fact that his son was taken in by his sister in Luxembourg did not break the family life tie which existed between them.[13] Similarly, in *Ahmut v the Netherlands*, the fact that the applicant's father had left Morocco when he was six years old, leaving him in the care of his former wife and then his mother, did not disrupt their tie of family life.[14]

The Court also appears to have accepted in principle that the concept of family life includes the relationship between siblings.[15] This appears to be implicit also from the Commission's opinion in these cases.[16] However, it is apparent from earlier cases that family ties other than those between parent and child will not lead to the automatic entitlement to the protection of Article 8 § 1. This view appears to persist in the immigrant context at

---

[10] *Berrehab* judgment, *op cit*, § 21. See also No *10730/84 Berrehab* v the *Netherlands*, Comm Rep, 7.10.86, Series A no 138, p 21, § 72.

[11] Eur Court HR *Boughanemi v France*, judgment of 24 April 1996, Reports 1996-II no 8, p 593, 22 EHRR 228.

[12] See Eur Court HR *Gul v Switzerland*, judgment of 19 Feb 1996, Reports 1996-I, no 3, p 159, 22 EHRR 93.

[13] Eur Court HR *C v Belgium*, judgment of 7 August 1996, Reports 1996-III, no 12, p 915.

[14] Eur Court HR *Ahmut* v *the Netherlands*, judgment of 28 Nov 1996, Reports 1996 no 24, p 2017, 24 EHRR 62.

[15] *Boughanemi* judgment, *op cit*. See also Eur Court HR *Moustaquim v Belgium*, judgment of 18 Feb 1991, Series A no 193, 13 EHRR 802.

[16] See Liddy (1998), 'The Concept of Family Life Under the ECHR', *European Human Rights Law Review*, **1**, pp 15-25, at pp 18-19.

least, and evidence of the sincerity and importance of these ties is necessary before Article 8 will apply to such cases.[17]  Thus the apparent lack of dependency between family members has caused the Commission to reject the claims of family life between adult children and their parents;[18] between siblings;[19] grandchildren and grandparents;[20] nephews and uncles, and children and their adoptive parents.[21]  The fact that these relationships have been found to amount to family life in some purely domestic cases suggests that a strict line is taken on the existence of family life in immigration cases, particularly those involving reunification, where the burden is on the applicant to establish that such a relationship exists.[22]

It appears to be exclusive to immigration cases that applicants must prove the genuine nature of their family ties, although this requirement presumably aims to identify the bogus from the genuine claims.  In the *Nsona* case, the applicants were unable to substantiate their claim that they were aunt and niece and the Commission rejected their case under Article 8 as a result.[23]  The Court reached a similar conclusion, although it found that because the applicants had first alleged to be mother and child, their deceit invalidated any claim of family life.[24]  Those seeking entry for the purposes of family reunification must thus be able to prove their family life tie therefore, although it is uncertain whether refugees who arrive without any identity papers would be under the same obligation.  Conversely, the existence of a legal tie in the form of adoption papers will of itself be

---

[17]  *Ibid.*

[18]  No *10375/83 S & S v UK*, Dec 10.12.84, DR 40 p 196; No *14852/89 Akhtar & Johangir v the Netherlands*, Dec 7.4.93, DR 74 p 29.  *cf* no *13654/88 RR & SR v the Netherlands*, Dec 8.9.88, DR 57 p 287 where family life between a mother and her two adult daughters was found to exist.

[19]  No *9492/81 Family X v UK*, Dec 14.7.82, DR 30 p 232

[20]  No *8244/78 Uppal & Singh v UK*, Dec 9.7.80, DR 20, p 29, 3 EHRR 391.

[21]  No *7229/76 X & Y v UK*, *op cit.*  The Commission has also accepted that Article 12 does not guarantee the right to adopt children from another country, to legal recognition of that adoption in the home country or to the issuing of residence permits for the children.  See No *11041/84 L v the Netherlands*, Dec 13.12.84, unreported.

[22]  See further Liddy, *op cit*, p 17.

[23]  No *23366/94 Nsona v the Netherlands*, Comm Rep, 2.3.95, Reports 1996-V no 23, p 2010, § 59.

[24]  Eur Court HR *Nsona v The Netherlands*, judgment of 28 Nov 1996, Reports 1996-V no 23, p 1979, § 113-114.

insufficient to support a claim of family life in certain circumstances, notably when the child's parents are living and able to care for the adopted child.[25] It is likely that parties to genuine inter-country adoptions may be able to invoke Article 8 if the child is refused entry to a Convention State. However, in the past it has rejected that an adopted child has a right to enter in order to establish a new family relationship, where it suspects that the adoption is a 'sham'.[26]

The Strasbourg institutions have faced few challenges to the traditional notion of the family in determining the existence of family life in immigration cases, where marriage is still perceived to present the strongest evidence of family ties to immigration officials. Frequently, the institutions' main task appears to be deciphering the genuine from the bogus claims of family life and this explains their strict approach to the applicability of Article 8. The difficulty of the balancing exercise in immigration cases is highlighted by the frequent lack of consensus among the members of the Commission and the Court.[27] It is important, therefore, that the cases of *Berrehab* and *Boughanemi* signify the adoption of a principled approach to the existence of family life in this area. It is significant too that in determining the existence of family life, the Court has begun to take into account the interests of the children and particularly the detrimental impact which deportation of a parent can have on their relationship. Although many questions remain unanswered in relation to the existence of family life, the establishment of a presumption in favour of family life between all parents and their children, together with the implicit acceptance that family life may extend beyond the nuclear family, are both positive developments, which set the standards for future cases.

## The Compatibility of Immigration Measures with Article 8

An order deporting someone from a Convention State where their children reside, or refusing to allow a parent or child to join the other there will interfere with their family life.[28] Such a measure will only be incompatible with the Convention, however, where it fails to fulfil the requirements of

---

[25] No *7229/75 X & Y v UK, op cit.*
[26] *Ibid.*
[27] See further below.
[28] On the former, see *Berrehab* judgment, *op cit* and the latter, see No *14501/89 A & A v the Netherlands*, Dec 6.1.92, DR 72, p 118 and *Ahmut* judgment, *op cit.*

Article 8 § 2.[29] The fulfilment of the first of these conditions, i.e. that the measure be in accordance with law, requires that it have a legal basis and provide protection from arbitrariness. The legality of an immigration measure has rarely, if ever, been questioned on this basis. In relation to the requirement that the measure pursue a legitimate aim, the Convention institutions have generally accepted that immigration orders aim either to protect the country's economic well-being, to prevent disorder or crime, or sometimes both.[30] Measures falling into the former category include expulsion following the expiry or revocation of a residence permit where its conditions are no longer valid.[31] However, the broad scope of the aim to preserve public order, together with its overlap with effective immigration control, means that this aim is most frequently invoked by States in such immigration cases.[32] Moreover, although the Strasbourg institutions do not distinguish expressly between measures on the basis of their perceived aim, the case law appears to suggest that an expulsion prompted by criminal activity (protecting public order), rather than the expiry of a residence permit for reasons such as divorce (protecting economic well-being), is less difficult to justify.

## Interests of the Child?

With regard to children, the case law highlights a clear distinction between the application of Article 8 in immigration cases to that in all other areas of family life. In particular, measures which interfere with family life in the area of adoption, for example, aim to protect the interests of the child and they are examined in this context. In immigration cases, however, the interference with family life aims to protect the general interests of the State and the effect of this distinction on the way a case is decided is significant. In particular, considering whether the balance achieved between protecting the general interest and respecting family life involves

---

[29] See further Chapter 9, pp 199-204.

[30] See No *8245/78 X v UK*, Dec 6.5.81, DR 24 p 98 and No 26922/95 *Ebibomi & Others v UK*, Dec 29.11.95, unreported.

[31] This aim is associated with concerns about population density and is frequently invoked by the Dutch Government in this context. See *Berrehab* judgment, *op cit*, § 26 and *Ahmut* judgment, *op cit.*

[32] However, the aim was considered inappropriate in No *14830/89 Yousef v UK*, Comm Report, 30.6.92, unreported.

reconciling the interests of the family with those of the State. Notwithstanding that the common issue is whether the separation of a child from his/her parents is compatible with Article 8, the consideration of immigration measures consequently lacks the child focus evident in other areas.

The institutions appear to attach little significance to the child's respect for family life when determining whether the immigration measure is compatible with the Convention and thus, the detrimental impact on children of an order deporting or refusing entry to a parent plays little part in the way in which the Strasbourg application is decided. While the absence from the Convention of a right to enter or reside in a Convention State means that anything, other than a strict approach, will be perceived as an attempt to read rights into the Convention that are beyond its scope, there is arguably room for adopting a more child-friendly approach in these cases. In addition to taking a more flexible approach to the existence of family life commensurate with other areas of Article 8 case law, it is submitted that the child's needs and interests should be given greater weight when determining whether the interference with family life is proportionate with the aim which it pursued. It is also arguable that the Court should investigate with scrutiny whether the need to take the measure of immigration control which interfered with family life was well-founded, in addition to whether it was proportionate.[33]

*Berrehab* provides an example of good practice in this regard.[34] Having found family life to exist between a divorced father and his daughter due to their close relationship, the Court then noted that the effect on his family life of the decision to deport him was very serious. Although he had succeeded in maintaining contact with his daughter since his expulsion to Morocco, the Court considered that nevertheless his deportation threatened to break the close ties which he shared with his daughter. Although it was clearly relevant that the applicant's expulsion resulted from his divorce, rather than any illegal or criminal conduct, the girl's young age and her need to remain in contact with her father were significant factors in the Court's conclusion that the deportation was disproportionate to its aim. Moreover, even though this judgment preceded the UN Convention on the Rights of the Child, it reflects clearly its principles and provisions,

---

[33] It is argued that States should have to submit evidence in order to substantiate this issue. See Warbrick (1998), 'The Structure of Article 8', *European Human Rights Law Review*, **1**, pp 32-44, at p 41.

[34] *Berrehab* judgment, *op cit*, § 27-29.

particularly Article 9, which provides for the child's right to maintain contact and personal relations with both parents unless it is contrary to the child's best interests.[35] This principle is also evident in the *Mehemi* case.[36] Here, although the applicant's criminal conviction counted heavily against him, the Court found that in the light of a number of factors, 'above all' the fact that he would be separated from his minor child and wife, his deportation from France violated Article 8.

The Commission has noted that when the family life concerned is that between a parent and a child, regard must be had to the interests of the latter in considering the compatibility of an immigration measure with Article 8.[37] It has also held that when assessing the proportionality of the interference, the national authorities must take sufficient account of their interest in continuing to enjoy existing, extensive contact. The articulation of these principles brings the immigration jurisprudence closer in theory, if not in practice, to areas of family life where denial of contact is seen as a drastic and far-reaching measure to be justified only by relevant and sufficient reasons. However, this approach is not yet established practice, although there are substantial reasons for doing so, not least the need to adopt a uniform approach to the application of Article 8.

*Proportionality*

Although it is the role of the Convention authorities to assess whether an immigration measure is compatible with Article 8, it is not the function of the Court to pass judgment on domestic immigration law or policy. Its role is to examine individually any interference with family life which forms the substance of the complaint under Article 8, in particular by weighing the legitimate aim pursued against the seriousness of the interference with the right to respect for family life. Any relevant factors will be taken into account in applying the proportionality principle in this regard. In immigration cases, factors such as the strength of family ties and other links with the country ordering the deportation, the reasons on which the order is based and the extent of the person's ties with the country to which

---

[35] See also Article 10, UN DOC A/44/25.

[36] Eur Court HR *Mehemi v France*, judgment of 26 Sept 1997, Reports 1997-VI, no 51, p 1959.

[37] No *12411/86 M v Germany*, Dec of 4.3.87, DR 51 p 245; No 29192/95 *Ckikz v the Netherlands*, Comm Rep, 20.5.98, unreported.

s/he is being deported will be taken into account. In relation to the latter issue, where a person's links with the deporting country are precarious at the time of establishing family life, there appears to be a presumption that s/he cannot expect to be able to pursue family life there. For example in the *Bouchelkia* case, the fact that the applicant had married and had a child *after* his deportation was ordered meant that these facts could be disregarded by the Court when considering whether his expulsion was compatible with Article 8.[38] As a result, any interference with family life caused by the expulsion in these circumstances may well be consistent with Article 8,[39] although it is arguable that where one parent and the children enjoy nationality, then the other parent's deportation should be justified only in exceptional cases.[40]

Notwithstanding a parent's genuine interest in maintaining contact with a child, where their relationship becomes distant following divorce and the ties are weakened due to a parent's behaviour, the seriousness of the interference will be reduced, making it easier to justify under Article 8 § 2.[41] Other factors that appear to be relevant here include whether contact was permitted before deportation and whether any denial of visitation rights was contested.[42] Similarly, where custody of the child has previously been relinquished by the parent seeking to reside in a particular country either by placing them in voluntary care[43] or with another relative,[44] then this will be taken into account in determining the proportionality of the immigration measures.

Whether the removal of a parent or child from, or a refusal to admit such a person to, a Convention State is consistent with Article 8 will depend on a number of factors. In particular, the Court has regard to the extent to which the measure effectively ruptures family life, whether there

---

[38] Eur Court HR *Bouchelkia v France*, judgment of 29 Jan 1997, Reports 1997-I no 28, p 47, 25 EHRR 686.

[39] No *9088/80 X v UK*, Dec 6.3.82, DR 28 p 160 and No *20002/92 Charfa v Sweden*, Dec 5.4.95, unreported.

[40] See No *27299/95 Singh v UK*, Dec 4.3.98, unreported, which was found admissible in this regard.

[41] No *17124/90 G v Switzerland*, Comm Rep, 12.10.92, unreported, § 59-60, and No *12411/86 M v Germany, op cit.*

[42] *Ibid*, § 60. It is also relevant that the point in time for determining the existence of family life is the making of the deportation order. Eur Court HR *El Boujaidi v France*, judgment of 26 Sept 1997, Reports 1997-VI.

[43] No *23734/94 Rahmonaj & Makshana v Switzerland*, Dec 11.5.94, unreported.

[44] No *14507/89 B v UK*, Dec 2.4.90, DR 65, p 296.

are insurmountable obstacles in the way of the family living in the country of origin, and whether there are factors of immigration control in favour of exclusion. The first factor involves balancing the interference with family life with the general aim pursued by the immigration measure and as such, it has been discussed above. A discussion of the other two factors follows.

*Obstacles to Living Elsewhere*

In determining whether the removal of a parent to a Convention State is consistent with Article 8, it is established practice for the institutions to consider whether there are obstacles in the way of the family living in their country of origin which it is possible to surmount.[45] Thus, it is taken into account whether it is practical and reasonable for family members to accompany the person being deported, so that they can enjoy family life elsewhere.[46] Central to this approach is the ability of family members, usually children, to adapt to the country of origin and this involves considering the age of the children, the nationality of the other family members[47] and the length[48] and lawfulness[49] of the family's stay in the country ordering the expulsion. Economic or cultural disadvantages will usually be insufficient to prevent family members from joining the expelled member abroad.[50] However, it is arguable that factors such as the adequacy of medical facilities should be taken into account where a family member, particularly a child, suffers from an on-going medical condition, which will require attention.[51] Harris et al argue that the test of hardship

---

[45] Storey calls this the 'elsewhere' approach, *op cit*, pp 336-337.

[46] No *22791/93 Maikoe & Baboelal v the Netherlands*, Dec 30.11.94, unreported. See also Eur Court HR *Beldjoudi v France*, judgment of 26 March 1992, Series A no 234-A, 14 EHRR 801.

[47] In No *8245/78 X v UK*, *op cit*, the Commission accepted that the German nationality of the American applicant's wife and daughter constituted a serious obstacle which hindered them from accompanying him. Cf No *24698/94 HG v Switzerland*, Dec 6.9.94, unreported.

[48] On integrated aliens see further Sherlock, *op cit* and Warbrick, *op cit*, at pp 38-40 and below.

[49] No *9492/81 Family X v UK*, Dec 14.7.82, DR 30, p 232.

[50] No *23938/94 Sorabjee v UK*, Dec 23.10.95, unreported.

[51] *Ibid* and No *26985/95 Poku v UK*, Dec 15.5.96, 22 EHRR CD 94. In No *13078/87 Fadele Family v UK*, Comm Report, 4.7.91, DR 70, p 159 the father was granted leave to return to the UK to rejoin his children, after they had

under Article 8 should be kept distinct from that under Article 3, in order to recognise that what is at stake is a family relationship, and not the treatment of an individual family member.[52] In line with this approach, the Commission has considered the links which the deported person and other members of the family have with the country of destination, in particular whether there are other family members or relatives there.[53] It is also pertinent whether family members enjoy the nationality of the State ordering the expulsion,[54] although the Commission has yet to find that the deportation of a parent from a State where their child enjoys the right to reside affects the consistency of the measure with Article 8.[55]

With regard to the feasibility of a parent and child carrying on family life elsewhere, the Commission has noted that young children are likely to accompany their mother if she is deported and it has concluded, albeit with little evidence, that children of three or four years are adaptable in this regard.[56] Although the Commission purports to consider whether there are any effective obstacles to children accompanying their parents in such circumstances, its conclusions, including for instance, that a child of ten who has been integrated into the school system will be likely to adapt to his new environment, raise genuine questions on this.[57] The fact that States are not required to submit reasoned opinions as to the adaptability of a child in an individual case adds to the apparent arbitrariness of this approach.[58]

Article 3 of the Fourth Protocol prohibits a State from expelling its own nationals.[59] However, a measure ordering the deportation of a mother, whose young child was born in the Convention State, will not raise an issue under this provision, notwithstanding that the child enjoys nationality

---

followed him to Nigeria and suffered *inter alia* problems relating to poor medical treatment.

[52]  Harris O'Boyle & Warbrick, *op cit,* p 332.

[53]  See Warbrick, *op cit*, and Sherlock, *op cit.*

[54]  No *22791/93 Maikoe & Baboelal v the Netherlands, op cit.*

[55]  No *23938/94 Sorabjee v UK, op cit* and No *24865/94 Jaramillo v UK,* Dec 23.10.95, unreported.

[56]  *Ibid.*

[57]  No *26985/95 Poku v UK, op cit.*

[58]  See Warbrick, *op cit,* p 41.

[59]  Protocol No 4 is excluded from the Human Rights Act 1998.

of that State.[60] The Commission's reasoning here is that it is the parent, rather than the child, who is the subject of the deportation order and consequently, it has refused to treat the issue as one of effective expulsion, even though the child's decision to accompany a parent may be inevitable in the circumstances.[61] This is particularly the case where a child wishing to reside in a Convention State, of which s/he is a national, would have to be placed with alternative carers should his/her parents be deported. However, an issue might arise under Article 8 where a child who enjoys family life with both parents must choose between accompanying the deported parent, or remaining with the other parent, who also enjoys a right to reside in the Convention State. This argument has yet to enjoy success,[62] despite the fact that the situation forces the child to choose between family life with one parent and the other. Instead, the Commission has found that where there are no effective obstacles to the deported person's spouse and children accompanying him/her to their country of origin, then no issue will arise under Article 8, even where the accompanying family members must leave the State in which they have a legal right to reside.[63] Should there be an impediment, such as a risk of ill-treatment, to the family's return to their country of origin, then the situation would not be so clear cut.[64] Similarly, if a parent's deportation interrupts his/her frequent and regular contact with a child from a previous marriage, then this would raise an issue under Article 8 also. In particular, the child's complaint that s/he cannot accompany his/her father without forfeiting family life with his/her mother and new family would arguably deserve consideration.[65] Important factors in such a case would include the strength of the family tie between the parent being deported and his/her child, as well as the possibility of them maintaining contact afterwards. The conduct which led to the deportation would also be taken into account, particularly where it was criminal in nature. While the outcome will depend on the circumstances of the case, it is submitted that, in line with *Berrehab* and other cases, weight should be attached to the right of the

---

[60] See Mole (1995),'Constructive Deportation and the European Convention', *European Human Rights Law Review* 1, pp 63-71.

[61] No *22791/93 Maikoe & Baboelal v the Netherlands, op cit.*

[62] See No 27299/95 *Singh v UK, op cit.*

[63] No *26985/95 Poku v UK, op cit.*

[64] See below, pp 229-231.

[65] No *26985/95 Poku v UK, op cit.*

child to enjoy contact with both parents as far as possible and, where such contact can only be effective by both parents living in the same country, then this should weigh in favour of finding the deportation to be inconsistent with Article 8.

On a more general level, there is scope to argue that the 'elsewhere' test itself is contrary to the Convention. In particular, nowhere does the Convention differentiate between rights which can be enjoyed within Contracting States and those which can only be enjoyed 'elsewhere'.[66] A move away from this approach is encouraged, particularly in cases like *Berrehab,* which lack a strong public order factor, to ensure uniform application of Convention provisions as far as possible, and to enhance the level of protection which Article 8 currently offers children in this area.

### Factors of Immigration Control

*Public Order*: The importance of immigration control is well recognised throughout Strasbourg case law, and the Court has consistently found that it is for the Convention States to maintain public order by

> exercising their right, as a matter of well-established international law and subject to their treaty obligations, to control the entry and residence of aliens. For that purpose, they are entitled to order the expulsion of such persons convicted of criminal offences.[67]

In examining the compatibility of immigration measures with Article 8, the different reasons for making an expulsion order have played a role. In *Berrehab* for example, the Court noted that the father was being expelled, not because of any criminal activity or breach of immigration law, but due to the Government's refusal to renew his residence permit following his divorce from his Dutch wife.[68] The innocent nature of his conduct thus made the serious interference with his family life which it caused difficult to justify. In contrast, the scales appear to tip the other way where the people being expelled have repeatedly taken measures in breach of immigration rules. According to the Commission, such people must, to a large extent, be held responsible when their expulsion separates them from

---

[66] See Storey, *op cit*, p 337

[67] *Bouchelkia* judgment, *op cit*, § 48.

[68] *Berrehab* judgment, *op cit*, § 29.

their children.[69] In several other cases, notably those concerning integrated immigrants,[70] the Strasbourg authorities have found the expulsion of a parent for involvement in criminal activity to be proportionate to the often serious interference with their family life which it causes, particularly where the behaviour is persistent[71] and violent.[72] Where the family member being expelled has been involved in serious criminal activity over a long period of time, particularly, where he has committed drugs offences,[73] it is not difficult to justify the deportation, regardless of his strong family ties with the country and the seriousness of the interference likely to result from his departure.[74] However, the Court is prepared to make certain allowances where the criminal conduct which gave rise to the expulsion was undertaken at a young age and thus immaturity may act as a mitigating factor in some circumstances.[75]

*Cases of Expulsion and Family Reunification*

A survey of the case law highlights that it is the Commission, rather than the Court, which appears to adopt a more sympathetic line as to whether the deportation of an integrated immigrant, who has family and considerable social ties with the Convention State, is justified by virtue of his criminal behaviour.[76] However, both institutions appear to make a

---

[69] No *11970/86 v UK*, Dec 13.7.87, 11 EHRR 48.

[70] See further Warbrick, *op cit*, pp 38-40.

[71] No *17124/90 G v Switzerland* Comm Rep, *op cit*, § 58.

[72] No *22696/93 Lumumba v Sweden*, Dec 10.10.94, unreported; *Bouchelkia* judgment, op cit and Eur Court HR *Boujlifa v France*, judgment of 21 Oct 1997, Reports 1997-VI, no 54.

[73] For example, No 7816/77 *X & Y v Germany*, Dec 19.5.77, DR 9, p 219; No *21212/94 Karadag v Germany*, Dec 2.9.94, unreported; No *25161/94 SZ v Switzerland*, Dec 30.11.94 and No *23775/94 Aghopian v France*, Dec 31.8.94, unreported.

[74] See *Boughanemi* judgment, *op cit*, and *Bouchelkia* judgment, *op cit*.

[75] Eur Court HR *Moustaquim v Belgium*, judgment of 18 February 1991, Series A no 193, 13 EHRR 802, § 44-45.

[76] In the following cases, for example, the Commission found a violation of Article 8 but the Court did not: No *16152/90 Lamguindaz v UK*, Comm Rep, 13.10.92, Series A no 258, p 100; No *22070/93 Boughanemi v France*, Comm Report, 10.1.95, Reports 1996-II no 8, p 617, 22 EHRR 228.; No *13446/87 Djeroud v France*, Comm Report, 15.3.90, Series A no 191.

distinction between interferences with family life caused by expulsion and those caused by a refusal to permit entry. The former have enjoyed a greater degree of success in Strasbourg, suggesting that the expulsion of a person, who enjoys family life in the country in question, is more difficult to justify, than a refusal to allow entry in the first place.[77] This difference arises principally from the applicants' ability to enjoy family life elsewhere, as well as the Court's reluctance to require States to permit the entry of family members for the purpose of reunification.

In comparison with the approach taken by the Commission in expulsion cases[78] a strict approach is evident in cases of family reunification, which concern the consistency with Article 8 of refusing to permit children to join parents already lawfully resident in a Convention State. The claims of such children that the refusal to permit family reunification in this way breaches Article 8 have not enjoyed much success in Strasbourg. In the majority of cases, the complaints have failed because of an inability to prove the existence of family life with the parent or relative they seek to join. For example, this may be because the children concerned have reached majority and further elements of dependency are lacking,[79] or because there are insufficient links between the parent and the child seeking to gain entry to attract the scope of Article 8.[80] Moreover, according to the Commission, the protection of family life guaranteed by Article 8 presumes the coherency of interests between parents and children in their care.[81] As a result, although parents who left their children behind when emigrating to a Convention State may find it possible to establish family life, they will find it difficult to prove that their links with their children require respect under Article 8. In considering whether this is the case, the Court will take into account whether there are family members still living in the child's country of origin[82] and whether such a relative is

---

[77] For example, *Ahmut* judgment, *op cit*, and *Gul* judgment, *op cit*. See further Warbrick, *op cit*, pp 40-43.

[78] See further Harris, O'Boyle & Warbrick, *op cit*, pp 333-334 and pp 351-353.

[79] No *14852/89 Akhtar & Johangir v the Netherlands, op cit*; No *12139/86 v the Netherlands*, Dec 5.10.87, 11 EHRR 78 and No *16249/90 FEB v Switzerland*, Dec 1.10.90, unreported.

[80] No *23701/94 Bicilir v Switzerland*, Dec 22.2.95, unreported. See above, pp 215-219.

[81] *Ibid.*

[82] *Ibid* and No *14852/89 Akhtar & Johangir v the Netherlands, op cit.*

able and willing to care for him/her there.[83] If the parent can prove that the child cannot be cared for except in the Convention State, then his/her claim under Article 8 is likely to be successful. If the contrary is the case, however, then it will arguably fail.[84]

The treatment of immigration cases has attracted deserved criticism, both within the institutions themselves and academically.[85] However, the wide range of conflicting, general and individual interests makes it difficult to argue realistically that the interests of the child should be paramount in such cases. The strict approach taken by the Commission and Court to Article 8 in immigration cases generally makes this even more unlikely. There are positive aspects to the case law however, not least the weight increasingly attached to the family life between parent and child in cases involving the expulsion of integrated aliens. It is important, therefore, that these principles are taken on board at domestic level, where these decisions are most frequently made.[86]

## Expulsion and Protection under Article 3

There is considerable jurisprudence on the treatment of immigrants and refugees under Article 3, which prohibits torture, inhuman and degrading treatment or punishment. In the *Soering* case, the Court first enunciated the principle that the expulsion of someone in circumstances in which they will face a real risk of treatment contrary to Article 3 will violate that provision.[87] Moreover, because Article 3 is an absolute right, the activities

---

[83] See, for example, No *21702/93 Ahmut* v the Netherlands, Comm Rep, 17.5.95, Reports 1996-VI, no 24, p 2039, § 52; *Nsona* Comm Rep, *op cit*, § 58. See also No *23701/94 Bicilir v Switzerland, op cit*; No *24968/94 Lambrati v the Netherlands*, Dec 18.5.96, unreported.

[84] See *Ahmut* Comm Report, *ibid*, where the Commission found a violation of Article 8. cf *Ahmut* judgment, *op cit* when different facts emerged before the Court, which led to it reaching the opposite conclusion on this point.

[85] See Sherlock, *op cit*, pp 70-72 and Warbrick, *op cit*, generally.

[86] See further Blake (1997) 'Judicial Review of Discretion in Human Rights Cases', *European Human Rights Law Review*, **4**, pp 391-403.

[87] Eur Court HR *Soering v UK*, judgment of 7 July 1989, Series A No 161, 11 EHRR 439. See also Eur Court HR *Cruz Varas v Sweden*, judgment of 20 Mar 1991, Series A No 201, 14 EHRR 1; Eur Court HR *Vilvarajah v UK*, judgment of 30 Oct 1991, Series A No 215, 14 EHRR 248.

of the individual in question, however undesirable or dangerous, cannot be a material consideration in the assessment of the risk of ill-treatment which s/he faces.[88]

Despite these dynamic and important principles, the claims of child refugees that their expulsion, either alone or in the company of family members, will violate Article 3 in this way have enjoyed no success to date. Families who have fled from situations of persecution in Yugoslavia,[89] Turkey,[90] Iran,[91] Syria[92] and Uganda[93] have had their claims rejected by the Commission, on the basis that they faced no real risk of ill-treatment on the facts. Although the children concerned have been listed as applicants in such cases, the merits of their individual claims have rarely considered separate from the risk faced by the head of the family unit. Nor has the protection of Article 3 of Protocol No 4, which prohibits collective expulsion, been applied successfully in cases involving children. In particular, the Commission has been satisfied that an issue of collective expulsion is not raised as long as the respondent State agrees to have each individual case decided on its merits.[94]

However, in 1997, the Court demonstrated the flexibility of its approach in applying Article 3 to expulsion cases. *D v UK* concerned the proposed removal of an alien drug courier who was dying of AIDS to his country of origin. The Court found that the poor medical facilities in St Kitts and his lack of family and social support there would hasten his death and expose him to a real risk of dying under the most distressing circumstances and thus to inhuman treatment contrary to Article 3.[95] This judgment does not grant an alien, who is subject to an expulsion order, the right to benefit from medical, social or other forms of assistance provided by the expelling State. Nevertheless, it represents a significant expansion

---

[88] Eur Court HR *Chahal v UK*, judgment of 15 Nov 1996, Reports 1996-V, no 22, p 1831, 23 EHRR 413 and Eur Court HR *Ahmed v Austria*, judgment of 17 Dec 1996, Reports 1996-VI, 24 EHRR 278.

[89] No *22178/93 Daferofski v Germany*, Dec 31.8.94, unreported; No *23521/94 Milic v Sweden*, Dec 5.7.94, 18 EHRR CD 222.

[90] No *27442/95 Tunc Family v Sweden*, Dec 19.10.95, unreported and No *27776/95 AG v Sweden*, Dec 26.10.95, DR 83, p 101.

[91] No *27683/95 v Switzerland*, Dec 6.9.95, unreported.

[92] No *28239/95 Shabo & Ors v Sweden*, Dec 26.10.95, unreported.

[93] No *27249/95 Lwanga & Sempungo v Sweden*, Dec 14.9.95, unreported.

[94] No *7011/75 Becker v Denmark*, Dec 3.10.75, DR 4, p 215.

[95] Eur Court HR *D v UK*, judgment of 2 May 1997, Reports 1997-III, no 37, p 777, 24 EHRR 456.

of the scope of Article 3 and it has obvious implications for children. For example, it is arguable that the expulsion of children suffering from HIV/AIDS to a country without adequate medical facilities may raise an issue under Article 3. Similarly, the expulsion of a child with a parent who is terminally ill may also fall within the scope of Article 3 in this context. It may also be possible to argue that children being expelled to certain countries will face a real risk of exposure to inhuman and degrading treatment in the form of dangerous living conditions. An applicant in a recent case argued, for example, that her return to Sri Lanka would result in her being subjected to prostitution.[96] However, claims under Article 3 will only be successful where it can be proven that there is a real risk, and not simply a mere possibility, that they will face treatment which is inhuman or degrading.[97]

*Conditions of Expulsion*

Notwithstanding that the deportation of a minor may be consistent with the Convention, an issue may arise in relation to the treatment of such children both before and during the expulsion process. Although ill-treatment must reach a minimum level of severity to breach Article 3, factors such as the nature and context of the treatment, the manner and method of its execution, its duration, physical or mental effects, and in some instances, the sex, age, and state of health of the victim will be taken into account in reaching that conclusion.[98] This highlights the potential for applying the Article 3 standard in children's cases, although there is little evidence, as yet, of success in this regard.

The difficulty in attaining the minimum level of severity necessary to breach Article 3 is evident from *Nsona v the Netherlands*, decided by the Court in 1996.[99] Following her arrival from Zaire, nine year old Francine Nsona was refused entry into the Netherlands, and an order was made for her expulsion. Consequently, she was separated from her escort, placed in

---

[96] No *35149/97 Kanagarathnam v Switzerland*, Dec 7.4.97, unreported. Her claim was found to be unsubstantiated.

[97] *Cruz Varas* judgment, *op cit*. See further Harris, O'Boyle & Warbrick, *op cit*, pp 73-80.

[98] See Eur Court HR *Ireland v UK*, judgment of 18 Jan 1978, Series A No 25, 2 EHRR 25, § 162. See further Chapter 8, pp 160-166.

[99] See *Nsona* Comm Rep, *op cit*, and judgment, *op cit*.

a hotel and then a nursery for seven days, until finally, she travelled alone back to Kinshasa, where she spent a further three days in the company of a stranger before being returned to friends. Neither the Commission nor the Court found her treatment to be severe enough to amount to a violation of Article 3, although the former institution expressed concern that the girl's expulsion involved a certain degree of hardship and was carried out without due concern for her care.[100]

## Friendly Settlements

Under the Convention, the Court (previously the Commission) is obliged to place itself at the disposal of the parties with a view to securing a friendly settlement, following the achievement of which, the case is struck off its list.[101]  A case concerning a challenge to the expulsion of two 17 year old boys under Article 3 highlights the Convention's potential to protect children in this way.[102]  The Swedish authorities had rejected the boys' claims for asylum, so they complained to the Commission that their deportation would result in their suffering inhuman and degrading treatment in violation of Article 3.  Without giving its opinion on the merits of their claim, the Commission reached a settlement, which involved attaching conditions to the boys' expulsion, to ensure their protection from ill-treatment. According to the agreement between the Commission and the Swedish government, the expulsion was subject to written instructions from the police authority, which were in turn subject to the Aliens Appeals Board, which included the requirement that the minors would be met on their return to Uganda by representatives of both the Child Welfare Authority and the Swedish Embassy.  Assuming that no expulsion would take place without assurances that both of these conditions were met, the Commission found it reasonable to assume that their return to Uganda would not violate Article 3.  Although the boys were found to be suffering from depression while in detention pending the enforcement of the order, the Commission was reassured by the fact that a chief physician was responsible for their care and that he would have the opportunity to assess their state of health at the time of the expulsion.

---

[100] *Nsona* Comm Rep, *op cit*, § 52-54.  Unlike the Court, the Commission found that the Netherlands authorities had failed to investigate her personal situation in Zaire and to take adequate measures in respect of her arrival there.

[101] See Article 38.

[102] No *27249/95 Lwanga & Sempungo v Sweden, op cit.*

Although the Commission's approach to this case served to protect the unaccompanied minors from hardship it would have been preferable to secure the guarantee that no expulsion would take place without the requisite conditions being met.    In general, however, the friendly settlement procedure plays a constructive role in the resolution of immigration cases involving children and, where possible, it has resulted in the granting of residence permits and permission for family reunification in the Convention State.[103]    The requirement that a case be declared admissible before the parties seek to secure a settlement means that the remedy is only available where there is *prima facie* evidence that the expulsion may itself breach the Convention.  Nevertheless, the remedy is extremely valuable given that the resolution of a complaint in this way is usually of more benefit to the applicant than the finding of a violation.[104] In any event, the reaching of a settlement will always depend on the circumstances of each case, as well as the desire of the State concerned to avoid adverse publicity.[105]


## Detention of Immigrant and Refugee Children

Despite the international consensus that children seeking asylum should not be detained,[106] the European Convention does not appear to prohibit

---

[103] See for example, No *24930/94 Sari v Switzerland*, Dec 6.9.95, unreported, No *11026/84 Taspinar v the Netherlands*, Dec 9.10.85, DR 44, p 262; No *23065/93 KD v Finland*, Dec 10.3.94, unreported.

[104] See No *9330/81 Bulus v Sweden*, Dec 17.11.83, DR 35, p 13, 6 EHRR 587, in which a young illegal immigrant was found to be in such a poor psychological state that deporting him with his brothers would have hindered his development. The case was settled with his two brothers being returned to Sweden and all three boys being granted residence permits. *Bulus* Comm Rep, 8.12.84, DR 39, p 75.  See also No *17532/90 M,S,P,M & Ors v the Netherlands*, Dec 11.7.91, unreported.

[105] Although the *Nsona* case was unsuccessful in Strasbourg, the overwhelming public support invoked by a campaign set up in her name led to her return to the Netherlands and the award of a residence permit. See Kilkelly (1996),'Nsona v The Netherlands: The Treatment of Minors and the European Convention on Human Rights', *International Journal of Refugee Law*, 8(4), pp 640-650.

[106] European Council on Refugees and Exiles 1996 (1997) 'Position on Refugee Children' *International Journal of Refugee Law* 9 pp 74-81.  See also UNHCR

such treatment.   Article 5 § 1 (f) permits detention in order to prevent illegal entry to a Convention State or prior to deportation and there is little to suggest that this does not apply to children.   While it is unlikely that the detention of children awaiting deportation, or on arrival into a Convention State, would itself be contrary to Article 5, it is arguable that detention which is lengthy or otherwise arbitrary would be capable of challenge.[107] In any event, everyone detained under Article 5 is entitled to have the lawfulness of their detention reviewed under Article 5 § 4 and reference to international principles on the detention of children may be taken into account by the Court in this context.[108]

**Procedural Rights**

Article 6 does not apply to procedural matters or the determination of disputes regarding immigration rules, because the right to enter and reside in a country is not a 'civil right' within the meaning of the provision. However, the absence of an effective remedy to test a substantive family life claim concerning immigration law or policy may raise an issue under Article 13, which guarantees an effective remedy for breaches of the Convention at domestic level.[109]   Little case law exists on this exact subject, although it is established that where immigration rules fail to make provision for entry on specific grounds, such as to allow access to a child following divorce, and leave to enter is granted only as a matter of discretion, this does not offer sufficient guarantees of efficacy to satisfy the requirements of Article 13.[110]

With regard to the nature of immigration clearance procedures, the Commission considers that a Convention State, which has accepted the principle of family reunification, is entitled to establish a domestic verification procedure for the family claims of prospective or settled

---

Guidelines on Refugee Children in Van Bueren (ed)   (1993), *International Documents on Children Vol 1*, Dordrecht: Martinus Nijhoff, p 356.

[107] See Fortin (1999) , 'Rights Brought Home for Children', *Modern Law Review* **62,** pp 350-370, at p 356.

[108] See further Chapter 3, pp 46-52.

[109] See further Blake, *op cit.*

[110] *Yousef* Comm Rep, *op cit,* § 46-51.

immigrants.[111]   Thus, the Court may review whether the exercise of the functions of relevant domestic authorities was within what may reasonably be expected of them under Article 8, even where the right to respect for family life itself is not itself in question.   In this regard, as long as the applicant has had a fair opportunity to present his case and the authorities did not act perversely, arbitrarily or otherwise so as to deny the right to respect for family life, then no violation of Article 8 will occur.

The fact that Article 6 rights do not apply to immigration proceedings means that the Convention's potential for influencing the way in which such decisions are taken is limited.   For example, in the event that Article 6 guarantees to the child the right to participate in the decision making process concerning his/her civil rights and obligations, this would not apply to decisions concerning his/her asylum or residency application. The Court has established, however, that there are considerable procedural safeguards implicit in respect for family life under Article 8.[112]   Insofar as immigration measures impinge on the right to respect for family life, it is arguable that, *mutatis mutandis*, parents, at least, must be involved in this decision-making process to ensure the protection of their rights under Article 8, particularly given what is at stake in such proceedings.

Moreover, there is evidence to suggest that the Convention is not powerless in this context and the friendly settlement mechanism has, in the past, been used effectively to improve immigration procedures.   In 1975, a case challenging the collective expulsion of a large number of Vietnamese children from Denmark was settled before the Commission.[113] Importantly, during the Commission's examination of the application, the respondent Government announced its intention to analyse individually the application of each child for refugee status and to give consideration to the wishes and best interests of the individual children involved as part of this process.   This suggests that the Commission had some influence on the Danish Government's handling of the affair and illustrates the benefits that can accrue from the making of such an application.

---

[111] *8378/78 Kamal v UK*, Dec 14.5.80, DR 20 p 168.

[112] See further Chapter 9, pp 206-207.

[113] No *7011/75 Becker v Denmark, op cit.*

## Rights of Immigrant and Refugee Children while in a Convention State

It is of great significance that by guaranteeing its rights to everyone, Article 1 of the Convention ensures that immigrant and refugee children enjoy the rights and freedoms set out in the Convention and its Protocols, notwithstanding their nationality or other status. Moreover, Article 14 of the Convention prohibits discrimination in the enjoyment of Convention rights and the non-exhaustive list of grounds on which differential treatment is forbidden is open ended. There is thus little doubt that refugee and immigrant children must enjoy Convention rights regardless of their status, however precarious. Children or families who are illegal entrants and over-stayers are also entitled to enjoy all Convention rights on this basis.

The absence from the Convention of rights that are particularly relevant to refugee children, particularly in the area of social, economic and cultural rights, reduces its usefulness in alleviating the difficulties which they face. Nevertheless, Article 3 of the Convention, which prohibits inhuman and degrading treatment, may play a constructive role here, especially in the light of the *D* case.[114] In particular, it may be argued that the denial of basic welfare services or medical treatment to refugees or immigrants will raise a serious issue under this provision.

The right to education, which cannot be denied to anyone under Article 2 of the First Protocol, taken alone or in conjunction with Article 14, also takes on significance in the case of refugee children. This is due to the role which education plays in integrating the child into the community and equipping the child with the skills necessary to provide him/her with equality of opportunity in the event of a prolonged stay in the host country. It is unfortunate, for this reason, that the Convention does not oblige States to provide education of a specific type or in a particular language.[115] Nor does it require States to respect the linguistic preference of minorities. However, where a child does not enjoy an understanding of a national language sufficient to ensure that his/her education is meaningful, then a question may arise under Article 2 of the First Protocol. For instance, if a child arriving from Kosovo is granted refugee status by a Convention State and is then sent to school without any additional tuition in the national

---

[114] See above.

[115] Eur Court HR *The Belgian Linguistic Case*, judgment of 23 July 1968, Series A no 6, 1 EHRR 252. See further Chapter 4, pp 81-84.

language, it is not difficult to imagine the hindrance which the language barrier would pose to the child's ability to receive such instruction. Effective obstacles to education under this provision would appear to offer the State a choice of means in complying with the right to education, which would allow either special tuition in the child's own language, or alternatively intensive education in the language of the Convention State, either prior to or coinciding with the child's ordinary schooling.

## Future Challenges

The continuing humanitarian crises in various parts of the world, as well as on the fringes of Europe, together with the tightening of border controls in European States mean that the already large number of cases challenging immigration decisions under the Convention is likely to continue to grow. As a consequence, the danger of opening the flood gates to such applicants is likely to confirm the Court in its cautious approach in this area.

Nevertheless, there are important trends emerging in the case law, in particular with regard to the significance of maintaining the relationship between parent and child, and it is thus important that the Court continue to address the needs of children in this context, where the many conflicting interests of state and individual tend frequently to suppress the important children's issues.  Moreover, the Court has adopted a more principled approach to the existence of family life in recent cases and this broadens the provision's potential to protect children, notwithstanding that it is difficult to prove that interferences with family life caused by immigration measures are unjustifiable.  For this reason, it is likely that the procedures, according to which immigration decisions are made, will be the subject matter of future cases in this area.  Given that Article 6 is not applicable to immigration cases, the principle under Article 8 that requires adequate involvement by the parties in decision making processes regarding the family may have a significant role to play in this area.  The treatment of unaccompanied minors may also raise an issue of compatibility with the Convention, under Articles 3 and 5 with regard to detention or other ill-treatment suffered, but also in relation to issues of family reunification under Article 8.  In this context, it is arguable that a child who has secured a residence permit, but who is unable to have other family members join him/her in the Convention State may complain to the Court under Article 8 or alternatively, taking this provision with Article 14, where parents in similar circumstances enjoy the right to be joined by their children.

It is important that all children, including immigrants and refugees, are guaranteed Convention rights, in particular with regard to the right to enjoy effective rights, such as education, freedom of religion and private and family life.  The potential of the Convention's provisions in this context has yet to be examined by the Court and the extent of the obligation to respect family life is also uncertain.  It is possible to argue, however, that where a child arrives into a Convention state alone, without information of the whereabouts of his/her parents, Article 8 requires the adoption of appropriate measures to promote his/her reunification with parents. The circumstances of the case will obviously determine the existence of such an obligation and its scope, but a dynamic approach to such children's cases should not be ruled out.

# 11    Custody and Contact

## Introduction

It is well established that the family is located within the private sphere, where parental disputes about the care of their children are traditionally resolved. However, there are situations in which this cannot be achieved and state intervention, or interference will be required.[1] Such intervention normally involves a judicial or administrative body settling the dispute between the parties and because it will usually be resolved in favour of one parent, the decision will, by its nature, constitute an interference with the family life of the other. It is important, therefore, that Article 8 provides protection from certain types of state interference, and that the respect for family life, which the Convention guarantees, is neither diminished nor destroyed by separation or divorce. The fact that decisions of domestic authorities on matters of custody or contact interfere with family life means that their actions fall squarely within the scope of that provision. In this way, they will require justification under Article 8 § 2, with particular reference to the welfare and best interests of the child.

## The Right to Complain to the European Court

Although Article 8 is typically invoked by parents seeking to challenge an award of custody, the fact that such measures disrupt the family life of the children means that they are also entitled to bring a complaint before the Court. Article 25[2] of the Convention provides that the Commission is entitled to examine an application lodged by a person claiming to be the victim of a violation of the Convention.[3] As such, there is nothing to

---

[1]  See the dissenting opinion of Judge Bonnici in Eur Court HR *Hoffmann v Austria*, judgment of 23 June 1993, Series A No 255-C, 17 EHRR 293.

[2]  Since Protocol 11, this provision has been replaced with Article 34 which makes the same provision in relation to the Court.

[3]  See further Rogge, 'The 'Victim' Requirement in Article 25 of the European Convention on Human Rights', in Matscher & Petzold (eds) (1988), *Protecting Human Rights: The European Dimension, Studies in Honour of Gerard J Wiarda*, Koln: Heymanns, pp 539-545.

prevent children either themselves, or through their independent representatives, from bringing their own complaints to Strasbourg, although this has hitherto been a rare occurrence. Instead, it is common practice for parents to introduce an application on their child's behalf, and insofar as they enjoy custody of their children they are entitled to do so. Where a parent does not hold rights of care or custody in relation to his/her children, however, the Commission has refused to accept their right to complain on their children's behalf, unless it is established that they are especially empowered to that effect.[4]

Implicit in the Commission's approach is the principle that complaints introduced together must be capable of being considered together. It is only possible for parents to introduce a complaint on behalf of their children, in addition to their own application, therefore, where their complaints are strongly similar.[5] The Commission understands that parents and children will only share concerns in this way where the parent has rights of care and custody. For this reason, the parent without custody rights is prevented from introducing a claim on his/her child's behalf, unless there is evidence that s/he is especially entitled to do so. One of the consequences of this approach is that the case law in this area is dominated by the complaints of parents and hence it has a distinctly paternalistic flavour. While the case law would be less one-sided were the institutions to consider separately the complaints of children, to an extent, this is dependent on children making such applications. Even without the individual complaints of children, however, it is argued that an approach which had greater focus on children's issues would help to remedy the imbalance. In this regard, there is support for awarding independent representation to children at the centre of cases before the Court.[6] Children's issues could be more adequately dealt with by taking measures short of this step however, and in particular, giving serious consideration to the right of children to family life and to enjoy personal relations with both

---

[4]  No *8045/77 X v Sweden*, Dec 4.5.79, DR 16, p 105; No *28319/95*, Dec 20.5.96, DR 85, p 153; No *28422/95 Hoppe v Germany*, Dec 14.1.98, unreported. See further Chapter 6, pp 123-126.

[5]  See No *10812/84 D v Germany*, Dec 11.7.85, DR 44, p 211.

[6]  See the view of Judge Bonnici in  Eur Court HR *Kroon & Others v the Netherlands*, judgment of 27 Oct 1994, Series A no 297-C, 19 EHRR 263, and Judge Pettiti in Eur Court HR *X, Y & Z v UK*, judgment of 22 April 1997, Reports 1997-II no 35, 24 EHRR 143.

parents, for example, would help to raise the profile of children in Article 8 cases before the Court.

## Custody and Article 8

Family life does not cease with divorce and thus the right to respect for family life under Article 8 is to be enjoyed by married, as well as separated, spouses together with their children.[7] Although the Convention does not provide for the right to custody of one parent, as opposed to the other,[8] it is inevitable that the question of custody will be decided in favour of one party only, in the event of divorce or separation. As a result, Article 8 cannot be invoked by one parent to justify showing preference to his/her claim for custody, although, as a natural consequence, awarding custody to one parent will constitute an interference with the right to respect for family life of the other.[9] Such an interference must pursue a legitimate aim under Article 8 § 2, and the Commission and the Court have consistently accepted that a decision awarding custody aims to protect the interests of the child.[10] A custody order will only be compatible with the Convention, however, where an appropriate balance is reached between the interference with family life which it causes and the protection of the child, which it aims to achieve, and accordingly, it must be based on relevant and sufficient reasons.[11]

It is the task of the Strasbourg authorities to review an award of custody in the light of the obligation to respect family life, although its consideration of this issue is influenced heavily by the margin of appreciation which the State enjoys in this area.[12] In this, the Court does not substitute its view for that of the domestic court. Thus, although it refers to the authorities' basis for awarding custody to one particular parent,

---

[7] No *8427/78 Hendriks v the Netherlands*, Comm Rep, 8.3.82, DR 29, p 5, 5 EHRR 223.

[8] No *1449/62 X v the Netherlands*, Dec 16.1.63, 6 Yearbook, p 262.

[9] See for example, No *12246/86 Irlen v Germany*, Dec 13.7.87, DR 53 p 225 and *Hoffmann* judgment, *op cit*, § 29.

[10] See further Chapter 9, pp 201-203.

[11] Eur Court HR *Hokkanen v Finland*, judgment of 23 Sept 1994, Series A No 299-A, p 31, 17 EHRR 293, § 64.

[12] No *5486/72 X v Sweden*, Dec 8.73, Collection 44, p 128; No *12495/86 Jonsson v Sweden*, Dec 7.12.87, DR 54 p 187; No *12246/86 Irlen v Germany*, *op cit*. See further Chapter 1, pp 6-8 and Chapter 9, pp 204-206.

the Court does not itself review whether the measures were actually in the child's best interests.   In the *Hokkanen* case, for example, the reasons advanced for awarding custody - the length of the girl's stay with the grandparents, her strong attachment to them and her feeling that their home was her own - were noted by the Court to be relevant and sufficient.[13] However, it did not assess the merits of the expert opinion upheld by the domestic court - that custody should be awarded to the child's grandparents, rather than her father - but merely accepted the domestic decision as lawful, proportionate and within the exercise of state discretion. It is possible to conclude, therefore, that in many cases the European institutions defer to the national authorities the determination of what is in the child's best interests.   They do not do so expressly, however, and in principle, they always reserve the right to subject the issue to more detailed scrutiny.

*Best Interests of the Child*

There is implicit acceptance in Convention case law that a decision to entrust care of a child to a particular parent is justifiable under Article 8 § 2 only with reference to the child's welfare.[14]   However, it is unclear what weight should be attached to the child's best interests in this respect. International law, in the form of the UN Convention on the Rights of the Child, has recognised that the best interests of the child must be **a** primary consideration in all matters concerning the child, including custody.[15]   The European Court appears to have suggested a higher standard in this respect and in particular, it has found that the interests of the child are paramount in determining the outcome of a custody dispute.[16]   The Commission, similarly, has referred to the child's interests as dominant and it has found that:

---

[13] *Hokkanen* judgment, *op cit*, § 64.

[14] See *Hoffmann* judgment, *op cit* and below.

[15] Article 3, UN Doc A/44/25.   See Wolf, 'The Concept of the 'Best Interests' in Terms of the UN Convention on the Rights of the Child' in Freeman & Veerman (eds) (1992), *The Ideologies of Children's Rights*, Dordrecht: Martinus Nijhoff, pp 125-133.

[16] It made this statement with reference to Article 5 of Protocol No 7, which provides that parental equality as to their children does not prevent States from taking measures as are necessary in the interests of the children. See *Hoffmann* judgment, *op cit*, § 35.

where there is a serious conflict between the interests of the child and one of its parents which can only be resolved to the disadvantage of one of them, the interest of the child must prevail.[17]

As long as the domestic authorities treat the interests of the child as the predominant consideration in such cases, they enjoy apparent discretion as to the factors which they consider critical to the protection of the child.[18] Although the effect of this discretion is to reduce the level of scrutiny undertaken by the Strasbourg authorities, it is nevertheless an important recognition that such matters are most appropriately considered at domestic level. This is particularly pertinent given that, although evidence of abuse or ill-treatment will make the decision regarding custody straight forward,[19] in most cases, there will be little to tip the balance in favour of one parent or the other. In this context, the Commission has signified the relevance of factors, such as the importance of continuity of development[20] or consistency in the child's upbringing.[21] However, the case law shows that, for the most part, the Commission and Court rarely take an active approach with regard to the factors that should be taken into account in the domestic determination of the custody issue.[22] They have yet to insist upon or even recommend that the child's wishes be taken into account[23] and in this regard, their approach arguably reflects the traditional notion of the child's best interests, rather than the dynamic concept set out in the UN Convention on the Rights of the Child.[24] At the same time, an award of custody made in the face of serious opposition from the child, or any other decisive factor, would raise an issue of arbitrariness. As such, it would fall to be considered under Article 8 § 2, with which it would arguably be incompatible.

---

[17] *Hendriks* Comm Rep, *op cit*, § 124.

[18] No *12875/87 Hoffmann v Austria*, Comm Rep, 16.1.92, Series A No 255, p 69, § 91.

[19] No *1449/62 X v the Netherlands, op cit.*

[20] No *11526/85 W v Germany*, Dec 10.10.86, DR 50, p 219.

[21] No *19471/92 H & BM v Germany*, Dec 6.4.94, unreported. See also No *9867/82 X v UK*, Dec 10.82, 5 EHRR 489.

[22] See further Chapter 6, pp 117-120.

[23] For further criticism see Gomien (1989), 'State Powers and the Best Interests of the Child under Article 8 ECHR', *Netherlands Quarterly of Human Rights*, 7, pp 435-450, at pp 440-443.

[24] See Van Bueren (1995a), *The International Law on the Rights of the Child*, Dordrecht: Martinus Nijhoff, pp 45-46.

*Religious Discrimination*

The Convention prohibits the domestic authorities from awarding, or rather refusing to award the custody and care of children to a particular parent on religious grounds. This was established in the important, albeit somewhat problematic case of *Hoffmann v Austria*.[25] The applicant in this case was a Roman Catholic woman, who married a Catholic man and together, they had their children baptised and brought up in the Catholic religion. However, she later became a Jehovah's Witness and divorced her husband, taking her children with her. The couple contested custody in the Austrian courts and the lower courts awarded custody to the mother. The Supreme Court reversed this decision, however, being persuaded, in part, by the negative effects of the mother's religion on the children, including its opposition to blood transfusions and public holidays and its position as a social minority. It also considered that the lower courts had ignored a relevant piece of legislation, which provided that neither parent had the right to change the religion of a child from that shared by both parents when they married, or in which a child had hitherto been raised.

The European Court found, by a majority of five votes to four, that the decision of the Supreme Court was incompatible with the Convention insofar as it amounted to discrimination on the basis of religion.[26] In reaching this conclusion, the Court looked both at the decision of the Supreme Court, which had treated the legislation on the religious education of children as decisive and that of the lower courts, which, in contrast, awarded custody to the mother and appeared overall to take a more balanced approach to the issue. In particular, the Court noted that the lower courts had relied on expert opinion as to what was in the children's best interests, as well as the extent to which the mother was willing to compromise in order to minimise her religion's deleterious effects on her children.[27] Taking this into account, it appeared to be the way in which the higher court reached its decision, especially the extent to which the domestic court had relied on the legislation in question, that caused the European Court most concern.

---

[25] *Hoffmann* judgment, *op cit.*

[26] *Ibid*, § 30-36. The Commission reached the same conclusion by eight votes to six. *Hoffmann* Comm Rep, *op cit*, § 72-104.

[27] *Hoffmann* judgment, *op cit*, § 32. She agreed to permit the celebration of public holidays when in the care of their father and agreed also to concede to a court order should a blood transfusion be necessary.

The contrasting approaches which the domestic courts took to the custody issue served to highlight the difference in treatment experienced by the parents in this case. While this established a prima facie case of discrimination under the Convention, the difference in treatment would not violate the Convention if it pursued a legitimate aim, to which it was proportionate. In this regard, the aim of the Supreme Court's decision was to protect the health and rights of the children, which, the European Court recognised, are paramount in cases of this nature.[28] Moreover, while it did not deny that certain social factors concerning membership of the Jehovah's Witnesses might tip the scales in favour of one parent when awarding custody,[29] the Court held that any distinction between parents based essentially on a difference in religion alone was unacceptable. The means, which the domestic court employed to pursue its legitimate aim were considered to be disproportionate therefore, and a violation of the Convention was established.

Ironically, it was their concern for the welfare of the children that prompted some members of the Commission and the Court to dissent from the majority.[30] The distinction between these views is a subtle one, lying somewhere between the mother's membership of the minority religion - which the majority found could not form the basis of the custody decision - and the consequences for her children of her religion - which the minority believed could be decisive in this regard.[31] The final decision was thus finely balanced, somewhere in between these two opposing view points.

Insofar as the dominant issue in *Hoffmann* was discrimination, the Court appeared to attach greater importance to the principle of religious freedom, than to the best interests of the children in determining the compatibility of the custody order with the Convention. Respect for democratic principles notwithstanding, the outcome of the case is problematic from a child's perspective. In particular, it leaves unresolved what factors may be used to determine custody where both parents are

---

[28] *Ibid*, § 35.

[29] It referred to the factors which the Austrian Supreme Court had found decisive, ie, the possible effect on the children's social life of being associated with a religious minority and the hazards attached to the mother's total rejection of blood transfusions in the absence of a court order. *Ibid* § 32-33.

[30] See the separate, dissenting opinions of Judges Valticos, Walsh and Matscher in *Hoffmann* judgment, *op cit* and that of Mr Ermacora and Mr Loucaides in *Hoffmann* Comm Rep, *op cit*.

[31] See also Bainham (1994), 'Religion, Human Rights and the Fitness of Parents', *Cambridge Law Journal*, **53**, pp 39-41, at p 40.

equally apt to undertake the task, if issues indicating a risk to the child's health and well-being may not. Mr Schermers, dissenting from the Commission, makes this point and also asks, similarly, whether talk of discrimination is appropriate in the light of the inherently discriminatory way in which custody between parents is regularly decided.[32]

Regardless of the above criticism, the opposite conclusion, namely that the decision of the Austrian Supreme Court was compatible with the Convention, would have raised concern about the well-being of *all* children in the custody of Jehovah's Witnesses, or other religious minorities deemed similarly hazardous. This is clearly an implausible prospect. However, a way out of this dilemma may lie in the extent to which parents with minority religious views are prepared to compromise in order to satisfy serious concern about the welfare of children in their care.[33] However, a more strict approach may be justifiable with regard to minority religions, which are prohibited by law.[34]

A final point about *Hoffmann* is worth noting: although the applicant invoked Article 8, both alone as well as together with Article 14, the Commission and the Court found it appropriate only to consider her complaint under the two provisions combined. Had the compatibility of the decision to transfer custody been examined under Article 8 alone, it is arguable that the interference with the mother's right to respect for family life caused by the Supreme Court's decision would have been justifiable with regard to the need to protect the interests and health of the children under Article 8 § 2. The reasoning behind the decision of the Commission and the Court to treat the issue as one of discrimination is apparent.

*Discrimination on the Grounds of Marital Status*

Although *Hoffmann* established that a decision to award custody to one parent over another on religious grounds was incompatible with the Convention, it is unclear whether a refusal to award custody on other grounds prohibited by Article 14 would be similarly offensive. For example, it is arguable that refusing to award joint custody to unmarried parents amounts to discrimination reading Article 8 with Article 14. Yet,

---

[32] *Hoffmann* Comm Rep, *op cit*. See his similar dissenting opinion in No 8695/79 *Inze v Austria*, Comm Rep, 4.3.86, 8 EHRR 498.

[33] See Bainham, *op cit*, p 40 and above.

[34] See No *27496/95 MM v Bulgaria*, Dec 10.9.96, unreported.

the case law on this matter points to the opposite conclusion.[35] In particular, the Commission has found that the inability of unmarried parents to enjoy joint legal custody of their child responds to the circumstances which prevail where a child is born outside marriage. Such treatment has thus been found to be consistent with the Convention, even where both parents wish to have their factual situation of shared parental responsibility recognised in law.[36] Its reasoning is based on two factors. Firstly, the granting of a joint right to custody involves a strengthening, not of the relationship between the father and his child, but of his legal position vis-à-vis the child's mother, which would operate to her detriment should the relationship break down. Secondly, and linked to the first point, is the Commission's view that if both parents wish to maintain family relations with the child, they are free to marry so as to obtain the relevant legal advantages. However, where they choose not to do so, then they themselves are responsible for the consequences.

The merit of these arguments notwithstanding, this interpretation of the Convention is arguably out of line with both the Convention and its dynamic interpretation in other areas. In particular, the Court has clearly found that Article 8 applies to non-marital relationships and has also established that the children of such relationships must be placed 'legally and socially in a position akin to that of a legitimate child'.[37] These principles, together with the fact that it would ensure greater consistency in Article 8 case law, support the argument that Article 8 requires the legal recognition of a factual situation with regard to an award of joint custody. Practice among Convention States,[38] as well as the express recognition in international law of the principle of shared parental responsibility, add further weight to this argument.[39]

---

[35] No *9519/81 v Germany*, Dec 3.84, 6 EHRR 599. See also Nos *7658/76 & 7659/76 X v Denmark*, Dec 5.12.78, DR 15, p 128.

[36] *Ibid*. cf No *13557/88 N v Denmark*, Dec 9.10.89, DR 63, p 167.

[37] Eur Court HR *Johnston v Ireland*, judgment of 18 Dec 1986, Series A no 112, 9 EHRR 203, § 72. See further Chapter 2, pp 29-32.

[38] For example, Danish law was amended in 1978 to allow for joint custody. See Nos *7658/76 & 7659/76 X v Denmark, op cit*.

[39] Article 18 § 1 UN Convention on the Rights of the Child, *op cit*. See also Recommendation No R (84) 4 of the Committee of Ministers on Parental Responsibilities, particularly Principle 7, in Council of Europe (1996) *The Rights of the Child: A European Perspective*, Strasbourg: Council of Europe, pp 322-324.

The inherently discriminatory way in which the issue of custody is determined makes it difficult to prove that the refusal to award custody in a particular case amounts to unjustifiable discrimination under the Convention. Given the number of fathers who seek to challenge the award of custody before the Commission, it is surprising that this issue of indirect or covert discrimination has never arisen. It would arguably be difficult to prove that a presumption in favour of awarding custody to the mother is being applied in practice, particularly where the domestic authority appears to carry out a reasoned assessment of the custody issue having due regard to interests of the children involved. A legislative presumption that children should remain with their mother following divorce may be inconsistent with Article 8 however.[40] In this regard, it is relevant that under the Convention, domestic authorities called upon to determine custody must consider the interests of the child.[41] Thus, although they may consistently conclude that the welfare of the children is better safeguarded by them residing with their mother, it is arguable that a legal presumption that this is the case would be inconsistent with Article 8 where it precludes examination of the interests of the child.[42]

Given the discretion which the State enjoys in the determination of matters relating to the welfare of children, it would be difficult to establish that bias in favour of raising a child in a marital unit was responsible for the award of custody to a mother and her new husband, over the child's unmarried father, for example. As long as the domestic authorities weigh up the interests of the child and the interference with family life is justified on these grounds, then no issue will arise under Article 8. Thus it is acceptable to attach significance to factors such as the need to protect the child from conflict between birth parents,[43] the degree to which the child is

---

[40] It is argued to be unsatisfactory that a domestic decision regarding respect for family life was based on a legal rule and not a full examination of the merits of the particular case. See Jacobs (1975), *The European Convention on Human Rights*, Oxford: Clarendon Press, p 136.

[41] See above.

[42] While Article 5 of the Seventh Protocol provides for equality between spouses, it is not to prevent States from taking such measures as are necessary in the interests of the children. In this regard, a maternal presumption in law may aim to protect children from highly traumatic legal proceedings. See Elster (1978), 'Salamonic Judgement: Against the Best Interests of the Child', *University of Chicago Law Review*, **54**, pp 1-45 and Dupaix (1987), 'Best Interests Revisited: in Search of Guidelines', *Utah Law Review*, 3, pp 651-573.

[43] No *10148/82 Garcia v Switzerland*, Dec 14.3.85, DR 42, p 98.

integrated into the mother's 'new' family,[44] as well as the extent to which it is possible to maintain contact with the other birth parent,[45] when awarding custody.

## An Effective Right to Custody

While Article 8 imposes a negative obligation on the State to refrain from arbitrary and unlawful interference with family life, it is well established that domestic authorities may also be required to take positive measures to ensure that family life is respected.[46] In the context of custody, Article 8 has been found to oblige the State to take active measures with a view to enforcing such a court order. Although straightforward in practice, this principle raises difficult issues in practice, particularly where the child has resided for a period of time with another parent or family member. In that situation, there is an inevitable clash between the need for stability in the child's upbringing and the right to respect for family life of the parent awarded legal custody, but denied it in fact. Even before that stage however, the failure to enforce custody raises a fundamental issue of justice and respect for the rule of law, in the light of the fact that the matter, having been determined legally by the courts, is decided opposingly by default.

These issues all arose in the *Hokkanen* case,[47] where the applicant father argued that his inability to enforce the orders awarding him custody of his daughter constituted a lack of respect for his family life under Article 8. The facts were that his daughter had gone to stay with her grandparents on a temporary basis following the death of her mother, the applicant's wife. When the time came for her to return to her father's care, however, the grandparents refused, notwithstanding that he had secured several court

---

[44] No *9530/81 v Germany*, Dec 3.84, 7 EHRR 134.

[45] No *9867/82 X v UK*, *op cit*. In this case, the Commission justified the decision of the 'new' family to move to a foreign country thereby frustrating the birth father's access.

[46] See further Chapter 9.

[47] No *19823/92 Hokkanen v Finland*, Comm Rep, 22.10.93, Series A no 299-A, p 31, 19 EHRR 153. Other cases had failed to proceed beyond the Commission. See No *2707/66 Kurtz & Seltmann v Germany*, Dec 4.4.67, Collection 25, p 28, which was settled and also No *8257/78 X v Switzerland*, Dec 10.7.78, DR 13, p 248 (custody dispute between birth mother and foster mother) and No *9993/82 v France*, Dec 5.10.82, DR 31, p 241, 5 EHRR 302 (custody dispute between birth mother and adoptive father).

orders confirming his right to custody. In assessing whether the State had done enough to fulfil its positive obligation to respect the applicant's family life in this case, the Commission noted that regard must be had to the individual interests of the child and her father, as well as the general interest in upholding the rule of law.[48]     In particular, while coercive measures should be avoided where they conflict with the child's interests, the Commission found that a contrary approach could have the effect of encouraging child abduction as a means of eventually obtaining parental rights and this would be incompatible with the rule of law. In this regard, it was satisfied that the applicant had himself taken reasonable steps to have his rights enforced but, in contrast, it was struck by the absence of effective measures taken in response to his requests for enforcement. In relation to the wishes of the child, the Commission considered it important that they be given consideration in such a case, although it found that the circumstances in which the child had expressed a preference about where she wanted to live were such that weight could not be attached to her opinion.[49]     In conclusion, the Commission found that the domestic authorities had failed to achieve a fair balance between these competing interests and more importantly, perhaps, they had failed to take adequate and effective measures sufficient to ensure fulfilment of the positive obligation to respect the father's family life.[50]

The reasoning employed by the Court differed from that of the Commission, not least because it dealt separately with the issues of non-enforcement of contact, and custody. The Court also had an additional complaint to examine, however, given that by the time the application came before it, the Finnish courts had granted *de jure* rights of custody to the child's grandparents and it considered the challenge to this decision with the failure to enforce custody together under Article 8. Both measures were found to be justified in light of the length of the child's stay with her grandparents, and her significant emotional attachment to them.[51]     In reaching this conclusion, the Court found it significant that the obligation on the State to take positive measures to ensure respect for family life could not be absolute, and it noted, in particular, that preparatory measures

---

[48] *Hokkanen* Comm Rep, *ibid*, § 124-147.

[49] *Ibid*, § 143.     She had expressed her views only in the presence of her grandparents. See further Chapter 6, pp 118-119.

[50] The Commission considered together the non-enforcement of custody and contact, finding the overall situation to breach Article 8.

[51] *Hokkanen* judgment, *op cit*, § 63-65.

may be required where a child has lived with others for some time. The nature and extent of such preparation should depend on the circumstances of the case, and while domestic authorities

> must do their utmost to facilitate such co-operation, any obligation to apply coercion must be limited as all interests and rights (particularly of the child) must be taken into account.[52]

Given that six years had passed during which the child had lived with her grandparents and had little contact with her father, the domestic courts' transfer of her legal custody to them was arguably a well-grounded and practical decision. The conclusion of the Court that this measure was compatible with Article 8 also reflects that an appropriate balance had been met between the competing individual interests, notwithstanding its undoubtedly traumatic nature for the child's father. Its finding that non-enforcement of the custody order was consistent with the Convention is more contentious. In particular, it appears to place an official seal on the interference with the father's family life which the grandparents' actions caused by deliberately avoiding the enforcement of a court decision made on the basis of the child's best interests. It is positive, therefore, that the Court recognises the importance of undertaking preparatory work with regard to reuniting parents with their children and to that extent, at least, the issues of contact and custody are almost indivisible. In any event, the importance of acting in accordance with the child's view is given express recognition by both the domestic authorities, as well as the European Court here, and this is a clearly positive development. In contrast, the importance of the child's right to know and be cared for by her father is not so clearly acknowledged. Although it may have been considered implicitly as part of the child's best interests, express recognition of this important principle should be encouraged to ensure a fully balanced approach to such issues under the Convention.

## Contact and Article 8

It is a well established principle that, in the event of family breakdown, children need to have contact with both parents to allow them to identify with the non-custodial parent and to ensure their harmonious

---

[52] *Ibid*, § 58.

development.[53] The fundamental nature of the link between a parent and child means, therefore, that where family life has come to an end in the sense of living together, continued contact between parents and their children is desirable and should in principle remain possible.[54] To date, the Convention institutions have dealt only with the rights of parents in this regard and, similar to the custody case law outlined above, the right of the child to have contact with both parents has not yet been given express recognition, although this is arguably due more to the lack of individual complaints brought by children in this area, than any other factor.

It is important in this context that the parental right to contact with his/her children is neither absolute nor free from restrictions. In particular, it is justifiable to interfere with family life, by limiting or prohibiting contact in special circumstances, or where strong reasons relevant to the interests of the child exist.[55] As in other areas, an appropriate balance must be reached between respect for family life and the need to protect both the interests and the rights of the child. Similarly, the State's margin of appreciation is generous in the area of contact, and its practical effect is to limit the capacity of the Court when considering the compatibility of restrictions on contact with respect for family life under Article 8 as to whether it is based on reasons which are relevant and sufficient.[56]

*Best Interests of the Child*

As in many areas of children's rights, the legitimacy of the State's role in disputes regarding access or contact has given rise to much academic debate.[57] The Commission's view is that it is the function of law in a

---

[53] No *10148/82 Garcia v Switzerland, op cit,* and *Hendriks* Comm Rep, *op cit,* § 94. See also Article 9 § 3 Convention on the Rights of the Child, *op cit* and Fortin (1998) *Children's Rights and the Developing Law,* London: Butterworths, pp 327-333.

[54] *Hendriks* Comm Rep, *op cit,* § 95.

[55] See No *911/60 X v Sweden, op cit; Hendriks* Comm Rep, *op cit,* § 95 and No *21548/93 Malchin v Germany,* Dec 11.1.94, unreported.

[56] See Chapter 9, pp 204-206.

[57] See Dickens (1981), 'The Modern Functions and Limits of Parental Rights', *Law Quarterly Review,* **97,** pp 462-485; Bainham (1990a), 'The Privatisation of the Public Interest in Children', *Modern Law Review,* **53**(2), pp 206-221 and Duncan, 'The Child, The Parent and the State: The Balance of Power' in Duncan (1987), *Law and Social Policy: Some Current Problems,* Dublin: DULJ, pp 19-37.

democratic society to provide safeguards in order to protect children from any harm or mental suffering resulting from the break-up of the parents' relationship.[58] This is particularly true of those children whose tender age makes them vulnerable in this way. While it is clearly acceptable to prohibit a parent's contact with his/her children where the relationship is violent or abusive,[59] the aim of protecting health or morals under Article 8 § 2 has also been interpreted to justify state interference with family life where the child's psychological, as well as physical, well-being is in question. The former applies especially to the suffering which may result from divorce,[60] and it is consistent with Article 8 therefore to suspend the right to contact where conflict exists between parents, and visits with the children would lead to tension in the family of the custodial parent and/or to a conflict of loyalties in the child.[61] The Commission recognises that this situation may cause a parent distress, particularly where contact is being frustrated by the custodial parent. Nevertheless, it has established clearly that where there is a serious conflict between the interests of the child and one of its parents which can only be resolved to the disadvantage of one of them, then the interests of the child must prevail.[62]

It is central to the Strasbourg review of domestic decisions that the State enjoys a wide margin of appreciation in determining the proportionality of measures taken in the child's best interests.[63] The breadth of the discretion enjoyed was illustrated clearly in the *Hendriks* case in 1982, in which the Commission found that refusing to permit contact between the applicant and his child following divorce was compatible with Article 8 insofar as it was proportionate to the best interests of the child. Although the Commission acknowledged the

---

[58] See No *10148/82 Garcia v Switzerland, op cit* and No *12495/86 Jonsson v Sweden, op cit*. It is unclear whether this approach would allow the Commission to sanction state intervention where it was not requested.

[59] No *7911/77 X v Sweden*, Dec 12.12.77, DR 12, p 192 (history of severely maltreating the children at a very young age); No *1449/62 X v the Netherlands*, Dec 16.1.63, 6 Yearbook, p 262 (father convicted of indecently assaulting his daughter). However, see No *2792/66 X v Norway*, Dec 6.10.66, Collection 21, p 64, where the prohibition of access was justified on the grounds that the father's 'abnormal personality traits' could be detrimental to the children's psychological balance.

[60] *Hendriks* Comm Rep, *op cit*, § 120.

[61] *Ibid*, § 121 and No *10148/82 Garcia v Switzerland, op cit.*

[62] *Hendriks* Comm Rep, *op cit*, § 124.

[63] See further Chapter 9, pp 203-206.

frustration and distress of the applicant, its review of the domestic decision was superficial and its conclusion had the effect of sanctioning a lack of contact between a father and child, which had been instigated by a mother determined to frustrate his access.[64]     However, four members of the Commission dissented from the majority in this case, and their particularly dynamic opinion serves to set the standard for other decisions in this area. Firstly, their opinion contained a clear statement of the importance of the principle that after divorce the child must be able to enjoy contact with both parents in order to grow up harmoniously.   In this regard, they questioned whether the Dutch legislation, according to which contact was refused, provided sufficient guarantees of this principle in order to meet the requirements of Article 8.[65]     Secondly, the dissenting voices expressed concern that under the applicable law, the father's right to contact was a privilege, rather than a right.   Finally, although the child's interests had been considered, the dissenting members of the Commission subjected the process by which they were determined to very strong criticism.[66]   In this latter respect, they expressed the view that the child's interests had been determined in a 'purely static manner (his protection from psychological stress)', with no consideration being given to the dynamic concept that it was in his interests to maintain contact with his father.   The dissenting opinion was strong and positively worded and reflected clearly the principles of the UN Convention on the Rights of the Child,[67] notwithstanding that it preceded it by over 15 years. The minority of the Commission held the clear view that strong reasons were required to justify a prohibition on contact between a parent and a child.   While they accepted that the right to contact is not absolute, they appeared to set a higher threshold than the majority of the Commission with regard to the justifiable limits which could be placed on parent-child contact under Article 8.   In particular, although they accepted that an exception should be made in the

---

[64]   See the opinion of the Human Rights Committee which also considered Mr Hendriks' complaint under Articles 23 and 24 of the International Covenant on Civil and Political Rights, UN Doc A/43/40 in McGoldrick (1991), 'The UN Convention on the Rights of the Child', *International Journal of Law and the Family*, **5**, pp 132-169, at pp 136-137 and Van Bueren (1995a),   *The International Law on the Rights of the Child*, Dordrecht: Martinus Nijhoff, pp 75-76.

[65]   Dissenting opinion of Messrs Melchior, Sampaio, Weitzel and Schermers in *Hendriks*, Comm Rep, *op cit*, pp 238-241.

[66]   See further Gomien, *op cit*, p 441.

[67]   See particularly Articles 9 and 12, *op cit*.

case of maltreatment or abuse, it was their view that the creation of tension within the new family could not in itself warrant the denial of access.

Although there has been considerable development of Convention jurisprudence in relation to the restrictions on contact with children in the care of the State, opportunities to rewrite *Hendriks* along the lines suggested by the minority have been rare. The margin of appreciation would arguably prevent the Court from reviewing the factual grounds for the decision to deny contact in such a case, increasing emphasis on the way in which decisions are reached and reference to the principles of children's rights in international law have the potential to change the perspective in such cases.

## An Effective Right to Contact

While a parent may be successful in obtaining recognition of a right to contact, this may not always be sufficient to ensure the enjoyment of this right. This is evident from the *Ouinas* case, which concerned the right of a prisoner to enjoy the contact with his daughter, which he had been awarded by the courts and which she also favoured.[68] The prisoner's right of access applied to one particular prison only, and so difficulties arose when he was transferred to another institution and found that his right of access was no longer enforceable. His requests to be returned to the original prison in order to see his daughter were rejected and he complained to the Commission that this constituted a violation of his right to respect for family life. Although it found that the decisions taken by the prison authorities were justifiable with regard to the State's discretion in the prevention of disorder and crime, the Commission expressed reservations about the applicant's treatment. In particular, it noted that the authorities

> did not seem to have done everything in their power to guarantee the effective exercise of the applicant's right of access to his daughter.[69]

Moreover, it wondered whether greater efforts to move the applicant closer to his daughter's home might not have been possible and compatible with prison security.[70]

---

[68] No *13756/88 Ouinas v France*, Dec 12.3.90, DR 63, p 265.
[69] *Ibid.*
[70] *Ibid.* See also No *5712/77 X v UK*, Dec 18.7.74, Collection 46, p 112 and No *24889/94 McCullough v UK*, Dec 12.9.97, 25 EHRR CD 34.

The *Hokkanen* case had raised a similar issue about the authorities' failure to enforce a father's legal right of access to his daughter, although this situation had a wholly private beginning. Here the Court, like the Commission found that the domestic authorities had not made reasonable efforts to facilitate the applicant's contact with his child in violation of Article 8.[71] While it acknowledged that there were difficulties arranging contact as a result of the animosity between the parties, at the same time, the Court found that the applicant could not be considered responsible for the failure of the relevant court decisions in bringing about contact. The Court went on to reject the Government's claim that it could not be held liable for the obstacles created by the child's grandparents and as a result

> the inaction of the authorities placed [a] burden on the applicant to have constant recourse to a succession of time-consuming and ultimately ineffectual remedies to enforce his rights.[72]

In conclusion, therefore, the failure to take reasonable efforts to promote the reunion of father and daughter over a three year period amounted to a violation of Article 8. This violation appeared to cease, however, with the decision of the Finnish Court of Appeal that the child had become sufficiently mature for her views to be taken into account and that access should therefore not be accorded against her own wishes.[73] In contrast with the Commission, therefore, the Court clearly accepted that the State enjoyed a wide margin of appreciation in this area and the domestic courts' determination of the issue was found to be decisive.

In addition to recognising the importance of an effective right to contact under Article 8, the Court in *Hokkanen* also clarified the extent of the positive obligation on the State to facilitate contact between a parent and child, where it is considered to be in the child's best interests. Importantly, this obligation includes the situation where access is being frustrated by the custodial parent, although it is not yet clear what the position is in relation to other obstacles, such as the issue of security in a prison regime.[74] Where obstacles are created by the difficulties between the parties themselves, the

---

[71] *Hokkanen* judgment, *op cit*, § 60-62. The Commission had reached the same conclusion. *Hokkanen* Comm Rep, *op cit*. See above.

[72] *Ibid*, § 61.

[73] See further Chapter 6, pp 118-119.

[74] See No 28555/95 *Togher v UK*, Dec 16.4.98, unreported, concerning the separation of a new born baby from her mother, a Category A prisoner.

Commission has found that there is no positive obligation on the State to make available effective family counselling to families so as to enable them to enjoy the right of access.[75]

The *Fidler* case illustrates how an issue relating to the effective right to contact may arise under Article 6 of the Convention, which guarantees the right to have civil rights determined within a reasonable time. Here the Commission considered that the State, in failing to deal with a request for contact with appropriate and necessary expedition, may be responsible for denying the effective right of access to a court under Article 6 of the Convention.[76] The Austrian courts were found to have acted in violation of the Convention because they waited until January before determining the request for Christmas contact between the applicant and her grandchild, making the granting of her request impossible.

### Respect for the Views of the Child

A factor ignored by the Commission in *Hendriks* was the age of the applicant's son who, at 16 years old, should arguably have had his wishes as to contact given serious consideration.[77]   While the best interests principle was applied in this case, a more appropriate application of this test would arguably have involved ascertaining the views of the child, and giving them due weight in accordance with his/her age and maturity.[78]

This case notwithstanding, the case law of the Commission shows that the wishes of the child are not always ignored in its determination of whether an interference with family life, caused by a restriction on contact, is proportionate to the child's best interests under Article 8. Moreover, most cases in which the child's wishes have been considered relevant have involved the child's opposition to contact.[79]   Admittedly, the child's opposition to contact may be more relevant than the child's support in assessing a parent's complaint about the restriction on contact. It is thus important that the Commission has recognised that it is not in the child's

---

[75] No 28244/96 *Myszk v Poland*, Dec 1.7.98, 26 EHRR CD 76.

[76] No 24759/94 *Fidler v Austria*, Comm Rep, 3.12.97, unreported.

[77] *Hendriks*, Comm Rep, *op cit.*

[78] See Article 12 Convention on the Rights of the Child, *op cit*, and Chapter 6, pp 117-120.

[79] See No *9530/81 v Germany*, *op cit.*

interests to force him/her to see a parent where s/he repeatedly refuses to do so.[80]

Although it is not yet an implicit requirement under the Convention that the domestic authorities take the wishes of children into account when reaching decisions about contact, the Commission has acknowledged the view of such courts that, for instance, it is important for children of a certain age to have a say on the issue of contact. While the child's wishes may be a persuasive factor in the determination of whether a refusal of contact is compatible with Article 8,[81] the views of the child may play a more decisive role depending on the circumstances of the case. In *Hokkanen* for example, the Court considered that the domestic authorities had failed to take sufficient action to ensure the enforcement of the applicant's right of contact with his daughter. This obligation to secure contact ceased, however, once it was established by the domestic court that the child was opposed to such contact.[82] As a result, the child's opposition to contact with her father was found by the Court to be decisive in relation to whether the failure of the authorities to bring about access violated Article 8. The Commission, in contrast, found that the importance to be attached to the child's wishes was diminished by the fact that she had expressed her view as to where she wanted to live in the presence of her current custodian only.[83] Despite the fact that the Commission's approach involves affording a narrower margin of appreciation to the State as to what weight is attached to the interests of the child, it is significant, nevertheless, that respect for the wishes of the child regarding contact and custody matters has featured in the case law of both institutions.

## International Child Abduction

1980 saw the adoption of two international conventions which sought to address the problem of child abduction by expediting the return of children under the age of 16 to their country of usual residence following their wrongful removal from a contracting state.[84] Both the Hague and the

---

[80] No *9018/80 X v the Netherlands,* Dec 4.7.83, DR 33, p 9, 6 EHRR 133.
[81] No *26169/95 Wielgosz v Poland,* Dec 18.10.95, unreported.
[82] *Hokkanen* judgment, *op cit,* § 61.
[83] *Hokkanen* Comm Rep, *op cit,* § 129.
[84] The Hague Convention on the Civil Aspects of International Child Abduction, 1980 and the European Convention on the Recognition and Enforcement of

European Conventions on Child Abduction require States to establish a central authority responsible for receiving and dealing with applications[85] and there is thus a mechanism in place in many ECHR States to deal with the abduction of children from one Convention State to another.[86]   This does not prevent the European Commission and Court from examining complaints relating to child abduction, but the existence of a proper and efficient forum for their consideration serves to reduce the number of complaints brought before the Strasbourg Court.

Child abduction is contrary to the best interests of the child principally because it involves the sudden removal of the child from familiar surroundings, and a complete change of family, home and school environment for a child with possible traumatic and psychological consequences.[87]  As a result, the Commission has found that a decision to deny contact between a child and a parent, who lives in a different country, may be justified under Article 8 by the need to protect the child's well-being.   In particular, the risk of abduction may itself justify restricting contact, where there is a possibility that, should the children be permitted to visit a parent in his/her own country, they would not be returned.[88]   The threat to the child's health and psychological well-being, posed by the abduction means that measures refusing contact which aim to reduce the risk of abduction may indeed be compatible with Article 8.[89]   As regards the assessment of such a risk, the Commission has acknowledged that it

---

Decisions Concerning Custody of Children and Restoration of Custody of Children, 1980 (ETS No 105).   See Jones (1981), 'Council of Europe Convention on Recognition and Enforcement of Decisions Relating to the Custody of Children', *International and Comparative Law Quarterly*, **30**, pp 467-475 and Schuz (1995), 'The Hague Child Abduction Convention, Family Law and Private International' Law, *International and Comparative Law Quarterly*, **44**, pp 771-802, 771-802.   See generally Davis, Rosenblatt, & Galbraith, (1993), *International Child Abduction*, London:Sweet & Maxwell.

[85] For an English case study in this regard see Lowe & Perry (1999) 'International Child Abduction - the English Experience', *International & Comparative Law Quarterly*, **48**, pp 127-155.

[86] Admittedly not all ECHR States have also ratified the child abduction conventions.

[87] See Van Bueren (1995a), *op cit*, pp 90-93.

[88] No *911/60 X v Sweden*, *op cit*; No *8045/77 X v Sweden*, *op cit*.

[89] No *5608/72 X v UK*, Dec 14.12.75, Collection 44, p 466.

may arise as a result of a previous incident of abduction[90] or where the domestic court has found it possible that the parent in question would not positively assist in returning the children following their visit.[91]

Decisions made subsequent to a parent's abduction of a child to another country may be tested before the Court with regard to their consistency with the Convention. Such complaints will generally be decided in the same manner as other custody disputes under Article 8 and the proceedings themselves will be open to challenge under Article 6.[92] The existence of the Hague and European Conventions may complicate the Strasbourg proceedings although it is clear that the European Court has no jurisdiction to examine direct complaints concerning the implementation of these instruments. Nevertheless, the decisions made by national authorities pursuant to their obligations under either Convention will fall under the jurisdiction of the Commission and Court in the normal way. Where such a decision involves an interference with family life of a parent or child, therefore, it must be justifiable under Article 8 § 2 with reference to the child's best interests or some other aim under that section. To date, little use has been made of the extra avenue of complaint which this provides for aggrieved parents and children. Although the European Convention does not oblige Convention States to combat the illicit transfer and non-return of children abroad,[93] it is arguable that the positive obligation under Article 8 to allow family ties to be maintained may require public authorities to do all that could be reasonably expected of them to locate the whereabouts of an abducted child and have the child returned.[94]

The recognition by the Commission and Court of the limited use of coercion in the enforcement of domestic custody and contact decisions applies equally to abduction cases. Moreover, the wishes of the child who is sufficiently old and mature, have been considered relevant in cross-border custody disputes. Thus, where the express wish of the child is not to return to one parent, following abduction by another, this must be respected under Article 8.[95] The Commission has also found that a

---

[90] No *24606/94 RS v UK*, Dec 6.9.95, unreported; No *7639/76 X v Denmark*, Dec 5.10.77, DR 11, p 169.

[91] No *8045/77 X v Sweden, op cit.*

[92] No *27095/95 Koutsofotinos v Norway & Greece*, Dec 10.9.97, unreported.

[93] Cf Article 35 Convention on the Rights of the Child, *op cit*

[94] No *7547/76 X v UK*, Dec 15.12.77, DR 12, p 73. On positive obligations see further Chapter 9, pp 198-199

[95] No *20592/92 Olsson v Norway*, Dec 5.4.95 unreported.

domestic authority which places emphasis on the wishes of the child in such circumstances is not acting contrary to Article 6, and the custody proceedings which follow the abduction cannot be deemed unfair as a consequence.[96] Nor does the decision by the domestic court to hear the children in the absence of their parents violate the parent's right to a fair hearing of itself, and what is of overriding importance in this context is that the views of the child be heard in circumstances most likely to give rise to a true picture of their opinions. The importance of the child's opinion is acknowledged in Article 13 of the Child Abduction Convention which provides for the refusal to order the return of a child where the child objects to being returned and has attained an age and maturity at which it is appropriate to take account of its views. Express recognition of the child's right to be heard in proceedings under the Hague Convention is reflected in the importance attached to the child's views in the proceedings before the Commission. Thus, faced with a challenge to the application of this provision, the Commission has pointed to the importance of the qualifying criteria by finding that although a domestic court may

> base a decision on the views of children who were palpably unable to form and articulate an opinion as to their wishes, the 'necessity' for such a decision may not be readily apparent. [97]

However, it has not yet found a custody decision to be incompatible with Article 8 in this way and in the case in question, it could not exclude that children of ages 7 and 9 may be capable of 'holding and expressing firm and coherent views on where they wish to live'. As it found nothing in the domestic decision to indicate that the views of the boys were not genuine and tenable, it concluded that the decision to refuse custody had indeed been based on reasons which were relevant and sufficient under Article 8.

## Future Challenges

While the Commission and the Court have developed considerable jurisprudence around the sensitive and complex disputes about custody and contact matters, these principles have been developed largely from an adult or parents' perspective. The Commission's refusal to consider complaints

---

[96] No *26376/95 Laylle v Germany*, Dec 4.9.96, unreported.
[97] *Ibid.*

introduced by non-custodial parents on behalf of their children, together with the low number of complaints introduced by or on behalf of children themselves, help to explain the adult focus of Convention case law in this area. However, these factors also highlight a point which is more fundamental to the enjoyment by children of their Convention rights, namely the importance of providing children with independent legal representation both at domestic level, to enable them to participate effectively in domestic proceedings, as well as before the European Court in Strasbourg. While the interests of children are represented in care proceedings, measures aimed at increasing the level of child participation in private family law proceedings have not been particularly successful.[98] However, until child applicants introduce their own complaints in this area, the Court will not be encouraged to afford express recognition to the child's right to be heard with regard to respect for his/her family life.

The issues likely to arise in this area include further challenges to the scope of the obligation under Article 8 to recognise the rights of custody and contact in an effective manner. This may require the Court to clarify the measures, which a State is required to adopt in order to ensure that both parents and children enjoy the custody or contact legally recognised by the domestic courts. Moreover, the proportionality between the interference with family life caused by matters of security and the prevention of crime and disorder, such as where contact between parents in prison and their children is prohibited, may also prove contentious in the future. Finally, while bias or covert discrimination in favour of awarding custody to mothers, family units based on marriage, and against members of minority religions which are illegal or deemed socially harmful may be difficult to establish, it may nonetheless raise an issue under the Convention where its result is to avert a balanced assessment of the matter with regard to what is in the child's best interests.

---

[98] The European Convention on the Exercise of Children's Rights, 1996 has only been ratified by two of the three States necessary to allow it to come into force. See further Chapter 6.

# 12    Alternative Care

## Introduction

The principal purpose of Article 8 is to protect the individual's private and family life against arbitrary interference by public authorities. While it is clear that many other areas fall within its scope, the situation to which Article 8 applies most directly is that involving the removal of children from the family home by the public authorities in order to place them with alternative carers. The Convention does not make express provision for the rights of children who are removed from their home environment in this way.[1] However, in their consideration of this and related issues, the Commission and Court have developed a number of important principles with regard to family life and the scope of the state's obligation to respect it, both in negative and positive terms. These standards hang on the rule that family life survives the removal of children from the family home and their replacement with alternative carers. They concern the basis for the child's removal from the home, the implementation of the care order, the importance of continuing contact with the child's family while in care, as well as facilitating the child's return once a care order is no longer necessary. In addition, considerable procedural safeguards have been found to be implicit in Article 8 in this area and these have become an important part of the right to respect for family life under the Convention.

## Removing Children from the Family

The removal of a child from the family environment will be compatible with the Convention only where it is necessary in a democratic society in order to protect the interests of the child and has, what the Court describes as, a relevant and sufficient basis. In addition, however, the discretion, which the State enjoys in guaranteeing respect for family life, is

---

[1]  *Cf* Convention on the Rights of the Child, particularly Article 20, UN Doc A/44/25. On this provision see Walsh (1991), 'UN Convention on the Rights of the Child: a British View', *International Journal of Law and the Family*, 5, pp 170-194, at pp 182-184.

particularly wide in this area and as a result, the Court will find a care order to fall outside the margin of appreciation only in exceptional situations.[2]

The scope of the State's discretion in the making of a care order is apparent from a survey of the case law in this area. It shows that in the vast majority of cases where children have been taken into care, the bases for these decisions have been accepted by the Commission and Court, which have gone on to find the interference with family life complained of to be justified under Article 8 § 2. Nevertheless, the institutions consider in each case whether the reasons advanced in favour of the care order are relevant and sufficient.

### Abuse or Neglect

In extreme cases, it will not be difficult to find the interference with family life to be proportionate to the need to protect the child. Where, for example, the child is known to have been sexually abused by a parent, the removal of the child from the family home will clearly be compatible with Article 8.[3] Equally, where the physical injury to a child can be explained either by the action of the parent in deliberately causing the abuse, or alternatively, by the parent's failure to protect the child from such injury, either reason may be considered relevant and sufficient for the purposes of Article 8.[4] Where injury is not visible, allegations of abuse made by neighbours may be sufficient to justify taking the children into care for observation.[5]

The removal of children from the family home where they live in circumstances of neglect (such as deplorable conditions, without light or heat) has also been accepted as consistent with Article 8 § 2.[6] So, too, has the fact that the child suffers neglect or other ill-treatment as a result of a parent's alcohol or drug addiction.[7]

---

[2]   See further Chapter 9, pp 204-206 and Chapter 1, pp 6-8.

[3]   No *11630/85 v Sweden*, Dec 10.85, 9 EHRR 267. See Chapter 8, pp 171-172, for details of the proof required in such cases.

[4]   No *16184/90 Lavender v UK*, Dec 7.5.90, unreported; No *12805/87 Nowack v Sweden*, Dec 13.3.89, DR 60, p 212.

[5]   No *14013/88 Family T v Austria*, Dec 14.12.89, DR 64, p 176.

[6]   No *8059/77 X & Y v Germany*, Dec 3.10.78, DR 15, p 208.

[7]   No *25054/94 ED v Ireland*, Dec 18.10.95, unreported; No *12651/87 Grufmann v Sweden*, Dec 9.5.89, DR 61 p 176, and No *24721/94 Burlind v Sweden*, Dec 4.7.95, unreported.

*Fulfilment of Needs*

While it may not be difficult to conclude that a care order made on the above grounds is compatible with Article 8, the proportionality of domestic decisions based on more ambiguous grounds is not so easily determined. For example, it is not readily apparent that taking a child into care because his/her parent suffers from a mental condition, which either prevents him from understanding the child's needs,[8] or may lead to the development of similar problems in the child[9] is justified under Article 8. The difficulty in balancing the interests of the child with the family life of the parent is even greater where the child is removed from a parent with such a condition shortly after birth.[10] The Commission has recognised the severity of the interference with family life, which such a measure causes, and in assessing its compatibility with Article 8, it has taken into account whether the social authorities provided assistance to the parents or took other preventive measures prior to the removal of the child from their care.[11] In addition, the Court has consistently maintained that an interference with the right of the parents to continue to take care of their child cannot be justified simply because the child would be better off with foster parents.[12] However, it is not yet clear whether authorities, which fail to take such measures in advance of removing a child from parental care, would be found to have acted arbitrarily under Article 8. It is at least significant that in order to determine whether a care order is arbitrary, the Court will attach

---

[8] See No *17383/90 Johansen v Norway*, Comm Report, 17.1.95, Reports 1996-III, no 13.

[9] No *25047/94 EL v Germany*, Dec 22.2.95, unreported.

[10] No *18562/91 Karppinen & Johnsson v Sweden*, Dec 1.12.93, unreported, and No *11704/85 Krol v Sweden*, Comm Rep, 5.7.88, DR 56, p 186. Gomien criticises the State in such cases for acting *ultra vires* in assuming greater control over a child than the circumstances warrant. See Gomien (1989), 'State Powers and the Best Interests of the Child under Article 8 ECHR', *Netherlands Quarterly of Human Rights*, 7, pp 435-450, at p 443.

[11] No *10141/82 v Sweden*, Dec 10.84, 8 EHRR 253. This reflects Article 18 § 2 of the Convention on the Rights of the Child which provides that States Parties shall render appropriate assistance to parents in the performance of their child-rearing responsibilities. See McGoldrick, *op cit*, p 143.

[12] No *10141/82 v Sweden, op cit.*

importance to the fact that the authorities did not intervene without adequate prior knowledge of the case.[13]

It is apparent from the case law that a high level of state intervention in the family may be consistent with Article 8 as long as it aims to protect the child, and arbitrariness in the manner in which this is achieved is prevented. For example, among the infinite number of Swedish care cases examined under the Convention, the following justifications for removing children from the family home have been found to be compatible with Article 8: the child's 'need for stimulation [wa]s not being satisfied in the home environment'[14] there existed a 'clear risk of impairment of health and development' of the child,[15] and the parents were unable to realise the child's special needs.[16] In contrast to clear cases of physical or emotional abuse, these less clear-cut grounds for taking a child into care highlight the difficulty of the Court's task in reviewing their compatibility with Article 8. These cases also illustrate the appropriateness of permitting local authorities a degree of discretion in the area of alternative care, although it may still be decisive for the outcome of the case that the care order is open to challenge before domestic courts and that it is only made following a thorough investigation of the circumstances, in order to preclude arbitrariness.[17]

*Conflicts of Interests*

According to the case law of the Commission, it may be consistent with Article 8 to place a child in the care of the State in order to avoid the friction and tension of a post-divorce situation.[18] Moreover, where there is conflict between those caring for the child and the social authorities this may, combined with other factors, justify a care order under Article 8.[19] Although it is not difficult to imagine that parents, who are themselves

---

[13]  See Eur Court HR *Olsson v Sweden*, judgment of 24 March 1988, Series A no 130, 11 EHRR 259, § 72 and No *18562/91 Karppinen & Johnsson v Sweden, op cit.*

[14]  No *12651/87 Grufmann v Sweden, op cit.*

[15]  No *24721/94 Burlind v Sweden, op cit.*

[16]  No *23977/94 Stombrowski v Sweden*, Dec 5.4.95, unreported.

[17]  See No *11350/85 X v Sweden*, Dec 10.85, 9 EHRR 265.

[18]  No *4396/70 X v Germany*, Dec 14.12.70, 33 Collection, p 88. Unfortunately this (early) decision is so brief as to provide little detail of the nature of the family environment from which the child had to be removed.

[19]  No *11350/85 v Sweden, op cit;* No *23977/94 Stombrowski v Sweden, op cit.*

experiencing difficulties, might refuse to cooperate with the authorities in the removal of children from their care, it is unlikely that a parent's uncooperative attitude could ever constitute the sole justification for such a measure, unless this was placing the children in danger. This is so principally because the authorities' initial intervention must itself have a reasonable and sufficient basis and it is this decision to intervene which would require consideration under Article 8 therefore. This is illustrated by the Swedish case of *Gustavsson* in which the Commission found that a care order, necessitated by the conflict of interests between the social authorities and the child's grandparents, was compatible with Article 8.[20] The background to the case was that criminal proceedings were ongoing against the grandparents' son for sexually abusing his child. The grandparents, who believed in his innocence, were unwilling to permit the child to undergo rehabilitative therapy for sexual abuse, and thus their failure to cooperate had the effect of denying the child the care which the domestic authorities believed he needed. Thus, although the final reason for implementing the care order was the grandparents' attitude, the problem stemmed from the child's allegations of sexual abuse by his father. This decision illustrates how decisions made in a proactive, interventionist child care system may indeed be consistent with the Convention in the light of the State's margin of appreciation. It demonstrates also how state interference with family life may be compatible where it aims to secure the child's right to health or rehabilitative treatment.

The Commission revisited this view in 1996 when it rejected a complaint made by the parents of a child who was taken into care so that he could receive surgical treatment to which his parents objected.[21] What is clearly decisive here is the depth of the investigation undertaken at domestic level, in particular, the consideration of the matter by the courts, including the testimony of expert witnesses. In this case, the facts that the authorities had not intervened without adequate knowledge of the case, and they had subjected the necessity of the care order to the courts for a hearing were decisive in finding it to be justified under Article 8. The absence of such factors in another case may raise a query as to whether the decision to remove the child into care was consistent with the Convention.[22]

---

[20] No *21009/92 Gustavsson v Sweden*, Dec 5.4.92, unreported.

[21] No *16071/93 Wedberg & Hillblom v Sweden*, Dec 11.4.96, unreported.

[22] See No *28945/95 TP & KM v UK*, Dec 26.5.98, 26 EHRR CD 84, in Chapter 8, pp 171-172, 180.

*Consent of the Parent and the Child*

Where a parent consents to the placement of their children in care, the Commission appears to be precluded from examining the compatibility of the care order with the Convention. Once a parent revokes their consent, however, the continuation of the placement may raise an issue under Article 8, which will fall to be justified in the usual way.[23] Where a child is even indirectly in favour of the placement, such as where s/he expresses a persistent wish not to live with a parent, this factor may be relevant to the justification of a care order insofar as it creates a suspicion of serious deficiencies in that person's parenting ability.[24] However, it is unlikely that a care order could justifiably be based on the wishes of the child alone, unless the child has reached an age and maturity which made any other conclusion arbitrary.

The fact that the above case law does not include one successful application before the Commission - all justifications submitted by the authorities having been accepted by the Commission as proportionate to the aim of protecting the child's health and other interests - suggests that Article 8 places a heavy burden on parents to show that the grounds on which a care order is based are arbitrary, irrelevant or insufficient. It also illustrates the breadth of the Commission's interpretation of the best interests principle, which clearly ranges from protecting the child from sexual abuse to ensuring necessary surgery is carried out; from providing the child with an adequate standard of living to ensuring the child's proper educational and moral development. The approach of the Commission and the Court also highlights their generous approach to the exercise of state discretion with particular regard to decisions of this kind.[25]

*The Olsson Case*

The case of *Olsson v Sweden* illustrates the manner in which the margin of appreciation operates in care cases and it usefully highlights the two possible extremes of the Strasbourg approach. On the one hand, the Commission's opinion implies that its review of a case under Article 8

---

[23] No *21687/93 BH v Norway*, Dec 12.10.94, unreported.

[24] No *10141/82 v Sweden, op cit.* The child here was 13 years of age and experts reported that the reason for her attitude was likely to be psychological pressure from her mother through her unbalanced behaviour and her excessive demands towards her daughter.

[25] See further Chapter 9, pp 204-206.

extends beyond procedural matters to include issues of substance and fact.[26]   The judgment of the Court, on the other hand, reaffirms the considerable discretion enjoyed by the State under Article 8 and the fact that it is not a court of fourth instance.[27]   Details of the contrasting approaches taken by the Commission and the Court highlight this distinction and a detailed consideration of the case is thus useful.

The basis of the complaint made in this case was that the State's decision to take the three Olsson children into care amounted to an arbitrary interference with the right to respect for their family life.[28]   The Commission did not dispute that the care order constituted an interference of a serious nature, or that its purpose was an important one, namely to protect the children's interests. However, in determining whether there was proportionality between these two factors, it made the following detailed observations. It began by expressing the view that parents have the right under Article 8 to take care of and educate their children. This right, it said, must be exercised in the interests of the children and can only be restricted by the State if it is clearly shown that the parents exercise it in a contrary manner. According to the Commission, the separation of children from their parents cannot be justified simply because the children would be better cared for by foster parents; the reasons for doing so must be strong and sufficient and of such a weight as to be necessary in a democratic society in the interests of the child. In this context, it made the important observation that separating a child from his/her parents will, in itself, have a negative effect on the child, but found that with regard to determining other aspects of the child's well-being, both the domestic courts and the Convention institutions must rely to a great extent on the evidence of doctors and psychologists. In this regard, the Commission considered that the most important element in its examination of the case was the reasons indicated in the judgments of the domestic courts in justification of the care order and it considered each one in turn.[29]   In relation to the first such reason - that the children's home environment was unsatisfactory - it agreed with the domestic court that it may, in theory, justify placement in care. However, it found it essential that the unsatisfactory elements of the home environment be clearly set out and it considered also that its detrimental

---

[26] No *10465/83 Olsson v Sweden*, Comm Rep, 2.12.86, Series A no 130, 11 EHRR 301

[27] *Olsson* judgment, *op cit.*

[28] *Olsson* Comm Rep, *op cit*, § 145-151.

[29] *Ibid*, § 154-163.

effects must be so severe that a lesser measure than a care order would not suffice. Looking at the second reason - that two of the children were retarded in their development - the Commission noted that the facts on which this conclusion was based were not included in the judgment and that the Government's explanation provided on request was drawn from a report written after the care order had been made. With regard to the third reason - that there was a great risk of the third child developing unfavourably if she remained at home - the Commission considered that this amounted to no more than a prediction of possible unfavourable development. Looking at the case as a whole, the Commission was unconvinced that the factual situation was so grave as to justify a care order. In this regard and with respect to other complaints of contact, it found a violation of Article 8.[30]

The judgment of the Court appears brief in contrast to that of the Commission.[31] While it found that the reasons relied on in support of the care order were relevant, it reiterated the view of the Commission that, in addition, the splitting up of a family must be supported by 'sufficiently sound and weighty considerations' in the interests of the child. It confirmed also that it was not enough that the child would be better off in care. Having regard to the case as a whole, however, the Court noted that the Swedish authorities had not intervened without adequate knowledge of the background of the case, and in light of the margin of appreciation which they enjoyed it concluded that they were reasonably entitled to think that it was necessary to take the children into care.

The strong principles enunciated by the Court in the *Olsson* case make it clear that domestic authorities may disrupt the family only in exceptional circumstances and where they have adequate background knowledge to the effect that no lesser measure would suffice in order to protect the interests of the children. Nevertheless, it is arguably more notable that the judgment established the practice of applying the doctrine of the margin of appreciation in a way which effectively precludes the Court from examining whether a decision to remove children from their parents' care was necessary in fact. In this regard, the judgment is the antithesis of the Commission's more detailed analysis of the facts, which is in itself noteworthy as a unique example of how Article 8 could and should be applied dynamically in this context.[32]

---

[30] *Ibid*, § 178.
[31] *Olsson* judgment, *op cit*, § 72-73.
[32] See Gomien, *op cit*, pp 444-446.

*A Requirement to Intervene?*

One important issue which has yet to be considered by the Court is where the line is to be drawn between refraining from intervening in the family without adequate prior knowledge of the situation, and protecting the welfare of the child. This obviously raises important and complex issues about the obligation of the state to protect children from harm and the need to respect the integrity of the family under Article 8. In such cases, however, it is the issue of the child's ill-treatment or abuse which is central and it may be more relevant to invoke either Article 8, which protects physical integrity, or Article 3, which prohibits inhuman and degrading treatment. There is a challenge of this nature currently awaiting determination in Strasbourg brought by children who complain that the State failed to protect them from abuse and neglect by their parents.[33] Whether the Court will interpret either provision to oblige the domestic authorities to intervene in the family to protect the child, even where it has adequate knowledge of the background to the situation, is unlikely. Its determination of such a complaint will arguably centre on the availability of domestic remedies, or legal protection, from such abuse.

## Placing Children in Care

While domestic authorities enjoy considerable discretion under the Convention when making a care order, the margin of appreciation is narrowed with regard to the manner in which care orders are implemented. Moreover, the Court has set down a number of important principles in this respect based on the understanding that the relationship between parent and child is a fundamental aspect of family life, which is not terminated by the child's placement in care.[34] The most important principle is that as long as the care order is intended to be temporary in nature, its implementation must be guided by the ultimate aim of family reunion. Only in exceptional cases can it be justified to act as if a care order should never be lifted and thus, even if it is necessary for the child to spend a long period of time in care, the aim of lifting the order must inform all arrangements made during that time.

---

[33] No *29392/95 KL and Others v UK*, Dec 26.5.98, 26 EHRR CD 113. See further Chapter 6, pp 173-174.

[34] *Olsson* judgment, *op cit*, § 81.

The practical application of this principle is illustrated by the *Olsson* case in which three children were removed from their parents with a view to providing them with alternative care.[35] Difficulties arose when the children were placed with foster families a great distance from their parents and from each other. In particular, the practical impediment to contact caused by the distance between them resulted in family relations almost being cut off between family members. Considering whether this situation was justified under Article 8, the Court found that the authorities had acted in good faith in implementing the care decision in this manner. However, it rejected that administrative difficulties, such as a lack of appropriate foster families, could play more than a secondary role in the implementation of a care order.[36] Thus, despite the uncooperative nature of the parents, the measures taken by the authorities were not supported by sufficient reasons for them to be proportionate to the aim pursued and this, the Court found, gave rise to a violation of Article 8.[37]

The fact that one child was placed 900 km from his siblings undoubtedly raised concern about respect for the family life of all three children. Indeed, the complaint under Article 8 was made with regard to the separation of the children from each other, as well as from their parents, and the Commission expressed clear dissatisfaction with the inadequacy of the domestic court's justification for separating the siblings.[38] However, like the Court, the Commission refrained from finding that the siblings' separation from each other was unjustifiable in itself, and preferred to conclude generally that the placement of the children with families very far away from their parents as well as each other without convincing reasons for such serious interferences, was inconsistent with Article 8 § 2.[39]

It is of great practical significance that the Court refused to accept inadequate fostering arrangements as a justification for separating siblings from each other and their parents. However, it remains unclear whether the risk of parents interfering with the foster family would permit the authorities to place the children such a distance from their parents. Where

---

[35] See above.

[36] *Ibid*, § 82.

[37] Judges Ryssdal, Thor Vilhjalmsson and Golculklu, dissenting, found that the children's placement was merely 'unfortunate'.

[38] *Olsson* Comm Rep, *op cit*, § 176. Six members of the Commission (Messrs Norgaard, Frowein, Jurundsson, Trechsel, Schermers and Danelius) found the likelihood that the parents would interfere with the foster parents to be a relevant and sufficient justification under Article 8.

[39] *Ibid*, § 178.

the care order is a temporary arrangement then arguably any measure which has the potential to damage family life irreparably will raise an issue under Article 8, unless it can be justified with specific regard to the welfare of the child.   In any event, the importance of the *Olsson* case is clear insofar as it places a direct obligation on the local authorities to fulfil the children's need for alternative care in a manner which allows them to maintain direct and frequent contact with other family members.[40]

**Respect for the Child's Background**

According to Article 2 of the First Protocol to the Convention, the State is obliged to respect the religious and philosophical convictions of parents in the education and teaching of their children.   The broad interpretation of the terms 'education' and 'teaching' by the Court means that this provision has implications for the manner in which children are raised.[41]   As a result, when the State assumes responsibility for the upbringing of children by taking them into care, the care order must be implemented in a manner which respects the religious and philosophical convictions of the child's parents. Article 9, which guarantees freedom of thought, conscience and religion, may require that the beliefs of the child be respected also, although no case law exists yet to this effect.[42]

*Religious Convictions*

Parents seeking to challenge the implementation of a care order on the basis that it conflicts with the way in which they wish to raise their children face a significant burden in doing so under the Convention.   According to the Court, they must be able to prove firstly, that their religious convictions are seriously held and secondly, that the upbringing received by their children in their foster home is clearly contrary to those beliefs.   In *Olsson*, the parents complained that the placement of children with a religious family was incompatible with their wish to provide their children with a non-religious upbringing.   Their claim failed, however, because the Court

---

[40]   Other related problems are identified in Gallagher (1998) 'Care Orders and the State's Responsibilities' *New Law Journal*, pp 670-672.

[41]   See Eur Court HR *Campbell & Cosans v UK*, judgment of 25 Feb 1982, Series A no 48, § 33, 4 EHRR 293.   See generally Chapter 4, pp 70-75.

[42]   On related case law see further Chapter 6, pp 132-136.

could not find any serious indication that this was in fact the parents' wish.[43] Nor were they able to show that the education their children received in care in any way diverged from what they would have desired. Evidential problems notwithstanding, however, the placement of children whose parents have raised them in one religion, with a foster family who follow a different faith, is likely to contravene the Convention, unless special arrangements are made to enable the children's own religion to be respected.

Despite the case law that the practical difficulties of finding a suitable foster home cannot justify placing the children a considerable distance from their parents, this principle does not seem to extend to respect for religious convictions. Moreover, it appears that as long as the authorities have made a reasonable effort to comply with the express wishes of parents with regard to the religious beliefs of the foster family, taking into consideration the need to find a home within visiting distance of the parents, then there will be no breach of Article 2 of the First Protocol.[44] In addition, where a parent has rejected the arrangements made for visiting the children, thereby declining to take an active part in ensuring their children's education in accordance with their convictions, then no issue will arise under this provision.

### Parents' Philosophical Convictions

In the light of the fact that Article 2 of the First Protocol obliges the State to protect the parent's philosophical as well as their religious convictions, it is arguable that such beliefs must also be respected as appropriate in the implementation of a care order. Although the meaning of philosophical convictions is unclear, the case law has established that they may include views that are part of a serious and coherent thought process, relating to physical punishment for example.[45] However unlikely the prospect, it is arguable that the placement of a child with foster parents who administer physical punishment to children will raise a serious issue under the Convention where birth parents have made the authorities aware of their opposition to such treatment.

---

[43] Although they claimed to be atheists, the applicants were members of the Church of Sweden where the children had been baptised, and these factors cast doubt on the genuine nature of their claim before the Court. *Olsson* judgment, *op cit*, § 94-95.

[44] *No 16031/90 Tennenbaum v Sweden*, Dec 5.93, 18 EHRR CD 41.

[45] See further Chapter 4, pp 76-81.

*Cultural Identity*

The Convention may also oblige the domestic authorities to have regard to other parental convictions in the manner in which care orders are implemented, where such beliefs are found to fall within the scope of Article 2 of the First Protocol. For example, it is possible to argue that the authorities must take into account the child's ethnic or racial background, insofar as this reflects the deeply held convictions of the child's parents, which must be respected under the Convention. Recognition of the importance of ensuring consistency in the child's upbringing at international level supports this argument[46] although the European Convention provides no express protection of this kind. An Irish case involving the placement of a child with a Traveller background with a settled foster family raised these issues before the Commission.[47] The protesting father argued that the placement violated his rights under Article 10 to impart information about the culture of the travelling community to his children, as well as under Article 11 insofar as the long-term placement would prevent the children from associating with other members of that community.[48] Moreover, the applicant also complained that the failure to place the child with an adoptive family, which shared the Traveller identity, amounted to discrimination under Article 14 taken with Article 8. However, as it was accepted by the parties that the child had already bonded with his foster parents by the time the adoption proceedings were underway, and that it was unrealistic to suggest that the child should be moved to a different family, this complaint was dismissed.[49] These technicalities notwithstanding, the complaints raised in this case were both interesting and genuine, and they will be difficult to resolve should they reappear before the Court, particularly given the absence of clear protection for minorities in the Convention.[50] Some sense of its reasoning in a future

---

[46] See above, and Rosenblatt (1996), 'The Needs of Black and Ethnic Children', *Family Law*, **26**, pp 641-642, and Richards (1987), 'Family, Race and Identity', *Adoption & Fostering*, **11**(3), pp 10-13.

[47] No *25054/94 ED v Ireland, op cit.*

[48] These complaints were found to be out of time. On the application of Articles 10 and 11 to children, see Chapter 6.

[49] His failure to raise this complaint in the domestic proceedings before bonding occurred meant that he had failed to exhaust domestic remedies, *op cit.*

[50] See Baka, 'The Convention and the Protection of Minorities under International Law' in Macdonald et al (eds) (1993), *The European System for the Protection of Human Rights*, Deventer: Kluwer, pp 875-888.

case of this kind may be taken from the discussion by the Commission of the Article 8 argument in this case. In particular, weighing up the factors for and against the child's adoption and acknowledging that the adoption would preclude the parent from passing on his Traveller heritage to his child, the measure was found, on balance, to be in the child's best interests, albeit to the detriment of the child's right to identity.[51]

## Contact with Children in Care

It is well established that the child who is separated from his/her parents must be allowed to maintain personal relations and direct contact with them on a regular basis, unless it is contrary to the child's best interests.[52] The fundamental nature of family life between parent and child under the Convention means that where a child is placed with alternative carers, contact between them must continue, not least, in order to facilitate the ultimate aim of reuniting the family.

### Principles under Article 8

Article 8 guarantees parents and children a right of mutual contact when a care order is in place and thus a decision which denies or regulates such contact will interfere with family life and fall to be justified by considerations pertaining to the child's best interests under Article 8 § 2.[53] Moreover, particularly harsh restrictions on contact can only be applied in exceptional circumstances and they will only be justified under Article 8 where they are motivated by an overriding requirement pertaining to the best interests of the child.[54] The principle of proportionality requires, therefore, that a decision to deprive parents and children from mutual contact on a permanent basis must be supported at the time by 'particularly strong reasons' in order to be compatible with the Convention.[55] Furthermore, the balancing of interests in the application of Article 8 must

---

[51] See further Chapter 13, p 308.

[52] See also Article 9 § 3 Convention on the Rights of the Child, *op cit.*

[53] No *12963/87 Andersson v Sweden*, Comm Rep, 3.10.90, Series A no 226-A, 14 EHRR 634, § 85.

[54] Eur Court HR *Johansen v Norway,* judgment of 17 Aug 1996, Reports 1996-III no 13, p. 979, 23 EHRR 33, § 78 and Eur Court HR *Andersson v Sweden,* judgment of 24 Feb 1992, Series A no 226-A, 14 EHRR 615, § 95.

[55] *Johansen* judgment, *op cit,* § 74.

thus be undertaken in the light of the circumstances obtaining at the time the decisions were taken, rather than with the benefit of hindsight. This helps to ensure, among other things, that the process by which domestic decisions are reviewed by the Court is fair. In addition, any decision to restrict parental access to a child in care must be viewed in the light of the reasons on which the initial care order, and any subsequent decision to maintain it in force, were based.[56] The Court has also held that when considering whether the placement of specific restrictions on parental contact with a child in care, such as a prohibition on telephone contact, is justified under Article 8 § 2, the measures must be considered in the broader context of the restriction on contact as a whole.[57]

Where contact with a parent would harm the child's interests, the national authorities must strike a balance between the interests of the child in remaining in public care and the interests of the parent in being reunited with the child.[58] In carrying out this balancing exercise, the Court attaches particular importance to the best interests of the child which, depending on their nature and seriousness, may override those of the parent. In particular, the parent cannot be entitled under Article 8 to have such measures taken as would harm the child's health and development.[59] However, it is insufficient to argue that contact might disturb the calm and stable foster-home environment when access arrangements can be implemented outside the foster home.[60] The measure restricting contact must thus be necessary in all the circumstances.

It is not sufficient for the purposes of Article 8 that a restriction on contact, which creates an interference with family life, is considered necessary to protect the interests of the child. Article 8 § 2 also requires that any interference with family life be in accordance with law, requiring that the measure which causes it has a basis in domestic law. It must also be 'accessible' to the persons concerned and be formulated with 'sufficient precision' to enable them, if necessary with appropriate advice, 'to foresee to a degree that is reasonable in the circumstances the consequences which a given action may entail'.[61] Where it is unclear whether the social

---

[56] *Johansen* judgment, *op cit*, § 79.

[57] *Andersson* judgment, *op cit*, § 95.

[58] Eur Court HR *Olsson (No 2) v Sweden*, judgment of 30 Oct 1992, Series A no 250, 17 EHRR 134 § 90.

[59] *Johansen* judgment, *op cit*, § 78.

[60] *Ibid*, § 74.

[61] *Andersson* judgment, *op cit*, § 75.

authorities have the power to extend or apply a particular restriction, such as extending a general restriction on contact to include telephone and written communication, it is primarily for the national authorities to interpret and apply the domestic law. If contested limitations are upheld by the domestic courts, this will normally constitute sufficient protection from arbitrariness for the purposes of Article 8 § 2.[62]

It is much celebrated that the Convention guarantees rights that are effective and practical in nature[63] and this principle also applies to the contact enjoyed by parents and their children. The extent to which practical impediments can frustrate contact between family members and cause a violation of their right to family life was illustrated in the *Olsson* case. Here it will be remembered that although access was not prohibited, the fact that the foster families with whom the children were placed lived a significant distance from their parents and from each other meant that it was extremely difficult for them to maintain meaningful contact.[64] This principle places a heavy burden on the domestic authorities to ensure that the care order is implemented appropriately and in a manner which guarantees the right to respect for family life of both children and adult family members, particularly given the Court's judgment that practical difficulties caused by the lack of suitable foster parents are not relevant. The responsibility of the State will be mitigated or even discharged altogether, however, where the parents are themselves responsible for failing to maintain contact.[65]

*Justification for Restricting or Prohibiting Contact*

Although Article 8 does not make express provision for the use of the welfare principle, it is clear from Convention case law that measures which restrict or prohibit parental contact with their children in care are most commonly justified where their purpose is to protect the best interests of the children. Despite their implicit acceptance of the best interests test, therefore, the Strasbourg bodies have not established criteria for its application, and as a standard, it is broadly indeterminate in nature.[66] The

---

[62] *Ibid*, § 80-85. *Cf* the opinion of the Commission that the law's lack of precision itself cast doubt over the legal basis of the additional restrictions on contact. *Andersson* Comm Report *op cit*, § 90-102.

[63] See Chapter 1, pp 11-12.

[64] *Olsson* judgment, *op cit*, § 81-83. See above, pp 268-270.

[65] See below, pp 283-284.

[66] See Chapter 9, pp 201-203 and also Chapter 11, pp 242-243, 252-255.

breadth of the margin of appreciation enjoyed by the State in this area has the apparent effect of precluding the Court from examining whether the measures adopted by domestic authorities to protect the children's interests did so in fact and typically, case law highlights few incidences where the domestic decision was queried on this ground. As a result, the arguments put forward by the State and accepted by the Commission and the Court as to the basis for restricting parental contact with their children are varied. They include, for example, the need for stability in the child's upbringing, and this is frequently recognised to be a relevant and sufficient reason upon which to base a restriction or prohibition on parental access.[67] Other justifications for interfering with family life in this way include the need to remove children from the influence of their parents when they are under observation;[68] the need to keep a child away from a situation which could be detrimental to his/her mental development due to a loyalty conflict vis-à-vis one or both parents or the foster parents,[69] and where a conflict of interests exists with regard to the care of the child.[70]

The Convention authorities may also attach importance to the wishes of the child, where the child's age and maturity permit, when balancing the child's best interests against the parent's right to contact. In this regard, the reluctance expressed by a 12 year old girl[71] and a 15 year old boy[72] to see their respective mothers constituted relevant and sufficient reasons for denying such contact. The arrangement of more frequent contact contrary to the child's wishes may also be unacceptable under Article 8, not least because it may make future attempts to reunite parent and child impossible to realise. In this way, the Commission attempts to reconcile the denial of access with the aim of reuniting parent and child in the long term.[73] The responsibility of the social authorities to arrange meetings between parent and child is also diminished where a parent's demands are unreasonable or inconsistent with the wishes of the child. For example, where a child refused to meet her mother outside the foster home and the mother rejected the authorities' alternative arrangements, the Commission found that they

---

[67] No *12805/87 Nowack v Sweden, op cit,* and *Johansen* judgment, *op cit,* § 80.

[68] No *14013/88 Family T v Austria, op cit.*

[69] No *22597/93 Thorbergsson v Iceland,* Dec 1.94, 18 EHRR CD 205.

[70] No *16580/90 Boyle v UK,* Comm Rep, 9.2.93, Series A no 282-B, 19 EHRR 181.

[71] No *21078/92 Lundblad v Sweden,* Dec 9.94, 18 EHRR CD 167.

[72] No *19762/92 Asplund v Sweden,* Dec 9.94, 18 EHRR CD 111.

[73] No *21078/92 Lundblad v Sweden, op cit.*

had made sufficient attempts to bring about meetings having regard to the wishes of the mother and daughter and they could not be blamed for any failure in this regard.[74] In any event, although the Commission will accept the position adopted by domestic courts with regard to attaching significance to the child's opinion, Article 8 has yet to be found to require that account be taken of the child's wishes in such circumstances.[75]

When a child is placed in care, the discretion to allow contact between grandparents and grandchildren, which normally resides with the child's parents, passes to the local authority as a result of the care order. Restricting contact between children and their grandparents will not always raise an issue under Article 8 however. Thus, although their relationship may amount to family life under Article 8, the fact that it is different in degree to that between parent and child means that the same obligations do not flow from that relationship. As a result, denying a grandparent access to his/her grandchild in care will not necessarily interfere with their family life, although that will, necessarily, depend on the nature of their relationship.[76]    For example, an interference may occur if contact is considered to be reasonable in all the circumstances and necessary to preserve their relationship. Where family life exists and the restriction on contact interferes with that relationship, then it will fall to be examined under Article 8 in the usual way. In particular, it may be justified in order to protect the interests of the child, even if the child lived with the grandparent before being placed in care.[77]

## Removing Children from Care

Respect for family life must govern the placement of a child in care and ensure that all measures taken by the authorities in this regard are guided by the overriding aim of reunification, where it is in the interests of the child. Particular problems arise, however, in the interim period between the lifting of a care order and the child's return to the family environment when the domestic authorities prohibit the child's removal from care on a temporary basis. Such a decision has been found to interfere with the

---

[74] No *21608/93 Johansen & Others v Sweden*, Dec 22.2.95, unreported.
[75] See the dissenting view of Mr Schermers in No *12366/86 Rieme v Sweden*, Comm Report, 2.10.90, Series A no 226-A, 16 EHRR 169.
[76] No *12402/86 Price v UK*, Dec 9.3.88, DR 55, p 224. See Chapter 9, pp 196-197.
[77] See No *12763/87 Lawlor v UK*, *op cit*, where a grandfather, no longer able to look after his granddaughter, placed her for adoption but still desired contact.

family life of both parents and children, and although it falls to be examined under Article 8 in the usual way, the essential balancing of interests is a difficult and complex matter in such cases.

The Court has accepted implicitly that a child should not be returned to his/her family unless the reasons for the child's initial removal into care are no longer relevant or the conditions for lifting the care order are not yet in place. Thus, an order prohibiting the child's return will be consistent with Article 8 where there is a risk, not of a minor nature, that his/her health or development would be jeopardised if s/he returns to his/her family immediately after the care order has been terminated.[78] This is particularly the case where children are placed in care at a very young age,[79] where they are separated from their natural parents for a considerable period, or where there has been little contact between them.[80] The refusal to terminate the placement may also be justifiable if the improvement in the circumstances which originally gave rise to the care order do not appear with reasonable certainty to be stable.[81] It is clearly in the interests of the child that the authorities be cautious in returning him/her home in such circumstances.[82]

Although a prohibition on removal may be justified during a transitional period, it is a measure which

> by its very nature is likely to increase the tension between those involved in the transfer of the child, notably the child, the foster parents and the natural parents.[83]

If such a situation prevails for a long period, there is a great risk that conflicts will increase, making it gradually more difficult to establish the close relationship between the child and the birth parent, which is a necessary condition for the transfer. In determining whether the prohibition on removal is consistent with Article 8 therefore, emphasis is placed on the length of time which the prohibition remains in force. In this regard, the Commission has found it to be 'understandable' that a care order was not lifted after a lapse of two years[84] and at the other extreme, it has suggested

---

[78] *Rieme* Comm Rep, *op cit*, § 59.
[79] *Johansen* judgment, *op cit*, § 72.
[80] No 11373/85 *Eriksson v Sweden*, Comm Rep, 14.7.88, Series A no 156, § 195.
[81] *Olsson* judgment, *op cit*, § 76.
[82] *Olsson* Comm Rep, *op cit*, § 165.
[83] *Eriksson* Comm Rep, *op cit*, § 211.
[84] *Olsson* Comm Rep, *op cit*, § 165. For a stricter view see the opinion of Mrs Thune in *Rieme* Comm Rep, *op cit*.

that a prohibition in removal lasting five years will only be justified in exceptional circumstances.[85]    Although each case will be taken on its merits, the facts that the children have lived with alternative carers from a very young age and for a significant portion of their young lives, must weigh in favour of a longer transitional period than would otherwise be acceptable.  Logically therefore, the shorter the period of care and the older the child when the care order is made, the shorter the period of transition to be justified under Article 8.

## *The Link between Contact and Removing the Child from Care*

Contact between family members and the child in care is necessary in order to maintain personal relations and promote reunion so that the child's return home can be facilitated and carried out with minimum disruption. Contact during this period is thus fundamental to the successful completion of the child's placement and return home.  To this extent, the link between parental contact with children in care and the circumstances in which a care order may be terminated is inextricable.

Once the decision to return a child home has been taken, it is in the interests of all parties that it be implemented as quickly as possible.  In this regard, Article 8 has been found to include a right to have measures taken with a view to reunion and the importance of having a transitional period during which essential preparation for reuniting parents and children following the revocation of a care order can take place.  Moreover, the provision places a corresponding obligation on domestic authorities to take such steps without delay,[86] given that inaction on their part in relation to preparing reunion may give rise to uncertainty about the child's future.[87] This situation is potentially harmful to all parties, particularly the child, and disregard for the child's interests in this way may be particularly significant in the determination of whether the right to respect for family life of the child has been violated under Article 8.[88]  Moreover, an authority, which takes measures which effectively obstruct the child's reunification with his/her parents will be acting in violation of Article 8.[89]  An example of

---

[85]  *Rieme* Comm Rep, *op cit*, § 63.

[86]  *Olsson (No 2)* judgment, *op cit*, § 90.

[87]  *Eriksson* Comm Rep, *op cit*, § 220.

[88]  Eur Court HR *Eriksson v Sweden*, judgment of 2 June 1989, Series A no 156, 12 EHRR 183, § 89.

[89]  No *12574/86 Nyberg v Sweden*, Comm Rep, 31.8.90, Series A no 181-B, § 125-126.

offensive action in this regard is the institution of proceedings to have custody of the children transferred to the foster parents. However, Article 8 was been found to be violated where the authorities failed to actively promote a reunion between the natural parents and their child, notwithstanding that tense relations between the foster and birth parents made reunion difficult.[90] Neither the rights of parents nor of the domestic authorities are absolute in this context and, although the nature and extent of the preparation which must occur before the child is returned to his/her family will depend on the circumstances, the process will always require the active understanding and co-operation of all concerned.[91]

With regard to the wishes of the child, the Court has found that, as long as some measures have been taken in order to create closer contacts between parent and child, the child, should be able to determine the pace at which their relationship should develop.[92] This obviously depends on the child's age and maturity. However, certain members of the Commission have criticised measures which place a burden on the child in this regard,[93] and it is important in this context that the child should have the right to express his/her view, but not an obligation to do so.

While the domestic authorities must do their utmost to bring about co-operation, the Court has found that the possibility of applying coercion is limited since the interests, rights and freedoms of all the parties under Article 8, particularly children, must be taken into account. Where contact with the parent would harm these interests, it is for the authorities to strike the appropriate balance in this respect. Moreover, what is decisive in this regard is whether, considering the State's margin of appreciation,

> the national authority has made efforts to make the necessary preparation for reunion as can reasonably be demanded under the special circumstances.[94]

Such circumstances may include the behaviour of uncooperative parents and it is clear that the State will not be held responsible for failures not attributable to its agents in this regard. This occurred in the second *Olsson* case, where the parents refused to accept the contact arrangements made by

---

[90]  *Rieme* Comm Rep, *op cit*, § 61.

[91]  *Olsson (No 2)* judgment, *op cit*, § 90.

[92]  Eur Court HR *Rieme v Sweden*, judgment of 22 April 1992, Series A no 226-B, 16 EHRR 155, § 73-74.

[93]  See the dissent of Mrs Liddy and Mr Loucaides in *Rieme*, Comm Rep, *op cit*.

[94]  *Olsson (No 2)* judgment, *op cit*, § 90.

the authorities, demanded access which they knew was unacceptable to both the authorities and the children, and neglected contact by telephone.[95] In the light of this behaviour, the Court refused to hold that responsibility lay with authorities for failing to take measures with a view to reunification. The Commission, by contrast, considered that the lack of meaningful contact between the family members, and the failure by the authorities to take other effective measures to resolve the problems which existed did, in fact, violate Article 8.[96]    It appeared to attach less significance than the Court to the parents' difficult behaviour therefore, and its interpretation of the obligation on the domestic authorities to facilitate family reunion also differed from that of the Court.    These factors notwithstanding, however, the main feature distinguishing the two opinions in this case was arguably the margin of appreciation offered to the domestic authorities. The Court clearly envisaged the arrangement of contact in such difficult circumstances to fall within the State's discretion, whereas the Commission held the opposite view.

## Procedural Protection of Parents' Rights

Although the object and purpose of Article 8 is to protect family life from unlawful and arbitrary state interference, the sensitive and complex nature of care proceedings means that domestic authorities must enjoy discretion as to the appropriate procedure to be followed.    Protection from arbitrariness is crucial, however, because such decisions and decision-making processes can have a drastic effect on the relations between parent and child, which may prove irreversible.  For this reason, the Court has established that there is a procedural element implicit in respect for family life under Article 8.[97]    In particular, the decision-making process must ensure that the views and interests of parents are made known and taken into account by the relevant domestic authority, and they must also be given time to exercise available remedies.[98]  Importantly, the development of this procedural requirement allows the Court to review the fairness of the procedure followed and to assess the extent to which it is consistent

---

[95]    *Ibid*, § 91.

[96]    *Olsson (No 2)* judgment, *op cit,* § 129.

[97]    See Reid (1993), 'Child Care Cases and the ECHR', *Journal of Child Law*, 5(2), pp 66-70, at pp 66-67.

[98]    Eur Court HR *W v UK*, judgment of 8 July 1987, Series A no 121, 10 EHRR 29, § 63.  See further Chapter 9, pp 206-207.

with respect for family life under Article 8, notwithstanding the wide margin of appreciation, which the State enjoys in this area.[99]

According to the Court in *W v UK*, what falls to be considered under Article 8 is whether, given the particular circumstances and the serious nature of the decisions to be taken,

> the parents have been involved in the decision-making process to a degree sufficient to provide them with a requisite protection of their interests.[100]

With regard to the way in which such involvement takes place, the Court has recognised that regular contact between social workers and parents provides an appropriate channel for the communication of the parents' views. It appears to accept therefore that in some cases parental involvement at this level may be sufficient to satisfy the procedural requirement under Article 8. The Court has also noted the importance of regular parental involvement in the decision-making process, given that decisions as to the child's welfare may evolve from a continuous process of monitoring on the part of the local authority. A final factor which is relevant here is whether the participation of a parent in the decision-making process is either meaningful or possible. This is arguably a recognition that, in certain circumstances, constant parental involvement may be neither important nor useful. According to the facts of *W*, the applicant's child was taken into care because of his wife's protracted illness and once parental rights had been transferred to the local authority, it proceeded to take a series of decisions - placement in long term foster care with a view to adoption, restriction and termination of access - without advance consultation or discussion with either parent. The child's mother meanwhile began a remarkable recovery and once their situation at home had improved, they applied for access, which was refused. Considering the compatibility of this process with Article 8, the Court criticised the failure of the authorities to consult and involve the parents in critical stages of decision-making about their relationship with their daughter. The consequence of this neglect was that the authorities had not afforded them the requisite consideration of the father's view or the protection of his interests. This gave rise to a violation of Article 8.

---

[99] *Ibid*, § 62.

[100] *Ibid*, § 64. The Court's judgment in *W* is reflected in five other similar cases in which judgment was handed down on the same day.

The consequence of the *W* case was to establish the right of parents to be consulted and heard about important decisions regarding their children, unless there are convincing reasons to exclude them from such consultation or information.[101] Failure to consult or provide a parent with adequate information during the decision-making process will thus constitute an interference with respect for family life, which requires justification under Article 8 § 2 in the normal way. Accordingly, where the decisions from which the parent is excluded are particularly serious, strong and weighty reasons relevant to the interests of the child will be required in order to justify the interference with family life which this causes.[102] Examples include decisions which are decisive not only for immediate contact between parent and child, but also for the long term question of the children's rehabilitation with their parents, such as the termination of contact, or placement of a child with foster or adoptive parents.

The effectiveness of a parent's participation in the decision-making process concerning the care of a child may be led to question where they receive inadequate information about decisions taken in this context. Notwithstanding that family proceedings may be informal and non-contentious, the Court established in the *McMichael* case that a parent's lack of access to reports or documents which are relevant to the welfare of the child and parental capacities, may affect his/her participation in the decision-making process thereby raising an issue under Article 8. Moreover, it may also frustrate attempts to seek advice as to the possibility of a ground of appeal.[103] The denial of such information may also be contrary to Article 6 § 1 in the light of the general principle that the right to a fair, adversarial trial include the opportunity to have knowledge of, and comment on, the observations filed or evidence adduced by the other party.[104] It was left open in *McMichael* whether the refusal to disclose certain documents to parents can be justified where it contains material which may be detrimental to the interests of either parents, or perhaps more

---

[101] S 22 Children Act 1989, which was adopted subsequent to the Court's judgment in *W*, places a duty on local authorities to consult parents before making any decision with respect to a child in their care.

[102] No *9749/82 W v UK*, Comm Rep, 15.10.85, Series A no 121, § 105-111.

[103] Eur Court HR *McMichael v UK*, judgment of 24 Feb 1995, Series A no 308, 20 EHRR 205, § 85-93.

[104] *Ibid*, § 75-84.

likely, the child.[105]   The Court would arguably treat such an argument as one of the factors to be taken into account in considering whether the competing interests were appropriately balanced under the Convention.

*The Scope of the Right to be Consulted*

The applicant father in *McMichael* complained that he was discriminated against because, as an unmarried father, he had no right to be consulted in the care proceedings concerning his daughter due to the fact that he was not granted automatic parental rights.  His complaint was essentially directed at his status as an unmarried father under Scots law and this was the perspective adopted by both the Commission and the Court in considering and rejecting his claim under Article 14.[106]  In particular, both institutions noted that a system which required unmarried fathers to apply for a parental rights resolution helped to identify meritorious fathers and to protect the interests of the child.  It thus had the necessary objective and reasonable basis and was justified under Article 14. However, in the light of the *Keegan* judgment which found the unmarried father's lack of standing in adoption proceedings to violate Article 6, the consistency of the Court's conclusion with its previous jurisprudence must be questioned.[107]

The right of other family members, such as grandparents, to participate in the decision-making process appears to depend on the nature of their relationship with the child in care.[108]  Due to the fact that the relationship between grandparents and grandchildren differs from that between parents and their children, the domestic authorities will not normally be required to consult or involve the former in the decision-making process to the same degree as the latter.[109]  However, once family life is established, it appears

---

[105] No special reasons were put forward to justify withholding information from the applicants. See No 16424/90 *McMichael v UK*, Comm Rep, 31.8.93, Series A No 205, 20 EHRR 225, § 104.

[106] *McMichael* Comm Rep, *op cit*, § 122-127 and judgment, *op cit*, § 94-99.

[107] See also the dissenting opinion of Mrs Liddy, joined by Mr Soyer, who noted that had McMichael applied for parental rights there was no guarantee that he would have been successful. See also No *11468/85 K v UK*, Dec 15.10.86, DR 50, p 199 where the Commission found that the fact that an unmarried father could not invoke his right to apply for custody and access in order to challenge a care order meant that such rights were ineffective in care proceedings, resulting in a violation of Article 6.

[108] See Reid, *op cit*, p 68.

[109] No *12402/86 Price v UK*, *op cit*.

that some degree of participation by the grandparents will be required to fulfil the requirements of Article 8. For example, in the *Price* case, the children's grandparents made representations to the local authority on several occasions and had these views taken into account in the decisions made regarding their care. The degree of their involvement was thus sufficient to protect their interests under Article 8, as access to court was not considered to be necessary.[110] The same principle applies to the involvement of aunts or uncles in the process, although where several family members request involvement, then favour is likely to be shown to those, with whom the child's relationship is considered to be particularly important.[111] The situation will be different, however, where a family member, who enjoys a relationship of family life with the child, is denied the opportunity to participate in the decision making process regarding his/her care because of the exclusion of the parents from the process. This occurred in the *Boyle* case, where the mother's refusal to acknowledge that abuse had occurred rendered the available consultation mechanism nugatory. As a result, there was no forum in which the applicant, who was the boy's uncle, could participate in the decision making process and this meant that he had no means of protecting his interest in the boy's welfare, in violation of Article 8.[112]

*Delays in Proceedings*

A procedural delay in the resolution of proceedings involving children may result in them being determined on a factual, rather than legal basis. In recognition, the Court has established that effective respect for family life requires that:

> future relations between parent and child be determined solely in the light of all relevant considerations and not by the mere effluxion of time.[113]

This principle means that the length of the administrative and the judicial decision-making process at domestic level will be taken into account by the Court when considering whether the domestic authorities have acted in a manner consistent with respect for family life under Article 8. Delays in care proceedings may also fall foul of Article 6 insofar as they are

---

[110] *Ibid.*

[111] No *12763/87 Lawlor v UK*, Dec 14.7.88, DR 57, p 216.

[112] *Boyle* Comm Rep, *op cit*, § 52-58.

[113] *W* judgment, *op cit*, § 65.

inconsistent with the right to a fair hearing within a reasonable time. Indeed, the delay may give rise to a violation of both provisions in certain circumstances, where it has resulted in a *de facto* determination of the issue.[114]

## Procedural Protection of Children's Rights

Despite the importance which the Court has attached to the right of the parent to be consulted and involved in care proceedings, it has yet to extend this right to the subjects of the proceedings, the children themselves. Although it is arguable that, insofar as they coincide, parental participation in care proceedings aims to protect their children's interests as well as their own, this may not always be the case. On the other hand, it may be argued that it is the domestic authorities which act in the child's interests, but here too, the interests are not necessarily identical. As a result, the issue of affording independent and impartial representation to children is highly significant in care proceedings[115] and although it has been highlighted by international legal provisions,[116] the Court of Human Rights has, as yet, had little opportunity to elucidate the level and type of independent representation to be enjoyed by children in care proceedings.

The *Andersson* case did concern a related issue, however, namely the complaint of a child that he did not enjoy an effective remedy under Article 13 with regard to the restrictions placed on his contact with his mother while he was in care. The basis of his complaint was that although Swedish law entitled a child to appeal against such a decision in principle, due to his young age, he could not make such an application on his own. In this regard, the Court noted that Article 13 did not require that a twelve year old could be able to institute and conduct such proceedings on his own, but found it sufficient that a legal representative could do this on the child's behalf.[117] The fact that it was possible for his mother, being his legal guardian, to appeal against the prohibition on his behalf convinced

---

[114] *Ibid*, where the delay in the proceedings gave rise to violations of Articles 6 and 8.

[115] See Fortin (1998) *Children's Rights and the Developing Law*, London: Butterworths, pp 178-182, for details of the provision for the representation of children in such care proceedings under the Children Act 1989.

[116] See Article 12 Convention on the Rights of the Child, *op cit*, and Chapter 6.

[117] *Andersson* judgment, *op cit*, § 101.

the Commission and a slim majority of the Court that this was sufficient to offer him an effective remedy under Article 13.[118]

Notwithstanding the merit of this principle, dissenting members of the two Convention bodies raised an important objection to its practical application in this case. In particular, they expressed the view that the lack of contact between parent and child meant that the child's entitlement to be represented by his mother could not be used effectively to exercise his right to a remedy under Article 13.[119] This is all the more relevant considering that the decision he sought to challenge was the prohibition on contact, which had been found by the Court to be in violation of Article 8. Given that the level of contact between a mother and son was so poor as to breach their right to respect for family life, it is unclear how the same level of communication can be considered sufficient for one to instruct the other in legal proceedings affecting the fundamental rights of the child. Moreover, it is hardly conceivable that the same level of contact between a prisoner and a legal advisor would be considered adequate to ensure respect for the guarantees in Article 6 and 13 and the justification for such a difference in treatment is not readily apparent.

## Care Proceedings and Article 6

The fact that Article 8 offers procedural protection with regard to both administrative and judicial proceedings concerning the family means that its scope is broader than the Convention's fair trial provision, Article 6.[120] However, there is undoubtedly a degree of overlap in the protection offered by the two provisions in family law and as a result, procedural matters often fall to be examined under both provisions. Whatever the arguments as to the scope of the procedural protection enjoyed under each respective provision, Article 6 and Article 8 appear in some ways mutually compatible, insofar as the right to respect for family life is considered to be a right of a non-pecuniary nature to which Article 6 applies.[121]

---

[118] *Andersson* Comm Rep, *op cit*, § 111-115 and *ibid*, § 98-104.

[119] See the dissenting opinion of Mr Schermers, joined by Mrs Thune in *Andersson* Comm Rep, *ibid*, and the partly dissenting opinion of Judge de Meyer, joined by Pinheiro Farinha, Pettiti and Spielmann in *Andersson* judgment, *ibid*.

[120] *McMichael* judgment, *op cit*, § 91.

[121] See Harris, O'Boyle & Warbrick (1995), *Law of the European Convention on Human Rights*, London: Butterworths, p 180.

*The Scope of Article 6*

Article 6 guarantees the right to a fair trial within a reasonable time in the determination of civil rights and obligations. One clear limitation of Article 6 is that it applies only to proceedings affecting rights which are recognised in domestic law and so, it does not create new substantive rights which are absent in the relevant State.[122] However, the term 'right' is given an autonomous interpretation under Article 6 and it is not decisive for the purpose of this provision whether a benefit is characterised as a right in domestic law. For example, in *W v UK*, where a care order had resulted in parental authority being transferred to the local authority, the parents complained under Article 6 that they were unable to have their right of contact determined by a court. The Court noted that subsequent to the making of the care order the parental right of access became a matter of discretion for the local authority, but found that this did not in itself preclude the applicability of Article 6. It went on to find that, because a right to contact would still arise as a fundamental part of family life guaranteed by Article 8, and as a general feature of family law in the Contracting States even after a parents rights resolution had been passed, the possibility which the parent had under English domestic law to enjoy contact with his child at the discretion of the local authority could reasonably be characterised as a right under Article 6.[123]

It does not appear that grandparents can claim to have a civil right of access to their grandchildren within the meaning of Article 6.[124] Notwithstanding that they may be able to take legal proceedings in relation to the welfare of their grandchildren, where domestic law does not treat this as a right which accrues to them by virtue of their status as grandparents, it is not considered to be a civil right for the purposes of Article 6. Conversely, where domestic law confers a right of access on grandparents, it is unclear whether this would be sufficient to attract the protection of

---

[122] *W* judgment, *op cit*, § 73 and Comm Rep, *op cit*, § 115.

[123] *Ibid*, § 76-78 and § 118-120 respectively. It is noteworthy that following this line of cases, s 34 of the Children Act 1989, which provides for the parents' right to have the access question determined by a court, came into force allowing settlements to be reached in similar cases. See No *11240/84 Campbell v UK*, Comm Rep, 13.5.88, DR 56, p 108 and No *15407/89 RTB & ASB v UK*, Dec 5.10.90, unreported. See also Reid, *op cit*, p 67.

[124] No *12763/87 Lawlor v UK, op cit.*

Article 6 due to the autonomous interpretation of 'civil rights' under this provision.[125]

## Compatibility with Article 6

Insofar as issues relating to the parent/child relationship constitute civil rights within the meaning of Article 6, parents must be able to challenge the decisions of a local authority in a court of law. It is not clear what kind of proceedings are necessary to comply with the 'determination' of a parent's right of contact in this context, although the Court has clarified what proceedings are inadequate for this purpose. In particular, neither the institution of wardship proceedings nor a challenge to a parental rights resolution fulfil the requirements of Article 6 on the grounds that their scope is too broad and complex and they are not directed at the issue of contact specifically.[126] Nor is judicial review sufficient in this regard, because it only permits the court to decide on the fairness of the decision taken and allows no review of the merits of the contact issue.[127]

The more fundamental issue of permitting access to a court in order to challenge the actions of the care authorities is currently before the Strasbourg institutions in the form of two separate applications.[128] Both sets of applicants sought to challenge the negligence of the local authority before the domestic courts, but had their action rejected by the House of Lords, on the basis that it would be contrary to public policy to allow them to proceed.[129] They are now pursuing this action before the Strasbourg Court, *inter alia,* on the basis that it deprives them of their right of access to a court to have the civil rights determined, as required by Article 6. Insofar as they complain that their right of access to a court has been disproportionately restricted, the Court's judgment in the *Osman* case

---

[125] See further Harris, O'Boyle & Warbrick, *op cit,* pp 174-186 and Van Dijk & Van Hoof (1998), *Theory and Practice of the European Convention on Human Rights,* 3rd ed, The Hague: Kluwer, pp 398-406.

[126] *Eriksson* judgment, *op cit,* § 80-82 and *W* judgment, *op cit,* § 80-81.

[127] *Ibid.*

[128] No *28945/95 TP & KM v UK, op cit,* and No *29392/95 KL & Others v UK, op cit.* See also above and Chapter 8, p 180.

[129] *X (Minors) v Bedfordshire County Council & M (A Minor) v Newham Borough Council & Ors* [1995] 2 AC 633. See further Wright (1998) 'Local Authorities, the Duty of Care and the European Convention on Human Rights', *Oxford Journal of Legal Studies* **18**, pp 1-28.

would seem to apply *mutatis mutandis*.[130]  Whether a violation of Article 6 will result in these cases, therefore, will arguably depend on whether they were able to have the merits of their claim in negligence examined by the domestic courts or whether, in the alternative, they had access to other appropriate means of having their rights determined under Article 6.

## Future Challenges

Despite the wealth of important and decisive case law handed down in relation to the public care of children, the absence of a child's rights approach is noticeable.  This gap is especially apparent with regard to the procedural aspects of Article 8, which focus exclusively on the rights of the parents in the decision-making process.  So far, the Convention has not been found to oblige the domestic authorities to respect the right of the child to be involved and independently represented throughout care proceedings, depending on factors of age and maturity.  Notwithstanding that many Convention States already have such structures firmly in place, consistent with the requirements of the UN Convention on the Rights of the Child as well as the European Convention on the Exercise of Children's Rights, this consensus should arguably help, rather than hinder the Court's development of such principles in future cases.

The challenge to the availability of remedies for injuries and harm suffered as a result of care authorities' action or inaction currently before the Court will affect the way the care system is organised at domestic level should it succeed.  In any event, this area of Strasbourg jurisprudence is one in which the possibility of invoking Convention arguments in the domestic courts should enhance such proceedings. The exercise of judicial restraint by the Court in relation to examining state intervention into the family should not play such a dominant role in domestic cases, although it is inevitable that the margin of appreciation doctrine will also be used here to a certain extent.

On a general level, the case law of the Court would benefit from increased reference to the UN Convention on the Rights of the Child, which offers much useful child-specific guidance here.  Although the best interests principle is well established in Strasbourg case law, there is a clear need to give express recognition to the right of the child to maintain contact

---

[130] Eur Court HR *Osman v UK*, judgment of 28 Oct 1998, Reports 1998-VIII, no 95. See further Chapter 7, pp 143-145.

with both parents and other family members when in care so that the child's reintegration into the family always remains possible and desirable. Further challenges to the way in which care orders are implemented are to be expected before the Court, with particular regard to the issue of maintaining consistency in the child's upbringing, as well as his/her religious and ethnic background. The limits of the Court's ruling that practical or administrative difficulties cannot justify placing children a long distance from their families will undoubtedly be tested here.

# 13 Adoption

## Introduction

Like other international human rights instruments of its time, the European Convention on Human Rights contains no specific references to adoption, either from an adult or a child perspective. There is no shortage of standards relating to adoption in regional and international law however, and in relation to the former, the Council of Europe adopted the European Convention on the Adoption of Children in 1968.[1] There has also been considerable activity in international law in recent years, and attempts to regulate domestic and inter-country adoption have led to the Hague Convention on Jurisdiction, Applicable Law and Recognition of Decrees relating to Adoptions in 1978 and, in light of the increasing adoption of children from other countries, the Hague Convention on International Cooperation and Protection of Children in Respect of Inter-country Adoption in 1993.[2] Moreover, the highly ratified UN Convention on the Rights of the Child, 1989, whose relevant standards recognise the rights *of* the child, as opposed to the right *to* a child, in the adoption process, reflects an important shift in emphasis in international law in this regard.[3] However, although these instruments establish important standards in relation to the administration of the adoption process, the lack of available remedies for any violation of their standards is disappointing. It is important in principle, therefore, that the Commission and Court of Human Rights may examine any complaints related to the adoption process, which fall within its scope.

Challenges to domestic and inter-country adoptions have been considered under Article 12, which guarantees the right to marry and found a family, and Article 8, which safeguards respect for family life. In the latter context, placing a child for adoption will interfere with a parent's family life and require justification with regard to the best interests of the

---

[1] ETS No 58.
[2] On the development of international law on adoption see Van Bueren (1995a), *The International Law on the Rights of the Child*, Dordrecht: Martinus Nijhoff, pp 94-103.
[3] UN Doc A/44/25.

child. However, in contrast to the case law in other areas of family life, notably alternative care, the Commission and Court have failed to develop clear principles with regard to the rights of parents and children in the adoption process. In addition, Convention law reflects the consideration of adoption from the adult's perspective[4], although this may be partly explained by the lack of complaints brought by children. Notwithstanding the potential of the Convention in this area, therefore, many questions, such as the proper role of the unmarried father, the application of suitability criteria to children and adults and contact with birth families following adoption, have yet to be resolved.

## The Right to a Family?

Although each child is entitled to respect for his/her family life under Article 8, this applies only to existing family life and does not guarantee to any child a right to a family.[5] Thus, unlike the Convention on the Rights of the Child[6], the European Convention fails to offer a child who is without a family for whatever reason, the right to a replacement family, either on a temporary or a permanent basis. Insofar as the adoption of a child and his/her integration into a family may be perceived as the founding of a family within the meaning of Article 12, that provision may be said to encompass the right to adopt a child.[7] This right is not absolute, however, and like the right to marry and found a family, its exercise is subject to national laws.[8] Moreover, notwithstanding that Article 8 encompasses family life irrespective of marital status, Article 12 has not been interpreted in the same way. In particular, the right to marry and found a family has been found to constitute one simple right, which cannot be divided into its

---

[4]  See Van Bueren (1995a), *op cit*, p 95.
[5]  Nor is this right guaranteed by international law generally. *Ibid*, p 95.
[6]   See Article 20 which guarantees to such a child the right to special protection and assistance including options such as foster care and adoption, *op cit*.
[7]  No *7229/75 X & Y v UK*, Dec 15.12.77, DR 12, p 32. See generally Harris, O'Boyle & Warbrick, *Law of the European Convention on Human Rights* (London: Butterworths, 1995) pp 425-442 and Van Dijk & Van Hoof (1998), *Theory and Practice of the European Convention on Human Rights*, 3rd ed, The Hague: Kluwer, pp 601-617.
[8]  *Ibid* and *8896/80 X v the Netherlands*, Dec 10.3.81, DR 24, p 176. See also Douglas (1988), 'The Family and the State under the ECHR', *International Journal of Law and the Family*, **2**, pp 76-105, at p 84.

component parts,[9] although the right to marry obviously exists even where there is no possibility of procreation.[10] As a result, the Commission's view that a law, according to which only married persons may adopt, is consistent with Article 12 still stands,[11] although it is likely that, by attaching significance to the existence of family ties, as opposed to marriage, the Commission has left the door open to unmarried persons together to mount a challenge in this regard.[12]

## Adoption and Article 8

The greatest number of challenges to the placement of a child for adoption are brought by the child's birth parents under Article 8. In particular, they complain that the child's adoption without their consent constitutes an interference with their right to respect for family life, which is disproportionate to the best interests of the child. No challenge has yet been brought by children themselves and however unlikely this prospect, it is not inconceivable that the child's independent representative in the domestic proceedings would wish to make a complaint on the child's behalf in certain circumstances. In this regard, there is significant overlap between the issues raised by long-term foster care and adoption in relation to the welfare of the child and this complicates the process of assessing the child's best interests. In particular, where children have spent considerable time in care, the odds inevitably become stacked against parents wishing to have them returned, adding a further determinant to the best interests test.

As in other areas of family life, the domestic authorities enjoy a wide margin of appreciation with regard to the circumstances in which they overrule a parent's objections to adoption. Although Article 8 § 2 requires

---

[9] No *6482/74 X v Belgium & the Netherlands*, Dec 10.7.75, DR 7, p 75 and No *7229/75 X & Y v UK, op cit.*

[10] Harris, O'Boyle & Warbrick, *op cit*, p 435 and Fawcett (1987), *The Application of the European Convention on Human Rights*, 2nd ed, Oxford: Clarendon Press, p 285.

[11] No *6482/74 X v Belgium & the Netherlands, op cit.*

[12] It is arguable that this case, which was decided in 1975, no longer reflects common practice. See Duncan, in Bainham, Pearl & Pickford (eds) (1995), *Frontiers of Family Law,* Chichester: Wiley, at p 41 and Department of Health (1993), *Adoption: The Future,* London: HMSO, p 9 on the possibility which has existed since 1926 in England and Wales for single people to adopt.

that such measures have a legitimate purpose, it is arguable that only reasons relevant to the child's welfare, and not the wishes of the adoptive parents for example, may justify such an interference with family life. In this regard, as long as the overriding objective is to protect the rights, welfare and interests of the child concerned, then the particular basis for making an adoption order will fall within the discretion of the State.[13] Moreover, the national authorities enjoy discretion as to what aspects of the child's welfare - financial, emotional or physical - they choose to emphasise in finding the adoption order necessary and it is also a matter of domestic law whether the child's best interests are paramount or merely of 'special importance' in such matters.[14] In any event, the case law highlights a familiar assumption that the interests, and in some cases the wishes, of the child are accurately determined at domestic level although the Court always reserves the right to review whether the reasons for an adoption order were truly relevant and sufficient for the purposes of Article 8 in any individual case. As in other areas of family life, however, its practice is to accept the child's best interests as determined by the domestic authorities and to focus instead on the proportionality of the adoption, as well as the procedural safeguards implicit in respect for family life.

## Family Life and the Applicability of Article 8

### *The Unmarried Father*

Although the Convention makes no provision for the right of a child to be adopted, Article 8 permits the placement of a child for adoption where it is in his/her interests. Birth parents seeking to complain about such a measure under Article 8 must first establish that a relationship of family life exists between them and the child. While there is a well established presumption that mothers and married parents enjoy family life with their children by the fact of birth, the unmarried father has not always benefited from the same presumption.[15] While there is growing evidence of support for this approach in the Court, it has yet to formally extend the presumption of

---

[13] See for example No *7626/76 X v UK, op cit* and No *9993/82 X v France,* Dec 5.10.82, DR 31, p 241, 5 EHRR 302.

[14] *Ibid.* However, more recently in No 22430/93 *Bronda & Bronda Kaiser v Italy,* Comm Rep, 21.1.97, unreported, the interests of the child were (in French) 'primordiaux'.

[15] See further Chapter 9, 189-191.

family life to unmarried fathers in such cases. However, it is important that it does so to enable such parents to have the merits of their claims examined under Article 8, particularly given the irrevocable nature of the adoption process.

In the past, the Commission has rejected the family life claims of allegedly unmeritorious single fathers who were unable to provide evidence of commitment to their children, in addition to the blood link. Fathers who did not demonstrate this commitment from the earliest possible stage, who did not enjoy regular contact with their children, or whose relationship with the child's mother was casual have all had their attempts to challenge the placement of their children for adoption thrown out at this initial stage.[16]  By contrast, an unmarried father who demonstrated his continued interest in his child notwithstanding the periodic interruption of their contact was found to have done enough to establish the existence of family life between them.[17] Moreover, where the father's attempts to enjoy contact with his child are frustrated by the mother, then the potential for family life may be sufficient to attract the protection of Article 8 where his relationship with the mother contained the constituent elements of family life.[18] While this is an important extension of the application of Article 8 in relation to unmarried fathers, the fact that potential family life will only be recognised where the child's parents can be said to have enjoyed such a relationship arguably treats children differently on the basis of their parents' behaviour. Given the potential consequences of recognising family life, it is worrying that this approach may deny the protection of the Convention to children whose parents are not committed to each other, but who are committed to them. Moreover, in the light of the fact that a father's claim may nonetheless fail on the merits, this discriminatory application of Article 8 would appear to be without reasonable and objective basis. By contrast, the presumption in favour of the existence of family life between all parents and their children, emerging in the Court's case law, would ensure a more objective and consistent application of Article 8. Such an approach would also enable the Court to

---

[16]   See No *24848/94 Bellis v Greece*, Dec 22.2.92, unreported and No *18280/91 MV v Malta*, Dec 9.4.92, unreported.

[17]   No *9966/82 X v UK*, Dec 7.82, 5 EHRR 299.

[18]   Although the parents split up before the child was born, it was decisive that they had cohabited, planned the pregnancy and planned to marry. Eur Court HR *Keegan v Ireland*, judgment of 26 May 1994, Series A, no 290, 18 EHRR 342. See further below.

undertake a more balanced assessment of whether the interference with the father's family life was proportionate to the child's welfare, in particular taking into account the nature of the relationship between father and daughter, the child's right to know his/her birth parents, as well as other moral, physical and psychological considerations relevant to the child's welfare. Indeed the Court appears to have adopted this approach in the *Söderbäck* case[19] where having noted only that there existed 'certain ties' between the unmarried applicant and his daughter, the Court went on to deal with the merits of the case under Article 8 § 2. [20]

*Adoptive Parents*

The Commission has found that the relationship between an adopted child and his/her adoptive parents is, in principle, of the same nature as the family relationship protected by Article 8.[21] However, in the context of immigration at least, the evidence of an adoption order may not always be sufficient to establish the existence of family life between a child and an adoptive parent. [22] In such circumstances, it may be important to look behind the immigration context to discover whether there was a genuine need for the adoption. The existence of family life may then depend on factors such as whether the child's parents are still alive and whether they are willing and able to take care of him.

Where family life is found to exist between members of an adoptive family, the obligation to respect that family life appears to be purely negative in nature and the State is thus under no obligation to adopt legal safeguards, which ensure the child's integration into the family. At the same time, the Court clearly recognises the effect of adoption in terms of consolidating and formalising existing family life ties, although it is unlikely to require the adoption of such measures except where it would be

---

[19] Eur Court HR *Söderbäck v Sweden*, judgment of 28 Oct 1998, Reports 1998-VII, no 94. In particular, the Court referred to the fact that the arguments before the Court centred on the issue of the compliance and not the applicability of Article 8, § 24.

[20] See further below.

[21] No *9993/82 X v France, op cit* and No *6482/74 X v Belgium & the Netherlands, op cit.* It has also found that the adoption of a child by a couple and the integration of that child into the family could conceivably amount to the founding of family life under Article 12. No *7229/75 X & Y v UK, op cit.*

[22] No *7229/75 X & Y v UK, ibid.*

entirely consistent with the interests of the child.[23] In particular, although the State may not separate two people united by means of formal adoption without engaging responsibility under Article 8, it would not appear to be under a positive obligation to grant a particular status to a child and a prospective adoptive parent.[24]

## The Effect of Consenting to Adoption

Where family life exists under Article 8 § 1 it is unclear whether voluntary adoption will interrupt these ties or even cause them to cease altogether. The Commission has left open whether the tie which naturally exists between a mother and her child will continue to exist following the child's adoption. Thus, where a mother initially consented to her child's adoption, and then later underwent a change of heart and sought the child's return, the Commission accepted that the tie of family life had been re-established between them.[25] It is likely, therefore, that the relationship between a mother and her child will fall outside the scope of Article 8 in exceptional circumstances only.

## Justifying Adoption under Article 8

There are two clear situations in which a child's adoption is justifiable. The first is in the care context, where the welfare of the child requires his/her removal from her family and placement with alternative long-term carers and eventually adoptive parents. The second situation relates to adoption as a purely legal measure and it concerns the process by which the child's integration into one parent's 'new' family is facilitated. Here, the adoption will commonly involve overruling any objection held by the father in relation to the adoption of his child by the mother's new husband.

---

[23] See *Söderbäck* judgment, *op cit*, § 33.

[24] No *6482/74 X v Belgium & the Netherlands*, *op cit*. The wording of Article 12 apparently precludes such an interpretation. See O'Donnell (1995a), 'Protection of Family Life: Positive approaches and the ECHR', *Journal of Social Welfare and Family Law*, **17**(3), pp 261-280, at p 164.

[25] No *7626/76 X v UK*, Dec 11.7.77, DR 11, p 160.

*Exceptional Grounds*

It is well established in international law that the placement of a child for adoption in the absence of parental consent should take place in exceptional circumstances only.[26] This principle is reflected in Strasbourg case law too and thus the making of an adoption order, despite parental opposition, will constitute an interference with the parent's right to respect for family life of a particularly serious nature which only exceptional grounds may justify.[27] The severity of the interference is derived from the fact that it is a consequence of state action (against which it is the purpose of Article 8 to protect) which adversely affects, or renders impossible, the resumption of family life between a parent and child. It is a further aggravating factor that the adoption process is usually irrevocable. The burden is on the State to establish that the far reaching interference with family life is proportionate to the need to protect the child and the presence of 'exceptional grounds' necessary to justify overruling parental consent has not proved difficult to establish in practice.[28]

Evidence of gross and continuous violations of parental duties, such as a child's seriously retarded development, physical injuries and poor health will generally be found to constitute the 'exceptional grounds' needed to justify overruling parental objection to adoption.[29] The Commission has also found less severe situations, in which a child's moral, material or educational well-being was at stake, to be sufficient in this regard,[30] although it has argued that only the most pressing grounds may be considered sufficient to justify the disruption of existing family ties in a democratic society, even where the material conditions of a family are poor.[31] In addition, the Commission appears to attach significance to the parents' will or intent to provide for their children, rather than their financial capacity to do so and in assessing the proportionality of overruling parental objection, the Commission has taken into account whether they accepted the assistance and medical treatment offered to them

---

[26] See Article 21 Convention on the Rights of the Child, *op cit*.

[27] In No *7626/76 X v UK*, *op cit*, the Commission relied on Article 5 of the European Convention on Adoption in this respect, *op cit*.

[28] Cf *Keegan* judgment, *op cit*, where a father's *inability* to consent was found to violate Articles 6 and 8.

[29] No *11588/85 U & GF v Germany*, Dec 15.5.86, DR 47, p 259.

[30] No *7626/76 X v UK*, *op cit*.

[31] *Ibid* and No *8059/77 X & Y v Germany*, Dec 3.12.78, DR 15, p 208.

and their children.[32]    This appears to permit a distinction between the ability of a parent to care for his/her children and the desire to do so, although even where relations between the parents are difficult and their relationship with the social authorities has broken down, these factors will not by themselves justify the decision to order adoption without their consent.[33]    What will be decisive, however, is the situation of the child and, where the child is in a state of abandon as a result of a lack of moral and material care by the birth parent, then the balance will tip easily in favour of justifying the child's adoption, notwithstanding strong parental objection.[34]    Similar, in this regard, is the situation where the child's life, health or development is at risk.

*Integration into a 'new' Family*

Where the adoption process is used to integrate a child legally into the 'new' family of the mother, and to the extent that this involves dispensing with the consent of the child's birth father, it will raise an issue under Article 8.    However, relevant case law suggests that it will not be particularly difficult to justify the interference with the father's family life created by such an adoption given the importance of providing the child with the opportunity to grow up in a complete family unit with one birth parent, into which the adoption makes full integration possible.    Whether such an adoption is proportionate to the interference with the father's family life however will depend on all the circumstances, including the nature of his relationship with his child and any other relevant factors.    For example, in 1977 the Commission found that it was consistent with Article 8 to dispense with the consent of the child's birth father, who was serving 18 years in prison, so that his former wife's new husband could adopt his children.[35]    Finding that the adoption was in the children's best interests, particular regard was had to the fact that the father was a long-term prisoner convicted for violent offences, that communication with his children was only authorised through their mother, and that they had been very young when he was first arrested.

---

[32] No *11588/85 U & GF v Germany, op cit.*
[33] No *16609/90 Intrieri v Italy*, Comm Rep, 18.10.95, unreported.
[34] Interestingly, the child in *Intrieri* attained majority during the course of the proceedings and returned to live with his mother, raising concern about the lack of consultation with the child during the adoption process.
[35] No *7610/76 X v UK*, Dec 9.5.77, DR 9, p 166.

Notwithstanding the justification of the adoption on the basis of the child's best interests, the Commission's treatment of this case is problematic insofar as it does not consider the relationship between the prisoner father and his child or the importance and potential of future contact between them.[36]    Although adoption does not preclude such contact, particularly when the children are older and can act with greater autonomy, the balancing exercise undertaken by the Commission appears to favour strongly the interests of children in having a two parent family to the detriment of maintaining contact with their birth father.[37]    Moreover, to the extent that the adoption serves to regularise the legal position between the children and their mother's new husband, it can be contrasted with consistent Convention case law that emphasises the factual, rather than the legal ties between parents and their children.[38]

These issues were arguably picked up by the Commission in its opinion in the *Söderbäck* case, in which the birth father challenged the adoption of his daughter by the child's step-father under Article 8.[39]    Here, it considered that the adoption order was not sufficiently justified with regard to any overriding requirement in the child's best interests and concluded that the Swedish authorities had overstepped the margin of appreciation which they enjoyed under Article 8 in ordering the child's adoption.    Although it acknowledged that the adoption of a child may be necessary to secure a stable family environment for the child in certain circumstances, the Commission could not find any evidence to suggest that the applicant intended to disrupt his daughter's family situation.    In particular, it believed that he only wished to have access to his daughter, access which the Social Council said would be beneficial and important to her and which was unlikely to change her feelings towards her social father.    By choosing to ignore this vital information, and notwithstanding that the reasons on which

---

[36]    See Article 9 § 3 of the Convention on the Rights of the Child, *op cit*.  Although adoption does not preclude such contact, it may involve the child moving some distance from the prison where any future communication between parent and child is unlikely.  On access between prisoner parents and their children see generally Shaw (ed)    (1992), *Prisoner's Children: What are the Issues?*, London: Routledge.

[37]    These concerns are expressed also in Bainham (1990a), 'The Privatisation of the Public Interest in Children', *Modern Law Review*, **53**(2), pp 206-221, at pp 214-215.

[38]    See further below.

[39]    No 24484/94 *Söderbäck v Sweden*, Comm Rep, 22.10.97, Reports 1998-VII, no 94.

it based its decision were relevant to the issue of necessity under Article 8 § 2, the Commission found that the adoption order itself was incompatible with Article 8.

The Court, however, reached the opposite conclusion.[40] It found a distinction between an adoption order, which severs the link between a child taken into public care and his/her mother (the scenario highlighted above), and the present case, where the effect of the adoption is to sever the links between an unmarried father and a child who has been in the care of his mother since she was born and in relation to whom he has neither care nor custody rights. The Court then went on to consider that the contacts between the applicant and his daughter were infrequent and limited in nature and that when the adoption was granted he had not seen her for quite some time. On the other hand, the child had lived with her mother since birth and with her adoptive father since she was eight months old. The child regarded him as her father and, at the time of the adoption order, they were found to have enjoyed *de facto* family ties, which the adoption consolidated and formalised, for over six and a half years. As a result, the Court found that the adverse effects of the decision to grant the adoption order on the applicant's relations with his daughter could not be said to be disproportionate to the aims which it sought to achieve.

This judgment is positive insofar as it illustrates the Court's new approach to family life under Article 8, whereby issues previously considered relevant to whether family life existed, such as the nature of the father's relationship with his daughter, have been taken into account in determining whether the interference with that family life was justified.[41] However, although the Court noted the importance of the adoption order insofar as it consolidated the child's relationship with her 'new' father, its judgment appears to contradict that handed down in the case of *X, Y & Z v UK* in 1996.[42] In that case, the Court refused to find that Article 8 entitled the members of a *de facto* family arrangement to have their relationship placed on a legal footing due to concern about whether such a measure was in the child's best interests. Admittedly this case concerned the recognition of the relationship of the child born by AID with her transsexual father, but the Court's implicit concern with the right of the child to knowledge about his/her origins and parentage, is equally relevant here. It is not

---

[40] *Söderbäck* judgment, *op cit*, § 31-35.

[41] See further Chapter 9, pp 193-194.

[42] Eur Court HR *X, Y & Z v UK*, judgment of 22 April 1997, Reports 1997-II, no 35, 24 EHRR 143. See also Chapter 5, pp 98-101 and Chapter 9, pp 195-196.

unimportant that the Court's finding in *Söderbäck* assured the child's welfare and right to grow up in the care of her mother and her 'new' family. Nevertheless, in the light of the stable nature of this relationship, it is arguable that their inability to have their *de facto* situation legally recognised would not have had a disproportionately detrimental effect on the child.[43]   As a result, it is submitted that the Commission's opinion, which found the adoption to be disproportionate under Article 8, is preferable in this case, not least because it attaches clear significance to the issue of future contact between the child and her birth father, which, the domestic authorities believed, would have been mutually beneficial and desirable.   While the adoption order does not itself preclude the possibility of such contact, the fact that the child's mother had frustrated contact in the past does not make this likely.

The facts of the *Söderbäck* case, and the different conclusions which the Commission and the Court reached in considering them, highlight the complexities of adoption cases where there are competing family life claims.  However, given the irrevocable nature of adoption itself, it is arguable that the Court should be more cautious in approving the decisions of the domestic authorities in the absence of strong reasons relating to the child's best interests.  This latter concept should itself be capable of broad interpretation and it should at least include reference to the long term welfare of the child in terms of the child's right to know and maintain contact with his/her parents clearly recognised in the UN Convention on the Rights of the Child.[44]

### Adoption and Long-Term Foster Care

Adoption often takes place as a continuation of the process which aims to fulfil the child's need for long-term alternative care.  In such cases, the grounds advanced for the adoption order itself will include consideration of the reasons which prompted the child's removal from his/her family environment in the first place.[45]   However, the additional factor of time, insofar as a child placed with carers, may establish bonds with them which it will not be in his/her interest to break, may play a significant role in determining whether the decision which results in the extinction of all ties

---

[43]   Indeed, this view has enjoyed much support in Convention case law over the years. See for example, *X, Y & Z* judgment, *op cit.*

[44]   See Article 9, *op cit.*

[45]   No *11588/85 U & GF v Germany*, *op cit.*

between a child and his/her birth family is justified. The Court has warned of the impact which the time factor can have in such cases, and has stressed the importance of exercising caution from the outset when placing a child with alternative carers.[46]  In any event, once a child has lived with a foster family or prospective adopters for a period of time, the process of balancing the child's interests with those of the birth parent seeking the child's return will undoubtedly be prejudiced by the duration of this placement, the child's recognisable need for stability and the child's attachment to his/her 'new' family. Once the goalposts have been shifted in this way, the question is no longer whether the child's interests will be served by adoption, but rather, having lived for some time in the adopted family, is the interest of the child in being adopted - both from the point of breaking its links with its birth parents and that of consolidating its links with the adopters - so clear that the adoption should be ordered against the parent's will destroying all possibility of family life between the parent and the child?[47]  The original grounds for the child's placement away from the family, such as an unsettling relationship between the child's parents giving rise to concern about the child's health, become consolidated with the child's integration into his/her foster family and as a consequence, the child's strong need for stability may often justify breaking his/her links with a birth parent.[48]

The factor of stability clearly plays a role in the decisions made at domestic level regarding the child's care. Thus, the Commission has found it to be in the child's interests to prefer adoption to long-term fostering where the child would benefit from the removal of 'any residual security in the child by reason of the fear that he might be removed from the foster parents'.[49]  The suggestion here is clearly that adoption will be in the child's interests where his/her need for stability demands it. However, this factor is likely to be relevant only in relation to choosing between different types of long-term care, rather than the making of an adoption order on its own merits.

---

[46] *Keegan* judgment, *op cit*, § 55.

[47] No *7626/76 X v UK, op cit.* See also above discussion of *Söderbäck* case.

[48] No *9966/82 X v UK, op cit; No 11588/85 U & GF v Germany, op cit.* See also *Bronda & Bronda Kaiser* Comm Rep, *op cit.*

[49] No *25054/94 ED v Ireland*, Dec 18.10.95, unreported.

## Ensuring Consistency in the Child's Upbringing

Although the use of eligibility criteria to determine prospective adoptive parents is consistent with Article 8, the principle of choosing adopters who share the child's background has not yet emerged in Convention case law. The failure to take the need for consistency in the child's upbringing into account was the subject of a challenge brought under the Convention by a member of the Traveller (or gypsy) community in Ireland.[50] The father's complaint centred on the placement of his child with adoptive parents who came from the settled community, and because this would lead to his child's identity being lost, in particular that the child's name would be changed, he argued that the adoption order was contrary to the child's best interests. While the Commission acknowledged the importance of the child's identity, it considered that the likely loss of the child's Traveller heritage was only one factor to be weighed up in determining the necessity of the adoption order, the making of which was justified by the hopeless circumstances of the parents who suffered from alcoholic and drug addictions. It is unclear whether a reasonable attempt was made in this case either to seek adoptive parents who shared the child's Traveller identity, or to find those who were willing to ensure contact with the Traveller community to prevent it being lost. Nevertheless, it appears that once an adoption order is found to be consistent with Article 8, the issue of maintaining consistency in the child's background is sidelined. However, it may be possible to argue that the placement of a child with adoptive parents who have different religious or philosophical convictions from the child or his/her parents raises an issue under Article 2 of the First Protocol, which guarantees respect for such parental convictions in the education and teaching of their children. Such claims have failed thus far because the parents' beliefs were not genuine enough to warrant respect as the case law requires. Where the parent's views can be said to amount to strong and genuinely held convictions, then the applicant may enjoy greater success.[51]

## Regulating Adoption

International law on adoption highlights the fact that regulation of the adoption process at both domestic and inter-country levels is fundamental

---

[50] *Ibid.*
[51] See further Chapter 12, pp 273-274.

to protecting the interests and rights of the child.[52] Notwithstanding that the text of the Convention makes no express acknowledgement to this effect, the Commission has accepted the need to regulate the adoption process and it has recognised the legitimate role of the State in this area.

The founding of a family within the meaning of Article 12 incorporates the adoption of children, as well as their birth.[53] Thus, in the same way that the right to marry and found a family is guaranteed only insofar as it is in accordance with national law, the regulation of adoption, including the use of eligibility criteria to distinguish between prospective adoptive parents, is also consistent with Article 12.[54] Relevant case law suggests that Convention States enjoy complete freedom as to the criteria to be used in this context, as well as the manner in which they are applied, as long as they are set out in domestic law. However, Article 12 does not appear to require either that the child's interests be paramount in the setting and application of such criteria, or that the wishes of the child be respected regardless of age.[55]

In its consideration of the application of eligibility criteria in adoption procedures under Article 8, it has accepted that, although States enjoy discretion with regard to the administration of the adoption process, consideration for the child's interests must be the overriding factor.[56] In particular, the Commission found that a requirement that a child being received for inter-country adoption should not have reached school-going age was acceptable because it was based on the idea that children of different cultural and social environment should receive their basic school education, in particular their language instruction, at the same age as it becomes compulsory for national children. Moreover, it has found nothing arbitrary in attaching significance to the different interests at stake in placing a child for adoption and has concluded that a procedure, which attributes importance to prospective parents' personalities, their age and health situations, their views, their relationship with the child and the

---

[52] See above.
[53] No *7229/75 X & Y v UK, op cit*; No *8896/80 X v the Netherlands, op cit*, and No *11041/84 L v the Netherlands*, Dec 13.12.84, unreported.
[54] No *8896/80 X v the Netherlands, op cit*.
[55] *Ibid*, where it was considered sufficient for the purposes of Article 12 that the criteria applied were set out in law.
[56] See No *22206/93 Lang-Lussi v Switzerland*, Dec 6.9.95, unreported.

situation in the future, in pointing to whether adoption was in the child's best interests, is entirely consistent with Article 8.[57]

The Commission has also found that imposing an age requirement on children for the purposes of inter-country adoption will be consistent with Article 8 where its aim is to facilitate their integration into their new society and minimise any detrimental effects of their departure from their country of origin.[58]   However, it is not clear what other criteria may be legitimately applied to children involved in inter-country adoption procedures, although it is interesting, nevertheless, that the Commission's use of the best interests principle in this area seems to aim at protecting the collective, as well as the individual, interests of children.[59]   Given that the regulation of adoption is a matter for the domestic authorities in which they enjoy a wide margin of appreciation, the Commission is not likely to impose its views on States as to the acceptability of specific criteria.   It is more likely to accept the use of eligibility criteria which are imposed to protect the child's interests, as long as there is no evidence of arbitrariness in their application.[60]   On the other hand, it is inconceivable that a system of adoption which is unregulated by the State could be compatible with the Convention and this argument is strengthened further by the consensus at international level that the regulation of adoption is the only way to ensure protection of the child's best interests.[61]

## Adoption Procedures

### Respect for Family Life

The availability and fulfilment of adequate procedural guarantees is crucial to the determination of whether adoption is compatible with respect for family life under Article 8.[62]   Thus, in order to consider whether an adoption order made in the face of parental opposition is compatible with the Convention, it is necessary to take into account whether the parents enjoyed procedural guarantees sufficient to provide them with a protection

---

[57]   *Ibid.*

[58]   No *8896/80 X v the Netherlands, op cit.*

[59]   See further Chapter 9, pp 201-203.

[60]   See Hale (1996), *From the Test Tube to the Coffin: Choice and Regulation in Private Life*, London: Sweet & Maxwell, 4-44, particularly pp 28-33.

[61]   See Duncan, in Bainham, Pearl and Pickford, *op cit*, p 51.

[62]   *Söderbäck* judgment, *op cit,* § 33.

of their interests. It is particularly important in this regard whether they were represented and/or present during the course of the adoption proceedings.[63]

The *Keegan* case examined this point at its most basic level, in relation to the right of the unmarried father to have knowledge of and consent to the placement of his child for adoption. The case concerned the relationship of family life between an unmarried father and his child, born to his former girlfriend, V, with whom he had lived and who he planned to marry. However, prior to the birth of their child, V left their home and after the child was born, placed her for adoption. Due to his lack of standing in the adoption process under Irish law, the father was unable to challenge the adoption and he took the only action available to him, namely the institution of proceedings for guardianship and custody. However, his application was rejected on the grounds that it was not in the best interests of the child and he complained under Article 8 that this violated his right to respect for family life. The fundamental problem raised by this case, according to the Court, was not the decision of the domestic courts in relation to custody, but rather the fact that Irish law permitted the placement of the applicant's child for adoption after birth without his knowledge or consent.[64] This situation meant that the child was placed immediately with prospective adopters with whom she began to form bonds and by the time his application came before the courts, the child was found to be secure and established in the adoptive home. Thus, the legal situation not only

> jeopardised proper development of the applicant's ties with his child, but also set in motion a process likely to prove irreversible, thereby putting the applicant at a distinct disadvantage in the contest for custody.[65]

Regardless of the merits of placing the child for adoption, therefore, the procedural impropriety caused by the failure to consult or inform the unmarried father about his child's placement amounted to a failure to respect his family life under Article 8.[66]

---

[63] No *18280/91 MV v Malta, op cit.*

[64] *Keegan* judgment, *op cit*, § 54-55.

[65] *Ibid*, § 55.

[66] *Ibid. Cf* No *17771/91 R v Switzerland*, Comm Rep, 9.9.93, unreported.

*Fair Trial Rights*

In addition to his complaint that he had failed to enjoy the procedural protection implicit in his right to respect for family life under Article 8, Mr Keegan also complained under Article 6 that he had no standing in the adoption proceedings in which his civil right to the custody of his daughter was being determined. The Court had little difficulty finding that adoption proceedings fell within the scope of this provision and the fact that he was excluded from both administrative and judicial proceedings in which he sought to challenge the adoption was found to violate Article 6.[67]    In particular, the Court held that because the applicant could not possibly have his objection to the adoption process determined by either the Adoption Board or the High Court, he did not have at his disposal a procedure satisfying the requirements of Article 6 in respect of his dispute as to the placement of his daughter for adoption.

While it is clear that the lack of any procedure according to which an adoption can be challenged will violate Article 6, it is also possible that the proceedings which are available will fall short of the requirements of that provision. For example, the lack of an oral hearing will raise an issue under the fair trial provision and the inability to comment on statements of the opposing party will similarly breach Article 6, where it places the parent at a significant disadvantage in contesting the adoption proceedings.[68]

It may also be possible to challenge adoption proceedings on the grounds that their confidential nature is in breach of fair trial standards under Article 6. This may arise for example where the identity of the adoptive parents remains secret throughout the process. However, Article 6 provides for such hearings to take place in private where it is considered to be in the children's interests. Thus, as long as confidentiality is necessary to safeguard those interests and it does not prejudice the applicant in the proceedings, it will not violate the principle of a public trial enshrined in Article 6.[69]

The *Keegan* case highlights the significance of the passing of time in adoption cases and the fact that any delay in the proceedings may be prejudicial to the welfare of the child as well as the rights of the parent

---

[67] *Keegan* judgment, *op cit*, § 58-60. The Commission reached the same conclusion. *No 16969/90 Keegan v Ireland*, Comm Rep, 17.2.93, Series A no 290, p 26, § 61-67.

[68] No *17771/91 R* Comm Rep, *op cit*, at § 41-52.

[69] No *18280/91 MV v Malta*, *op cit*.

seeking to oppose the adoption order.[70] Article 6 also requires that a dispute regarding the adoptive process be determined within a reasonable time. Thus, long, drawn out proceedings may have serious implications both for the family life between parent and child under Article 8, as well as their right to a fair trial under Article 6. While acknowledging the importance of these interests, the Commission has recognised that adoption proceedings concern important and sensitive questions relating to the welfare of the child, which require careful consideration and sometimes investigation by the courts. In striking a balance between the right to a fair trial on the one hand, and the importance of giving all the issues due consideration in the light of what is at stake for both parent and child, Article 6 requires that each case be decided with reasonable expedition. The Commission found in one case that adoption proceedings lasting two years and nine months did not violate the applicant's right to a fair trial within a reasonable time.[71] By contrast, however, proceedings lasting from June 1986 to July 1992 were found not to have been conducted with the requisite diligence and efficiency to satisfy the requirements of Article 6 § 1.[72] Whether the duration will be compatible with the reasonable time requirement will thus depend on the circumstances of each case, in particular its complexity and the conduct of all the parties, including the State.

**Future Challenges**

Many of the challenges with which the Court has yet to be confronted in this area concern the position of the child in the adoption process. For example, it is unclear whether respect for the child's private and family life under Article 8 requires the child to be awarded independent representation in adoption proceedings, either at the administrative or the judicial stages, or both. Other issues likely to be contentious include the selection of adoption parents so as to ensure continuity in the child's upbringing, as well as respect for the child's religious and ethnic background.

---

[70] See the importance of the time factor in *Hokkanen v Finland*, judgment of 23 Sept 1994, Series A No 299-A, p 31, 17 EHRR 293, Chapter 11, pp 241-242 and pp 249-251.

[71] *Ibid.*

[72] *Intrieri* Comm Rep, *op cit.*

The nature of the obligation to respect family life in the context of adoption is still undetermined, particularly where it aims to facilitate the integration of the child into his/her parent's 'new' family.  The question of the importance to be attached to the right of the child to maintain contact with his/her birth parents following adoption in this context remains unanswered.  In the same way, the rights of the unmarried father, who is committed to maintaining contact with his child following adoption, must also be addressed in the light of adoption in these circumstances. Similarly, the right of the child to access information regarding his/her birth family, dealt with in Chapter 5, is also awaiting resolution.

# Convention for the Protection of Human Rights and Fundamental Freedoms (Selected Provisions)

**Article 1**

The High Contracting Parties shall secure to everyone within their jurisdiction the rights and freedoms defined in Section I of this Convention.

**Article 2**

1. Everyone's right to life shall be protected by law. No one shall be deprived of his life intentionally save in the execution of a sentence of a court following his conviction of a crime for which this penalty is provided by law.

2. Deprivation of life shall not be regarded as inflicted in contravention of this article when it results from the use of force which is no more than absolutely necessary:

a in defence of any person from unlawful violence;

b in order to effect a lawful arrest or to prevent the escape of a person lawfully detained;

c in action lawfully taken for the purpose of quelling a riot or insurrection.

**Article 3**

No one shall be subjected to torture or to inhuman or degrading treatment or punishment.

**Article 5**

1. Everyone has the right to liberty and security of person. No one shall be deprived of his liberty save in the following cases and in accordance with a procedure prescribed by law:

a the lawful detention of a person after conviction by a competent court;

b the lawful arrest or detention of a person for non- compliance with the lawful order of a court or in order to secure the fulfilment of any obligation prescribed by law;

c the lawful arrest or detention of a person effected for the purpose of bringing him before the competent legal authority on reasonable suspicion of having committed an offence or when it is reasonably considered necessary to prevent his committing an offence or fleeing after having done so;

d the detention of a minor by lawful order for the purpose of educational supervision or his lawful detention for the purpose of bringing him before the competent legal authority;

e the lawful detention of persons for the prevention of the spreading of infectious diseases, of persons of unsound mind, alcoholics or drug addicts or vagrants;

f the lawful arrest or detention of a person to prevent his effecting an unauthorised entry into the country or of a person against whom action is being taken with a view to deportation or extradition.

2. Everyone who is arrested shall be informed promptly, in a language which he understands, of the reasons for his arrest and of any charge against him.

3. Everyone arrested or detained in accordance with the provisions of paragraph 1.c of this article shall be brought promptly before a judge or other officer authorised by law to exercise judicial power and shall be entitled to trial within a reasonable time or to release pending trial. Release may be conditioned by guarantees to appear for trial.

4. Everyone who is deprived of his liberty by arrest or detention shall be entitled to take proceedings by which the lawfulness of his detention shall be decided speedily by a court and his release ordered if the detention is not lawful.

5. Everyone who has been the victim of arrest or detention in contravention of the provisions of this article shall have an enforceable right to compensation.

## Article 6

1. In the determination of his civil rights and obligations or of any criminal charge against him, everyone is entitled to a fair and public hearing within a reasonable time by an independent and impartial tribunal established by law. Judgment shall be pronounced publicly but the press and public may be excluded from all or part of the trial in the interests of morals, public order or national security in a democratic society, where the interests of juveniles or the protection of the private life of the parties so require, or to the extent strictly necessary in the opinion of the court in special circumstances where publicity would prejudice the interests of justice.

2. Everyone charged with a criminal offence shall be presumed innocent until proved guilty according to law.

3. Everyone charged with a criminal offence has the following minimum rights:

a to be informed promptly, in a language which he understands and in detail, of the nature and cause of the accusation against him;

b to have adequate time and facilities for the preparation of his defence;

c to defend himself in person or through legal assistance of his own choosing or, if he has not sufficient means to pay for legal assistance, to be given it free when the interests of justice so require;

d to examine or have examined witnesses against him and to obtain the attendance and examination of witnesses on his behalf under the same conditions as witnesses against him;

e to have the free assistance of an interpreter if he cannot understand or speak the language used in court.

## Article 8

1. Everyone has the right to respect for his private and family life, his home and his correspondence.

2. There shall be no interference by a public authority with the exercise of this right except such as is in accordance with the law and is necessary in a democratic society in the interests of national security, public safety or the economic well-being of the country, for the prevention of disorder or crime, for the protection of health or morals, or for the protection of the rights and freedoms of others.

## Article 9

1. Everyone has the right to freedom of thought, conscience and religion; this right includes freedom to change his religion or belief and freedom, either alone or in community with others and in public or private, to manifest his religion or belief, in worship, teaching, practice and observance.

2. Freedom to manifest one's religion or beliefs shall be subject only to such limitations as are prescribed by law and are necessary in a democratic society in the interests of public safety, for the protection of public order, health or morals, or for the protection of the rights and freedoms of others.

## Article 10

1. Everyone has the right to freedom of expression. This right shall include freedom to hold opinions and to receive and impart information and ideas without interference by public authority and regardless of frontiers. This article shall not prevent States from requiring the licensing of broadcasting, television or cinema enterprises.

2. The exercise of these freedoms, since it carries with it duties and responsibilities, may be subject to such formalities, conditions, restrictions or penalties as are prescribed by law and are necessary in a democratic society, in the interests of national security, territorial integrity or public safety, for the prevention of disorder or crime, for the protection of health or morals, for the protection of the reputation or rights of others, for preventing the disclosure of information received in confidence, or for maintaining the authority and impartiality of the judiciary.

## Article 11

1. Everyone has the right to freedom of peaceful assembly and to freedom of association with others, including the right to form and to join trade unions for the protection of his interests.

2. No restrictions shall be placed on the exercise of these rights other than such as are prescribed by law and are necessary in a democratic society in the interests of national security or public safety, for the prevention of disorder or crime, for the protection of health or morals or for the protection of the rights and freedoms of others. This article shall not prevent the imposition of lawful restrictions on the

exercise of these rights by members of the armed forces, of the police or of the administration of the State.

### Article 12
Men and women of marriageable age have the right to marry and to found a family, according to the national laws governing the exercise of this right.

### Article 13
Everyone whose rights and freedoms as set forth in this Convention are violated shall have an effective remedy before a national authority notwithstanding that the violation has been committed by persons acting in an official capacity.

### Article 14
The enjoyment of the rights and freedoms set forth in this Convention shall be secured without discrimination on any ground such as sex, race, colour, language, religion, political or other opinion, national or social origin, association with a national minority, property, birth or other status.

### Article 1, Protocol No 1
Every natural or legal person is entitled to the peaceful enjoyment of his possessions. No one shall be deprived of his possessions except in the public interest and subject to the conditions provided for by law and by the general principles of international law. The proceeding provisions shall not, however, in any way impair the right of a State to enforce such law as it deems necessary to control the use of property in accordance with the general interest or to secure the payment of taxes or other contributions or penalties.

### Article 2, Protocol No 1
No person shall be denied the right to education. In the exercise of any functions which it assumes in relation to education and to teaching, the State shall respect the right of parents to ensure such education and teaching in conformity with their own religious and philosophical convictions.

### Article 3, Protocol No 4
1 No one shall be expelled, by means either of an individual or a collective measure, from the territory of the State of which he is a national.
2 No one shall be deprived of the right to enter the territory of the State of which he is a national.

### Article 5, Protocol No 7
Spouses shall enjoy equality of rights and responsibilities of a private law character between them, and in their relations with their children, as to marriage, during marriage and in the event of its dissolution. This Article shall not prevent States from taking such measures as are necessary in the interests of the children.

# List of Cases of the European Commission of Human Rights

# List of Cases of the European Court of Human Rights

# Bibliography

Abdullali An-Na'im (1994), 'Cultural Transformation and Normative Consensus on the Best Interests of the Child', *International Journal of Law and the Family*, **8**, pp 62-81.

Abramson (1994), *The Invisibility of Children and Adolescents: The Need to Monitor our Rhetoric and our Attitudes*, Unpublished Ghent Conference Paper.

Alston (1980), 'UNESCO's Procedure for Dealing with Human Rights Violations', *Santa Clara Law Review*, **20**, pp 665-696.

Alston (ed) (1992), *The UN and Human Rights: A Critical Appraisal*, Oxford: Clarendon Press.

Alston (1994), 'Best Interests Principle: Towards a Reconciliation of Culture and Human Rights', *International Journal of Law and Family,* **8**, pp 1-25.

Alston, Parker & Seymour (eds) (1992), *Children, Rights and the Law,* Clarendon: Oxford University Press.

Andrews & Sherlock (1995), 'Respect for Family Life and Presumptions Regarding Paternity of Children', *European Law Review*, **20**, pp 414-416.

Archard (1993), *Children, Rights and Childhood,* London: Routledge.

Arts (1993), 'The International Protection of Children's Rights in Africa: The 1990 OAU Charter on the Rights and Welfare of the Child', *African Journal of International and Comparative Law,* **5**, pp 139-162.

Azer (1994), 'Modalities of the Best Interests Principle in Education', *International Journal of Law and the Family*, **8**, pp 227-258.

Bainham (1989), 'When is a Parent not a Parent? Reflections on the Unmarried Father and his Child in English Law', *International Journal of Law and the Family*, **3**, pp 208-239.

Bainham (1990a), 'The Privatisation of the Public Interest in Children', *Modern Law Review*, **53**(2), pp 206-221.

Bainham (1990b), *Children - The New Law: The Children Act, 1989*, Bristol: Family Law.

Bainham (1994), 'Religion, Human Rights and the Fitness of Parents', *Cambridge Law Journal*, **53**, pp 39-41.

Bainham, Pearl & Pickford (eds) (1995), *Frontiers of Family Law,* Chichester: Wiley.

Balton (1990), 'Convention on the Rights of the Child: Prospects for International Enforcement', *Human Rights Quarterly*, **12**, pp 120-129.

Barsch (1989), 'The Draft Convention on the Rights of the Child - A Case of Eurocentrism in Standard Setting', *Nordic Journal of International Law*, **58**, pp 24-34.

Barton (1989), 'Children: The International Perspective', *Family Law*, **19**, p 369.

Beddard, (1993), *Human Rights and Europe*, Cambridge: Grotius.

Bennett (1987), 'A Critique of the Emerging Convention on the Rights of the Child', *Cornell International Law Journal,* **20**, pp 1-64.

Bergman (1994), 'Proposals for Optional Protocols to the Convention on the Rights of the Child', *The International Journal of Children's Rights,* **2**(4), pp 425-427.

Bernhadt (1995), 'Reform of the Control Machinery under the ECHR: Protocol No 11', *American Journal of International Law,* **89**, pp 145.

Blake (1997), 'Judicial Review of Discretion in Human Rights Cases', *European Human Rights Law Review,* **4,** pp 391-403.

Bleiman (1993), 'Conference Report - Is it better to travel hopefully than to arrive?', *Family Law,***23**, pp 6.

Bloed, Leicht, Nowak & Rosas (eds) (1993), *Monitoring Human Rights in Europe: Comparing International Procedures and Mechanisms,* Dordrecht: Martinus Nijhoff.

Bonner (1979), 'The Beginning of the End for Corporal Punishment', *Modern Law Review,* **42**, pp 580-586.

Boucaud (1989), 'The Council of Europe and Child Welfare: The Need for a European Convention on Children's Rights', *Human Rights Files No 10,* Strasbourg: Council of Europe.

Broekhuijsen-Molenaar (1996), 'Who are the Parents of a Child? The Law of Descent in the Netherlands', *Journal of Social Welfare and Family Law,* **18**(3), pp 341-352.

Brownlie (ed) (1992), *Basic Documents on Human Rights,* 3rd Ed, Oxford: Clarendon Press.

Buquicchio De Boer (1996), 'The Impact of the European Convention on the Rights of Children', *International Symposium on Children's Rights,* unpublished.

Calciano, (1992), 'UN CRC - Will it help Children in the US?', *Hastings International and Comparative Law Review,* **15**(3), pp 515-534

Cantwell & Scott (1995), 'Children's Wishes, Children's Burdens', *Journal of Social Welfare and Family Law,* **17**(3), pp 337-354

Case Comment, (1996), Hussain & Singh v UK, *European Human Rights Law Review,* **3**, pp 331-335

Cashmore & Bussey (1994), 'Perception of Children and Lawyers in Care and Protection Proceedings', *International Journal of Law and Family,* **8**, p 319-336.

Cerda (1990), 'The Draft Convention on the Rights of the Child: New Rights', *Human Rights Quarterly,* **12**, pp 115-119.

Chaponniere (1982), 'A Question of Interests: Inter-Country Adoption', *International Children's Rights Monitor,* pp 2-5.

Chen (1989), 'The UN Convention on the Rights of the Child: A Policy-Orientated Overview', *New York Law School Journal of Human Rights,* **7**(1), pp 16-28.

Children's Legal Centre (1987), 'European Boost to Children's Rights', *Childright,* **39**, p 3.

Clapham (1995), 'The Privatisation of Human Rights', *European Human Rights Law Review,* **1**, pp 20-32.

Clarke (1986), 'Freedom of Thought in Schools: A Comparative Study', *International and Comparative Law Quarterly*, **35**, pp 271-301.

Clarkson & Thomas (1995), 'Press Reports of Young Offenders Under S 49', *Childright*, **113**, pp 5-6.

Clements (1994a), 'European Convention: Human Rights and Family Law Cases', *Family Law*, **24**, pp 452-453.

Clements (1994b), *European Human Rights: Taking a Case under the Convention*, London: Sweet & Maxwell.

Clesney-Lind (1989), 'Female Status Offenders and the Double Standard of Juvenile Justice', *International Review of Criminal Policy*, **39-40**, pp 105-112.

Cohen (1983), 'The Human Rights of Children', *Capital University Law Review*, **12**, pp 369-403.

Cohen (1990a), 'The Role of NGOs in the Drafting of the Convention on the Rights of the Child', *Human Rights Quarterly*, **12**, pp 137-147.

Cohen (1990b), 'UN Convention on the Rights of the Child: Introductory Note', *International Commission of Jurists, The Review*, **44**, pp 36-41.

Cohen (1993), 'UN Convention on the Rights of the Child: A Guide to the Travaux Preparatoires', *American Journal of International Law*, **87**, p 477.

Cohen, Hart & Kosloske (1992), 'The UN Convention on the Rights of the Child: Developing an Information Model to Computerize the Monitoring of Treaty Compliance', *Human Rights Quarterly*, **14**, pp 216-231.

Coker (1995), 'Major flaw fails Minor', *Law Society Gazette*, **92**(4), p 12.

Connelly (1986), 'Problems of Interpretation of Article 8 of the ECHR', *International and Comparative Law Quarterly*, **35**, pp 567-593.

Connelly (1993), 'The European Convention on Human Rights and the Protection of Linguistic Minorities', *Irish Journal of European Law*, **2**, pp 277-293.

Connors (1994), 'The UK's Initial Report and UK Agenda for Children', *Journal of Child Law*, **6**, p 140

Conway (1998), 'The Concept of Child Protection', *New Law Journal*, pp 1012,1025.

Cooke (ed) (1994), *Human Rights of Women: National and International Perspectives*, Philadelphia: University of Pennsylvania Press.

Corcos (1991), 'The Child in International Law: A Pathfinder and Selected Bibliography', *Case Western Reserve Journal of International Law*, **23**, pp 171-196.

Council For Social Welfare (1991), *The Rights of the Child: Irish Perspective on the UN Convention*, Dublin: The Council for Social Welfare.

Council of Europe CDPS III.8 Obs (1996) 1 *Ages at which Children are legally entitled to carry out a series of acts in Council of Europe member countries.*

Council of Europe Doc H (1995), 12, *Case Law on Cultural Rights.*

Council of Europe CDPS III.8 (1994), 9 *Children and their Families; Children and Society.*

Council of Europe CDPS CP (1996), 1 *Children's Rights and Childhood Policies in Europe.*

Council of Europe CDPS CP (1996), d 9 *Children's Rights in Residential Care.*

Council of Europe *Collected Edition of the Travaux Preparatoires* Vol I - VI (The Hague: Martinus Nijhoff, 1975-1985).

Council of Europe Doc MMF-XXIII (1993), 1/Coll *Conference for European Ministers Responsible for* Council of Europe: *Family Affairs,* XXIIIrd Session (1993) *National Replies to the Questionnaire Family Policies, Children's Rights, Parental Responsibilities.*

Council of Europe CDPS III.8 (1994), *Conference: Evolution of the role of children in family life: participation and negotiation.*

Council of Europe DF (1995), 1 *Council of Europe Achievements in the Field of Law: Family Law.*

Council of Europe CDPS CP (1996), 7 *Education.*

Council of Europe CDPS CP (1996), 11 *The Interests of the Child: Child Day Care and Family Policies.*

Council of Europe CDPS CP (1996), 6 *Legal Affairs.*

Council of Europe CDPS CP (1996), 8 *Mass Media.*

Council of Europe CDPS CP (1996), 4 *Migration.*

Council of Europe Doc 7473 (1996), *Parliamentary Assembly Opinion Strategy for Children.*

Council of Europe (1996), *The Rights of the Child: A European Perspective,* Strasbourg: Council of Europe.

Council of Europe CDPS CP (1996), 3 *Social Protection, Family Polices.*

Council of Europe CDPS CP (1995), 1 *Television and Children.*

Cousins (1996), *Seen and Heard: Promoting and Protecting Children's Rights in Ireland,* Dublin: Children's Rights Alliance.

CRDU Column (1993), 'Hard task faces the UN Committee', *Childright,* 97, p 19.

Cretney (1989), 'Gillick and the Concept of Legal Capacity', *Law Quarterly Review,* 105, pp 356-364.

Cullen (1993), 'Education Rights or Minority Rights', *International Journal of Law & the Family,* 7, pp 143-177.

Cumper (1989), 'Muslim's Knocking at the Class Room Door', *New Law Journal,* 140, pp 1067-1071.

Cumper (1998), 'School Worship: Praying for Guidance', *European Human Rights Law Review,* 1, pp 45-60.

Danelius (1969), 'Conditions of Admissibility in the Jurisprudence of the European Commission', *Human Rights Journal,* 2, pp 284-336.

Davidson (1993), *Human Rights,* Buckingham: Open University Press.

Davis, Rosenblatt, & Galbraith, (1993), *International Child Abduction,* London: Sweet & Maxwell.

Defence For Children International (1993), *Selected Essays on International Children's Rights,* Vol 1, Geneva: DCI.

Defence For Children International (1990), *Seminar on the Implementation of the Convention on the Rights of the Child,* Syracusa Italy, 24-28, September, 1990.

De Hondt & Holtrust (1986), 'The European Convention and the 'Marckx-Judgment' Effect', *International Journal of the Sociology of Law*, **14**, pp 317-328.

Delmas-Marty (ed) (1992), *The European Convention for the Protection of Human Rights: International Protection versus National Restrictions*, Dordrecht: Martinus Nijhoff.

Deng & An-N'aim (eds) (1990), *Human Rights in Africa: Cross Cultural Perspectives*, Washington: The Brookings Institute.

Department of Health (1993), *Adoption: The Future*, London: HMSO.

Department of Health /Welsh Office (1992), *Review of Adoption Law, Report to Ministers of an Interdepartmental Working Group: A Consultation Document*, London: HMSO.

Department of Health/Welsh Office (1994), *Placement for Adoption - A Consultation Document*, London: HMSO.

Detrick (ed) (1992), *The UN Convention on the Rights of the Child: A Guide to the Travaux Preparatoires*, Dordrecht: Martinus Nijhoff.

Dickens (1981), 'The Modern Functions and Limits of Parental Rights', *Law Quarterly Review*, **97**, pp 462-485.

Dickson (1997), *Human Rights and the European Convention: The effects of the Convention on the United Kingdom and Ireland*, London: Sweet & Maxwell.

Doek (1994), 'Child Abuse and Neglect: Article 19 CRC', *The International Journal of Children's Rights*, **2**, pp 88-99.

Douglas (1988), 'The Family and the State under the ECHR', *International Journal of Law and the Family*, **2**, pp 76-105.

Drzewicki, Krause & Rosas (eds) (1994), *Social Rights as Human Rights: A European Challenge*, Abo: Institute for Human Rights, Abo Akademi University.

Duffy (1982), 'The Protection of Privacy, Family Life and Other Rights under Article 8 of the European Convention on Human Rights', *Yearbook of European Law*, **2**, pp 191-238.

Duncan (1986), 'Family - the Child's Rights to a Family - Parental Rights in Disguise', *Dublin University Law Journal* , pp 76-86.

Duncan (1987), *Law and Social Policy: Some Current Problems*, Dublin: DULJ.

Dupaix (1987), 'Best Interests Revisited: in Search of Guidelines', *Utah Law Review*, **3**, pp 651-573.

Durrant (1994), 'The Abolition of Corporal Punishment in Canada: Parents' Versus Children's Rights', 2(2) *The International Journal of Children's Rights*, **2**(2), pp 129-136.

Dutch Ministry for Foreign Affairs (1994), *First Steps Policy Memorandum on Children in Developing Countries*, Ministry for Foreign Affairs: The Hague.

Edge (1994), 'Dancing to the Beat of Europe', *New Law Journal*, **144**, p 770.

Editorial (1993), 'Corporal Punishment and the Abuse of Children', *Practitioner's Child Law Bulletin*, **6**, pp 26-27.

*The Education of Migrant Workers' Children* (1980), Strasbourg: Council of Europe.

Eekelaar (1986), 'The Emergence of Children's Rights', *Oxford Journal of Legal Studies*, **6**, pp 161-182.

Eekelaar (1991), 'Are Parents Morally Obliged to Care for their Children?', *Oxford Journal of Legal Studies*, **11(3)**, pp 340-353.

Eide, et al (eds) (1995), *Economic, Social and Cultural Rights: A Textbook*, Dordrecht: Martinus Nijhoff.

Elster (1978), 'Salamonic Judgement: Against the Best Interests of the Child', *University of Chicago Law Review*, **54**, pp 1-45.

Emery (1996), 'Representation for Children', *International Legal Practitioner*, **21**, pp 29-31.

Enrich (1993), 'Rights of the Child: UK Implementation of the Goals Agreed by the World Summit for Children', *Family Law*, pp 536.

Enrich Mas (1990), 'The Protection of Minors under the ECHR: Analysis of Case Law', *ICML and CIAS Conference, November 1989*.

Enrich Mas (1995), 'La Protection des Enfants Mineurs en Europe', *Bulletin des Droits de l'Homme*.

Evans (ed) (1996), *Blackstone's International Law Documents*, 3rd ed, London: Blackstone Press.

Eya Nchama (1991), 'The Role of NGOs in the Promotion and Protection of Human Rights', *Bulletin of Human Rights, 90/1*.

Fawcett (1987), *The Application of the European Convention on Human Rights*, 2nd ed, Oxford: Clarendon Press.

Farran (1996), *The UK Before the European Court of Human Rights: Case Law & Commentary*, London: Blackstone.

Fischer (1982), 'Reporting under the Covenant on Civil and Political Rights: The First Five Years of the Human Rights Committee', *American Journal of International Law*, **76**, pp 142-153.

Flekkoy (1992), 'Working for the Rights of Children in Norway', *Juridical Review*, **2(2)**, pp 127.

Flekkoy (1993), 'Monitoring Implementation of the UN Convention on the National Level', *The International Journal of Children's Rights*, **1(2)**, pp 233-236.

Forder (1993), 'Constitutional Principles and the Establishment of the Legal Relationship between the Child and the Non-Marital Father', *International Journal of Law and the Family*, **7**, pp 40-107.

Forder (1995), 'Steps in International Law to Combat Paedophiles and Steps Towards Children's Rights', *Maastricht Journal of European and Comparative Law*, **3(4)**, pp 323-328.

Fortin (1998), *Children's Rights and the Developing Law*, London: Butterworths.

Fortin (1999), 'Rights Brought Home for Children', *Modern Law Review* **62**, pp 350-370.

Fortuyn & De Langen (eds) (1992), *Towards the Realisation of Human Rights of Children,* Amsterdam: DCI Netherlands.

Fox (1990), 'Remarks for the Opening Session of the Beijing International Conference on the Protection of Children's Rights', *Boston College International and Comparative Law Quarterly,* **13**, p 47.

France (1990), *Inter-Departmental Review of Adoption Law, Background Paper No 1: International Perspectives,* London: Department of Health.

Franklin (ed) (1995), *The Handbook of Children's Rights Comparative Law and Practice,* London: Routledge.

Freeman (1984), 'The Unborn Child and the ECHR: To Whom Does Everyone's Right to Life Belong?', *Emory International Law Review,* **8**(2), pp 615-665.

Freeman (1994), 'The European Court Upholds School Beating', *The International Journal of Children's Rights,* **2**, pp 81-83.

Freeman (1994), 'The Philosophical Foundations of Human Rights', *Human Rights Quarterly,* **16**, pp 491-514.

Freeman (ed), (1996), *Children's Rights: A Comparative Perspective,* Aldershot: Dartmouth.

Freeman & Veerman (eds) (1992), *The Ideologies of Children's Rights,* Dordrecht: Martinus Nijhoff.

Freestone (ed) (1990), *Children and the Law. Essays in Honour of Professor HK Bevan,* Hull: Hull University Press.

Furmiss & Blair (1997), 'Sex Wars: Conflict in and Reform of Sex Education in Maintained Secondary Schools', *Journal of Social Welfare and Family Law,* **19**(2), pp 189-202.

Gallagher (1998), 'Care Orders and the State's Responsibilities', *New Law Journal* pp 670-672.

Gearty (1993), 'The European Court of Human Rights and the Protection of Civil Liberties: An Overview', *Cambridge Law Journal,* **52**(1), pp 89-127.

Ghandi (ed) (1995), *Blackstone's International Human Rights Documents,* London: Blackstone Press.

Glazebrook (1984), 'Human Beginnings', *Cambridge Law Journal,* p 209.

Gledhill (1994), 'The Naming of Juvenile Delinquents', *New Law Journal,* **144**, pp 365-368.

Gomez (1995), 'Social Economic Rights and Human Rights Commissions', *Human Rights Quarterly,* **17**, pp 155-169.

Gomien (1989), 'Whose Right (and Whose Duty) is it? An Analysis of the Substance and Implementation of the CRC', *New York Law School Journal of Human Rights,* **7**, pp 161-175.

Gomien (1989), 'State Powers and the Best Interests of the Child under Article 8 ECHR', *Netherlands Quarterly of Human Rights,* **7**, pp 435-450.

Gomien (1993), *Broadening the Frontiers of Human Rights: Essays in Honour of Asbjorn Eide,* Oslo: Scandinavian University Press.

Goodman (1992), 'Analysis of the First Session of the Committee on the Rights of the Child', *Netherlands Quarterly of Human Rights,* **1**, pp 43-62.

Goonesekere (1994), 'The Best Interests of the Child: a South Asian Perspective', *International Journal of Law and Family*, **8**, pp 117-149.

Gray (1981), 'Remedies for Individuals Under the ECHR', *Human Rights Law Review*, **6**, p 153.

Greer (1995), *Public Interests and Human Rights in the ECHR*, Strasbourg: Council of Europe.

Grewock (1996), 'Judicial Process and Political Whim', *Childright*, **125**, pp 18-20.

Guedala (1994), 'Representing Unaccompanied Refugee Children in the Asylum Process', *Childright*, **112**, p 11.

Guggenheim (1994), 'The Right to be Represented but not Heard: Reflections on Legal Representation for Children' *New York University Law Review*, **59**, p 76.

Haimes (1988), 'Secrecy: What Can Artificial Reproduction Learn From Adoption?', *International Journal of Law and Family*, **2**, pp 46-61.

Haimes (1991), 'Gamete Donation and Anonymity', *Bulletin of Medical Ethics*, **66**, pp 25-27.

Hale (1996), *From the Test Tube to the Coffin: Choice and Regulation in Private Life*, London: Sweet & Maxwell.

Hamilton (1995), *Family Law and Religion*, London: Sweet & Maxwell.

Hamilton & Watt (1995), 'A Discriminating Education - Collective Worship in Schools', *Child and Family Law Quarterly*, **7**(4), pp 28-42.

Hammarberg (1990), 'The UN Convention on the Rights of the Child and How to Make it Work', *Human Rights Quarterly*, **12**, pp 97-105.

Hammarberg (1994), 'The Work of the Committee on the Rights of the Child', *The International Journal of Children's Rights*, **2**, pp 83-87.

Hannum(ed) (1992), *Guide to International Human Rights Practice*, 2nd ed, London: Macmillan Press.

Harris, O'Boyle & Warbrick (1995), *Law of the European Convention on Human Rights*, London: Butterworths.

Haskey (1995), 'Trends in Marriage and Co-Habitation: the Decline in Marriage and the Changing Pattern of Living in Partnerships', *Population Trends*, **80**, pp 5-15.

Heffernan (ed) (1994), *Human Rights: A European Perspective*, Dublin: Round Hall Press.

Henderson 'Immunisation: Going the Extra Mile' (1998), *The Progress of Nations*, New York: UNICEF.

Hodgson (1993), 'The International Protection of the Child's Right to a Legal Identity and the Problem of Statelessness', *International Journal of Law and Family*, **7**, pp 255-260.

Hodgson (1995), 'Combatting the Organisation of Sexual Exploitation of Asian Children: Recent Developments and Prospects', *International Journal of Law and the Family*, **9**, pp 25-53.

Hoggett (1993), *Parents and Children: The Law of Parental Responsibility*, 4th ed, London: Sweet & Maxwell.

Hoyal (1993), 'The Children Act 1989 and the European Convention', *Legal Action*, pp 22-23.

Hunt (1997), *Using Human Rights Law in English Courts*, Oxford : Hart.

Jacobs (1975), *The European Convention on Human Rights*, Oxford: Clarendon Press.

Janis, Kay & Bradley (1995), *European Human Rights Law: Text and Materials*, Oxford: OUP.

Johnson (1994), 'Child Victims of Human Rights Violations', *Childright*, **106**, pp 14-15.

Jones (1981), 'Council of Europe Convention on Recognition and Enforcement of Decisions Relating to the Custody of Children', *International and Comparative Law Quarterly*, **30**, pp 467-475.

Jones (1988), 'Artificial Procreation, Societal Reconceptions: Legal Insight from France', *American Journal of Comparative Law*, **36**, pp 525-545.

Jones (1994), 'Refugee Children: Treatment in International and Domestic Law', *Immigration and Nationality Law and Practice*, **8**(2).

Jupp (1991), 'Confronting the Challenge of Realizing Human Rights Now: Rights of Children: UNCRC: An Opportunity for Advocates', *Howard Law Journal*, **34**, pp 15-25.

Kektina, (1993), 'Latvia: are Children's Rights also Human Rights', *International Legal Practitioner,* **18**, p 35.

Khan (1995), 'Corporal Punishment in Schools', *Education and the Law*, **7**, p 1-11.

Kilkelly (1996), 'The UN Committee on the Rights of the Child - An Evaluation in the Light of Recent UK Experience', *Child and Family Law Quarterly*, **8**(2), pp 105-120.

Kilkelly (1996),'Nsona v The Netherlands: The Treatment of Minors and the European Convention on Human Rights', *International Journal of Refugee Law*, **8**(4), pp 640-650.

Kilkelly (1997), *Small Voices: Vital Rights, A Submission to the UN Committee on the Rights of the Child*, Dublin: The Children's Rights Alliance.

Killerby (1995), 'The Draft European Convention on the Exercise of Children's Rights', *The International Journal of Children's Rights*, **3**, pp 127-133

King (1985), 'Parental Rights, Child Protection and the European Convention', *Family Law*, **15**, p 150.

King (1994), 'Children's Rights as Communication: Reflections on Autopoietic Theory and the UN Convention', *Modern Law Review*, **57**, p 385.

King & Piper (1990), *How the Law Thinks About Children*, Aldershot: Gower.

King & Young (1992), *The Child As Client: A Handbook for Solicitors who Represent Children*, Bristol: Family Law.

Koren (1995), 'A Children's Ombudsman in Sweden', *The International Journal of Children's Rights*, **3**, pp 101-118.

Kubota (1989), 'The Protection of Children's Rights and the United Nations', *Nordic Journal of International Law*, **58**, pp 7-23.

Kunnemann (1995), 'A Coherent Approach to Human Rights', *Human Rights Quarterly*, **17**, p 323.

Kuper (1994), '[Children's Law] Centre Report to UN on Conditions for Young People in Custody', *Childright*, **103**, p 7.

Landy (1980), 'The Implementation Procedures of the International Labour Organisation', *Santa Clara Law Review*, **20**, pp 633-663.

Lansdown & Newell (eds) (1992), *UK Agenda for Children*, London: CRDU.

Lansdown (1995), 'CRDU Closes after Three Years', *Childright*, **114**, p 6.

Lansdown (1995), 'Implementing the UN CRC in the UK', *Child and Family Law Quarterly*, **7**, p 122.

Lavender (1997), 'The Problem of the Margin of Appreciation' *European Human Rights Law Review* **4** pp 380-390.

Leach (1994), *Children First: What Society must do - and is not doing - for Children Today*, London: Penguin.

Leblanc (1995), *The Convention on the Rights of the Child: United Nations Law making on Human Rights*, Lincoln: University of Nebraska Press.

Leckie (1991), 'An Overview and Appraisal of the Fifth Session of the UN Committee on Economic, Social and Cultural Rights', *Human Rights Quarterly*, **13**, pp 545-572.

Ledogar (1993), 'Implementing the CRC through National Programmes of Action for Children', *The International Journal of Children's Rights*, **1**, pp 377-391.

Leonardi (1996), 'The Strasbourg System of Human Rights Protection: Europeanisation of the law Through the Confluence of the Western Legal Traditions', *European Review of Public Law*, **8**(4), pp 1139-1196.

Lester (1989), 'Unequal Treatment ...?', *Childright*, **61**, pp 7-8.

Lester (1996), 'The European Convention in the New Architecture of Europe', *Public Law*, pp 5-10.

Lewis (1999), 'Relationship Breakdown, Obligations and Contracts', *Family Law*, pp 149-152.

Liddy (1998), 'The Concept of Family Life Under the ECHR', *European Human Rights Law Review*, **1**, pp 15-25.

Liu (1994), 'The Parentage of Children Born as a Result of Natural and Assisted Reproduction', *Hong Kong Law Journal*, **23**(4), pp 356-371.

Livingstone (1997), 'Article 14 and the Prevention of Discrimination in the European Convention on Human Rights', *European Human Rights Law Review*, **1**, pp 26-34.

Loucaides (1995), *Essays on the Developing Law of Human Rights*, Dordrecht: Martinus Nijhoff.

Lowe (1994), 'Problems Relating to Access Disputes under the Hague Convention on International Child Abduction', *International Journal of Law and the Family*, **8**(3), pp 374-385.

Lowe & Perry (1999), 'International Child Abduction - the English Experience', *International & Comparative Law Quarterly*, **48**, pp 127-155.

Luciano (1980), 'The Law of the Child - in a Changing World', *Catholic Lawyer*, **25**, pp 144-153.

Lurvey & Rutkin (1993), 'First World Congress on Family Law and Children's Rights', *Family Advocate*, **15**(4), p 14.

Macdonald et al (eds) (1993), *The European System for the Protection of Human Rights*, Deventer: Kluwer.

Mahoney & Mahoney (1993), *Human Rights in the Twenty First Century: A Global Challenge*, Dordrecht: Martinus Nijhoff.

Matscher & Petzold (eds) (1988), *Protecting Human Rights: The European Dimension, Studies in Honour of Gerard J Wiarda*, Koln: Heymanns.

McGoldrick (1991), 'The UN Convention on the Rights of the Child', *International Journal of Law and the Family*, **5**, pp 132-169.

McSweeney (1993), 'The Potential for Enforcement of the UN Convention on the Rights of the Child: The Need to Improve the Information Base', *Boston College International and Comparative Law Review*, **76**, pp 467-496.

Meeusen (1995), 'Judicial Disapproval of Discrimination Against Illegitimate Children A Comparative Study of Developments in Europe and the United States', *American Journal of Comparative Law*, **43**, pp 119-145.

Melton (1991), 'Lessons from Norway: the Children's Ombudsman as a Voice for Children', *Case Western Reserve Journal of International Law*, **23**(2), pp 197-254.

Melton (1993), 'Young Children's Political Rights', *Childright*, **93**, pp 17-19.

Merrills (1988), *The Development of International Law by the European Court of Human Rights*, Manchester: MUP.

Middleton (1995), 'A Disabling Childhood', *Childright*, **113**, pp 25-27.

Miljeteig-Olssen (1990), 'Advocacy of Children's Rights - The Convention as more than a Legal Document', *Human Rights Quarterly*, **12**, pp 148-155.

Minow (1986), 'Rights for the Next Generation: A Feminist Approach to Children's Rights', *Harvard Women's Law* Journal, **9**, p 1.

Mole (1995), 'Constructive Deportation and the European Convention', *European Human Rights Law Review* **1**, pp 63-71.

Montgomery (1988), 'Children as Property', *Modern Law Review*, **51**, p 323.

Muller (1995), 'Strasbourg Human Rights Meeting', *International Legal Practitioner*, pp 35-36.

Mullerson, Andenas & Fitzmaurice (eds) (1997), *Constitutional Reforms and International Law in Central Europe*, Deventer: Kluwer.

Murdoch (1993), 'Safeguarding the Liberty of the Person: Recent Strasbourg Jurisprudence', *International and Comparative Law Quarterly*,**42**, pp 494-522.

Nowak (1980), 'The Effectiveness of the International Covenant on Civil and Political Rights - Stocktaking after the First Eleven Sessions of the UN Human Rights Committee', *Human Rights Law Journal*, **1**, pp 136-170.

Nowak (1993), 'The Activities of the UN Human Rights Committee: Developments from 1 August 1989 through 31 July 1992', *Human Rights Law Journal*, **14**, pp 9-19.

O'Boyle (1980), 'Practice and Procedure under the ECHR', *Santa Clara Law Review*, **20**, pp 697-732.

O'Doherty (1996), 'Recent Cases on Hearsay Evidence in Civil Child Sexual Abuse Proceedings', *Irish Law Times*, **14**(12), pp 284-287.

O'Donnell (1982), 'The Margin of Appreciation Doctrine: Standards in the Jurisprudence of the European Court', *Human Rights Quarterly*, **4**, pp 474-496.

O'Donnell (1995a), 'Protection of Family Life: Positive approaches and the ECHR', *Journal of Social Welfare and Family Law*, **17**(3), pp 261-280.

O'Donnell (1995b), 'The Unmarried father and the Right to Family Life', *Maastricht Journal of European and Comparative Law*, **2**(1), pp 85-96.

O'Flaherty (1994), 'The Reporting Obligation under Article 40 of the International Covenant on Civil and Political Rights: Lessons to be Learned from Consideration by the Human Rights Committee of Ireland's First Report', *Human Rights Quarterly*, **16**, pp 513-538.

O'Sullivan (1993), 'Irish Child Care Law: The Origins, Aims and Development of the 1991 Child Care Act', *Childright*, **97**, p 15.

Olson (1984), 'The Swedish Ban on Corporal Punishment', *Brigham Young University Law Review*, pp 447-456.

Osler (ed) (1994), *Development Education Global Perspectives in the Curriculum*, London: Cassell.

Packer & Myntti (eds) (1993), *The Protection of Ethnic and Linguistic Minorities in Europe*, Abo: Institute for Human Rights, Abo Akademi University.

Palmer (1996), 'Limitation Periods in Cases of Sexual Abuse: A Response under the European Convention', *European Human Rights Law Review*, **2**, pp 111-119.

Palmer (1996), 'What has happened to Children's Rights in the Criminal Justice System?', *Cambridge Law Journal*, **55**(3), pp 406-409.

Parker (1991), 'Child Support in Australia: Children's Rights or Public Interest?', *International Journal of Law and the Family*, **5**, pp 24-57.

Phillips (1994), 'The Case for Corporal Punishment in the UK, Beaten into Submission in Europe', *International and Comparative Law Quarterly*, **43**, p 153.

Pickford (1992), 'The Gaskin Case and Confidential Personal Information - whose secret?', *Journal of Child Law*, p 33.

Pogany (1982), 'Education: The Rights of Children and Parents under the ECHR', *New Law Journal*, pp 344-346.

Porterfield & Staunton (1989), 'The Age of Majority: Article 1', *Journal of Human Rights (NY Law School) Article Series on the UN Draft Convention*, pp 30-34.

Ramcharan (1989), *The Concept and Present Status of the International Protection of Human Rights,* Dordrecht: Martinus Nijhoff.

Reid (1993), 'Child Care Cases and the ECHR', *Journal of Child Law*, **5**(2), pp 66-70.

Richards (1987), 'Family, Race and Identity', *Adoption & Fostering*, **11**(3), pp 10-13.

Ridgers (1995), 'Civil Liberties for Young People', *Childright*, **113**, p 23.

Robertson (1950), 'The European Convention for the Protection of Human Rights', *British Yearbook of International Law*, **27**, pp 145-163.

Robertson (1951), 'The ECHR: Recent Developments', *British Yearbook of International Law*, **28**, pp 359-365

Robertson (ed) (1973), *Privacy and Human Rights*, Manchester: MUP.

Robertson (1994), 'Appointment of Solicitors for Children', *Family Law*, p 390.

Robertson & Merrills (1989), *Human Rights in the World*, Manchester: MUP.

Robertson & Merrills (1993), *Human Rights in Europe: A Study of the European Convention on Human Rights*, 3rd ed, Manchester: MUP.

Roche (1995), 'Children's Rights: in the Name of the Child', *Journal of Social Welfare & Family Law*, **17**(3), pp 281-300.

Rosenbaum & Newell (1991), 'A Link between Children and Government', *Childright*, **78**, p 7.

Rosenblatt (1996), 'The Needs of Black and Ethnic Children', *Family Law*, **26**, pp 641-642.

Rubinstein (1996) 'Art and Taste', *New Law Journal* 1610-1611, 1665-1666.

*Rules of Procedure of the European Commission of Human Rights* (1993), European Commission of Human Rights: Strasbourg.

Rwezaura (1994), 'Concept of the Child's Best Interests in the Changing Economic and Social Context of Sub-Saharan Africa', *International Journal of Law and Family*, **8**, pp 82-114.

Rwezaura (1994), 'The Legal and Cultural Context of Children's Rights in Hong Kong', *Hong Kong Law Journal*, **24**, p 276.

Santos Pais (1993), 'The Committee on the Rights of the Child', *The Review, International Commission of Jurists*, **47**, pp 36-43.

Saunders (1994), 'Working for Children', *Childright*, **109**, p 19.

Sawyer (1995), 'The Competence of Children to Participate in Family Proceedings', *Child and Family Law Quarterly*, **7**(4), pp 180-195.

Schaaf (1992), 'International Documentation - Convention on the Rights of the Child', *International Journal of Legal Information*, **20**(1), pp 57-60.

Schuz (1995), 'The Hague Child Abduction Convention, Family Law and Private International' Law, *International and Comparative Law Quarterly*, **44**, pp 771-802.

Shaw (ed) (1992), *Prisoner's Children: What are the Issues?*, London: Routledge.

Shelton (1991), 'Human Rights, Environmental Rights and the Right to Environment, *Stanford Journal of International Law*, p 103.

Sherlock (1998) 'Deportation of Aliens and Article 8 ECHR', *European Law Review*, **23**, pp 62-75.

Sieghart (1983), *The International Law of Human Rights*, Oxford: Clarendon Press.

Sieghart (1988), *Human Rights in the UK*, London: Pinter.

Sieghart (1989), *AIDS and Human Rights: A UK Perspective*, London: British Medical Association Foundation for AIDS.

Smith (1994), 'The Right to Life and the Right to Kill in Law Enforcement', *New Law Journal*, **44**, pp 354-356.

Smith (1999), 'To Smack or not to Smack? A review of A v United Kingdom in an International and European Context and its Potential Impact on Physical Parental Chastisement', *Web Journal of Current Legal Issues* **1**.

Starkey (ed) (1991), *The Challenge of Human Rights Education*, London: Cassell.

Steiner & Alston (1996), *International Human Rights in Context: Law, Politics, Morals*, Oxford: Clarendon Press.

Stentzel (1991), 'Prospects for US Ratification of the Convention on the Rights of the Child', *Washington and Lee Law Review*, **48**(4), pp 1285-1322.

Stewart (1992), 'Interpreting the Child's Right to Identity in the UN Convention on the Rights of the Child', *Family Law Quarterly*, **26**(3), pp 221-233.

Storey (1990), 'The Right to Family Life and Immigration Case Law at Strasbourg', *International and Comparative Law Quarterly*, **39**, p 328-344.

Sutherland (1992), 'Children's Charters', *Journal of Law Society of Scotland*, **37**, p 435.

Sutherland & McCall Smith (eds) (1990), *Family Rights: Family Law and Medical Advances*, Edinburgh: Edinburgh University Press.

Thoburn (1990), *Review of Research Relating to Adoption, Inter-Departmental Review of Adoption Law*, London: Department of Health.

Thorpe (1994), 'The Influence of Strasbourg on Family Life', *Family Law*, p 509.

Trechsel (1980), 'The Right to Liberty and Security of the Person - Article 5 of the European Convention on Human Rights in Strasbourg Case Law', *Human Rights Law Journal*, **1**, pp 88-135.

Turner (1992), 'The Rights of the Child under the UN Convention', *Law Institute Journal*, **1-2**, pp 38-45.

UNICEF (Bellamy) (1996), *The State of the World's Children*, Oxford: Oxford University Press.

United Nations, Bulletin of Human Rights, (1992), 91/2, *The Rights of the Child*, New York: UN.

Van Bueren (1991a), 'A New Children's Rights Treaty', *International Children's Rights Monitor*, **8**, p 20.

Van Bueren (1991b), 'The UN Convention on the Rights of the Child', *Journal of Child Law*, **3**(2), pp 33-36.

Van Bueren (1992a), 'The UNCRC: The Necessity of Incorporation into UK Law, *Family Law*, pp 373-375.

Van Bueren (1992b), 'Child Orientated Justice - An International Challenge for Europe', *International Journal of Law and the Family*, **6**, pp 381-399

Van Bueren (ed) (1993), *International Documents on Children Vol 1*, Dordrecht: Martinus Nijhoff.

Van Bueren (1995a), *The International Law on the Rights of the Child*, Dordrecht: Martinus Nijhoff

Van Bueren (1995b), 'Children's Access to Adoption Records - State Discretion or an Enforceable International Right', *Modern Law Review*, **58**, pp 37-53.

Van Bueren (1995c), 'The International Protection of Family Members' Rights as the 21st Century Approaches', *Human Rights Quarterly*, **17**, pp 732-765.

Van Bueren (1996), 'Protecting Children's Rights in Europe - A Test Case Strategy', *European Human Rights Law Review*, **1**, pp 171-180.

Van Dijk & Van Hoof (1998), *Theory and Practice of the European Convention on Human Rights*, 3rd ed, The Hague: Kluwer

Van Nijnatien (1989), 'Behind Closed Doors: Juvenile Hearings in the Netherlands', *International Journal of Law and the Family*, **3**, pp 177-184.

Van Nijnatien (1996), 'In the Name of the Third - Changing the Law on Naming Children in the Netherlands', *International Journal of Law, Policy and the Family*, **10**, pp 219-228.

Veerman (1992), *The Rights of the Child and the Changing Image of Childhood*, Boston: Martinus Nijhoff.

Veerman (1994), 'Proposals from Strasbourg to Brussels', *Childright*, **109**, p 7.

Verdoot (1996), 'The Right to Use a Language of One's Own Choice', *Proceedings of the 8th International Colloquy on the ECHR*, Strasbourg: Council of Europe.

Verhellen (1993), 'Children's Rights in Europe', *International Journal of Children's Rights*, **1**, pp 357-376.

Viccicia (1989), 'Promotion and Protection of Children's Rights through Development and Recognition of an International Notion of Juvenile Justice and its Child-Centred Perspective in the UN' *Nordic Journal of International Law*, **58**, pp 68-93.

Voegeli & Willenbacher (1993), 'Children's Rights and Social Placement: a Cross-National Comparison of Legal and Social Policy Towards Children in One Parent Families', *International Journal of Law and Family*, **7**, pp 108-124.

Walsh (1991), 'UN Convention on the Rights of the Child: a British View', *International Journal of Law and the Family*, **5**, pp 170-194.

Warbrick (1998), 'The Structure of Article 8', *European Human Rights Law Review*, **1**, pp 32-44.

Watt (1996), 'A Place for Children in Europe', *Childright*, **123**, pp 12-13.

Weil (1960), 'Decisions on Inadmissible Applications by the European Commission of Human Rights', *American Journal of International Law*, **54**, p 874.

White, Carr & Lowe (1995), *The Children Act in Practice*, 2nd ed, London: Butterworths.

Williams (1994), 'School Detention or False Imprisonment', *Childright*, **109**, p 15.

Woodhouse (1993), 'Children's Rights: The Destruction and Promise of Family', *Brigham Young University Law Review*, pp 497-514.

Woods (1988), 'Foster Family Rights: Recommendations by the Council of Europe', *Virginia Journal of International Law*, **28**, pp 561-584.

Wright (1998) 'Local Authorities, the Duty of Care and the European Convention on Human Rights', *Oxford Journal of Legal Studies* **18**, pp 1-28.

Zellick (1978), 'Corporal Punishment in the Isle of Man', *International Comparative Law Quarterly*, **27**, pp 665-671.

(1992), 'Draft European Charter of the Rights of the Child', *Childright*, **88**, pp 435-437.

(1993), 'Corporal Punishment and the Abuse of Children', *Practitioner's Child Law Bulletin*, **6**, p 26.

(1993), 'Human Rights: School Slippering not Degrading Punishment', *Research and Medical Injuries Law Letter*, **9**, p 27.

(1993), 'What's in a Name?', *Childright*, **96**, p 11.

(1997), 'Position on Refugee Children: European Council on Refugees and Exiles', *International Journal of Refugee Law*, **9**(1), pp 74-81.

# Index